HENRY VI

Shakespeare Criticism

Philip C. Kolin, *General Editor*

HENRY VI

CRITICAL ESSAYS

EDITED BY

THOMAS A. PENDLETON

ROUTLEDGE
NEW YORK AND LONDON

Published in 2001 by
Routledge
29 West 35th Street
New York, NY 10001

Published in Great Britain by
Routledge
11 New Fetter Lane
London EC4P 4EE

Routledge is an imprint of the Taylor & Francis Group.

Library of Congress Cataloging-in-Publication Data

Henry VI : critical essays / edited by Thomas A. Pendleton.
    p. cm.
    Includes bibliographical references and index.
    ISBN 0-8153-3301-3 (alk. paper)
    1. Shakespeare, William, 1564–1616. King Henry VI. 2. Henry VI, King
of England, 1421–1471—In literature. 3. Kings and rulers in literature. I.
Pendleton, Thomas A.

PR2813.H46   2000
822.3'3—dc21   00-061734

Printed on acid-free, 250-year life paper.
Manufactured in the United States of America.

10 9 8 7 6 5 4 3 2 1

Henry, the Lieutenant of the Tower and Gloucester. 3 Henry VI, 5.6. Design by
Henry Fuseli, engraved by James Neagle after Fuseli's lost drawing. London:
C & F. Rivington, 1803. By permission of the Folger Shakespeare Library.

Table of Contents

Acknowledgments

I owe thanks to a number of people. First of all, my contributors were good to deal with, pleasant and cooperative, and most important, talented people who gave me excellent work. At the end of the day, my liking and my respect for them all has grown all the stronger. The Faculty Resources Center here at Iona College rescued some texts for me from fearful electronic depths, and Bob Monteleone, Adrienne Franco, and others at the Ryan Library went literally as far as Phoenix to get me things on interlibrary loan. My coeditor on *The Shakespeare Newsletter* and friend of many years, John Mahon, was extremely generous in doing my share of our job as well as his own to give me some much needed time for the last fevered tasks on this volume. And Diane Grecco, our graduate assistant on *The Newsletter,* regularly saved me from word-processing disasters.

And, of course, my wife. It seems genre specific for writers to express their thanks to their wives—or, I suppose, husbands, if such is the case—but this does not make the gratitude any the less sincere. To get this finished off, I had to perform the very unloving act of ignoring my wife, and because she loves me, she let me do it. And that is worth remembering and cherishing: thank you, Carol, I love you.

GENERAL EDITOR'S INTRODUCTION

The continuing goal of the Shakespeare Criticism Series is to provide the most influential historical criticism, the most significant contemporary interpretations, and reviews of the most influential productions. Each volume in the series, devoted to a Shakespearean play or poem (e.g., the sonnets, *Venus and Adonis, The Rape of Lucrece*), includes the most essential criticism and reviews of Shakespeare's work from the late seventeenth century to the present. The series thus provides, through individual volumes, a representative gathering of critical opinion of how a play or poem has been interpreted over the centuries.

A major feature of each volume in the series is the editor's introduction. Each volume editor provides a substantial essay identifying the main critical issues and problems the play (or poem) has raised, charting the critical trends in looking at the work over the centuries, and assessing the critical discourses that have linked the play or poem to various ideological concerns. In addition to examining the critical commentary in light of important historical and theatrical events, each introduction functions as a discursive bibliographic essay that cites and evaluates significant critical works—essays, journal articles, dissertations, books, theatre documents— and gives readers a guide to research on the particular play or poem.

After the editor's introduction, each volume contains original essays (sometimes as many as 20 of them) by leading Shakespearean scholars, offering the most contemporary, theoretically attentive analyses of the play. Reflecting some recent critical approaches in Shakespearean studies, these new essays approach the play or poem from a multiplicity of perspectives, including feminist, Marxist, new historical, semiotic, mythic, performance/staging, cultural, and/or a combination of these and other methodologies. Some volumes in the series even include bibliographic analyses that have significant implications for criticism.

Each volume in the series has a section devoted to the play in performance which, again, is organized chronologically by publication date, beginning with some of the earliest and most significant productions and proceeding to the most recent. This section, which ultimately provides a theatre history of the play, should not be regarded as different from or rigidly isolated from the critical essays in the first section. Shakespearean criticism has often been informed by or has significantly influenced productions. Shakespearean criticism over the last twenty years or so has usefully been labeled the "Age of Performance." Readers will find information in this section on major foreign productions of Shakespeare's plays as well as landmark productions in English. Consisting of more than reviews of specific productions, this section also contains a variety of theatre documents, including interpretations written for a particular volume by notable directors whose comments might be titled "The Director's Choice," histories of seminal productions (e.g., Peter Brook's *Titus Andronicus* in 1955), and even interviews with directors and/or actors. Editors have also included photographs from productions around the world to help readers see and further appreciate the way a Shakespearean play has taken shape in the theatre.

Each volume in the Shakespeare Criticism Series strives to give readers a balanced and contemporary reading of a play in light of the most significant performance and cultural theories. The original essays included in each volume will, I hope, become part of critical legacy we pass on to future scholars.

Philip C. Kolin
University of Southern Mississippi

INTRODUCTION

Thomas A. Pendleton

Considering the source, the most significant criticism of the *Henry VI* plays may well be the closing lines of the Epilogue to *Henry V*:

> Henry the Sixt, in infant bands crown'd King
> Of France and England, did this king succeed;
> Whose state so many had the managing,
> That they lost France, and made his England bleed;
> Which oft our stage hath shown; and for their sake,
> In your fair minds let this acceptance take. (9–14)

The thematic emphasis is interesting, but there are two further implications relevant to this essay. The first is the popularity of the *Henry VI* plays, for which we also have the testimony of Nashe, Greene, and Henslowe's Diary—of which, more later. The appeal, even if formulaic, to fond remembrance of the earlier plays perhaps five years or so after they had left the repertory—and a busy repertory that continually presented new entertainments—argues for very considerable popularity. The reference to the loss of France would seem to include *Part 1*; indeed, the plurality of "for *their* sake" might well reflect the popularity of all the parts. The other implication, however, is negative: the time of that popularity is over. Our stage "oft hath shown" these plays, but the tense and the time are past.

The great misfortune of the *Henry VI* plays is that they were written very early in Shakespeare's career, and succeeded by other and better work. Almost immediately after *Part 3*, Shakespeare closed the sequence with *Richard III*, then and ever after one of his most popular plays. By the time the Epilogue to *Henry V* recalled the earlier histories, they had of course been superseded by the more mature, more complex, richer, and stronger plays of the Second Tetralogy. And shortly thereafter came the major romantic comedies and the great tragedies. The *Henry VI* plays quickly receded to the status of minor Shakespeare, which status they have held ever since and, I am sure, they will continue to hold even in spite of the work presented in this volume.

All lesser Shakespeare has for that very reason been considered less, although lesser consideration within Shakespeare criticism still amounts to more than formidable accumulation. But for most of their critical lifetime, the *Henry VI* plays have labored under the further disadvantage that questions of text and authorship preempted much of the conversation, and examination of the plays as plays was diminished.

For somewhat more than the past half-century, however, the climate has been improving, and in all probability these plays are now more discussed and more appreciated than at any time since their first appearance. In his essay in this collection, H. C. Coursen refers to them as "these wonderful plays," a comment largely evoked by their resuscitation on the twentieth-century stage (of which, also more later). In the current critical context the worst that might be said of Coursen's commendation is that it is extreme. Forty or even thirty years ago, calling *Henry VI* wonderful would have seemed, at the best, eccentric.

There have been perhaps half a dozen or so works most responsible for enabling this more productive criticism of the plays. The first and surely one of the most important is Peter Alexander's 1929 demonstration that the early quartos—*The First Part of the Contention* (1594) and *The True Tragedy of Richard, Duke of York* (1595)—were not, as had been thought since Edmond Malone's 1791 *Dissertation*, texts of the source plays which Shakespeare rewrote as *Parts Two* and *Three*, but rather "bad quartos": memorial reconstructions of the plays as they appear in the First Folio of 1623. Alexander's hypothesis has been accepted by virtually all editors of major editions since that time: Andrew S. Cairncross for Arden, Norman Sanders for Penguin, and Michael Hattaway for New Cambridge, as well as G. B. Evans and David Bevington for their Complete Works. There is a good deal of disagreement among editors on how the quartos may be properly utilized to supply stage directions and bases for emendations and on how quarto copy may have been utilized in the printing of the Folio texts, but Alexander's view of the basic nature of the quartos seems to have commanded unanimous acceptance among the editors. Notably, it has been accepted by Dover Wilson's "New" Shakespeare, although Wilson took a very different position on the separate but collateral issue of authorship, and by Wells and Taylor's Oxford edition (and the Norton that derives from it), an edition that strongly commits itself to reexamining and often dissenting from received opinion. Ronald Knowles's third-generation Arden edition of *Part 2* (which appeared while this was being composed) in effect also agrees; although Knowles is uncomfortable with the traditional bibliogrpahical assumptions and categories, in practice he takes the Folio as his copy text and allows no independent authority to quarto variants as such.

Recently the received opinion on the theory of memorial reconstruction in general has been vigorously doubted, by Laurie Maguire and Kathleen Irace, for example. In this collection, Steven Urkowitz, certainly one of the most notable dissenters from traditional textual theories, presents his latest commentary on the *Henry VI* plays and reasserts the general position that differences between Folio and quarto texts are better explained not by memorial reconstruction, but by progressive revisions by Shakespeare and/or his company of theatrical versions of the plays.

Urkowitz, citing the work of a number of scholars, foresees what in effect would be a revolution in textual studies, one already well under way since the revisionist consideration of the quarto and Folio texts of *Lear*. Whatever does eventuate, it is clear that the *Pax Alexandria* of the past half-century has had the salutary effect of promoting the *Henry VI* plays from Shakespeare's clumsy and probably plagiaristic redactions of pre-existing work to an early and remarkably ambitious undertaking that could be legitimately related to later achievements in the genre of history and in the canon generally.

Closely related to the textual situation are the overlapping problems of date and sequence and the question of authorship as well. Again, these considerations over time preempted scholarly attention and hence deflected traditional critical evaluation. Briefly, from Malone on, many commentators have found the stylistic unevenness of the *Henry VI* plays, and especially *Part 1*, evidence of the work of other playwrights, and there was for some time much collecting of parallels from Greene, Peele, Nashe, and Marlowe to establish their shares. With regard to dating, there are evidences of what seems a surprisingly late premiere of *Part 1*, which have been interpreted to deny the natural and immediate assumption that in composition as in story, it preceded *Parts 2* and *3*.

The Arden editions of Andrew S. Cairncross (*Part 1–1962, Part 2–1957, Part 3–1964*; the sequence is interesting) engaged these perennial concerns and by at least seeming to resolve them, established, perhaps even more significantly than Alexander, a critical context in which, without much apprehension, these concerns could be treated as for all practical purposes settled. This is precisely what many critics of the sixties, seventies, and even into the eighties proceeded to do: to deal with the *Henry VI* plays as an essentially unified sequence, authentically Shakespeare's. There are frequent referrals to Cairncross for those who wished further detail, and sometimes acknowledgments that perhaps some of these issues might be less than irrevocably resolved; but the usual procedure was simply to deal with the trilogy as with any Shakespeare plays, with Cairncross as the warrant for doing so. Cairncross was less innovator than consolidator: as he said in his introduction to *Part 3*: ". . . in the light of recent work on structure, decorum, and imagery, the literary and dramatic achievement emerges more powerfully" (vii). The recent work he relied on most heavily was that of Alexander, with whom he consulted extensively; Hereward T. Price's influential 1951 monograph that argued for a strong if novel dramatic structure in *Part 1*; and of course E. M. W. Tillyard's *Shakespeare's History Plays* (1944), itself the most famous and provocative work of the century on the subject.

With regard to dating, there is an odd sense that there is more evidence than can be comfortably assimilated in Cairncross's view. Thomas Nashe's *Pierce Penniless* (SR, August 8, 1592) praises a very popular "Talbot Play," Henslowe's Diary records a number of lucrative performances of the "ne" play *Harry the Sixt*, beginning in March of the same year, and—especially since Hanspeter Born's persuasive examination—there is general agreement that both refer to Shakespeare's *Part 1*. The problem arises with Robert Greene's famous attack on Shakespeare in *Groatsworth of Wit* (SR, September 20, 1592)—in fact posthumously, since Greene died on September 3. Greene's "His tiger's heart wrapped in a player's hide" seems patently to parody York's reference to Margaret of Anjou's "tiger's heart wrapped in a woman's hide" in Act 1, scene 4 of *Part 3*. The natural, indeed unavoidable, assumption is that Greene was alluding to a line made famous on stage; and all the more so since it comes from one of the play's high points, just moments before Richard, Duke of York, meets his true tragedy. Yet if *Part 1* premiered only in March of 1592, there hardly seems time for a line from *Part 3* to have become recognizable enough to parody by September of the same year, the matter being much exacerbated by the fact that plague closed the London theaters from June 23 until a brief resumption of playing in December.

These evidences have been explained by some investigators as indicating that *Part 1* was written after *Parts 2* and *3*, and to capitalize on their success. This leaves the generally acknowledged inferiority of *Part 1* unaccounted for and requires reading in the earlier narrative "recalls" rather than anticipations of the later narrative. Born defends the priority of *Part 1* by presuming that Greene was playing on a line he had read in manuscript or heard in rehearsal or at some provincial performance. But this seems so counterintuitive to what we would presume of parody as to justify Antony Hammond's elegant characterization—"intolerably speculative."

The question of sequence is also dealt with in Knowles's very recent edition of *Part 2*, but the examination is disappointing. Knowles's argument for the priority of the second and third parts to the first is largely just a reiteration of Dover Wilson's insistence that if *Part 1* had in fact preceded *Part 2*, the latter play would have included, as it does not, some reference to Talbot, the military hero of the former. Knowles repeats the linchpin of

Wilson's case: that it is "incomprehensible" that Talbot is not mentioned "even when in the first scene [of *Part 2*] Gloucester recounts the glorious dead who have given their lives to preserve Henry V's victories in France" (114; cf. Wilson, *Part 1*, xiii). In fact, Gloucester is not recalling the glorious dead; six of the eight names on his list (1.1.75–91) belong to the characters he is speaking to at the moment; the other two are his heroic brothers, Henry and Bedford, whose fraternity establishes Gloucester's own patriotism. (To give Wilson his due, his list was "of those who had shed their blood," a somewhat different claim.)

That Henslowe's "ne" *Harry the Sixt* in the spring of 1592 meant something other than the premiere of a recently composed work is perhaps a chancy proposition, because ordinarily it seems to mean just that. Still, Henslowe's "ne" looks like the least compelling of these evidentiary constraints, and the frequent supposition that the Folio text of *Part 1* contains later revision by Shakespeare might allow Henslowe's designation to mean something like newly revised for performance at the Rose. One will also encounter the assertion that a revised play could not have produced the takings recorded in the Diary, but in Michael Williams's infinitely useful words, that's more than we know.

In his recent essay "Shakespeare and Others," Gary Taylor both asserts the late composition of *Part 1*—that is, later than *Parts 2* and *3*—and also attacks Shakespeare's sole, or substantial, authorship of the play. Taylor presents a great deal of data on variations in the text, variations that he claims cannot be explained at the scribal or compositorial level and that therefore indicate multiple authorship. His investigation results in an apportioning of *Part 1* among four authors. Nashe is credited with the first act, and two anonymous contributors are assigned the bulk of the remainder: Y for Act Three and most of Act Five, and W for all but one scene of Act Two and for the first scene of Act Four. This leaves as Shakespeare's share Act Two, scene four (the Temple Garden scene) and all of Act Four except W's opening scene (thus the betrayal and death of Talbot); these are, incidentally, the portions of the play regularly attributed to Shakespeare by earlier disintegrators like Fleay and Dover Wilson, who proceeded, however, by different methods. Taylor's conclusion would make Shakespeare's participation quite small, something less than 20 percent of the play, and if it were to become generally accepted, would have the effect of moving *Part 1* to the margins of the canon.

Taylor considers a good deal of detail, and his accumulative method of presentation may well seem persuasive. The scenario he supposes, however, would require a number of atypical situations. Composition by a group of four or more writers is the least unusual; there are records in Henslowe's Diary of as many as fifteen such collaborations between 1598 and 1602 (out of 149 total plays). These are invariably credited to Drayton or Dekker or Chettle—almost always at least two are involved—with frequent help from Munday and/or Wilson. Whether this would have been a normal method for other playwrights six to ten years earlier seems at least open to question.

Writing a narratively antecedent continuation to a play—a "prequel" in contemporary demotic—was far less common. Taylor cites two examples: Chettle's *Rising of Cardinal Wolsey*, which followed his earlier Wolsey play very quickly; and Dekker's *First Introduction* (which might not be a full play) to his and Drayton's three-part *Civil Wars of France*. (All of these, incidentally, are lost.) With the likely addition of *Don Horatio* as a fore-piece to Kyd's *Spanish Tragedy*, these are the only instances we know of.

And finally, the extension of a dramatic narrative to as many as three plays is also very rare. Aside from Shakespeare's doing so, there are only Dekker and Drayton's *Civil Wars*, which one expects were done in imitation of Shakespeare's history sequences, and Heywood's series of five *Ages* plays, about twenty years later and themselves a most remarkable anomaly.

It should be remembered that Taylor is positing not just one but all of these unusual circumstances simultaneously, and in a play designed as an introduction to *Part 2*, which he presumes was then in the repertory of another company and thus unavailable for playing at the Rose. Further, since he dismisses the idea of *Part 1* as a later revised text, it would seem that he supposes the 1592 performances ended with Suffolk's plotting, which anticipates the opening of the unavailable *Part 2*. Taylor's challenge to the orthodox position on the authorship of *Part 1* is strong—it will surely be a basic document for further considerations of the matter—but it by no means answers all the questions.

One further point should be made. There have been, at least from the early sixties on, any number of critics who have used *Part 1* as their starting point in demonstrating the development of themes, characters, and images over the course of the *Henry VI* plays or even of the First Tetralogy; these include Brockbank, Berry, Kay, Riggs, Pierce, Ricks, R. Y. Turner, Danby, Talbert, Champion, Berman, and Richmond, among others. In the present collection, Harry Keyishian does so in tracing the theme of revenge through its various manifestations, and Nina daVinci Nichols follows the strange and various uses associated with paper in the three parts. Although not every critical argument is equally convincing, it is difficult to imagine that at least a good part of this work is not firmly based on what is validly there in the texts. It is comparably difficult to believe that *Part 1* could have provided the necessary first steps for these critical perceptions if in fact it had been produced by a consortium of four writers and after Shakespeare had already provided the necessary second and third steps.

In the present volume, J. J. M. Tobin presents a different perspective on the question of collaborative authorship of these plays by exploring Shakespeare's seemingly voracious appetite for Nashe's language and suggesting that greater emphasis on Nashe's indirect influence and less on his direct participation may well be the more productive approach.

The following survey of the critical fortunes of the *Henry VI* plays is indebted to a number of earlier surveys. Judith Hinchcliffe's 1984 Garland bibliography is remarkably thorough and includes brief but reliable annotations for almost all of the 921 items listed as well as helpful cross-references among them. Comparably valuable and surprisingly unnoticed is Laurie Lanzen Harris and Mark W. Scott's volume in the Gale Research *Shakespearean Criticism* series (also 1984). Harris and Scott provide selections from approximately sixty critics beginning with Thomas Nashe and ending with Marilyn French's *Shakespeare's Division of Experience* (1981). Some of the earlier items are, of course, just snippets, but the excerpts from later commentators are generous and well chosen, and there is a good deal of solid editorial comment on agreements and disagreements among critics. No one is likely to agree with every one of the choices for inclusion, but certainly most of the best is represented, and a list of about fifty-five further items, all with brief annotations, is appended.

Just one year later, in *Shakespeare Survey*, Dennis H. Burden did a thorough and well-considered review of criticism of the history plays from 1952 to 1983, using as a starting point the much admired retrospective of the criticism of the first half-century that Harold Jenkins had published in *Shakespeare Survey* for 1953. There is also much that is informative and even illuminating in the coverage provided by a number of guides edited by Stanley Wells. The 1986 *Cambridge Companion to Shakespeare Studies* contains a knowledgeable essay by Edward Berry tracing the fluctuations of the plays' critical fortunes, largely from Tillyard on; Berry's sanity and evenhandedness are attractive, although his judgment that "the histories have been relatively untouched by the more venturesome critical theories of the past forty years" (256) now seems somewhat premature. *The Cambridge Companion* is actually the third-generation work, succeeding *A New Companion to Shakespeare Studies*, edited by Kenneth Muir and S. Schoenbaum in 1971, which itself succeeded *A Companion* edited by Harley Granville-Barker and G. B. Harrison in 1934. The earliest *Companion* did not address criticism of the histories as a topic, and the next version had only a couple of well written pages by David Bevington on the plays of the First Tetralogy and a comment in passing, largely on Tillyard, by Stanley Wells in his overview of criticism since Bradley. By and large, it is only recently that tracing the criticism of the histories has seemed a necessity.

Wells's *Shakespeare: A Bibliographical Guide*, New Edition, published in 1990, demonstrates the new emphasis. It contains a chapter by Michael Hattaway on the First Tetralogy (and *King John*) in which Hattaway, in a relatively brief compass, analyzes and evaluates at least most of the more important issues raised about these plays; an extensive and obviously more current reading list is also provided. This volume, too, is the successor to an earlier work: Wells's oddly titled *Shakespeare: Select Bibliographical Guides* (1973). The 1973 *Guide(s)* includes a judicious essay by A. R. Humphreys which devotes a surprising amount of space and attention to what critical work had been done to date on Shakespeare's earliest histories.

The fondness for if not the compulsion to review and examine previous critical positions becomes more prominent in the eighties and nineties. Two last surveys will be mentioned. Robin Headlam Wells deserves inclusion, if only for his title "The Fortunes of Tillyard." Actually, he has a good deal more to recommend him, and although the date of his essay—1985—does not now sound very recent, he is very responsive to more recent trends in criticism and commendably sane in commenting on them. The most recent such work I have encountered is the 1998 "Shakespeare's Historicism: Visions and Revisions" by Paola Pugliatti, who has done a good deal of impressive work on these plays; her essay is in effect a review of reviews of criticism, perhaps indicative of the contemporary state of the art, and of course necessarily the most up-to-date.

For a quite long period of time, criticizing the *Henry VI* plays was tantamount to disagreeing with Tillyard; and, of course, for a considerable and earlier period it was roughly equivalent to agreeing with him. Tillyard both as stimulant and irritant has had an enormous effect on the criticism of these plays, and an effect that, in my judgment, has been notably salutary. There was, I think, nothing earlier that is really comparable to what he did in *Shakespeare's History Plays* in 1944. His focus was larger than just the plays considered here, which he presented as the penultimate stage of the long narrative of England's sin in deposing of Richard II, its long suffering of divinely imposed punishment, and its final restoration to grace with Henry Tudor's victory over the diabolical Richard III—the much noted "Tudor myth." However much his case is overstated, Tillyard performed an outstanding service by relating these plays to a broad and impressive background of religious, philosophical, and historical thought and by tracing in their long account of numerous, various, often confusing events a serious and coherent authorial purpose that made them worth the critical examination. After Tillyard, no one speaks of these plays as simply the heap of rubbish or the mere drum and trumpet things they had been claimed to be. Tillyard's work is of course of his time, but unless one takes the terminally relativistic view that as with the blind men and the elephant, there is nothing more permanent in the objects themselves than what a temporal (or perhaps political or sociological or genderal or other) perspective allows one to see, his work cannot be dismissed as just of its time. The time, incidentally, is the same year as Olivier's *Henry V*, with which Tillyard is sometimes linked and which, with comparable injustice, is sometimes dismissed as simpleminded jingoism: *pietas* is a virtue little practiced in Shakespeare studies.

Tillyard's influence was buttressed by Lily B. Campbell's arguments for the histories as "*Mirrors of Elizabethan Policy,*" which presented a view more alert to contemporary relevance but essentially compatible with Tillyard's in that it insisted on history as committed to moral instruction. Here, too, history is seen as disclosing divine justice, now by offering to rulers "mirrors" of moral and political instruction. Campbell had also just a few years earlier edited *The Mirror for Magistrates* (1938), a compilation of first-person laments of the great men and women of the fifteenth century, many of whom became the major characters of Shakespeare's tetralogy. The *Mirror* is in all probability an occasional source for Shakespeare's plays; at the least, as Tillyard insisted, it was a readily accessible text which read the happenings of the period as God's inevitable and individual judgments within the time frame of the tetralogy. Thus, along with Hall, Holinshed, and *The Civil Wars* of Samuel Daniel, it comprises a "literary background" which, Tillyard stresses, is saturated with the sense of God's providence. Tillyard's position was, as surveys of this material always seem to note, generally endorsed by Irving Ribner in *The English History Play in the Age of Shakespeare* (1957; 2nd. ed. 1965), and by M. M. Reese in *The Cease of Majesty* (1961). Both had some reservations to express: Reese on Tillyard's insufficient allowance for individual human agency, and Ribner on the implication that the history of the Second Tetralogy (most notably of course the deposition of Richard II), rather than the crimes portrayed in the plays themselves, is the motive power.

Still, both Reese and Ribner wrote in basic agreement with Tillyard, and the status their own books attained as critical resources tended to reinforce his hegemony. Further reinforcement came from Cairncross's editions, which adopted Tillyard's view and, as has been noted, incorporated it with a scholarly examination and seeming resolution of the traditional problems of text and sequence. And yet another substantiation seemed to be available in Geoffrey Bullough's standard work on the *Narrative and Dramatic Sources*. By the time Bullough presented the materials for the First Tetralogy (1960), he was somewhat more given to making literary-critical judgments; he frankly rejected Tillyard's idea of an eight-play epic of England, but, curiously, by insisting on Hall as the major source—and even more by reprinting Hall's full preface, emphasizing the disasters incurred by disobedience and rebellion—Bullough in fact appeared to be endorsing the critical importance of Tillyard's insistence on the observance of order and degree. The cumulative effect was that a student consulting most of what would have been seen (and in fair degree, still are seen) as the standard works on the topic would have found far more endorsement of rather than reservation from Tillyard's view.

Tillyard's work set the grounds for the critical conversation for a very long time; even today, although there are many new emphases, his focus is still often a shaping force. Clearly, he had claimed too much—a judgment that many subsequent commentators would feel is a litotes. Tillyard saw not just a divine purpose working itself out in fifteenth-century English history, but the significance of that history to be such that the cosmological implications of God's plan resonate in what might seem the most casual of details. Joan of Arc is a scourge not just because she inflicts pain on her enemies but because she is an instrument of God's punishment; and of course, as woman assuming male functions, she is an exemplar of the violation of degree. Refutation of Tillyard proceeded to such an extent that anti-Tillyardism became the new orthodoxy. Such critics as A. C. Hamilton, S. C. Sen Gupta, and James Winny all insisted that the plays themselves were governed by human motive and decision, not divine, and ordinarily by motive and decision of a decidedly self-seeking and pragmatic nature. There is, needless to say, much here that is indisputable, even if in some cases the refutation of Tillyard proceeded to questionable extremes. Robert Ornstein (who wrote most energetically and entertainingly) categorically announced that there was "no slightest hint" of the providential in these plays; and John Bromley saw the matter simply as successive Lancastrian generations being murderous, overreaching, and then inept. Both A. L. French (who wrote a series of energetic anti-Tillyard essays in the late sixties) and David Frey insisted that since the innocent Henry VI is allowed to suffer, Shakespeare must have meant to question the concept of a providential God operating in human affairs. But since a presumably providential God did in fact allow the innocent Henry to suffer, the matter here seems more the critics' than Shakespeare's inability to imagine the necessary deity.

At best, however, Tillyard as irritant motivated critics to supply their own and more accurate descriptions of what the plays were *really* about. A number of these anti-Tillyardian undertakings did indeed result in persuasive and permanently valuable work. Among these, pride of place should perhaps be given to J. P. Brockbank's "The Frame of Disorder," which presents a satisfyingly grim and comprehensive overview of the progressively more dire stages in the trilogy's story, of "the plight of individuals caught up in a cataclysmic movement of events." David Riggs's work is rooted in his research into the alliance of history and rhetoric that Shakespeare's schooling would have presented; this in turn leads to his reading the plays as an extended meditation on the decline of heroic idealism. Edward Berry's title, *Patterns of Decay,* recalls Brockbank's view of the continual worsening of England's condition, but Berry is by no means simply derivative. He explores more thoroughly—at book length rather than essay length—and he convincingly imposes salient categories on a very great deal of detail.

In general, later critics insisted that the *Henry VI* plays themselves and the cultural background behind them were far more complex than Tillyard had thought. Some of the perception of diversity of the plays' content certainly derived from readers trained in the methods of New Criticism: although neither Wilbur Sanders nor Norman Rabkin wrote on the *Henry VI* plays in detail, their comments on the ambiguities of the history plays in general have been quite influential. In this regard, however, clearly the most influential criticism has been the vigorously individual assertion by A. R. Rossiter of "Ambivalence: [as] The Dialectic of the Histories." A comparable point of view is very frequent in more recent criticism of the plays, which, however, tends not to proceed to the traditional New Critical resolution of disparities but to see the plays as irreconcilably ambivalent.

In a comparable way, the background of the plays has been much investigated to demonstrate a greater complexity than Tillyard had adduced. It is, however, not to the point to dismiss Tillyard's materials as mere commonplaces; commonplaces are in fact what an author can expect his audience to share. Still, he had been selective, certainly overly selective; and Robin Headlam Wells makes the telling point that historians of Tillyard's day had already demonstrated the diversity of Elizabethan thought in some detail. Henry Ansgar Kelly is sometimes put forth as the ultimate refuter of Tillyard. Kelly reread the chronicles and found in them far more diversity than Tillyard had asserted. One of the most cited of Kelly's judgments is his finding that there was not just a Tudor myth in the chronicles, but a Lancastrian and a Yorkist myth as well. One might argue here that this is more supportive than destructive of Tillyard; that chroniclers so often enlisted God's providence on any political side might well be seen as more important than that they did not all choose the same side. Kelly demonstrates Edward Hall, traditionally the main source of Shakespeare's supposed providentialism, to be far more skeptical than had been thought about judgments that God's hand was visible in some historical occurrence. Hall, probably more often, distances himself from such speculations with "men say" or some such phrase; yet he does clearly seem to think that God's displeasure is the best explanation of the disastrous results of Henry's marriage to Margaret of Anjou, and in his own voice, he presents Edward IV's false oath to gain entry to the city of York as the cause of his sons' murder. Hall is at times scornful of those who assume they can discern God's purposes in human affairs; but inscrutable is a far cry from inoperative.

A number of other critics have, like Kelly, broadened our view of the backgrounds Shakespeare may have drawn on. Riggs's work has already been mentioned. Emrys Jones explores the very rich heritage of classical, Christian, and humanist thought that was available, although his claim that Thomas Legge's *Richardus Tertius* was the model for structuring *Henry VI* in three parts is not persuasive. John D. Cox, arguing against the providentialist view, presumes that Shakespeare took a number of elements from medieval drama and relocated them in a secular context in which their inappropriateness comments on the non-providential nature of the world of the histories. This does of course assume that the details, which were available elsewhere, did in fact originate in mystery play and that their origin would have recognized by the audience. This may be right; I am somewhat the more disposed to think so by Nina daVinci Nichols's discussion in this volume of the mock-crucifixion killing of York in *Part 3*.

There is I think a fair amount that may be allowed—and a good deal more than is usually allowed—to Tillyard's way of seeing things, if not to his particular formulation of them. It is certainly true that things happen in the plays because human agents, usually for ignoble purposes, choose to make them happen. But, as a great many of the best readers of the play have insisted, there is also a process far larger than any individual judgment that continually advances both by means of these human decisions and in spite of them. No one character's destiny is the story of any one of the plays; the major players typically are introduced in one part and destroyed in the next; a few last for two more plays, and Margaret, the toughest of the lot, makes it into *Richard III* and survives to chuckle over her revenge in retirement. Although Henry's piety, until the latter acts of *Part 3*, ordinarily seems naive if not fatuous, the amoral, self-seeking pragmatists do not succeed either. The *winner*, so to speak, at the end of the trilogy is Edward IV, who makes a number of foolish mistakes and yet prevails. Yet this is not just the realm of the Goddess Fortuna. Crimes are always presented as crimes, and someone—even though he may have perpetrated the penultimate crime—always accuses the criminal at hand of disloyalty, betrayal, viciousness, inhumanity, sometimes even sin. Some kind of moral order is always being outraged; indeed, without some kind of moral order to be outraged, the actions would have no character worth remarking.

This is not quite Tillyard's providential cosmos, but it is by no means a morally neutral world. The various omens, prophecies, and curses of the plays are also relevant here. As A. R. Humphreys has it, "[Shakespeare's] structure is unified by retrospection, foreboding, irony and Nemesis (and so implies intelligence, not mindlessness, whether human or providential)" (242). Or, in H. M. Richmond's formulation, "the characters still exist in an ultimately ordered universe—although by no means as wholly subject to Providence as Henry imagines, or as the old morality plays had shown. Virtue may be destroyed often in the world of *Henry VI*, but Nemesis always overtakes the guilty" (46). Michael Quinn's article on general as opposed to particular providence is very useful here: there is a distinction to be made—and one that was often made in Christian texts—between the general providence of the attainment of peace with Henry VII's accession and the particular providence of happenings within the larger pattern. Usually the latter is difficult if not impossible to discern. There are a few instances in the *Henry VI* plays that seem as if they are intended to portray such particular providence: notably the death of Cardinal Beaufort, and perhaps the execution of the Duke of Suffolk as well. Even Kelly allows that they seem to be retribution for the murder of Good Duke Humphrey. But why, in terms of God's plan, things like the suffering of innocents occur is usually as unknowable in Shakespeare as in life. In this regard, Robert R. Reed's *Crime and God's Punishment* is instructive. However savage the idea may appear to us that God uses the evil of one man to punish the evil of another or that God avenges the sins of the father on the children or even grandchildren, Reed shows that there is ample warrant in the Bible and in the sermonizing of Shakespeare's time, and at least some reflection in the First Tetralogy.

What becomes crucial in this matter of judging how much, if at all, the *Henry VI* plays participate in the providential is their relationship to *Richard III*. The providential element is very strong in the later play: Richard is the scourge that punishes the lesser offenders, increases his own guilt by doing so, and is at last destroyed by God's captain at Bosworth. Rackin puts the matter well: "Pious and well-intentioned, Henry VI is confronted by a world ruled by Machiavellian *Realpolitik*. Ruthlessly clever, Richard III is subjected to the power of providential justice" (28). The evocation of the providential by no means requires Tillyard's insistence that, even as the action of *Part 1* begins, the curse of Richard II is already operative in the narrative and the minds of the audience. This surely was not the case, and as many have noted, the references to Richard II in the *Henry VI* plays are few—no more than half a dozen—and almost always presented as a cloud on the Lancastrian title, not a sin against God and His chosen deputy. And of course the dramatization of Bolingbrook's usurpation and its results had not yet been written, a circumstance that forced Tillyard to the desperate expedient of hypothesizing a lost early version of the Second Tetralogy.

In fact, the beginning we are given—the death of Henry V—is quite sufficient to initiate a narrative capable of demonstrating God's purpose working itself out in English history. After the disastrous death of the great king, his conquests are lost through internal dissension, faction and vengeance become ever more destructive, and finally the scourge and then the savior appear. If there are few mentions in these plays of Richard II, there is a plethora of references to Henry V—a remarkable thirty-seven in all. He is all but invariably portrayed as the ideal of kingship. (Mortimer does include him on the list of Lancastrian dispossessers.) That so glorious a reign existed so recently, and, so the best of the characters early in the sequence hope, might be re-established would seem to argue against critical views of the *Henry VI* plays that would see the beargarden world of *Part 3* as man's natural condition and Shakespeare interested only in how power is obtained. Phyllis Rackin refers to Henry V as "an emblem of lost glory," and makes the shrewd observation that by keeping him out of the narrative proper, Shakespeare avoids problematizing him through interaction with other characters, as is of course the case in the later histories.

A similar tactic is used with the ideal king of the other end of the sequence: Henry Tudor. He appears only briefly in the last act of *Richard III*; he wraps himself in an aura of sanctity by endlessly referring to God as his patron (literally eleven times); kills the villain in single combat; establishes a reign of peace to which God, as Henry has prayed, clearly says Amen; and exits the play with his heroic status intact but for the occasional feminist disapproval of his political marriage to Elizabeth of York.

The crucial question for seeing the First Tetralogy as at least something like Tillyard's providential narrative is whether Shakespeare intended in the writing of the *Henry VI* plays to dramatize the story of Richard of Gloucester as well. A quite strong case can be made that he did, even apart from the climactic ending of the union of York and Lancaster, which he inherited from Hall. Richard of course dominates the latter acts of *Part 3*; so much so that reader already familiar with *Richard III* (as we all are) cannot fail to recognize in Shakespeare's earlier comic-demonic soliloquies what in the later play which will reach full efflorescence. One even has the vague impression that Shakespeare is somewhat impatient with the fortunes of the saintly Henry and anxious to focus completely on his villain. (Young Henry Tudor also makes a brief appearance here in *Part 3* to receive the old king's blessing and the prediction of his post-Bosworth greatness and beneficence to his people.) More significant for this consideration, however, is the appearance of Richard toward the end of *Part 2* as a fierce full-grown warrior at a time when historically he was either two years old or yet unborn (Shakespeare conflates two different historical events here). Quite why he should have done so unless he intended to dramatize the Richard story is difficult to imagine.

The strongest argument for the kind of intimate connection between *Richard III* and its precedent plays that might justify seeing the First Tetralogy as a providential narrative derives from the very strange and strangely unnoted structuring of the *Henry VI* plays. To begin with there is, so far as we know, no precedent in the public theaters (and only Legge's *Richardus Tertius* in academic drama) for Shakespeare's extending a continuous narrative over as many as three plays; and there is precious little after, only Dekker and Drayton's *Civil Wars*, presumably in imitation of Shakespeare's history sequences, and Heywood's *Ages*, some twenty years after. What is even more unusual, in fact unique, is Shakespeare's ending each of the *Henry VI* plays by emphasizing some narrative concern that will be resumed immediately in the next play: *Part 1* ends with Suffolk planning to dominate the king by means of the marriage to Margaret of Anjou, and *Part 2* opens with his presentation of her to Henry; *Part 2* ends with the Yorkists, victors at the battle of St. Albans, encouraging one another to get to London before the Lancastrians, and *Part 3* opens with their doing so; *Part 3* ends with Richard's asides threatening to undermine the time of peace his brother Edward celebrates, and *Richard III* of course opens with his soliloquy announcing his commitment to destroying "this weak piping time of peace." The result is a narrative that is not just continuous from play to play but that is "to be continued," and no one else, not even Shakespeare himself in the Second Tetralogy (which is the closest approach), ever does this again.

Both Barbara Hodgdon and David Kastan have written at some length on closure in these plays. Much of Hodgdon's concern is with the "social text" of performance—both Elizabethan and modern—which she privileges equally with the printed text of the Folio; thus for her, open-endedness may be seen simply a variety of closure, a position of some interest but not of real relevance to my concern here (*End* 44–99). Kastan, however, sees open-endedness as genre specific: it is the "shape of time" that history play, as opposed to tragedy or comedy, imposes on its material; "this open-endedness is fundamentally the mark of the history play" (*Shapes* 47–48). To this he cogently contrasts the world of salvational history, especially in mystery play: in human history some further happening beyond the latest event dramatized is always intimated; but it is only in mystery play that time actually has a stop, that there literally is no tomorrow. In general, Kastan is surely right (he usually is) but his scheme allows insufficient distinction between "the lack of resolution in the military plot of *1 Henry IV*" (47) and the deliberately evoked anticipation at the close of *1 Henry VI* in Suffolk's great expectations from the imminent marrige of Margaret of Anjou. At the least, there is in the latter an insistence on, not just an implication of, the open-ended quality of the moment, an insistence that will be repeated at the ends of the next two plays. In fact, Shakespeare's method here approximates, about as well as secular drama can, the extratemporal implications of the mystery play's opening with Creation and closing with the General Judgment. The First Tetralogy opens with the recollection of a stasis, the time when Henry V ruled and all was well, and it closes with Henry Tudor's announcement that peace has been permanently restored and that we English will live, and for a century have lived, happily ever after. The final assurance that another stasis of perfection had been achieved would perhaps not have retained the audience's assent for much longer than it took to clear the theater; but that it was so intended may be shown by its difference from the stasis that momentarily concludes the Second Tetralogy. Here the great king, Henry V, is confirmed in his full glory, but the audience is permitted to savor his triumph no longer than the Epilogue's reflection on its brevity and fragility.

What happens in the First Tetralogy is also really a quite different matter from what happens in Elizabethan or Jacobean two-part plays, which have fairly often been investigated as models for Shakespeare's structuring (Crane, Leech, Hunter). These two-part plays are most often simply popular entertainments that begot unanticipated sequels. Of the thirteen that survive in whole or part, this is the case with at least nine, and none of the four that have some measure of continuity attempts the kind of narrative hook-and-eye linkage of the *Henry VI* plays. There was something of a vogue of two-part plays after Marlowe's *Tamburlaine*, and it is sometimes suggested that in imitation, *Parts 2* and *3* were also written as a two-part play. But it makes little sense to mount a two-part play that ends with an unattached linkage to a presumably not-yet-written *Richard III*; it makes even less sense that at some later time *Part 1* was designed to end with an unattached linkage to a play in another company's repertoire. The effect of continuity is so unavoidably the result of this unparalleled technique of connecting one play to the next that unless Shakespeare indeed wished to emphasize their continuity, it is more than difficult to imagine why he used it. And to return to the point at hand, since this same technique links *Part 3* with *Richard III* as it links *Part 1* with *Part 2* and *Part 2* with *Part 3*, it looks as if the general continuity was intend to include, not exclude, *Richard III*.

This is a less radical idea than it might sound: traditionally both in criticism and on stage, the three *Henry VI* plays are dealt with as one thing. Critics discuss them as a unit—as this volume does; to the best of my knowledge, no one has published a full-length book on any one of the three plays. Given the sheer volume of what Shakespeareans impose on one another, this is rather amazing, and it is not caused by restraint. Comparably, directors direct the three together, even if this requires radical cutting to fit them into two evenings of performance. The only exception I have heard of is the report by Dennis Kennedy of a 1994 Royal Shakespeare Company staging of *Part 3* billed simply as "*Henry VI; The Battle for the Throne*; ". . . if you didn't know that Shakespeare had written three parts, so much the better" (61).

My suggestion here is that the *Henry VI* plays, so frequent by considered one rather than three, might even better be considered three quarters. This hardly requires that all the plays were written before the first was staged or even that the ending with the triumph of Henry Tudor was from the beginning seen as the natural end of the sequence, although I think this by no means unlikely. At minimum, nothing more is being insisted on than that Shakespeare, by the time he wrote the end of the first play in sequence, realized that his narrative would require another play or, more probably, at least two, and committed himself to that completion, as the odd "to be continued" ending indicates.

What this means in terms of performance is of course unclear; no one I have read except Edward Berry seems to think that performance of three (or four) parts on consecutive days was feasible. But since there were in effect no other three-or four-part plays, we have no evidence for feasibility or otherwise. What we do have in Henslowe's records is evidence that second parts were played immediately after their first parts about two-thirds of the time they were performed, as if "continuity"—which in these cases would mean simply revisiting familiar characters and similar situations—had some considerable box-office appeal. We also have Henslowe's records of purchasing properties—which presumably indicated imminent perform-ance—for Dekker and Drayton's *Civil Wars*; on the basis of the dates we have, it looks as if the various parts succeeded each other in four to six-week intervals, and thus all may well have been in repertory at the same time. This is not much to go on but it suggests that Shakespeare's stage may quite possibly have oft shown the First Tetralogy if not on consecutive days, at least in close proximity within a playing season.

The *Henry VI* plays do not really seem to be the discrete entities recent critics often claim them to be (e.g., Hodgdon, *End* 46), but rather portions of a unified artistic conception. If this is so, then the ending with Bosworth, and to a lesser degree the beginning with the death of Henry V are more than just details numerically far outnumbered by other details demonstrat-ing human ambition and rapacity. And to the degree that this is so, a great deal more of Tillyard's kind of providentialism, if not his particular fomu-lation, is justified than is usually allowed; however tattered his ensign, it is not appropriately torn down. At least, so it seems from my own essential-ist, formalist, intentionalist, humanist, old-fashioned, old-historicist, guilty-on-all-counts theoretical stance (formerly point of view).

Having fulfilled Michael Hattaway's prediction that everyone who writes on these plays must necessarily wrestle with the idea of providence, it is appropriate to move on to critical work in which this theme is not paramount. The *Henry VI* plays, mostly perhaps because of their relative-ly minor status, seem often to be discussed in concert with other of Shakespeare's work. Most frequently of course, this means discussing them along with the later histories, but there is also an interesting group of treat-ments that associate them with the earliest of Shakespeare's plays, thus predominantly with the early comedies. A. C. Hamilton's *The Early Shakespeare* (1964) is a series of lectures on the plays of the early and mid-dle 1590s that includes a chapter on each of the parts of *Henry VI*. It is confessedly an exploratory consideration, but Hamilton moves gracefully through the criticism of the time, distancing himself from Tillyardian atti-tudes and providing sensible readings of the plays, though making only occasional connections to Shakespeare's beginnings in other genres. John Arthos's *Shakespeare: The Early Writings* (1972) covers much the same ground but continually explores relationships between the comedies and the histories. The emphasis is on Shakespeare as artist, as a poet sensitive-ly responding to the problems and possibilities of human experience, a more *belles lettres* approach but one productive of some valuable insights. Much the best of such examinations is, in my judgment, Robert Y. Turner's *Shakespeare's Apprenticeship* (1974), an impressive and much undervalued book. Turner approaches the early work from a kind of nuts-and-bolts pragmatism, investigating how Shakespeare engaged in these plays the demands to provide specific kinds of language (dialogue itself, speeches of emotion or moral instruction) and specific kinds of scenes (scenes of confrontation, scenes of persuasion). These are requirements that cut across the boundaries of genre—Turner includes even the narrative poems—and thus the sense is very strong that here we are dealing with authorship at an indisputably basic level. Needless to say, I find Turner's judgments on how Shakespeare met these demands convincingly rooted in the texts themselves.

F. W. Brownlow's *Two Shakespearean Sequences* (1977) surprisingly groups the First Tetralogy (and *John* and *Richard II*) with the final romances (plus *Henry VIII, Two Noble Kinsmen,* and *Timon*). The strategy is to use the "first plays" and the "last" to frame Shakespeare's career and to support Brownlow's semi-biographical conclusions. It will be noted that to do so, the first "sequence" is made to include *Richard II* and *Timon* becomes the "last" play, so that his burial by the sea may provide a return to "the tragic conflict between capacity and imagination of which Richard II, in prison, is so eloquent an expression" (9). John Wilders's *The Lost Garden* (1978) makes the most extreme connection: he sees in both the English and Roman history plays Shakespeare's development of a sense of human longing for lost and unattainable innocence that finds its full expression in the tragedies. Wilders writes evocatively, but his specific application—"The role of God in the history plays is comparable to that of the gods in *King Lear:* men hold conflicting views of Him and He remains inscrutable" (63)—makes little sense in the world of the *Henry VI* plays. Whether or not God is inscrutable, no character in these plays expresses (sincerely or otherwise) any belief other than traditional Christianity. As Kent advises Oswald, one must regard differences.

More recent criticism seems to take two contradictory directions. On the one hand, the New Historicist insistence on seeing the literary work as primarily a cultural document has led to the positing of any number of concerns and energies in Elizabethan society as operative and indeed constitutive in Shakespeare's work—logically, it would seem, willy nilly Will. Yet equally strongly, there has been an insistence on a remarkably self-reflexive Shakespeare. This latter strain was strongly asserted in an aesthetic context by James Calderwood in *Shakespearean Metadrama* (1971) and, with greater application to the First Tetralogy, by John W. Blanpied in *Time and the Artist in Shakespeare's English Histories* (1983). More recently, however, the self-reflexivity has more often been asserted with regard to Shakespeare's attitudes toward history itself: Shakespeare becomes not just historian but historiographer.

Bibliographies of *Henry VI* criticism regularly list Stephen Greenblatt's essay "Murdering Peasants"; given Greenblatt's status as founding father of New Historicism, this is to be expected. The essay, however, discusses *2*

Henry VI in a manner than charitably might be called less than elucidating. We are given a great deal of information about Dürer's proposed designs for a monument celebrating the victory of the nobility in the Peasants' War, the general proposition that defeating low-class enemies implicitly degrades the noble victor, and Sidney's and Spenser's "solutions"—in the *Arcadia*, Pyrocles and Mucidorus are disguised as Amazon and shepherd respectively while slaughtering the rabble, and in *The Faerie Queene*, Artegall consigns the destruction of the leveller Giant to his iron man servant Talus. Greenblatt sees Jack Cade as posing the same difficulty in *Part 2*: "How can such buffoons be put down without embarrassment to the victors?" (23). Shakespeare's "simple, effective, and, in its way, elegant" solution (24) is to make Alexander Iden, the property owner, rather than some aristocrat, Cade's slayer. Iden as property owner does indeed hold some interest, but since Cade has already engaged and defeated "the army of the King" (4.3.170), has knighted himself "To equal him [the royal commander, Sir Humphrey Stafford]" (115), has repeatedly proclaimed his own noble birth, has executed the royal counselor Lord Saye, has defiantly confronted yet another military force led by Clifford and Buckingham, and loses his following only when Clifford resorts to the chicanery of announcing a new and glorious expedition to France, it is hard to see how the dignity of the aristocracy has been preserved from the pollution of Cade's touch. Whatever Greenblatt's essay may tell us about attitudes of class in Shakespeare's society, it tells us worse than nothing about his play. And the play, so the very existence of this volume assumes, has its own autonomy.

There is no necessary reason that a largeness of approach result in inaccuracy in specific cases, although this is a very human failing. Such kinds of errors, however, do in fact seem to occur with some frequency in more recent criticism. In a very new book by Graham Holdernesss (*Shakespeare: The Histories*), we read that in *Part 1* "The brothers of Henry V, also heroes of Agincourt, Exeter and Bedford, lead a new French campaign" (115). In fact, Exeter was Henry V's great-uncle—he was actually Cardinal Beaufort's brother, but Shakespeare conceals that from us—and far from preparing for battle in France, he announces at the end of the first scene his intention to go "To Eltham, where the young King is" (1.1.170) to serve as Henry VI's "special governor." Exeter's only other appearances in *Part 1* are as choral commentator at the end of 3.1 and 4.1. If he is to be thought of as the same Exeter in *Part 3*, he is comparably non-martial: in 1.1, like Henry himself, Exeter is ready to flee the wrath of Margaret, and in 4.8, he is again in the King's company when Edward of York surprises and arrests him.

Holderness's having Talbot "Drawn up before Harfleur" (120) rather than Bordeaux is perhaps no more than faulty copyediting. But his defense of Joan as "the true centre" (133) of the play leads to denying "any obvious contextualising irony" to Joan's divine mission, although he quotes the locker-room snickering of the French lords in 1.2 and 2.1; seemingly accepting her claim of pregnancy though scornfully dismissing her related claims of multiple affairs with the French leaders (133); managing to read her famous "Done like a Frenchman—turn and turn again" (3.3.85) as "an admiring tribute to [Burgundy's] new-found patriotism" (132); and insisting that Joan, until her capture, is "virtually undefeated; and her supremacy in battle . . . unchallenged" (129), in spite of the English victories at Orleans and Rouen. (Joan asks: "At all times would you have my power alike?" [2.1.55]; Holderness presumably says "Yes.") The figure of Joan does indeed significantly problematize and subvert the assumptions of the male aristocrats in *Part 1*, but this cannot be established by invoking some "real" and symbolic Joan beyond the text and beyond the chronicles. However intriguing or broadening such historicist and/or feminist insights made be, they do not relieve the critic of the obligation to deal with the character with which the text presents us.

More recent, post-modernist, more theoretically based criticism seems to me in itself not necessarily worse or necessarily better than older, more traditional criticism; one can convict Tillyard of selectivity as egregious as what I have adduced of Holderness. I would, however, add the pre-postmodernist (and thus perhaps disabling) insistence that the criticism in some way elucidate the literature at hand. In the present collection, one will find some very contemporary approaches. Frances K. Barasch explores the use of the *mise en abyme* in these plays, M. Rick Smith investigates the history of *Part 2* in the light of Frederic Jameson's categories of the commodified and the recommodified, and James J. Paxson presents an impressive semiotic tracing of Joan of Arc's fiends in *Part 1* to an origin in misogyny. As Chaucer advises, if the churl's tale displeases, turn the page and choose another sort.

Feminist criticism of the First Tetralogy has been significant and successful; in many ways, these plays are made for a feminist approach. Shakespeare's own society and all the societies he creates for his plays, are at least strongly patriarchal. The histories are more than that: they are patrilineal, the father's nobility and virtue descending with his blood to his son. The topic of fathers and sons in the *Henry VI* plays has been well discussed by Berman and Pierce, among others, and its most obvious manifestation is the dialogue between Talbot and his son in *Part 1*; Talbot at least acknowledges a mother was involved in the transmission of his name and heroism; later, Henry IV will talk about Hal as if he created him by a process less messy than biology.

The histories descend from a chronicle tradition which is basically men recording the deeds of men for the edification of men. Phyllis Rackin develops this in an intriguing direction: she sees the male enterprise as one of inscribing a history of masculine heroism, and the women, especially the French women of *Part 1* as "anti-historians." The Good Duke would seem to agree: he sees the Anjou marriage as "canceling your fame,/ Blotting your names from books of memory,/ Razing the characters of your renown,/ Defacing monuments of conquered France" (*Part 2* 1.1.97–100). In this context, when a woman achieves notice, it is almost by definition unfavorable notice. Shakespeare certainly seems aware of and, to my reading, generally supportive of these presuppositions. He is constrained by the mere fact of the history he dramatizes to allow considerable attention to Joan of Arc and Margaret of Anjou; one could hardly retell the wars of the fifteenth century without them. But his portrayals are considerably more denigratory than his sources required, and his fictional Countess of Auvergne, who seeks fame—or infamy, the terms are synonymous here—further exemplifies the generality that the woman who achieves notice is transgressive in doing so. That she will be charged with sexual promiscuity is the further corollary.

The main lines of this approach have been in place for some time: David Bevington wrote a perceptive article in 1966 on the domineering women of *Part 1*, and Marilyn French's 1981 book states the general case quite well. To focus for the moment on Margaret—who is not quite the only character to appear in all four plays of the tetralogy; her husband, though dead, gets a couple of lines in *Richard III*— she has been discussed in a number of worthwhile articles: by Thomas H. McNeal, Patricia-Ann Lee, Marilyn Williamson, and others. Irene Dash—who is represented in this collection, but on another topic—devotes a chapter of her 1981 book to seeing Margaret's experience through Margaret's perspective; the result is the most sympathetic reading I have found. Here, Naomi Liebler and Lisa Scancella Shea trace Margaret through her appearances in the four plays as she embodies four Jungian archetypes, and relate the other women of the tetralogy to Margaret's centrally meaningful role. In her recent book *Women's Matters* (1998), Nina S. Levine attempts to shift the plays' disapproval of Margaret from a basis in mere anti-feminism to a more considered evaluation of how her actions affect the commonweal; Levine does, however, see notable misogyny in the plays' view of Margaret as the typically unruly woman.

Joan of Arc has of course also attracted a great deal of comment. Rackin has an energetic and persuasive discussion of the many articulations of her oppositional function: she "defin[es] the conflict between England and France as a conflict between masculine and feminine values: chivalric virtue versus pragmatic craft, historical fame versus physical reality, patriarchal age versus subversive youth, high social rank versus low, self versus other" (151). A bit further on, Rackin adds La Pucelle as nominalist versus realist: Joan believes in things, not words, although she uses words well to seduce Burgundy. Both Gabriele Bernhard Jackson and, at greater length, Leah Marcus have argued for La Pucelle as a representation of various aspects, some by no means adulatory, of Queen Elizabeth herself. Since

Marcus makes a strong point of returning to the old historicist idea of "Author's Intent or putative intentionality" (42), this linking of the dramatic character and the sovereign would seem to be the result of viewing *Part 1* as artifact, rather than culturally generated document. Joan's likeness to the queen who appeared in armor at Tilbury, who undermined the campaigns of 1590–1591 by lukewarm support, who entertained the Dukes of Alençon and Anjou as suitors, who was the subject of gossip about having borne illegitimate children, and so on—all here are claimed as parts of a "deliberate strategy" (68), "even though 'Shakespeare' in this play is inextricable from something that looks suspiciously like political sacrilege" (69). The quotation marks are a reminder that Marcus's privileging of "Author's Intent" does not extend to "its traditionally privileged position as the overriding determinant of meaning" (42). If authorial intent does not have this position, then it is hard to see much difference between Marcus's "local reading" and the typical New Historicist view of literature as culturally generated. On the other hand, to attribute such a strategy to the author as traditionally conceived is to assume that Shakespeare intended, his audience in some real sense understood, and the whole matter passed with impunity. At the least, this seems to imply a Shakespeare (or a "Shakespeare") so self-reflexively sophisticated that his success as a popular playwright is astonishing. It is worth remembering from time to time that these are extremely early plays in his career and that the one witness who reported a reaction, Thomas Nashe, spoke of tears for Talbot's heroism, not of ambiguation or containment of subversion or the resolution of anxieties and dark fantasies about the queen.

Investigation of the women of the First Tetralogy often naturally leads to consideration of others excluded from the official notice of the world of male, aristocratic, and usually martial power. Paola Pugliatti employs the useful term "marginals" (*Historian* 181–82), and much of her book is given over to investigating how the voices of those excluded from the history books enrich and complicate Shakespeare's version of history. Pugliatti's discussion is very complete and very valuable: she notes quite properly that these lower-class, largely anonymous personages enter the narrative often at the most crucial moments—it is the characters whose actions are not predetermined by the history books who offer the author the widest scope for his own determinations—and that they insist on another perspective apart from that of the warring nobility, often powerfully the perspective of basic humanity itself. The great example here is the father and son at Towton, although at this moment, Shakespeare adverts to something close to allegory, while his usual method is to make his marginals real, sometimes pungently real, and, as Pugliatti astutely notes, often vulnerable to forces that both disregard and destroy them. Whether the introduction of these officially unheard voices totally undermines the values and presuppositions of the aristocrats who are the plays' major characters is yet another consideration. Pugliatti has Shakespeare only "familiar and possibly in sympathy with the lower classes and their way of thinking" (187), but other critics make larger claims. Michael Hattaway, in a number of publications, has insisted on Shakespeare as a radical, and Annabel Patterson finds in the implicit allowance of the legitmacy of popular protest a basis to deny Shakespeare's traditional abhorrence of the crowd.

It might be noted in passing that recent writers on the plays often assert the strong presence of popular discontent in the London in which the *Henry VI* plays first appeared and as partial documentation cite the "Hackett rebellion" or "uprising" as evidence; Hackett shows up fairly prominently in both Patterson and Pugliatti. In fact, William Hackett was a religious maniac who, with a following of two (his prophets of justice and mercy), publicly announced that he had been sent by Christ to judge the world and, incidentally, to replace Elizabeth on the throne. He was arrested within about three hours of making his pronouncement, was tried and condemned ten days later, and, two days after that was executed not just to the approbation of the multitude, but to their exhortations that the full agony of a traitor's death be inflicted. It is difficult to see that his story illustrates anything except that Hackett was crazy and the law swift and merciless in punishing him.

The lower classes enter the tetralogy most spectacularly with the Jack Cade scenes of *Part 2*. Most critics still read the episode as vicious and chaotic—there is a very good interpretation in Maurice Hunt's essay in this volume—but certainly it broaches current popular concerns such as enclosure, the exemption from justice of the "clergy" (those who could read a neck verse), perhaps the rampant inflation of the times as well. Again, whether this offers sufficient grounds for Shakespeare as a radical or oppositional writer (Hattaway, Cartelli, Caldwell, in his way Greenblatt) seems very doubtful. It is also true that Cade is both York's stalking-horse and thus his analogue, but to equate the injustices the nobility have perpetrated with Cade's actions is to miss how autonomous he actually is once he appears on stage and to grossly underestimate the immense and destructive energy and chaotic fun he brings with him. The relationship of Cade to contemporary social and political complaint is valid, and Hobday has done a very good job with the tricky problem of establishing Shakespeare's access to the tradition of popular protest, a tradition belonging largely to the unlettered, with all the difficulty that entails. But to sympathize with poor hungry Jack Cade, done in by the defender of real estate rights who hypocritically espouses contentment but accepts advancement, is to bring one's own agenda to the episode, to deny it its own weight and emphasis. Far too often, recent criticism of these plays seems to be about what the characters and the audience *ought* to have felt.

The complexities, ambiguities, and even contradictions of the *Henry VI* plays have served as the basis for a number of recent critics to come to the judgment that Shakespeare is ultimately a historiographer, not simply reporting what for dramatic purposes is "the truth" of his history, but so vitally aware that in the mere telling of events, "the truth" is so radically conditioned by the telling that the proper meditation is on the telling, its divergence from other tellings, and the recognition that anything more is unattainable. Although I would not posit a Shakespeare incapable of such reflection, I cannot believe in a Shakespeare for whom such reflection was paramount—and especially at this point in his career; although I think the *Henry VI* plays have much to recommend them, I do not find in them the much noted unresolved ambiguities of the Second Tetralogy.

I regret that this may sound like my commitment to a dumbed-down Shakespeare; I also regret that it puts me in disagreement with Pugliatti, whose work I like, and Rackin, whose work I like very much, as the frequency with which I have quoted her would suggest.

In 1978, Homer D. Swander published an article with the interesting title "The Rediscovery of *Henry VI*." The piece was in appreciative reaction to Terry Hands's RSC production of the previous year. At least since the Birmingham Rep did the sequence in 1953 under the direction of Douglas Seale—and a brief piece by the producer, Sir Barry Jackson, appeared in *Shakespeare Survey* for that year—*Henry VI* has been rediscovered by audiences and critics every time a major production has been mounted. It has been re-established on the stage now for a half century, although productions are still infrequent enough that audiences are usually seeing the plays for the first time. This being the case, reviews by scholar-critics are of very real value: Barabara Hodgdon has written on *Henry VI* productions several times, and Herbert Coursen, whose latest commentary is included here, has done so as well. Coursen reviews two mid-1990s productions, Michael Kahn's at the Shakespeare Theater in Washington and Karin Coonrod's at the Public in New York; he supplies a great deal of detail about staging and acting and some vigorous evaluation as well. Coursen's view from the audience is nicely matched by an interview I conducted with Steven Skybell, who played York, and several minor roles, in the Coonrod production. Skybell's recollection of the practical difficuties of dealing with the role and the plays offers a perspective few can provide.

Performances are of course evanescent, but something can be preserved through visual media, and in the case of the *Henry VI* plays a surprising amount has been preserved. Patricia Lennox's essay investigates four different productions of the sequence that have been recorded and are available on videotape, though not as available as one would wish. Simply the fact that they exist would be worth writing about, but the essay proceeds to some intriguing further concerns, notably the origin of two of the productions as recreated stage performances and the other two as designed from the beginning as television plays.

Before the advent of photography, visualized Shakespeare meant paintings and drawings. This is a rich resource that Irene Dash explores in her investigation of Shakespeare and the art of illustration. Dash provides a number of handsome reproductions of this work, featuring her favorite artist, Henry Fuseli.

I find that I have, at least in passing, called some attention to all of the essays in this volume, with the single exception of Yoshio Arai's commentary on the reception of *Henry VI* in Japan. My oversight is not really an oversight: the impact of such work on a culture significantly different from our own is obviously a subject about which neither I nor, I think, most people are knowledgeable. The vagaries of the plays' translation, presentation, and critical reception in Japan have an obvious interest, and Professor Arai, who once publicly read the entire canon, guides us expertly.

The essays in this volume illuminate the *Henry VI* plays well and from a wide variety of perspectives; I would hope that might incline the reader to read the plays themselves, to study them, and—if the chance presents itself—to see them. I have become so immersed in the sequence that I tend to think of them as my own and, though not exactly rich and beautiful, not poor and ill favored neither.

TEXTS WITH TWO FACES
NOTICING THEATRICAL REVISIONS IN *HENRY VI, PARTS 2* AND *3*

Steven Urkowitz

> Can you not see? or will ye not observe
> The strangenesse of his alter'd Countenance?
> *2 Henry VI*, 3.1.4–5

This is a period of instability and revolution in the field of Shakespearean textual scholarship. Today the texts of the three *Henry VI* plays spin erratically through current debates, much to the present discomfiture and future benefit of readers of the plays. For roughly a century, one dominant paradigm, "memorial reconstruction and illicit printing," was used to explain the textual complexities of the group of Shakespeare's plays which have, like *Henry VI, Parts 2* and *3*, radically different versions in the earliest printed quarto and Folio texts. It was believed that variants in the extant printed versions resulted from printers' errors, from minimal playhouse adaptations, and from clumsy attempts at reconstructing the plays, made by actors intent on selling a manuscript to printers or to competing acting companies. Now, however, new research methods, such as Don Foster's analyses of the "rare-word" vocabularies of related texts, and new findings from more rigorous application of older methods, such as studies by Laurie Maguire, Grace Ioppolo, and Paul Werstine, challenge the premises and findings that support many traditional editions of Shakespeare's plays. Several critics, among them Don Foster, Yashdip Bains, and I, now suggest instead that something more like orderly and authorized revision better accounts for the significant changes in these texts. The new research challenges established principles of editing multiple texts and single text plays as well. More important, it attempts to bring contemporary readers into contact with the energetic processes of composing and revising for the theater that were practiced in Shakespeare's time.

During moments of such ferment in any intellectual field of study, both old and new models, patterns, or systems of explanation exist side by side. For a time, different practitioners of the editorial arts and crafts base their work on shifting and often contradictory principles, and the texts they pro-

duce for readers may assume unfamiliar hybrid forms. Since editorial practice is supposed to bring about trustworthy texts for scholars, students ,and
actors, a time of instability within the community of textual scholars seems
particularly disquieting. In the past, magisterial reputations of the great
university presses of Oxford and Cambridge and of figures such as W. W.
Greg, E. K. Chambers, Peter Alexander, Fredson Bowers, and others
seemed to guarantee that in all important ways we could trust the texts
produced by scholars. This is no longer the case: new names, new reputations, new methods, and new working editions of plays will now have to
be considered by readers unable to rely on the old patterns. The community interested in Shakespeare's plays will nevertheless benefit directly from
these re-evaluations with fresh and detailed insights into how plays were
composed, staged, and revised in Shakespeare's time.

The texts of *Henry VI, Parts* 2 and 3 offer particularly rich illustrations
of textual variation and theatrical transformation rarely examined in contemporary critical discourse. We have only a single version of *Henry VI,
Part 1*, first printed among the Histories in the First Folio of 1623, but versions of *Part 2* and *Part 3* radically different from the Folio were first printed almost thirty years earlier. In 1594 a text resembling what would come
to be printed in the Folio as *The second Part of Henry the Sixt* appeared as
a quarto volume titled *The first Part of the Contention betwixt the two
famous houses of Yorke and Lancaster.* In 1595, a text similar to the Folio's
Third Part of Henry the Sixt, was printed a year later as *The true Tragedie
of Richard Duke of Yorke* in a smaller octavo format. Both early printed
texts are about two thirds the length of their Folio equivalents. These two
playscripts were reprinted in 1600 without significant changes. They were
printed again, but as a single volume, in 1619 with a small number of interesting variants that more closely resemble equivalent passages later published for the first time in the Folio. What accounts for the different versions? Before examining the theories, it would be best to observe a sample
of the alternative forms.

The two versions of *Henry VI, Parts* 2 and 3 offer related but contrasting series of specific dramatic actions for players to perform. The excitement of examining the alternative scripts arises from recognizing how they
each command theatrically compelling activity for actors and audiences.
The alternative versions of *Henry VI, Parts* 2 and 3 offer hundreds of distinctly patterned passages representing a veritable casebook or anatomy of
stagecraft. In the opening scene of *2 Henry VI*, for example, the alternative
actions offer two different plans for the audience's perceptions of theatrical
characterization and courtly ceremony.

In the opening speech of *2 Henry VI*, identical in both texts, the Duke
of Suffolk kneels as he presents Queen Margaret as King Henry's bride.
Then, however, following the earliest printed version, the king bids Suffolk
to stand, he greets the queen, kisses her, and raises his head to address his

thanks to God for granting him a bride representing a "world of pleasures":

> *King*: Suffolke arise.
> [1]Welcome Queene Margaret to English Henries Court,
> [2]The greatest shew of kindnesse yet we can bestow,
> Is this kinde kisse: [3]Oh gracious God of heaven,
> Lend me a heart repleat with thankfulnesse,
> For in this beautious face thou hast bestowde
> A world of pleasures to my perplexed soule.

The king here welcomes Margaret [1]. If an actor is to follow the directions coded in the dramatic dialogue, the king must move towards her so he may bestow a "kinde kisse" [2]. And then [3] he must turn his face from her to address the heavens. He announces himself blessed, and his "perplexed soul" is relieved already by the pleasure he receives from the beauty of his bride's face.

Next, in this version, Queen Margaret responds to her husband's greeting with an elaborately ornamented and conventional claim of modesty:

> *Queene.*Th'excessive love I beare unto your grace,
> Forbids me to be lavish of my tongue,
> Least I should speake more then beseemes a woman:
> Let this suffice, my blisse is in your liking,
> And nothing can make poore Margaret miserable,
> Unlesse the frowne of mightie Englands King.

She says she loves him, she announces her desire to appear seemly, and she says she fears only the possibility of Henry's displeasure. For the audience, this initial view of a genteel, restrained queen will contrast starkly with the wild, violent anger seen later in her role. In the speech immediately following, Henry announces to others on stage the oddly lacerating emotional impact she has already had upon him [at 1]. He then invites her to sit down beside him [at 2], and he encourages his uncle and the attendant lords to greet her [at 3].

> *Kin.* [1]Her lookes did wound, but now her speech doth pierce,
> [2]Lovely Queene Margaret sit down by my side:
> [3]And unckle Gloster, and you Lordly Peeres,
> With one voice welcome my beloved Queene.
> *All.* Long live Queene Margaret, Englands happinesse.
> *Queene.* We thanke you all.
> > Sound Trumpets.

The script implies that the King and Queen have thronelike seats to settle on side by side. A pleased king, a modest queen, sitting monarchs, upright nobles: we see an array rich with narrative detail. The dynamic disposition of players across the stage is coded vividly in the dialogue. As we learn to read theatrical scripts, we recognize these cues for action.

The alternative script printed in the 1623 First Folio presents clearly distinct words and actions. For example, although the king greets his bride with the same kiss, his address to heaven closes with a conditional construction (here in italics):

> Suffolke, arise. Welcome Queene Margaret,
> I can expresse no kinder signe of Love
> Then this kinde kisse: 0 Lord, that sends me life,
> Lend me a heart repleate with thankfulnesse:
> For thou hast given me in this beauteous Face
> A world of earthly blessings to my soule,
> *If Simpathy of Love unite our thoughts.*

Unlike the relief for his perplexities celebrated in the earlier text, in the Folio Margaret's beauty will be a blessing only if it initiates marital concord, "Simpathy of Love." More than the simple exuberance of the first text, the king here draws on a more cautious vocabulary of wisdom as well.

In sharp contrast to the earlier version, the queen replies to King Henry in the 1623 Folio not with claims of modesty and trepidation but instead with a ringing exclamation of her immodest boldness:

> *Queen.*Great King of England, & my gracious Lord,
> The mutuall conference that my minde, hath had,
> By day, by night; waking, and in my dreames,
> In Courtly company, or at my Beades,
> With you mine Alder liefest Soveraigne,
> Makes me the bolder to salute my King,
> With ruder termes, such as my wit affoords,
> And over joy of heart doth minister.

The eloquent appeal to the conventional rhetoric of modesty in the first printed text becomes here instead a "ruder" celebration of the queen's rhetorical boldness and emotional daring. Her first appearance in the play in this version leads directly to the audience's apprehension of her adventurous and aggressive character in the action to follow, whereas in the earlier text that revelation comes later as a surprise.

The King next describes his emotionally dynamic experience of pleasure, though he seems excessively delighted with his bride after very minimal exposure to her. And as in the earlier text, he commands his peers to welcome the queen.

> *King.* Her sight did ravish, but her grace in Speech,
> Her words yclad with wisedomes Majesty,
> Makes me from Wondring, fall to Weeping joyes,
> Such is the Fulnesse of my hearts content.
> Lords, with one cheerefull voice, Welcome my Love.
> *All kneel.* Long live Qu. Margaret, Englands happines.
> *Queene.* We thanke you all.   Florish

If we are attentive to the lexicon of stage action found in the dialogue, we can see that in this 1623 version, however, the king does not ask Queen Margaret to sit beside him as in the earlier text. Indeed, at the equivalent point after the fourth line of his speech, there is no reference to any sitting at all. Further, although the nobles have the very same words to say, their speech heading in this text becomes a highly unusual embedded stage direction. Instead of "*All*" it reads "*All kneel.*"

In the visible geometry of courtly ceremony, the Folio version offers us a bold Queen Margaret and an exuberant king who stand erect while the visibly subordinated nobles kneel before them. In contrast to the modest queen seated beside the king surrounded by standing nobles, in this text at the equivalent moment we have an assertive queen standing upright with her monarch, visibly subordinating the kneeling, obedient lords. Distinct theatrical representations of psychological and political tensions distinguish the two versions of the passage.

Both texts "work" by leading an audience through an elaborate ceremonial display fraught with symbolic gestures of emotional attachment, sanctification, regal authority, and feudal obedience, but each displays a distinct pattern of language and coded gestures. Such fine-tuning of dramatic themes and actions are staples of professional theatrical writing.

Elsewhere we can see a parallel alternation between two equally viable stagings of a strikingly similar moment from *3 Henry VI*, 3.3. In this later episode from the dramatic narrative of the same Queen Margaret, she again arrives at a royal court, this time to be greeted by King Lewis of France. In the 1595 octavo version, Lewis invites her to "Sit by my side," and Margaret evidently agrees. In the 1623 Folio, however, the character first, with an ostentatious display of humility and despair, chooses to drop down to the ground; then King Lewis ceremoniously raises her to sit beside him. In the later version, as in the later version of the opening scene of *Part 2*, the script again allows Margaret to manipulate the dramatic moment counter to the expectations of polite decorum. The relatively conventional stage business of sitting down next to a king becomes an inventive evocation of emotional power.

Such alternatives abound throughout the versions of *Henry VI, Parts 2* and *3*, with variants affecting major characters such as King Henry and Richard of Gloucester as well as minor parts such as Alexander Iden and the murderers of Duke Humphrey. (Discussions of many further examples may be found in the work of Yashdip Bains cited in the bibliography as well as my own essays of 1988 and 1997.) The variants show us how to read and appreciate the particularly theatrical impacts of entrances and exits, stage business, stage properties, and psychological motivations of dramatic action.

Despite the evident interest and theatrical value of these variants, few readers of Shakespeare's earliest history plays are aware of the alternative texts. Although scores of passages in the versions of *Henry VI, Parts 2* and *3* show similarly thoughtful alternatives, the editorial tradition dominant in the twentieth century has until recently insisted on offering readers only single versions of these plays. Editors strenuously reject the explanation that *The Contention* and *The True Tragedy* represent discrete authoritative versions of *Henry VI, Parts 2* and *3*. Editors generally argue that only the Folio versions are worthy of study. Traditions of editing generally dictate that only a single version of a work should be presented as the most authoritative. Perhaps because not all alternative readings sound as appealing as the two greetings of Queen Margaret, or because many variants involve only single word substitutions, additions, or deletions, and because some passages found in the earlier texts present material that distorts details of the historical narrative found in the plays' sources, the editors have agreed that Shakespeare could not have had a hand in their derivation. Once the earlier versions were declared non-Shakespearean, they were sequestered from view away from discussion by readers who were not trained as bibliographic scholars.

Many emotionally charged arguments are offered to support the isolation of the first-printed versions and their subsequent suppression in critical or analytic discussions of the plays. For example, one particular passage in *The Contention*, equivalent to *2 Henry VI*, 2.2, where the Duke of York explains his ancestral rights to the throne of England, has been the basis of claims that the earliest printed versions are so bad that they could not possibly have been the product of a responsible author drafting a manuscript. Instead, on the basis of several factual errors and the relatively few clumsy passages where verse and prose are confused and where lines of verse have more or fewer than ten syllables, many critics have argued that the earlier-printed texts could have been generated only by "theatrical pirates."

According to this "piracy" theory, particular actors combined their good memories of their own roles and sketchy memories of other roles to produce "corrupt" manuscripts. These illicitly generated versions would then be sold to hypothetical unscrupulous printers eager to supply an imagined market clamoring for printed plays. Upholders of this theory proposed that they could identify "memorial errors" committed by the pirates. This imaginative scenario today forms the basis of virtually all modern editions of *Henry VI, Parts 2* and *3*.

The memorial reconstruction hypothesis gained widespread acceptance after it was tentatively adopted by W. W. Greg in his study of the quarto and Folio versions of *The Merry Wives of Windsor*. Despite his reputation as the founder of modern scientific bibliographic studies, in this matter Greg's speculations about memorial reconstruction were peculiarly impressionistic and irresponsibly imaginative. Despite its long-lasting appeal to editors, research has shown repeatedly that the "memorial reconstruction" narrative is both inherently unlikely and without factual basis in late sixteenth- and early seventeenth-century England (see particularly Maguire 73–94; Urkowitz, "Good News," Blayney, and Werstine, "A Century").

The "memorial reconstruction" case for *Henry VI, Parts 2* and *3* was argued most forcefully by Peter Alexander. Since it was published in 1929, Alexander's work has been cited as the primary basis for all subsequent editions. Despite its wide acceptance, Alexander's narrative about theatrical piracy has been questioned repeatedly, and new evidence shows that his arguments fail to warrant the credibility they have been accorded. But the imaginative appeal of his story as well as his daunting accumulation of inconsequential instances lends a continuing meretricious appeal, even in the face of strong counter-arguments. Shortly after Alexander's work on the texts was first published, Clayton Alvis Greer responded with an encyclopedic essay challenging the "memorial reconstruction" hypotheses of Peter Alexander and an ally, Madeleine Doran. Even though it appeared in *PMLA*, the foremost journal of the profession, Greer's arguments were and continue to be simply ignored by editors committed to memorial-reconstruction hypotheses. Until the last few years, the same outcome has faced subsequent challenges.

However, recent studies of the English book trade by Peter Blayney, studies of Renaissance acting companies by Scott McMillin and Roslyn Knutson, and examinations of Shakespeare's dynamic working vocabulary by Donald Foster give very strong evidence that the alternative texts could have resulted from normal theatrical and literary revision by Shakespeare and his acting company. And indeed most editors qualify their overall support for the memorial reconstruction hypothesis with demurrals admitting that at least some few alternative passages could most likely be explained as authorial revisions (see, for example, Hattaway, *The Second Part* 233; Cairncross, *Part II*, xlvi–xlvii).

Peter Alexander based his arguments on the then-popular but essentially unfounded idea of "memorial reconstruction" first given bibliographic credibility by W.W. Greg in his study of the First Quarto of *The Merry Wives of Winsor* (1910) and later reinorced by Greg's influential but equally flawed *Two Elizabethan Stage Abridgements*: The Battle of Alcazar and Orlando Furioso (1923). Following Greg, Alexander first claimed that competent authors do not make the kinds of theatrical or literary changes found in the quarto-Folio variants (55–106). Play scripts Alexander did not consult, however, offer strong evidence that Alexander was wrong. Eric Rasmussen has shown that extant manuscripts and printed texts record playwrights making exactly the kinds of changes observed between *The Contention* and *The True Tragedy* and the Folio *Henry VI, Parts 2* and *3* ("The Revision of Scripts," esp. 450–454). Ernst Honigmann demonstrated that many small-scale changes like those observed in the *Henry VI* texts occur when many fluent authors review, rewrite, or revise their own work. Grace Ioppolo also showed that patterns of revision in extant Elizabethan dramatic manuscripts resemble many of the alternative printed forms of the *Henry VI* plays (*Revising Shakespeare* 46–77).

Although Peter Alexander cited instances of play-piracy of Richard Brinsley Sheridan's *The Duenna* (1775) and *The School for Scandal* (1777) to bolster his case for piracy of *Henry VI, Parts 2* and *3*, the relationship between the extant pirated text of *The Duenna* compared with its genuine text is not at all like the relationship between the earlier and later versions of *Henry VI, Parts 2* and *3* (see Alexander 54, 68–69; Urkowitz "If I Mistake" 234–235). Further, Alexander was unaware of Sheridan's own earlier versions of *The School for Scandal*, extant in the form of two brief plays called *The Slanderers* and *Sir Peter Teazle*. Sheridan's revisions that led finally to *The School for Scandal* in fact strikingly resemble changes found in alternative versions of Shakespeare's plays (Alexander 70–71; Redford 9–14).

Alexander's claim most often cited as conclusive asserts that Shakespeare or indeed any responsible playwright could not have written a draft with major factual errors in the historical narrative. So claimed by Alexander and his followers, in an important moment in the Folio text of *2 Henry VI*, 2.2, the Duke of York tracks his ancestry back to King Edward III to demonstrate that he, rather than a descendant of the house of Lancaster, should rightfully be king. The genealogy given for the equivalent moment in the quarto traces Richard of York's pedigree through his mother back to the third son of Edward III. Although the track leading back through his mother's antecedents is drawn accurately, the quarto text mistakenly lists Edmund of Langley, Duke of York, as the second son of Edward III rather than as the third. (If Edmund of Langley had been the second son, York could have claimed his right to the throne through his father's line as well as through his mother's.) According to Alexander, such an error could have been committed only by a memorizing actor attempting unsuccessfully to recapitulate the genealogy. One might argue instead that the error could have been made by someone concentrating on a different aspect of the complex list, the matrilineal rather than the patrilineal line. But in any case, similar long lists of names (like the Salic Law speech in *Henry V*) may just as easily tangle the memory of a composing author as well as a hypothetical pirate. Indeed, so difficult are they for listeners on stage and in the audience, such lists are often followed by disingenuous statements of how clear or obvious their recitation must be. After the twenty-line genealogy in *The Contention*, the character Warwick exclaims: "What plain proceedings can be more plaine [?]" (see also Folio, and the end of the equivalent list of names related to the Salic law in *Henry V*, 1.2.). It seems likely that no one in the audience could follow the genealogy as given either in its erroneous quarto form or its more accurate Folio version.

Although Alexander claims that the error conclusively proves memorial reconstruction, there is no *a priori* justification for his assertion. Further, recent examination of play scripts used to regulate productions in professional theaters of Shakespeare's time reveals that such scripts frequently contain errors, anomalies, inconsistencies, and omissions sharply in contrast to the more orderly scripts of the nineteenth and twentieth centuries. William Long has argued that factual confusions in Elizabethan playhouse documents should no longer be accepted as signs of memorial reconstruction.

Other so-called "memorial reconstructions" in the earlier versions cited by Alexander turn out to be thematically and verbally closer to the chronicle sources than are the equivalent passages in the later-printed Folio (Alexander 63–64; Urkowitz, "If I Mistake" 240–242). For example, where the Folio text of *Henry VI, Part 3*, 2.6, has Clifford enter, "wounded" according to the stage direction, the equivalent direction in *The True Tragedie* indicates he come onstage "with an arrow in his neck." The detail of the arrow is drawn from the chronicle sources. Michael Hattaway, an adherent of the memorial-reconstruction hypothesis, proposes that Shakespeare, following the chronicles, coached the actors about how to perform the entry (*Third Part* 123). While the author may have neglected to record that detail in his own manuscript, which became the basis of the Folio, Hattaway implies, the imagined pirates seem to have remembered it in their recollected draft. Typically, this imaginative scenario requires more and more nonauthorial agents who, while they perform their piratical roles end up acting more and more like authors. Rather than evidence for memorial reconstruction, the variant forms of the stage direction could also result from a normal progression by a composing author working from sources towards more finished versions, adding, altering, and cutting as he moves through his text.

The memorial-reconstruction theory not only leads to strange or unlikely explanations, it also generates anomalous editorial practices. In the example of Queen Margaret's introduction drawn from the opening of *2 Henry VI* discussed at the beginning of this essay, the editor of the 1962 Arden edition, Andrew Cairncross, isolates the queen's greeting to Henry from its surrounding matrix of related variants. In an appendix, he prints the earlier version of that speech alone and concludes, "It would not be beyond the ability of a reporter to vamp the Q version" (5, 186). Because Cairncross omits any notice of the related standing/sitting/kneeling variants discussed at the beginning of this essay, his hypothetical reporter appears capable of only relatively simple alterations. But if we include the full context, we would have to consider that the reporter shows remarkable skills and a theatrical imagination suspiciously like that of William Shakespeare.

The recent Oxford editor, William Montgomery, goes a step further. He follows a more intricate originary narrative and editorial practice championed by Stanley Wells and Gary Taylor for the Oxford Shakespeare edition. Wells and Taylor, like Alexander and Cairncross, believe that the earliest versions of *Henry VI, Parts 2* and *3* (and several other plays) were memorial reconstructions. But they further imagine some of the resulting variant passages were not reconstructed from a performance that followed the script printed in the Folio. Instead, they feel that a few passages were reconstructed by the piratical actors from versions that Shakespeare had revised *after* he completed the texts found in the Folio. They feel furthermore that they must give readers those supposedly revised-by-Shakespeare passages in place of the equivalents from the Folio, since their chosen bits from the earliest printed texts hypothetically represent Shakespeare's own later wishes, which should be given priority (Wells and Taylor 177). Unfortunately they lift their snippets out of the earliest versions and plug them into later versions without regard to their patterned contexts.

In the passage discussed at the beginning of this essay, for example, William Montgomery, the Oxford editor responsible for this text, argues that out of the whole quarto version of the passage only Queen Margaret's modest salutation to the king, "Th'excessive love I beare unto your grace . . ." is Shakespeare's late revision (accurately remembered by the pirate) of the Folio's more boisterous "Great King of England, & my gracious Lord . . . ." But, Montgomery claims, the remainder of the exchange aside from this one speech was merely piratically invented rather than authorially or authoritatively revised (178). Typically, Montgomery does not discuss how he detects that the queen's speech is genuine within the false context of the pirate's memorial reconstruction. For Montgomery, the variant stage actions of the king sitting, his invitation for the queen to sit by his side, and the nobles standing erect while they greet the queen represent illicit nonauthorial inventions of the piratical actors. As a result, where *The Contention* gives us a stage image dominated by visually powerful nobles standing over the sedentary king and queen, and where the Folio (and all other modern editions) presents an upright king and his aggressive queen proudly erect above the momentarily humble nobles, the Oxford text invents a uniquely dominant king accompanied by an eloquently *modest* queen and greeted by a kneeling crowd of subservient nobles.

While certainly possible as a theatrical staging, Montgomery's stage action squanders the rich dramatic distinctions so clearly marked in *both* early versions. Repeatedly in the Oxford texts of *Henry VI, Parts 2* and *3*, we find passages from the earlier versions similarly interpolated into the Folio texts. These interpolations most often create theatrically clumsy grafts that confuse the coherent but distinct patterns of the earlier and later printed texts. (For further examples of these patterns relating to Queen Margaret, see Urkowitz, "Five Women"293–297.) The ultimate effect of these "memorial reconstruction" narratives and editorial practices drawn from them has been that attention is distracted from the earliest printed texts with their lively theatrical alternatives.

Though we have not yet finally determined whether Shakespeare or his company, or other playwrights, or indeed the hypothesized pirates created the divergent texts of *Henry VI*, today's scholarship now encourages us adventurously to examine these versions. As a result, editors now preparing new editions of the *Henry VI* plays for the Arden 3 series—Ronald Knowles for *Part 2* and Eric Rasmussen and John Cox for *Part 3*—intend to base their texts on the theory that Shakespeare and his company rather than memorial pirates were mainly responsible for the early versions as they appear in *The Contention* and *The True Tragedy*. In a related line of research, Donald Foster's work on Shakespeare's developing and changing vocabulary, using a database program called SHAXICON, promises to give firm evidence for the dates of composition and revision of the texts and the order of composition, and new information about literary and theatrical sources that lent vocabulary to these plays (see Foster's preliminary conclusions in "Reconstructing Shakespeare," and "SHAXICON 1995").

The most recent trend in editing all of Shakespeare's multiple-text plays with early versions, like *Henry VI, Parts 2* and *3*, has been to provide readers with all significant versions, either in facsimile or, better, edited according to the same principles as the primary copy texts. One such project is Jill Levenson's "mobile text" of *Romeo and Juliet* for Oxford University Press. She provides edited versions of the 1597 First Quarto and the 1599 Second Quarto designed to show the dynamic transformations of the play's literary and theatrical forms. For *The Contention, The True Tragedy*, and the Folio *Henry VI, Parts 2* and *3*, readers, directors, actors, and students of drama will benefit greatly when they can easily consult the alternative forms of these fascinating scripts. Audiences at any level of sophistication may learn much about *all* play texts when they read, analyze, perform, and observe these variant forms of theatrical action.

A Touch of Greene, Much Nashe, and All Shakespeare

J. J. M. Tobin

1 Henry VI is a special text for the nerve endings of Shakespearean enthusiasts, providing as it does possible grounds for arguing for multiple authorship as well as evidence for Shakespeare's single responsibility for the play as it now exists. The more than thirty years that elapsed between the Folio of 1623 and the play's likely first performance allow for an interpretation of a Shakespearean revisionary effort which does not perfectly conceal traces of possible original contributions by other dramatists. This last view of the case has a touch of having one's cake and eating it too, but the following discussions of a canonical symmetry and of the indirect role of Thomas Nashe may lead the reader towards an integrationist view.

The final three scenes of *1 Henry VI* are among those which several editors (and critics), including the Oxford editors, have deemed non-Shakespearean. Dover Wilson, for example, thought that 5.3.1–44 was possibly by Nashe but that the rest of the scene was Greene's, 5.4 was Greene's but revised by Shakespeare, and 5.5 was Greene's but the second half was a revision by Shakespeare. Taylor recently argues that 5.1 through 5.5, like 3.1.–3.4 (and possibly other sections) is the work of an unknown author "Y," whose work "has particular links with *Locrine* . . . [with] strong similarities to the dramatic writings of Robert Greene and George Peele" (Wells and Taylor, *Textual Companion* 217).[1] It is possible that we accept too easily the idea that these last scenes are non-Shakespearean, for there is a shapeliness in the arc of Shakespeare's career to be seen if we recognize that *The Tempest* echoes aspects of these passages from this early history. Of course, if one wishes to suggest that in Shakespeare's beginning was his end, whenever these last scenes were written/added to or not, *1 Henry VI* has to be considered the earliest of Shakespeare's work.

The similarities between this part of the history and those in the

romance include two pairs of lovers (Suffolk and Margaret, Ferdinand and
Miranda) in each of which one is the offspring of the King of Naples; both
women are "wonderful," with Margaret as "nature's miracle" (5.3.54)
who has Suffolk's "*wondrous* praise" (5.3.190) and will herself bereave
Henry's "wits with *wonder*" (5.3.195). Miranda's name indicates her wondrous nature, and she is addressed when first seen by Ferdinand, "O you
wonder" (1.2.426).Other similarities are the temporary impotence of each
of the male lovers, Suffolk's "I have no power to let her pass" (5.3.60) and
Ferdinand's "My spirits, as in a dream, are all bound up" (1.2.485); the
issue of love's trial in Suffolk's "How canst thou tell she will deny thy suit,/
Before thou make *a trial of* her love" (5.3.75–76) and Miranda's "O dear
father,/ Make not too rash *a trial of* him" (1.2.466–467), as well as her
father's "All thy vexations/ Were but my *trials of thy love*" (4.1.5–6). Both
male lovers talk of wood and servitude, albeit the bondage is of Margaret
in the first case and Ferdinand himself in the second: "Why for my king:
tush, that's a *wooden* thing," and "would you not suppose/ Your *bondage*
happy, to be made a queen" (5.3.89, 110–111), and Ferdinand, the patient
log man, saying that but for his love of Miranda he would not "endure/
This *wooden* slavery" (3.2.61-62). Indeed, Margaret, like Ferdinand, of
royal descent through Naples, shows a similar instinct for independence:
"To be a queen in *bondage* is more vile/ Than is a slave in base servility"
(5.3.112–113). Both male lovers, Suffolk as surrogate, Ferdinand in his
own person, offer to make the women queens (5.3.111, as just noted), and
in Ferdinand's "I'll make you/ The queen of Naples," (1.2.448–449). It will
also be remembered that Ferdinand, in the midst of his comparison and
contrast of Miranda with other women, speaks of their tongues having
"into *bondage*/ Brought my too diligent ear" (3.2.41–42), and that after
Miranda expresses her desire to have him as her husband, Ferdinand
replies: "Ay, with a heart as willing/ As *bondage* e'er of freedom"
(3.2.88–89). Both suitors use the adjective "*precious*" in dialogue with the
lovers. Suffolk speaks of the "*precious* crown" which Margaret will receive
if she should marry Henry, even as the earl confuses the pronouns "his"
and "my," while Ferdinand directly addresses Miranda as "*precious* creature" (3.2.25). Both women express their unworthiness; Margaret says "I
am *unworthy* to be Henry's wife" (5.3.122), while Miranda tells Ferdinand
that she weeps at her "*unworthiness*" (3.2.77). Both women describe themselves as maidens and willing servants; Margaret sends Henry "Such commendations as becomes a *maid,*/ A virgin and his *servant*" (5.3.177–178),
while Miranda tells Ferdinand, "If not, I'll die your *maid*. To be your fel-
low/ You may deny me; but I'll be your *servant*/ Whether you will or no"
(3.2.84–86). Of course, both marriages are to be "*solemnized*," as Suffolk
says at 5.3.168 and Prospero at 5.1.309.

Now, the tone of the remarks of Margaret differs from that of Miranda,
and the duplicity of Suffolk contrasts with the innocence of Ferdinand, but

the circumstances of love and status as well as diction are analogous in the first case and often identical in the second. Shakespeare may indeed have in an autoplagiaristic manner returned to his earlier work—*1 Henry VI*—with the lovers and a Neapolitan king, or he many have surrendered his resistance to using Greene, held to since the time of the attack in *A Groatsworth of Wit*, until the composition of *The Winter's Tale,* with its dependence upon *Pandosto,* and continued the relaxation in the writing of *The Tempest* by returning to the Greene-written section, Act V of *1 Henry VI*, perhaps even Greene-written originally but revised by Shakespeare himself.

Whichever or whatever the case, Shakespeare may have linked the writing of *The Tempest* with his recollection of *1 Henry VI* because of the fact that both plays have a dominant figure connected with magical powers—the white magician Prospero and the black magician Joan of Arc. Magic in and of itself is likely enough to draw upon a vocabulary naturally shared in *1 Henry VI* and *The Tempest*. La Pucelle appeals to "*ye charming spells*" (5.3.2), York cites her "*spelling charms*" (5.3.31), refers to her as a "*witch*" and speaks of her "*dainty eye*" (5.3.38) and calls her a "*hag*" (42). She replies with "*a plaguing mischief light* on Charles and thee!" and asks for "leave to *curse* a while" (43).

In *The Tempest* it is Caliban (whose "mother was a *witch*" [5.1.269]), "The damn'd *witch* Sycorax" (1.2.263), guilty of "*mischiefs* manifold" (264), "blue-eyed *hag*" (269), whose profit from having learned language is to "know how to *curse*" (1.2.364). He urges "All the *charms* of Sycorax *light*" (339–340) on Prospero, and the "the red-*plague*" (365) destroy him. Prospero promises to "*plague*" all his enemies (4.1.192), is told that his "*charm*" (5.1.17) has worked well on them, and calls upon his spirits "*Ye* elves" and so on in his speech of abjuration (5.1.33ff). And in his reference to "airy *charm*" (5.1.54), he sees the charmed enemy "*spell*-stopp'd" (61) and praises his "*dainty* Ariel" (95). Joan had also addressed her "*fiends*," while Sebastian speaks of fighting "one *fiend* at a time" (3.3.102).

All these terms, as I have said, could be merely the result of a common theme, the discussion of which necessitates similar vocabularies. However, there is a most unusual aspect which is shared by *1 Henry VI* and *The Tempest,* and that is the theme of escape from punishment of crimes by death because of the culprit's pregnant/"pregnant" condition. It will be recalled that both Sycorax and Joan are connected with this theme. Joan herself announces (falsely) "I am with child, ye bloody homicides;/ Murder not then the fruit of my womb" (5.4.62–63). Prospero reminds Ariel: "this blue-eyed hag was hither brought with child,/ And here was left by the sailors" (1.2.269–270), this was the "one thing she did/ [for which] They would not take her life" (266–267). An unusual topic, to say the least. One final point: Prospero destroys his art, returning to nature when he breaks his staff. At the end of the wooing scene Suffolk speaks of Margaret's "natural graces that extinguish art" (5.3.192). All together these parallels are suggestive and provide an elegant touch of artistic completeness to the career of one who may have died on the fifty-second anniversary of his own birth. The suggested circularity may appeal especially to those who see *1 Henry VI* as completely Shakespearean or at least a play completely revised by Shakespeare.

Some current scholars, led by Gary Taylor, building upon the work of John Dover Wilson and adding supportive material, argue on the basis of parallel passages, together with other unique features, that most of Act I of *1 Henry VI* is the work of Thomas Nashe. I believe that this reliance on the apparent presence of Nashean material in Act I—material that is indeed there—to determine Nashean authorship of this part of the play is a mistake and, indeed, that the material is more easily explained as yet another instance of Shakespeare's habitual incorporating of Nashe's prose into his own expressions, whether of prose or verse. The following examples of multiple uses by Shakespeare of several Nashean works, beginning with the most celebrated of the indictments of Gabriel Harvey, *Have with you to Saffron Walden*, illustrate the fact that Nashean presence is a sign of Shakespeare's borrowing.

Dover Wilson, citing George Steevens before him, finds in the Dauphin's opening remarks about the impossibility of predetermining a war's outcome, "Mars his true moving, even as in the heavens /So in the earth, to this day is not known" (1.12.1–2), a reflection of Nashe's phrasing in *Have with you to Saffron Walden* (1596), itself an echo of Nashe's source in Cornelius Agrippa's *De Incertitudine et Vanitate Scientiarnum*, "Neither hathe the true movings of Mars bene knowen untill this daie."[2]

Now, *Have with you to Saffron Walden* is a text Shakespeare borrowed from a number of times in the course of his career. As early as *Romeo and Juliet*, he incorporated a number of terms, from the very opening of the play with the taking-of-the-wall issue, but especially in 2.4, where Mercutio is at the height of his clever commentary as well as in his subsequent fateful collision with Tybalt, not to mention the description of the apothecary.[3] Then, in the composition of *The Merchant of Venice*, Shakespeare returned to Nashe's lampoon of Harvey:

> The number of parallel phrases, some unique in the canon, the general theme of revenge imaged in the letting of blood and cutting of flesh, the reference to the incubation of *Saffron-Walden* since "the hanging of Lopus" (18), an action of 1594 thought to be alluded to by Gratiano at IV.i.133ff., immediately following the mention of "Pythagoras," together suggest that although Shakespeare had his plot outline from *Il Pecorone* or some version of it, he made use of ideas and images from *Saffron-Walden* in the development of the texture of his play, finding less in Harvey that was like Shylock, but

much that was like Shylock in the attitude of Nashe and the Master Barber as they set about to phlebotomize the luckless Cambridge don.⁴

Even as the dramatist was working on Shylock, he had begun the creation of Falstaff in *1 Henry IV*, where Dover Wilson himself was among the first to see that Shakespeare had made use of this most successful and certainly the fullest of Nashe's attacks on Harvey. I suggest that the variety of elements in the play that are derived from *Saffron Walden* are the products of the following central fictional image of Harvey, so unlike the real Cambridge academic and so close to the *miles gloriosus* of *1 Henry IV* (and not unlike the Sir John Falstaff of *1 Henry VI*, 1.1.136, who "Cowardly fled, not having struck one stroke"). "Gabriel Harvey, of the age of fortie eight or upwards, (Turpe senex miles, tis time for such an olde foole to leave playing the swash-buckler") (55).⁵

It is perhaps enough to make the point that Shakespeare habitually borrowed from this particular text of Nashe, so that Nashean elements in *1 Henry VI* are more likely to be instances of Shakespeare's incorporation of these materials rather than signs of Nashe's own direct hand. This habitual manipulation of Nashean elements is quite clear even if we pass over other instances and cite simply *Saffron Walden* elements in *Hamlet*.

In the dialogue sections of *Saffron Walden* Nashe develops the theme of the Harvey family's humble origins in rope-making. With affected seriousness he has one of his interlocutors, Domino Bentivole, point out that although the ropes made by the Harveys are sometimes used in the course of criminal acts, the Harveys are not therefore guilty of any crimes themselves. Then Pierce Penilesse, the Respondent in this dialogue, makes some astute observations on the differences between cause and effect. In its rhythm and subject of logical tautology, with the added issue of insanity, this passage makes up the rhythm of Polonius's analysis of Hamlet's lunacy:

As though the cause and the effect (more than the superficies and the substance) can bee seperated, when in manie things *causa sine qua non* is both the cause and the effect, the common distinction of *potentia non actu* approving it selfe verie crazed and impotent herein since the premisses necessarily beget the conclusion, and so contradictorily the conclusion the premisses: a halter including desperation, and so desperation concluding in a halter; without which fatall conclusion and privation it cannot truly bee termed desperation, since nothing is said to bee till it is borne, and despaire is never fully borne till it ceaseth to bee, and hath depriv'd him of beeing that first bare it and brought it forth. So that herein it is hard to distinguish which is most to be blamed, of *the cause or the effect*; *the Cause* without the *effect*

beeing of no effect, and *the effect* without *the cause* never able to have
been. (59–60)[6]

Carneades, another of the interlocutors, urges the Respondent to continue with the live story of Gabriel Harvey and hopes that there will be no
interruption:

> Better or worse fortune, I pray thee let us heare how thou goest for-
> ward with describing the Doctor and his life and fortunes: and you,
> my fellow Auditors, I beseech you, trouble him not (anie more) with
> these impertinent Parentheses. (60)

Polonius is eager to describe the crazed desperation of Hamlet, inter-
rupting and delaying his narrative by parenthetical pieces of self-criticism.
His most comical lines are those devoted to premises which necessarily
beget tautological conclusions ("for to define madness, /What is it but to
be nothing else but mad") and to much play on the relationship of cause
and effect:

> Mad let us grant him then, and now remains
> That we find out *the cause* of the *effect*,
> Or rather say, *the cause* of this defect,
> For this *effect* defective comes by *cause*. (2.2.100–103)

No one has suggested that Nashe wrote parts of *Romeo and Juliet* or
The Merchant of Venice or *1 Henry IV* or *Hamlet*, yet the presence of the
same kind of Nashean source material has been too confidently used as evidence that Nashe was the direct author of a whole scene in *1 Henry VI*.

For example, Dover Wilson pointed to the conclusion of the Dauphin's
speech as also clearly Nashean, albeit from yet another Nashean work,
Christ's Tears over Jerusalem:

> Otherwhiles the famished English, like pale ghosts
> Faintly besiege us one hour in a month. (1.2.7–8)

He cites Nashe's "pale rawbone ghosts" (II. 69.23) in *Christ's Tears over
Jerusalem* (1593) and points out that "otherwhile" is used nine times by
Nashe and only this once in works attributed to Shakespeare. He is careful
to admit that "rawbone" also occurs in *The Faerie Queene,* and we know
that Spenser and his lengthy romance are frequent sources for Shakespeare.

This particular passage belongs to a set of pages in *Christ's Tears* which
concern themselves with the bloodshed and famine in Jerusalem at the time
of the siege of the city by the Romans under Titus and Vespasian, a set
which captured the attention of Shakespeare in at least three tragedies,

Titus Andronicus (1594), *Julius Caesar* (1599), and *Macbeth* (1606):

In *Christ's Tears* Nashe as moralist admonishes London for its sinfulness, likening its future to Jerusalem's past, particularly its divinely ordained siege, fall, and destruction in AD 70 at the hands of the Roman general Titus, the son of the newly crowned emperor Vespasian. As his chief illustrations of the terrors of such a fate Nashe tells the story of Miriam, a wealthy matron reduced by hunger and the imminent ignominy of Roman slavery to kill, roast, and serve up as dinner her only son. This is a Jerusalem from which *"Titus* ledde Prisoners to Rome" (78), a city ignorant of the danger represented by Vespasian, a mere general when he arrived in Judea but "by his own souldiers (against his wil) was there consecrated Emperour . . . leaving his sonne *Titus* behind to sack thee" (79), and a city in which a mother who is reduced to eating her son must explain to the child, "ratified it is (bad fated *Saturnine* boy) that thou must be Anthropophagiz'd by thyne owne Mother" (73). It is also a city whose ambition leads Nashe to reflect on the downfall of other ambitious figures of scripture and history: ". . . the truest image of thys kind of ambition was Absolom. Julius Caesar among the Ethnicks surmounted . . . and upon his returne to Rome was crowned Emperour . . . sent men skild in Geometry to measure the whole world a task not finished until . . . the Consulshyp of *Saturninus.* . . ." (82).

In the play the Roman general *Titus* is unwilling to accept his popular election as Emperor, and the Emperor *Saturninus*, sixteen times called *"Saturnine"* (a name, like *Saturninus*, unique in the canon to *Titus Andronicus*) is not the victim of maternal cannibalism, but is the appalled spectator to it. Historically, Saturninus, consul in 19 BC, was later Governor of Syria, in which capacity he presided over the trial of two of Herod's alledgedly treasonous sons, the victims of their father's wrath, although, as Flavius Josephus, one of Nashe's sources, tells us, "none supposed that Herod would carry his cruelty to the length of murdering his children."

Shakespeare in writing for the stage seldom scrupled about consistency in the naming of his characters, but Nashe in writing about a known historical event, the siege of Jerusalem in AD 70 was dependent upon the names which history and his historical sources gave him and they gave him a *"Titus"* and a *"Saturninus"* in a context of the choice of a reluctant emperor and the killing and eating of a child by its mother.[7]

In terms of Shakespeare's use of this section of *Christ's Tears over Jerusalem* in *Julius Caesar,* it is enough to note how much of Antony's forum speech and related scenes derive from Christ's oration over ungrateful Jerusalem.

Apart from *Hamlet,* no play has more evidence of manipulated Nashean material than does *Julius Caesar.* Elements from *The Terrors of the Night* and *Lenten Stuffe* are clearly incorporated into the soothsayer's prophecy and the thrice-offered crown, respectively, while *Christ's Tears* is particularly influential in the diction, syntax, and ironic tone of Marc Antony's oration in the Roman forum, a speech for which North/Plutarch notoriously provides no specific details. Dover Wilson in his Cambridge edition of *Julius Caesar* had pointed out that there are parallels of expression between Nashe's words on page 82 (McKerrow's edition) and a pair of remarks by Antony at 3.1.150–151 and 3.2.119–120. Dover Wilson does not argue for any causal link between the Nashean expression and those of Antony, but further scrutiny of this very page in *Christ's Tears* reveals Nashe's discussion of the nature of ambition, the theme of false honor (with the use of *"honorable"*), the explicit citing of *"Julius Caesar,"* the syntactical unit of proper name, copulative verb, and the adjective *"ambitious,"* as in *"David was ambitious,"* and *"Herod was ambitious"* (a structure followed at 3.2.78, *"Caesar was ambitious"*), together with *"fawning"* which anticipates the description of the behavior of Metellus Cimber in the previous scene of the assassination itself, "base spaniel *fawning,"* and also the reference to Caesar's triumphant return to Rome. Further, Nashe's work is, in its nature, an oration with Christ speaking in the first person, and it is explicitly called an *"oration"* on pages 21 and 60, and an oration which makes use of frequent apostrophes, a characteristic of the rhetoric of the tragedy, a prediction of violence to come to the city, as well as a number of words and phrases either absolutely unique in the Shakespearean canon or unique in their juxtaposition. Consider, for example, *"put to silence,"* *"lendest stonie eares,"* and *"prepare . . . I came not to shedde Teares but. . . ."* Even the rhetorical pausing by Antony is anticipated by that of Christ on page 54, the same page where there is a concatenation of bathing in blood, a *"burst"* vein, a *"heart,"* *"a hair,"* and a *"plucking,"* terms and actions which have become part of both Brutus's and Cassius's stooping, bathing, and washing in the blood of Caesar (3.1.106ff), Antony's description of the seeking of a hair of Caesar as a relic, Brutus's withdrawing, actually *plucking,* of his weapon from Caesar's body, and the bursting of Caesar's heart when the tyrant recognized Brutus as one of the assassins. There is in *Christ's Tears* on subsequent pages a reference to *"brutish beasts"* and honorable Romans who are the reverse of honorable, as well as a sequence of expressions *"So let it be,"* *"I fear,"* and *"shotte . . . beyond"* which have contributed to Antony's lines about the good oft being interred with the bones and his mock anxiety that he fears he has gone too far in telling the crowd of their share in Caesar's will. It is particularly important in terms of noting the very great number of Nashean elements absorbed into Antony's oration that this interring of the bones of Caesar is a violation of Roman funeral practices which, as Plutarch tells us, involved the burning of the corpse. Nashe it is who speaks of *"praises,"* *"bury,"* and *"inter."* And it is Nashe who has Christ indict the citizens of Jerusalem for their *"ingratitude,"* in spite of the fact that Christ had *"loved them,"* even as Brutus is indicted by Antony for his especial *"ingratitude,"* given "how dearly Caesar *loved him"* (3.2.185, 182). There is even Christ's preterition, "yet wil I not say . . . there may be ambition," even as he goes on to analyze extensively the ambition of Jerusalem, which has stimulated Antony's instances of the same device at 3.2.125, 131.

There is a good deal more in *Christ's Tears* that has affected the texture of *Julius Caesar*, but it is enough perhaps to conclude with the essential point that Shakespeare's plays, and this play particularly, are full of borrowings from *Christ's Tears over Jerusalem*, borrowings which cannot be instances of Nashe's authorship of the dramas in which they appear.[8]

There is yet another moment in the Scottish tragedy—the response to the discovery of the murdered Duncan—which shows the detailed influence of the passage in *Christ's Tears* descriptive of the combined offences of treason, murder, rape, and sacrilege.

When Nashe has Christ tell how the outlaw army not only slew the high priest, but murdered children brought "to the *Temple* . . . and . . . most *sacrilegiously* ravisht theyr mothers" (66), he provided Macduff with diction for his horrified announcement "*Most sacrilegious* murther hath broke ope/ The Lord's anointed *temple*. . . ." (2.3.67–68). These outlaws are "dreggy *lees* of Libertines" (65) and have reduced the Temple to "a pudlie *Vault* of *dead*-mens bones" (67), the description of which has affected Macbeth's artificial but ontologically true lament, "renown and grace is *dead,*/ The wine of life is drawn, and the mere *lees*/ Is left this *vault* to brag of" (2.3.94–96). Nashe's description of the polluted Temple with its "Lake of *blood* . . . *silver* gates . . . jellied *gore*"(66) has become part of Macbeth's description of the murder scene, "His *silver* skin lac'd with his golden *blood* . . . breech'd with *gore*" (2.3.112, 116).

The image of moral and physical corruption is yet another in the series of images of famine, murder, barnyard violence, carcase-swollen rivers with their shoals and banks, croaking ravens, and tongue-tied inarticulateness which derive from *Christ's Tears over Jerusalem*, and still one more element of Shakespeare's career-long manipulation of Nashean material, not of Nashe's writing parts of *Macbeth*.

Even the sonnets show the poet's use of *Christ's Tears*, as in sonnets 29, 55, 116, 144. Each of these poems builds upon words and images from the pamphlet. Especially suggestive in 29 are the themes of mistaken ambition and reluctant exchange and the words *"exchange my state," "kings," "scope," "heaven's gate,"* and *"scorn to."* For 55, in the midst of the theme of the vanity behind the building of transitory sculptured memorials, there is the juxtaposition not present in the other contributing sources of Ovid, Horace, and Propertius of "*marble*" and "*monuments.*" In 116, along with the tactic of negative definition, the theme of unchanging integrity, and the closely related terms "*admit,*" "*time,*" and "*sickle,*" there is the syntax of the personal guarantee of what has been said, "*I write, as no man . . .*" which expression has become part of Shakespeare's "*I never writ, nor no man. . . .*" Finally in 144, the themes of betrayal and isolation, the first-person point of view, the competition for an unfaithful loved one, as well as the diction of "*devil,*" "*pride,*" "*Hell,*" "*ill,*" and "*good angel out*" derive from the image and diction of the competition between Christ and the devil for the affections of that "gorgious strumpet" Jerusalem as presented in the pamphlet.[9] But this is sufficient for our purposes of denying the presence of Nashean material in a Shakespearean work as evidence of Nashe's direct involvement in the composition of the play or poem.

Others of Nashe's works, beyond *Saffron Walden* and *Christ's Tears*, show the same evidence of Shakespearean borrowing, borrowing often mistakenly interpreted as proof of Nashe's hand in a Shakespearean play. Dover Wilson, in order to bolster his argument that the Nashean elements are not accidentally present in 1.2, argues that Alençon's response to the Dauphin has still more extensive parallelism between *1 Henry VI* and Nashean texts, this time with *Four Letters Confuted* (1592) and *Summer's Last Will and Testament* (1592, published 1600). Dover Wilson cites both:

> They want their porridge and their fat bull-beaves:
> Either they must be dieted like mules
> And have their provender tied to their mouths,
> Or piteous they will look, like drown'd mice.(1.2.9–12)

And:

> pumpe over mutton and porridge into Fraunce? This colde weather our souldiors, I can tell you, have need of it, and, poore fielde mise, they have almost got the coliche and stone with eating of provant. (I, 331. 28–33)

He infers that "the similarity of diction evoked similarity of diction," but he does not infer that the similarity was evoked in the mind of Shakespeare as he was reading Nashe. Yet this very text of *Four Letters Confuted* fascinated the author of *The Comedy of Errors*, to the point where Act IV, scene iv, and elements of other scenes show Nashean theme and diction. And no one has yet suggested that Nashe wrote *The Comedy of Errors*, 4.4 or any other part of that early comedy.

It is customary to see arguments that say parallels in phrasing are the result of a common source for both the Nashean and Shakespearean texts or that the finite limitations of a culture's language together with the fact of similar themes naturally enough have led to similarities of expression, or indeed even that Nashe is the borrower from Shakespeare. Against these responses is the existence of very many instances of rare or unique terms not found in any known sources but belonging to both Nashe and Shakespeare, and of the clear and frequent evidence of Shakespeare's borrowing from Nashe, as we have indicated above, sometimes in plays composed not only after the publication of Nashe's works, but after his actual demise (1600 or 1601).

In the case of *The Comedy of Errors*, the editors of the play have sometimes made general observations of its Nashean quality, as in Stanley Wells's remark in his New Penguin edition of the play:

> The prose, too, is constructed with controlled artistry, rising in the description of the kitchen wench (III.2.92–154) to a virtuosic—and splendidly actable—piece of fantasy reminiscent of the best work of Shakespeare's contemporary, Thomas Nashe. (13)

And R. A. Foakes in his New Arden edition of the play, drawing upon the work of Dover Wilson in the New Cambridge edition and commenting on two unusual expressions, both in Act IV, scene iv, and both found in Nashe's *Four Letters Confuted* (1592) (also referred to as *Strange News)*, remarks: "In *Four Letters Confuted*, Nashe was attacking Gabriel Harvey, and it is odd that two of his jests against Harvey should turn up in this scene"(83). Foakes here is referring to Dromio of Ephesus's response to Adriana's statement that she had sent the money to redeem her husband— "*Heart and good will* you might, /But surely, master not *a rag of money*"(4.4.85–86)—which is paralleled in Nashe's words attributed to the deceased brother of Gabriel Harvey, a man who has left Gabriel and his other brother Richard "his old gowns" and his "notable sayings," among which was this one: "Vale Galene, mine owne deare Gabriell: Valete humanae artes, *heart and good will*, but never *a ragge of money*" (I, 301). Foakes had earlier noted, as had Quiller Couch, that Dromio of Ephesus's response to the arrival of Adriana in the company of Doctor Pinch, "Mistress, respice finem, respect your end, or rather, the prophecy like the parrot, 'beware the rope's end'" (4.4.41–42) was "alluding to two jokes of the time; one was the substitution of *respice funem* (a rope, i.e. hanging) for the common tag *respice finem* (think on your end, cf. Nashe's attack on Harvey in *Four Letters Confuted* (1592; McKerrow, I.268), "to bee . . . bid *Respice funem*, looke backe to his Fathers house" (Harvey's father was a ropemaker). . . ."(81). None of these editors notes that on this very same page of *Four Letters* there are references to a "Doctor," to Nashe's pamphlet *An Almond for a Parrot*, to another Harvey "brother," and to the issue of not being believed—"there's none will beleeve him"(268).

These references follow the expressions on the previous page, "ropes in Saffron Walden" (Harvey's hometown) and "the *surreverence* of his [Harvey's] works" (267); It is Dr. Pinch who has a "*saffron* face" (IV.iv.61) "*saffron*" is a rare term in the canon, unique in the sixteenth-century part of the Shakespearean canon. Dromio of Syracuse it is who uses "*Sir-reverence*" in his attempt to describe Nell the kitchen wench (3.2.91). On the page following the joke about the rope's end there is an expression, one of several from this pamphlet, that Shakespeare would later use in *Hamlet*. Nashe writes of how he can describe Harvey—"from the foote to the head I can tell how thou art fashioned"—who, in keeping his brother, "hast *crackt* thy credit *through the ring*, made thy infamy *currant* as far as the Queenes coyne goes" (269). Hamlet, in measuring the increased height of the boy actor who plays female parts, is concerned that "Pray God your voice, like a piece of un*current* gold, be not crack'd *within the ring*" (2.2.427-28). Of course, before *Hamlet*, Shakespeare used *Four Letters/Strange News* for *The Comedy of Errors*. G. H. Hibbard in his study of Nashe noted common elements, as had Dover Wilson before him, between *Strange News* and *1 Henry IV*:

> It is no accident that Shakespeare remembered *Strange News* when he was writing *Henry IV*. In some measure at least the disputation and slanging matches that the Prince and Falstaff engage in derive from the way Nashe goes to work here. Words such as "*therefore*" and "*ergo*," the small change of the logic schools abound. The whole thing is conceived in terms that recall either those used in a learned disputation or those used in a court of law. (*Thomas Nashe* 200–201)

The Comedy of Errors, an anticipation of that other Nashean-influenced comedy with a known law-school audience, *Twelfth Night*, delighted the law students at Gray's Inn in 1594. Without suggesting that Dr. Pinch, with his saffron face, was designed to evoke Gabriel Harvey, Doctor of Civil Law, in the eyes of that original law-school audience, no more than the Harveian elements in Malvolio were designed to evoke Harvey in his primping and self-congratulating but rather afforded material for generic laughter, I do want to point out that there are a good many other Nashean elements to be found in *The Comedy of Errors*. No one believes that Nashe had a hand in the composition of the play, but the logic of those who argue that the presence of Nashean material in Act I of *1 Henry VI* is direct evidence of Nashe's composition of that Act should lead the reader to accept Nashe's hand in this play and a good many other in the canon, some even his posthumous efforts.

Among the parallels between *Strange News* and *The Comedy of Errors* not already cited are "the *Doctor*," "a *Rope-maker*," and "*I conjure thee*" in the "Epistle Dedicatorie" (257–258). Comparing Adriana's "Good

Doctor Pinch, you are a conjurer" (4.4.47) and Dromio of Ephesus's "God and the *rope-maker* bear me witness (4.4.90) ("*rope-maker*" is a term unique in the Shakespearean canon), as well as Doctor Pinch's "*I conjure thee*" (4.4.57). Throughout the pamphlet Nashe refers to Harvey as "*the Doctor*," even as he calls him "*a mountebancke* of strange wordes, *a meere* merchant of babies and conny-skins" (261), even as Antipholus of Ephesus refers to Pinch as "*A meer* anatomy, *a mountebank*" (5.1.239). "*Mountebank*" is used only here in *Errors* in Shakespeare's sixteenth-century works. Between the Nashean references to "*rope-maker*" and "*mountebancke*" there is a reference to the animal, the "porcupine," spelled "*Porpentine*" (259). In *Errors* there are five references to the "Porpentine" as the name of the Courtesan's house. There is even a stimulating match for the egregious Nell of the play in the woman Harvey has slandered and who will revenge herself upon him—"a bigge fat lusty wench it is, that hath an arme like an Amazon, and will bang thee abhominationly, if ever she catch thee in her quarters" (289). One notes also that the pre-water-closet humor of the description of Nell—"where stood Belgia, the Netherlands? O, sir, I did not look so *low* . . . told me what *privy* marks I had about me. . . ."(3.2.138–139, 141) is precisely that of Nashe in general, as is indicated on the title page itself, "Of the Intercepting certaine letters, and a convoy of Verses as they were going *Privilie* to victuall the *Low* Countries"(253). Even the chief characteristic of the schoolmaster/conjurer from which he gains his name is paralleled in *Strange News* just after the reference to "heart and good will, but never a ragge of money" (301). Nashe refers to Harvey's description of Nashe as "Greene's inwardest companion *pinched* with want . . . in a raving and *frantike* moode, most desperately exhibiteth a Supplication to the Devill." Nashe then denies that he was "*pincht* with any ungentleman-like want when I invented *Pierce Pennilesse*" (303). From this passage Shakespeare has given Dr. Pinch the key term for his victim: "Go bind this man, for he is *frantic* too" (4.4.113). And this pamphlet, with brothers, skepticism, debts, insanity, conjuring, a fat wench, bathroom humor, legal diction, "ergo" and "therefore," specific jokes about ropes and ends, and with a "Doctor," concludes with a figurative use of a term which is literally operative in the plot of *Errors*, as Nashe describes Harvey as lately "*shipwrackt*," the very word used by Egeon to explain to the Duke the origins of his difficulties (1.1.114). Some or all of these elements might have prompted Shakespeare to use this particular pamphlet by Nashe in the composition of *The Comedy of Errors*. The borrowing from and manipulating of Nashe's works were career-long tactics of Shakespeare.

Dover Wilson adds that "the mules with their provender tied to their mouths" finds an echo in the typical pair of lines from *Summer's Last Will and Testament*:

Except the Cammell have his provender
Hung at his mouth, he will not travell on'. (III.270, 1152–1153)

But *Summer's Last Will and Testament* is an especially malleable source for
Shakespeare in the composition of several of his plays, beginning as early
as *Richard III*, where the villain protagonist's opening lines, as well as subsequent imagery-related verses, derive from Nashe's pageant play.

It is in *Richard III* that we have a sufficiently large Nashean presence in
an early Shakespearean work that appears to be Shakespeare's borrowing
from Nashe. *Richard III* was written shortly after Thomas Nashe's folk
play, *Summer's Last Will and Testament* (1592, but published first in 1600)
and its villain protagonist has some of the self-satisfied mocking attitude
found in Nashe's play. Richard begins the drama with one of Shakespeare's
most famous soliloquies;

Now is the winter of our discontent
Made glorious summer by this son of York:
And all the clouds that lowered upon our house
In the deep bosom of the ocean buried. (1.1.1–4)

And later in the soliloquy he contrasts himself with his amorous brother,
Edward:

He capers nimbly in a lady's chamber
To the lascivious pleasing of a lute. . . .
I, that am rudely stamped, and want love's majesty
To strut before a wanton ambling nymph.

These references to the seasons *winter* and *summer*, the *son* which is a pun
on *sun*, the adjective *glorious*, the *ocean*, the *lascivious* and *lute*, the *wanton*, and even the *nymph* owe much to the debate over succession and
usurpation amongst Summer, Winter, and Autumne on the one hand and
Sol on the other in Nashe's play. Summer tells Sol (called Hypocrisy and
base pride by Summer, fitting terms for Richard) with marked preterition:

How I have rais'd thee, Sol, I list not tell,
Out of the Ocean of adversitie,
To sit in height of honors glorious heaven. (450–453)

Autumne adds, "Lascivious and intemperate he is./ The wrong of Daphne"
(a nymph) "is a well-known tale" (487–488), and after many other indictments, "He setteth wanton songs unto the Lute" (496–497). Winter then
speaks:

Autumne had previously indicted Sol for arrogance:
> this sawcie upstart Jacke
That now doth rule the chariot of the Sunne. . . .
The sonne of parsimony and disdaine,
One that will shine on friends and foes alike,
That under brightest smiles hideth blacke showers. (472–473, 476–478)

When Richard asks for an almanac to determine the weather on the day of the battle of Bosworth Field, he reflects:

Then he disdains to shine, for by the book
He should have brav'd the east an hour ago,
A blacke day will it be to somebody. (5.3.278–280)

The sun will not be seen today. . . .
Not shine today? Why what is that to me
More than to Richmond? For the self-same heaven
That frowns on me looks sadly upon him. (5.3.282, 285–287)

The theme of indifference, the shining upon friend and foe alike, and the diction of *disdains*, *shine*, *sun*, and *black* together suggest that Shakespeare kept in mind this passage from *Summer's Last Will and Testament* both when he introduced the hypocritical Richard, sunlike in his ascendancy, and also when he sent him into eclipse. Interestingly enough, he had also available to him between the *lascivious* of line 487 and the *wanton* and *lute* of line 497 the attractive image of the oriental richness of the rising sun:

Then doubled is the swelling of his looks;
He overloades his carre with Orient gemmes
And reynes his fiery horses with rich pearle. (493–495)

Richard is given some of the diction of these lines not in his early and late associations with the shining and obscured sun but in his debate with Elizabeth on the issue of his marrying her daughter, his niece:

Repair'd with double riches of content.
What? We have many goodly days to see:
The liquid drops of tears that you have shed
Shall come again, transformed to orient pearl,
Advantaging their love with interest.
Of ten times double gain of happiness. (4.4.319–324)

Summer concludes the sixty-line section of the pageant of the seasons with the indictment, "Usurping Sol, the hate of heaven and earth" (502).

Shakespeare, impressed with this description of the sun and seeing the advantages of the association with the house of York and Richard in particular, gave to usurping Richard words which Nashe had written at about the same time.

C. L. Barber, long ago building on some observations of Dover Wilson himself, demonstrated how Bacchus in *Summer's Last Will and Testament* has become part of the nature of Falstaff in *1 Henry IV* and Kenneth Muir has shown further instances of borrowing from this part of the pageant in *2 Henry IV*.

It would be easy to cite further parallels that are indications of Shakespeare's borrowing from Nashe in still other plays, including *Richard II*, where Autumne of the pageant plays the role of Bolingbroke and Summer is in the identical role of the hesitant and ambivalent King Richard:

> Autumne be thou successor of my seat:
> Hold take my crowne—look how he grasps for it!
> Thou shalt no have it yet:—but hold it too,
> Why should I keep that needs I must forgo? (1240–1243)

Compare *Richard II*, 4.1.181ff, and note that these Nashean lines are only three pages later than those cited with the camel and the provender.

And not only is *Richard II* affected by *Summer's Last Will and Testament*, but *Troilus and Cressida* and *King Lear*, also. In the former is Ulysses' speech to Achilles regarding the inevitable transitoriness of power and glory, derived from Autumne's lecture to inhospitable Christmas, where the themes found in this passage in *Troilus* (3.3.145ff) of hospitality, transitoriness, and ingratitude, together with the diction of "*wallets*," "*backes*," "*ghests*," "*almes*," "*out of fashion*," and even the unique Ajaxian "*Milo*" are intertwined. In the case of *King Lear*, the old king's game of who loves me the most and his anger at Cordelia's "nothing" have been affected by the same section of Nashe's folk play.

The play involves the imminent passing of Summer, who must transfer his power to the other seasons, as is the nature of things. Summer calls his officers to account, querying especially Ver and Solstitium:

> Come neer, my friends, for I am neere my end.
> In presence of this Honourable trayne,
> Who *love* me (for I patronize their sports),
> Meane I to make my finall Testament:
> But first Ile call my officers to count,
> And of the wealth I gave them to dispose,
> Known what is left, I may know what to give.

First, Ver, the spring, unto whose custody
I have committed more than to the rest.
The choyse of all my fragrant *meades* and flowers,
And what delights soe're nature affords. (146–158)

Presumptuous Ver, uncivill nurturde boy,
Think'st I will be derided thus of thee?
Is this th' account and reckoning that thou mak'st? (222–224)

But say, Solstitium, hadst though nought besides?
Nought but dayes eyes and faire looks gave I thee?
Nothing, my Lord, nor ought more did I aske. (404–406)

Here, from a work often mined by Shakespeare, is an analogously structured dialogue revolving around the transference of kingly power, an ungrateful reply from a more highly favored youngest child (Ver/Cordelia), royal anger, and the keyword "Nothing." And this *Lear*-influencing passage follows immediately upon Summer's "Presumptuous Ver, uncivill nurturde boy," a line that has clearly shaped Gloucester's line to Eleanor in *2 Henry VI*, 1.2.42: "Presumptuous dame, ill-nurtur'd Eleanor."

Shakespeare frequently used several works of Nashe in the course of the composition of one play, so that the presence of several parallels in *1 Henry VI* from several works of Nashe is not only *not* proof that these parallels are evidence that Nashe wrote *1 Henry VI*, Act 1, but is in keeping with the career-long practice of Shakespeare of fusing several Nashean elements in the same text. Of course Taylor and others offer several different arguments, not merely Nashean parallels, in order to argue for Nashe's authorship of this part of *1 Henry VI*. Nevertheless the use of the Nashean argument seems less effective, indeed mistaken, if one accepts the contrary instances I have been adducing, and its would-be "proof" of Nashe's role seems a bit like the dubious case made by a conscious user of incorrectly interpreted evidence: "And this may help to thicken other proofs /That do demonstrate thinly."

The debate about the integrity of *1 Henry VI* is likely to continue for some time, but as it does, the sense one has of Nashe's indirect role should increase and his direct role diminish.

NOTES

[1] See also Gary Taylor, "Shakespeare and Others: The Authorship of *Henry the Sixth, Part One.*" *Medieval and Renaissance Drama in England* 7 (1995): 145–205.

[2] *Part 1*, New Cambridge ed. (1952) xxiii.

[3] Tobin, "Nashe and *Romeo and Juliet.*" *Notes and Queries* 225 (1980): 161–162.

[4] Tobin, "Nashe and Shakespeare: Some Further Borrowings," *Notes and Queries*, 237 (1992): 314.

[5] For other elements in *Saffron Walden,* see the forthcoming Festschrift for G. Blakemore Evans.

[6] References to *Have with You to Saffron Walden* are to McKerrow, vol. 3.

[7] Tobin, "Nomenclature and the Dating of *Titus Andronicus*," *Notes and Queries* 229 (1984): 186–187.

[8] For an expanded version of this note, see Tobin, "Antony, Brutus, and *Christ's Tears over Jerusalem,*" *Notes and Queries* 243 (1998): 324–331.

[9] For a fuller treatment of these instances of Nashe's influence upon the Sonnets, see Tobin, "Nashe and Some Shakespearian Sonnets," *Notes and Queries* 244 (1999): 222–226.

HENRY VI IN JAPAN

Yoshio Arai

I. INTRODUCTION

In the trilogy of English history plays, *Henry VI, Parts 1*, *2*, and *3*, William Shakespeare depicts such things as civil wars, power struggles, ambitions, vanity, and uncertainty which become the main subjects in his great tragedies, especially in *Macbeth* and *King Lear*. These two tragedies have been the most popular Shakespeare plays in Japan since his plays were first introduced over one hundred years ago. Akira Kurosawa's Japanese film versions of the two great tragedies, *Throne of Blood* (1957) and *Ran* (1985), have become world-famous. However, the *Henry VI* plays have never been as popular here as in England and other countries.

This trend has changed somewhat since World War II. With the success of the Royal Shakespeare Company's production of *The Wars of the Roses* under the direction of John Barton and Peter Hall, the trilogy has often been performed and has been discussed as much in Japan as in England, America, and other countries.

In this article, I would like to trace the brief history of the introduction of the trilogy into Japan. I shall also discuss the thematic affinity of the trilogy to the history and tradition of Japanese culture.

II. SHOYO TSUBOUCHI'S FIRST TRANSLATION

Shakespeare's *Henry VI, Parts 1, 2,* and *3*, were first translated into Japanese by Shoyo Tsubouchi in 1928 as a part of his Japanese version of the complete works of Shakespeare.[1] His interest in the history plays went back to the early stages of his Shakespeare translation. Tsubouchi attempted his first translation of Shakespeare in his university student days with *Julius Caesar* in 1888.

One of the aims of his Shakespeare translation was to employ Shakespeare's plays as a source and inspiration for the improvement of

Japan's traditional Kabuki plays and for the creation of new Japanese drama. As a result of his studies and translation of Shakespeare, Tsubouchi wrote three history plays under the influence of Shakespeare's history plays. They are *Kiri-hitoha* (*A Leaf of Paulownia*), *Hototogisu-kojo-no-rakugetsu* (*A Setting Sun over the Old Castle*), and *Maki-no-kata* (*The Shogun's Wife Maki*).[2]

Kiri-hitoha, written in 1894-1895 and first performed in 1904, is based on the famous power conflict between the Toyotomi Clan and the Tokugawa Clan in Medieval Japan. After the death of the strong leader Hideyoshi Toyotomi in 1598, the rival forces led by Ieyasu Tokugawa defeated the Toyotomi forces in the Battle of Sekigahara in 1600 and finally Ieyasu occupied the Shogunate. In this history play, Shoyo depicts the rise of Tokugawa and the fall of Toyotomi through the confrontation between hostile factions of royal warriors. The governing theme of the play is the uncertainty of worldly things as delivered in the speech of Katsumoto Katagiri, the most loyal subject of the Toyotomi Clan:

> Autumn has come in heaven and earth, and the leaves are
> falling in the garden. But a paulownia leaf, the symbol of my
> family name, never falls and my spirit of loyalty never
> changes. A flow will have an ebb. In all human things there
> is a rise and a fall! (Act III)

Almost the same notion of the uncertainty of worldly things finds expression in *Henry VI, Part 1*:

> Glory is like a circle in the water,
> Which never ceaseth to enlarge itself
> Till by broad spreading it disperseth nought. (1.2.133–135)[3]

Hototogisu-kojo-no-rakugetsu, written in 1897 and first performed in 1905, is the sequel to *Kiri-hitoha*. The main action of the play takes place on the day of the fall of Osaka Castle, built by Hideyoshi Toyotomi. It is the tragedy of a young and weak successor to Hideyoshi, Hideyori Toyotomi, and his mother, Yodo-gimi. Shoyo Tsubouchi created these two Kabuki history plays after careful research of Shakespeare's history plays, especially the *Henry VI* plays. The indirect influence of *Henry VI* upon these two plays is easily noticeable. Civil wars, power struggles, treacheries, intrigues, a young weak leader, royal subjects, and above all the theme of decline from prosperity are parallel themes in Shakespeare's *Henry VI* and Tsubouchi's history plays.

Maki-no-kata, written in 1897 and first performed in 1905, is again a play about a power struggle between the Kamakura Shogunate, Japan's first warrior government, and the rival leader Tokimasa Hojo. The title role

Maki-no-kata, the heroine created after Lady Macbeth, is the name of the second wife of Tokimasa. Tsubouchi wrote two more history plays as sequels to *Maki-no-kata*, *Nagori-no-hoshi-zukiyo* (*The Last Moonlit Evening*) and *Yoshitoki-no-Saigo* (*Yoshitoki's Death*). The former, written in 1917 and first performed in 1920, is about the assassination of the powerless Shogun Sanetomo, and the latter, written in 1918 and first performed in 1939, concerns the tragic death of the old Shogun Yoshitoki.[4]

Under the influence of *Henry VI, Richard III*, and *Macbeth*, Tsubouchi wrote this trilogy of the Kamakura Shogunate, which governed Japan from the 1180s until its overthrow in 1333. Tsubouchi's five Kabuki history plays, the two plays about the Toyotomi-Tokugawa conflicts and the trilogy of the rise and fall of the Kamakura Shogunate, are the fruits of his studies of the Shakespearean histories, especially the *Henry VI* plays.

III. NORIO DEGUCHI'S FIRST PRODUCTION

Shoyo Tsubouchi's Japanese version of the complete works of Shakespeare dominated reading circles and stage productions until the outbreak of World War II. But the *Henry VI* trilogy was never performed in Tsubouchi's lifetime. He died in 1935 after revising his complete Japanese version of Shakespeare, newly published by the Chuo-koron Publishing Company.

After World War II, the *Henry VI* plays were translated into Japanese again in 1967 as a part of the eight-volume version of the complete works of Shakespeare published by the Chikuma-Shobo Publishing Company. *Henry VI, Part 1*, translated by Jiro Ozu[5] and Tetsuo Kishi, *Henry VI, Part 2*, translated by Jiro Ozu and Kenji Oba, and *Henry VI, Part 3*, translated by Jiro Ozu and Naoe Takei, were included in Volume V. But again, they were never performed on stage in Japan.

Finally, in 1981, Norio Deguchi[6] directed the *Henry VI* plays for the first time in Japan. He commenced his direction of all the plays of Shakespeare with his own Shakespeare Theatre Company in 1975. It took six years to fulfill his dream of directing the thirty-seven Shakespeare plays newly translated by Yushi Odashima,[7] who was second after Shoyo Tsubouchi to translate the complete plays of Shakespeare into Japanese.

Deguchi directed the *Henry VI* plays at the Jean-Jean underground theatre of Shibuya, Tokyo, from the 10th to the 15th of April, 1981. The uniqueness of his production was that the *Henry VI* trilogy was performed in a single day with the same actors and actresses in contemporary costumes such as jeans. It took nine hours with several intermissions to finish the performance. The production by the young actors and actresses was so speedy, energetic and dynamic that it was very well received by the young audience. It was one of the most successful and impressive theatre performances of the year.

According to the director Deguchi, extremely violent fighting is necessary to dramatize the action of the trilogy. Therefore he devised the use of wooden and bamboo instead of iron swords in order to prevent fatal wounds. Because of this device, the fighting scenes, with just about twenty actors in the very small underground theatre, became most thrilling and unforgettable sequences. Thanks to the great success of his production of the trilogy, it was revived in 1982 at the Haiyuza Theatre in Roppongi, Tokyo, for five days from the 5th to the 9th of May.[8]

In April 1988, The Tokyo Globe Theatre debuted with the production of the English Shakespeare Company's *The Wars of the Roses,* directed by Michael Bogdanov.[9] Shakespeare's great cycle under the title of *The Wars of the Roses* consists of eight histories: *Richard II, Henry IV, Parts 1* and *2, Henry V, Henry VI, Parts 1, 2,* and *3,* and *Richard III.* For the first time in Japan, nearly all of Shakespeare's history plays were performed successively in fifteen days, in the original Shakespearean language. It was a monumental production in the stage history of Shakespeare in Japan.

IV. JUNJI KINOSHITA'S SHIGOSEN-NO-MATSURI

Junji Kinoshita[10] is not only a leading Japanese playwright but also a translator of Shakespeare. As a dramatist, he created the world-famous play *Yuzuru (The Twilight Crane),* which is also famous as an impressive opera.[11] Kinoshita translated sixteen Shakespearean plays into Japanese, starting with *Othello* in 1947.[12] His final eight-volume version of Shakespeare was published in 1986 by the Kodansha Publishing Company. Of these sixteen plays, he is most interested in *Macbeth;* he has written a number of essays, delivered a series of lectures, and held many seminars on the tragedy. This culminated in a long essay on his interpretation of the play, which accompanies his translation of *Macbeth* in the volume published in 1988.

Kinoshita's grandest venture is the creation of an epic drama for choral reading entitled *Shigosen-no-matsuri (A Ritual of the Meridian).*[13] This great epic drama is based on *Heike-monogatari (The Tale of the Heike),* the most famous epic classic in the history of Japanese literature. The influence of Shakespeare's histories and tragedies is reflected in the theme and scheme, style and speech, and the background of the creation of this grand epic drama. It was published in 1978 and first performed in April, 1979, by the Yasue Yamamoto Theatre Group.[14] The drama was so well received, winning a number of theatre awards, that it was revived several times.

The main theme of Kinoshita's epic drama is Life seen through eternal Time. He describes the tragic life of the loyal warrior Shinchunagon-Tomomori in the War of the Genji and the Heike Clans (1185) as one of the most fatal lives in recorded time. The sense of resignation and transience emerges in the speech of Kagemi, the shadowy female servant of Tomomori:

Only when we look at the heartless stars shining in the sky and think deeply about our life, we can realize the importance of our life and gain consolation and strength. Seen through the stream of eternal time, our life is also heartless. Look keenly at the heartless world. (Act III, Sc. 2)

The tragic hero Tomomori's last words, just before sinking into the Sea of Seto, are: "I have seen enough what I have to see. Now drowning, I kill myself" (Act IV).

After the success of his epic drama, Kinoshita undertook his translation into Japanese of *The Wars of the Roses,* adapted by John Barton for the Royal Shakespeare Company in 1970. Kinoshita's Japanese version was published by the Kodansha Publishing Company in 1997. With this translation, Kinoshita again expressed in Japanese the harsh world in which men never stop making wars. John Barton, in the Shakespearean lines from the last scene of *Richard III*, and Kinoshita, in his Japanese version, conclude *The Wars of the Roses* as follows:

Now civil wounds are stopp'd, peace lives again—
That she may long live here, God say Amen! (5.5.40–41)

From the very beginning of Kinoshita's life as a dramatist until his translation of *The Wars of the Roses*, his main concern has been "an irresistible force against men," in other words, "the tension between men and inevitability beyond men." This theme runs through the *Henry VI* plays, *Macbeth*, and many other Shakespearean plays.

V. STUDIES OF HENRY VI

Numerous short introductory essays and articles on the *Henry VI* plays have been written since Shakespeare was introduced in Japan. Among those essays, two articles the contributions of two scholars at least are worth mentioning here. Kenji Oba's article [15] on the *Henry VI* plays included in *Shakespeare Handbook*, edited by Jiro Ozu, was published in 1969 by the Nanundo Publishing Company as part of a collection of articles on all the works of Shakespeare. Oba discussed almost all the problems concerning the *Henry VI* plays: the multiple authorship, uncertainty about the order of their composition, and the bibliographical problems attending the surviving texts. However, he did not argue the theory that the trilogy was entirely composed by Shakespeare according to the natural chronological order of the events.

Yukiko Mori's three articles on the trilogy [16] are the most illuminating academic studies ever written in Japan on the Henry VI plays. Her first article "The Internal Enemy and the Foreign Enemy," included in the *Tsuda College Bulletin*, was published in 1991. As the subtitle of her article, "Joan of Arc in *Henry VI, Part 1*," suggests, she focused her attention on Joan to emphasize the symbolic meaning of the burning of the heroine. In her opinion, the dramatist changed some historical facts in order to make the execution of Joan of Arc manifest the strength of England, but ironically the strength displayed is also the weakness that led the country into the internal conflicts depicted in the Wars of the Roses in the *Parts 2* and *3* of *Henry VI*.

Mori wrote two more articles on *Henry VI, Part 1*: "On *Henry VI, Part 1*, Its Ending and Beginning," published by the Kenkyusha Publishing Company as a part of the book *Articles on the Complete Works of Shakespeare*, in 1992, and "The Age and History—On Joan of Arc in *Henry VI, Part 1*," as a part of *Shakespeare's History Plays*, published by the Kenkyusha Publishing Company in 1994. In these articles, Shakespeare's infusion of the character of Joan of Arc with strong and ambiguous aspects of Queen Elizabeth and the depiction of York as the seeker of fame and higher position are impressively interpreted from Shakespeare's text with well-researched historical facts and keen insight into the play. According to the writer, ambition for the crown, the governing theme of Shakespeare's histories, is already nascent in the characterization of York.

Professor Yukiko Mori's study of *Henry VI, Part 1* is one of the great accomplishments of Shakespeare studies in Japan.

VI. CONCLUSION—MY PUBLIC READINGS

It is ineffective and almost meaningless to start performing the *Henry VI* plays from *Part 2* or *Part 3*. No matter what Shakespearean scholars and critics may say about the order of the composition of the trilogy, all directors without exception made their productions of the *Henry VI* plays start with *Part 1*. I followed the current directorial consensus when I dedicated my reading of the trilogy to Sam Wanamaker's dream of rebuilding Shakespeare's Globe Theatre in Southwark. My public readings were a part of various fund-raising campaigns in Japan for the reconstruction of Shakespeare's Globe Theatre.[17] My readings of the complete works of Shakespeare started on April 23, 1987, at the Iwanami Cine Salon in Tokyo, with the Sonnets, from 1 to 32. After five years, I completed this project on January 25, 1992, with *The Two Noble Kinsmen*. In my readings of Shakespeare's history plays, I tried to emphasize the importance of executing the performance according to chronological order. I began with the reading of *Henry V* on the 27th of April, 1990. It was followed by *Henry VI, Part 1* on the 25th of May, *Part 2* on the 1st of June, *Part 3* on the 8th of June, and finally *Richard III* on the 22nd of June. In these consecutive weekly readings, the audience and I myself appreciated Shakespeare's consistent denunciation of the vanity of wars and power struggles. In addition to the lines already quoted, Shakespeare constantly expressed these themes in the following speeches:

Thus sometimes hath the brightest day a cloud,
And after summer evermore succeeds
Barren winter, with his wrathful nippings cold;
So cares and joys abound, as seasons fleet. (*3 Henry VI*, 2.4.1–4)

Why, what is pomp, rule, reign, but earth and dust?
And live we how we can, yet die we must. (*3 Henry VI*, 5.2.28–29)

Such feelings of the insecurity of power and the sense of waste are strongly expressed at the end of *Richard III*: "A horse! a horse! my kingdom for a horse!" (5.4.7). Seeking crown and kingdom, Richard kills a number of people, great and poor, but finally he realizes that on the battlefield a horse is more important than his crown and kingdom. What vanity and waste! The most impressive and meaningful speech Shakespeare ever wrote on this theme is the "Tomorrow and tomorrow" speech in *Macbeth* (5.5.19–28). In his last history play, *Henry VIII*, he again created the following unforgettable speech delivered by Wolsey:

I have touch'd the highest point of all my greatness,
And from that full meridian of my glory
I haste now to my setting. I shall fall
Like a bright exhalation in the evening,
And no man see me more. (3.2.223–227)

The same thought of the sense of vanity and uncertainty of life appears in Japanese classic literature. The most famous is the beginning of *Heikemonogatari* (*The Tale of the Heike*), the greatest epic in the history of Japanese literature:[18]

The bells of the temple of Gion
Seem to be singing, "All is vanity."
Green leaves and flowers signify
The fate of prosperity.
Those who are in power will decline.
Their lives are no more than dreams in a Spring night.
Even strong warriors have to die.
They are like dust before a rising wind.

Similarly, Basho, one of the most noted Haiku poets, expostulates on the vanity of war, as follows:

> A mound of summer grass:
> Are warriors' heroic deeds
> Only dreams that pass?[19]

The film director Akira Kurosawa portrays this sense of waste in his Shakespeare films, *Throne of Blood* and *Ran*. Kenji Mizoguchi's 1952 film *Saikaku-ichidai-onna* (*The Story of Oharu*), Yasujiro Ozu's 1953 film *Tokyo-monogatari* (*The Story of Tokyo*), and Takeshi Kitano's currently successful 1998 film *HANA-BI* (*Fireworks*) convey the same sense of waste.

Shakespeare's *Henry VI* plays and Japanese literature, theatre, and film coincide thematically with the sense of waste experienced everywhere in the world. Shoyo Tsubouchi and Junji Kinoshita, the two great Japanese translators of Shakespeare and dramatists in their own right, created Kabuki plays and a grand epic drama under the influence of Shakespeare's histories and tragedies. Moreover, their themes are Shakespearean motifs that thread through the *Henry VI* plays to his last play, *Henry VIII*.

The important difference between Shakespeare and Japanese adaptations of his histories and tragedies is that whereas Shakespeare ends his plays with the restoration of order and peace, Tsubouchi, Kinoshita, and film director Kurosawa end their plays and films in a shambles to emphasize the impermanence of worldly things which prevails in traditional Japanese literature and drama since the introduction of Buddhism in Japan in 538 (or 552).

In conclusion, I would like to say that the *Henry VI* plays are not lesser in the whole Shakespeare canon. Rather they are very powerful and effective on the stage when performed as a trilogy. Above all, *Part 1* is most important, as Professor Yukiko Mori analyzes it in detail from various angles in her three articles. In *Part 1*, as in *The Comedy of Errors* and *Titus Andronicus*, we can find many Shakespearean themes and techniques which he used in later plays. With this history play, Shakespeare appeared in London's theatre world as "an upstart crow" and probably became "the only shake-scene in the country," as Robert Greene said in his *Groatsworth of Wit* (1592).

NOTES

[1] Shoyo Tsubouchi (1859–1935) was one of the greatest cultural figures in the Meiji, Taisho, and the early part of Showa periods. He was also a novelist and professor at Waseda University.

[2] *Kiri-hitoha* and *Hototogisu-kojo-no-rakugetsu* are printed in *Shoyo*

Senshu (Collected Works of Shoyo), Vol. 1. Tokyo: Daiichi Shobo, 1977; *Maki-no-kata* is printed in *Shoyo Senshu*, Vol. 2.

[3] All quotations from Shakespeare are from *The Complete Works of Shakespeare*, ed. Peter Alexander. London: Collins, 1951.

[4] *Nagori-no-hoshi-zukiyo* and *Yoshitoki-no-Saigo* are printed in *Shoyo Senshu*, Vol. 2.

[5] Jiro Ozu (1920–1988) was a leading Shakespeare scholar and President of the Shakespeare Society of Japan from 1975 until his death in London in 1988.

[6] Norio Deguchi, born in 1940, after belonging to Bungajku-za Theatre Company, established his Shakespeare Theatre in 1975 and accomplished his grand ambition of directing all the plays of Shakespeare in 1981.

[7] Yushi Odashima, born in 1930, professor and Shakespeare scholar at Tokyo University, translated all the plays of Shakespeare (1973–1980).

[8] *Shakespeare in Japan Bibliography*, ed. Takashi Sasaki. Tokyo: Nihon Tosho-shuppan, 1995.

[9] The Tokyo Globe Theatre was opened at Shinokubo, Tokyo, in 1988. It is a covered concrete building making use of the latest stage technology. The theatre is based upon a design gleaned from information contained in the de Witt drawing of the Swan Theatre, the contract for the Fortune Theatre, and most importantly the etching of the Globe included in Wenceslaus Hollar's 1647 panorama of London. It is not a reproduction of Shakespeare's "Wooden 0," but a modern, concrete Globe.

[10] Junji Kinoshita, born in 1914, is Japan's leading dramatist and translator of Shakespeare.

[11] *Yuzuru* was first performed in 1949; the one-act opera, composed by Ikuma Dan, was first performed in 1952.

[12] Published by Shingetsusha Publishing Company, Tokyo, in 1947.

[13] Printed in *Kinoshita-Junji-Shu (Collected Works of Junji Kinoshita)*, Vol. 8. Tokyo: Iwanami-shoten, 1989.

[14] Originally called Budo-no-kai, it was established in 1945 by the actress Yasue Yamamoto and Junji Kinoshita.

[15] Professor of Meiji-gakuin University and a member of the Shakespeare Society of Japan.

[16] Associate professor of Tokyo No-ko University and a member of the Shakespeare Society of Japan.

[17] See "Editorial Column." *Asahi Evening News* September 12, 1991 and David Lazarus's "Seriously" Column, *The Japan Times*, December 15, 1991; The main purpose of the five-year public readings of the complete works of Shakespeare was fund-raising. So each year's program was a mixture of popular plays and unpopular ones. The *Henry VI* plays were read in the fourth year because they have been unpopular in Japan. Sam Wanamaker, the founder of Shakespeare's Globe, sent me a "Testimonial" dated September 6, 1991, when I completed the public readings of the

thirty-seven plays of Shakespeare: "On behalf of our Patron, His Royal Highness The Prince Philip, Duke of Edinburgh, KG., KT, and the Trustees and Directors of the Shakespeare Globe Trust and the International Shakespeare Globe Centre, I send you our warm greetings and congratulations on the completion of your magnificent achievement. The public reading of all of Shakespeare's thirty-seven plays is not only a phenomenal feat in its own right, but as an effort to help raise funds for the rebuilding of Shakespeare's Globe Theatre near its original site in London. It is a magnificent act of generosity and dedication."

[18] The most important of the Kamakura (1185–1333) and Muromachi (1333–1568) period prose tales known as *Gunki-monogatari* or "war tales," recited by *biwa* (lute) players.

[19] "Natsukusaya tsuwamonodomoga yumenoato," translated by Dorothy Guyver Briton in her book *A Haiku Journey*. Tokyo: Kodansha International, 1974. See also Basho, *The Narrow Road to the Deep North and Other Travel Sketches*, trans. and introduction by Nobuyuki Yuasa. Baltimore: Penguin Books, 1966.

THE PROGRESS OF REVENGE
IN THE FIRST HENRIAD

Harry Keyishian

The action of the *Henry VI* plays takes place in a nation in which central authority is weak, divided, and discredited, leaving autonomous individuals and factions free to pursue their own interests without regard to the good of the commonwealth as a whole. Such a world duplicates the earliest stages of society, when self-help, feud, vendetta, and vengeance were appropriate means, sometimes the only means, of settling quarrels, punishing crimes, and achieving justice. The normal pattern of social development requires individuals and clans to cede power to a central authority that substitutes the rule of law for the right of retaliation. In his first historical tetralogy, Shakespeare depicts the breakdown and reconstitution of legitimate authority. During the period of breakdown, each act of personal retaliation initiates another, the cycle ending only in the snake-pit world of Richard III, who is a false instrument of order. Richard gains temporary power but then self-destructs, leaving Henry Tudor to restore legitimate order.

The view of revenge Shakespeare takes in the *Henry VI* plays is not merely social, however, but personal. Shakespeare portrays injuries, insults, and wrongs as psychic traumas for which revenge seems, to the victim, the only remedy. Characters who have been victimized or violated, who have suffered malicious harm, look to revenge as a means to restore a sense of selfhood.[1] Focusing on the psychology of revenge, Shakespeare contends that this is how people behave when injured: through retaliatory actions, they try to restore a sense of selfhood and redeem an identity damaged by injury.

But though the psychology of revenge is consistent throughout the tetralogy, its results vary. Revenges against foreign foes are glorious; revenges against domestic enemies are odious; vindictive revenges, exercised for no valid reason, are most abhorrent of all. All three are manifested in the First Tetralogy, as the English shift the focus of their hostility from their French enemies to each other.

Revenge against the French—and especially revenge against Joan la Pucelle—is a fine thing indeed. *1 Henry VI* in fact opens with a call for vengeance for the death of Henry V, a catastrophic event that the English nobility cannot accept as an act of God. In their despair, they seek a target for their rage and find it initially in what Bedford calls the "bad revolting stars" (1.1.4). One cannot arraign the stars very conveniently, however; so the more pragmatic Exeter shifts the blame to "the subtle witted French/ Conjurers and Sorcerers, that, afraid of him, / By magic verses have contrived his end" (25–27). Whether he believes sincerely in French witchcraft or not, Exeter's tactic rallies the dispirited lords to defend England's recent conquests.

Their prime defender, Lord Talbot, is especially violent in his desire to avenge English losses. When the Master Gunner of Orleance fatally shoots Salisbury, Talbot is imaginatively stung to take action:

> [Salisbury] beckons with his hand and smiles on me,
> As who should say, "When I am dead and gone,
> Remember to avenge me on the French."
> Plantagenet, I will, and like thee, [Nero,]
> Play on the lute, beholding the towns burn:
> Wretched shall France be only in my name. (*1 Henry VI*, 1.4.92–97)

When it comes to foreign wars, like these against the rebellious French, comparison even to the lunatic Nero carries positive connotations. And the intervention of Joan la Pucelle only drives Talbot to further extremes; he vows to be a lunatic—a Tamburlaine, perhaps—of revenge:

> Pucelle or Puzzel, Dolphin or Dogfish,
> Your hearts I'll stamp out with my horse's heels,
> And make a quagmire of your mingled brains. (107–109)

When the English retreat before the maid's armies, Talbot denounces them as collaborators:

> You all consented unto Salisbury's death,
> For none of you would strike a stroke in his revenge. (1.5.34–35)

Describing their lack of revengeful passion as fundamental disloyalty, Talbot in effect accuses them of treason. He can, by contrast, boast that he has fulfilled his duty:

> Now have I paid my vow unto his soul;
> For every drop of blood was drawn from him,
> There hath at least five Frenchmen died tonight.
> And that hereafter ages may behold
> What ruin happened in revenge of him,
> Within their chiefest temple I'll erect
> A tomb, wherein his corpse shall be interr'd,
> Upon the which, that every one may read,
> Shall be engrav'd the sack of Orleance. (2.2.7–15)

Talbot's desire to inscribe his revenge in the body of France might be termed a Foucauldian gesture: a "coded action" that "made the body of the condemned man the place where the vengeance of the sovereign was applied, the anchoring point for the manifestation of power."[2] Talbot, as the representative of English royal sovereignty, exercises his obligation to make visible the guilt of the French. Clearly, therefore, revenge is an affirmative force when it motivates glorious deeds that advance the interests of the nation—and the bloodier, the better.

Domestic revenges are another matter. The squabbles between Duke Humphrey of Gloucester and Henry Beauford, Bishop of Winchester—the first the king's uncle, the second his great-uncle—are unseemly and disruptive. Gloucester accuses Beauford of lewdness and treachery ("saucy priest"); Beauford denounces Gloucester as ambitious and "unreverent." And their followers pursue their masters' quarrel; as the Mayor of London complains,

> The Bishop and the Duke of Gloucester's men,
> Forbidden late to carry any weapon,
> Have fill'd their pockets full of pebble stones;
> And, banding themselves in contrary parts,
> Do pelt so fast at one another's pate
> That many have their giddy brains knock'd out. (*1 Henry VI*, 3.1.76–81)

More dangerously, the nobles of the kingdom form the factions that will evolve into the antagonisms of the Wars of the Roses to follow. In the Temple Garden scene, the initiating quarrel surrounds Richard Plantagenet, whose father, Richard Earl of Cambridge, was executed for treason during the reign of Henry V. Dispossessed of his titles, Plantagenet is subject to insult by the other nobles. Somerset is particularly dismissive—"We grace the yeoman by conversing with him" (*1 Henry VI*, 2.5.81)—and the proud Planagenet vows to "redress" his "bitter injuries" (125–126). His determination is strengthened by a prison encounter with the dying Edmund Mortimer, a victim of Lancastrian ambition, who explains the wrongs the

House of York has endured.

When Plantagenet is restored to his titles and named Duke of York, the feuds only intensify. Though the king and Gloucester urge them to reconcile in the name of national unity, neither Somerset nor Planagenet is willing to aid the beleaguered Talbot in France. As a consequence he is killed in battle, and the tide turns against the English. Domestic broils have lost what Henry V had won.

The full destructive force of the continuing domestic turmoil begins to reveal itself when York decides to seek the crown. He does so with claims of right, as the avenger of the wrongfully deposed "Harmless Richard" who was "murthered traitorously" (*2 Henry VI*, 2.2.27). He will not rest until his "sword be stain'd/ With heart-blood of the house of Lancaster" (64–66). He is abetted by Warwick, who is aware that Duke Humphrey's death had been arranged by Queen Margaret's supporters and who vows to "do some service to [his] ghost" by killing her most ardent ally, Suffolk (*2 Henry VI*, 3.2.231).

Suffolk is banished and, on his way to France, captured by a pirate, Walter Whitmore, who aims to kill him on the spot:

I lost mine eye in laying the prize aboard,
And therefore to revenge it thou shalt die. (*2 Henry VI*, 4.1.26)

When Suffolk tries to escape death by offering a ransom, he only manages to enrage Whitmore further. It is, he says, a matter of family honor to take revenge:

Never yet did base dishonor blur our name
But with our sword we wip'd away the blot;
Therefore, when merchant-like I sell revenge,
Broke be my sword, my arms torn and defac'd,
And I proclaim'd a coward through the world! (4.1.39–43)

When Suffolk reveals his identity in an effort to awe his captors, matters become even worse for him, since the lieutenant who accompanies Whitmore is a patriot who longs to punish Suffolk for his sins against England—the greed, his support of Queen Margaret, his role in giving away English lands, his plots against Duke Humphrey:

Now will I dam up this thy yawning mouth
For swallowing the treasure of the realm. (4.1.72–73)

But mainly the lieutenant supports the claim of York to the throne, accusing the Lancastrians of "shameful murther of a guiltless king/ And lofty, proud, encroaching tyranny," against which the House of York

"Burns with revenging fire" (95–98). Revenge proceeds on two levels in this incident: the proud Whitmore cites personal honor, while the lieutenant demands revenge in the name of national interest.

Even as the murdered Suffolk's corpse is borne onstage, a remaining gentleman predicts that this "barbarous and bloody" act will lead to further killing:

> His body will I bear unto the King.
> If he revenge it not, yet will his friends;
> So will the Queen, that living held him dear. (4.1.145–147)

As York moves to seize power from the Lancastrians and their allies, the struggle takes on an increasingly personal and cruel tone. Events descend to petty retaliations calculated to inflict as much emotional pain as possible:

> The deadly-handed Clifford slew my steed;
> But match to match I have encount'red him,
> And made a prey for carrion kites and crows
> Even of the bonny beast he lov'd so well. (*2 Henry VI*, 5.2.9–12)

Still, when York and Clifford encounter each other in battle, they exchange courtly compliments:

> *Clif.* What seest thou in me, York? Why dost thou pause?
> *York.* With thy brave bearing should I be in love,
>   But that thou art so fast mine enemy.
> *Clif.* Nor should thy prowess want praise and esteem,
>   But that 'tis shown ignobly and in treason.
>   (5.2.19–22)

After he kills Clifford, York offers a benediction over his corpse:

> Thus war hath given thee peace, for thou art still.
> Peace with his soul, heaven, if it be thy will! (29–30)

As Stephen Urkowitz points out, these men, even as they destroy the political order, remain "exquisitely sensitive to nobility and grace."[3] But this exchange marks the end of an era: men who kill without conscience dominate the next generation.

One of the most vicious of these is Young Clifford, who calls on revenge to stir his troops when they suffer defeat:

> O war, thou son of hell,
> Whom angry heavens to make their minister,

Throw in the frozen bosoms of our part
Hot coals of vengeance! (*2 Henry VI*, 5.2.33–36)

In the heat of battle, he spies his father's body, and his calls for revenge
become even more fervent and personal:

> Even at this sight
> My heart is turn'd to stone; and while 'tis mine,
> It shall be stony. York not our old men spares;
> No more will I their babes. . . .
> Henceforth I will not have to do with pity.
> Meet I an infant of the house of York,
> Into as many gobbets will I cut it
> As wild Medea young Absyrtus did;
> In cruelty will I seek out my fame. (49–60)

Clifford soon makes good this promise. When he captures York's son
Rutland, he ignores the boy's pleas for pity:

> *Rut.* I never did thee harm; why wilt thou slay me?
> *Clif.* . . . Thy father slew my father; therefore die. (*3 Henry VI*, 1.3.38–47)

In his fury, Young Clifford has turned into an automaton of revenge. The
chivalric code of his father's generation is left far behind. And the energies
of revenge do indeed for the moment gain a victory for the Lancastrians, as
a wounded York, isolated from his allies, is cornered by the two who hate
him most, Margaret and Clifford.

York's many humiliations have been noted. For her part, Margaret too
has had to endure a goodly share of insults. As the daughter of a duke rich
only in titles, she is resented by many in the court of Henry VI, who see her
only as Suffolk's proud mistress wrongly installed as their queen. She had
felt humiliated by the protectorship of Duke Humphrey:

> Am I a queen in title and in style,
> And must be made a subject to a duke? (*2 Henry VI*, 1.3.46–47)

And she was especially angry at the pride of Humphrey's wife, Duchess
Eleanor, who "sweeps it through the court with troops of ladies,/ More like
an empress than Duke Humphrey's wife" (77–78). She despises her husband, King Henry—all the more because he so little resembles the man she
loves, Suffolk. When she loses Suffolk, first to banishment and then to
death after the murder of Gloucester, her sanity begins to waver: holding
Suffolk's severed head, she takes refuge in thoughts of vengeance:

Oft have I heard that grief softens the mind
And makes it fearful and degenerate.
Think therefore on revenge and cease to weep. (4.4.1–3)

As matters develop, her thoughts of revenge center more and more on York, who seems the main obstacle to her dominance. Margaret's great wish is to see her son, Edward, become king, so she is furious with Henry when he voluntarily disinherits him in order to retain his own place on the throne.

When these two great foes meet on the battlefield—York fatally wounded, and Margaret backed by Clifford and Northumberland, both of whom have lost fathers to York—the Queen's chance for personal revenge is at hand, and she makes the most of it. Her aim is not merely to kill York but to humiliate him—to crush his pride and diminish his spirit. She gets her physical revenge, certainly, but as the scene evolves, she loses the rhetorical battle: York will die with increased stature.

Fleeing his foes, York describes his present defeat in similes that depict him as the victim of overwhelming natural forces. His armies fly "like ships before the wind/ Or lambs pursued by hunger-starved wolves" (*3 Henry VI,* 1.4.4–5). His sons, though "they have demeaned themselves/ Like men born to renown by life or death" (6–8), suffer a similar fate, as he recalls their recent battle:

> We charged again; but out, alas,
> We bodg'd again, as I have seen a swan
> With bootless labor swim against the tide,
> And spend her strength with overmatching waves. (18–21)

These images of defeat are unlike his normal expansiveness, but it is utterly characteristic of him to use the royal image of the swan (white like the rose he bears) in describing his family, even in defeat.

Margaret, her son Edward, Clifford, and Northumberland immediately corner York. (Though Prince Edward has no lines in the scene, it is best to keep his presence in mind as he will ultimately be slaughtered in revenge of York's death.) York retains his pride, but now he will display it through his ability to endure suffering and overcome through stoical resignation:

> Come, bloody Clifford, rough Northumberland,
> I dare your quenchless fury to more rage.
> I am your butt, and I abide your shot. (27–29)

But Clifford is determined not to let York maintain his dignity in defeat. When Northumberland bids York yield to their "mercy," Clifford taunts him:

Ay, to such mercy as his ruthless arm
With downright payment show'd unto my father.
Now Phaëton hath tumbled from his car,
And made an evening at the noontide prick. (31–34)

The simile suits Clifford: the son of Apollo who stole his father's chariot but was unable to manage it was an apt symbol of presumption, and the sun was a Yorkist emblem. Thus a noontide tumble that turns day to night reflects the sudden reversal of Yorkist fortunes.

In response, York proposes a countermetaphor, one that confirms his sense of himself:

My ashes, as the phoenix, may bring forth
A bird that will revenge upon you all. (35–36)

The audience, knowing that the revenging "bird" will be the tyrant king Richard, may have a complex response to York's prophecy, but he speaks it without knowledge of future events. When York proceeds—"And in that hope I throw mine eyes to heaven,/ Scorning whate'er you can afflict me with" (37–38)—it is to affirm the justice of his cause and his strength of character.

The war of image and counterimage proceeds, with York picturing himself as the valiant battler, dangerous even in defeat ("Why come you not? What, multitudes, and fear?" [39]), and as a "true" man "o'ermatch'd" by thieves. Clifford counters by comparing York to a coward who fights only because he must, a dove caught by a falcon, a captured thief cursing the arresting officers (40–43), and a base cur, a stupid woodcock or cony.

Ultimately, the struggle ends in a verbal stalemate and Clifford moves in for the kill, but Margaret is having none of it. She aims, like a thorough revenger, to crush York's heart through invective, mocking his pretentions to power: "Come make him stand upon this molehill here/ That raught at mountains with outstretched arms/ Yet parted but the shadow with his hand" (67–69). She insults his adult sons, "the wanton Edward," "the lusty George," and especially "that valiant crook-back prodigy,/ Dicky, your boy, that with his grumbling voice/ Was wont to cheer his dad in mutinies" (74–77). And she finally unleashes her ultimate weapon: her knowledge of the death of Rutland. This she conveys by showing York a bloody handkerchief soaked with the blood of his youngest son.

Because her aim is to break him spiritually before killing him, Margaret does all she can to humiliate him. To his shocked silence, she replies:

Why art thou patient, man? Thou shouldst be mad;
And I, to make thee mad, do mock thee thus.
Stamp, rave, and fret, that I may dance and sing. (89–91)

And to turn him into an entertainment, she places a paper crown on his head and taunts his ambitions: "Ay, marry, sir, now looks he like a king!" (96).

As she mocks him for excessive ambition, he taunts her for unnatural cruelty. She is the "Shewolf of France" (111), "an Amazonian trull" (113), a "proud queen" (118, 125) lacking virtue and beauty, a "tiger's heart wrapp'd in a woman's hide" (137). Amazed at the level of cruelty Margaret has displayed, he exclaims, "even my foes will shed fast-falling tears" (162) when they hear of the killing of his child. Despite Margaret's reminder of "the wrong he did us all" (173), York's laments induce Northumberland's pity, and Shakespeare allows him to die becomingly when he is stabbed by Clifford and Margaret: "Open thy gate of mercy, gracious God!/ My soul flies through these wounds to seek out thee" (177–178).

York has a posthumous revenge when Richard of Gloucester stabs Margaret's son before her eyes, eliciting corresponding cries of outrage from her:

> They that stabb'd Caesar shed no blood at all,
> Did not offend, nor were not worthy blame,
> If this foul deed were by to equal it.
> He was a man; this, in respect, a child,
> And men ne'er spend their fury on a child. . . .
> You have no children, butchers; if you had,
> The thought of them would have stirr'd up remorse,
> But if you ever chance to have a child,
> Look in his youth to have him so cut off. (*3 Henry VI*, 5.5.53–66)

Shakespeare gives her the gift of prophecy—looking ahead to the death of Edward's heirs in the Tower—but he also makes her blind to her own previous behavior and the precedent she set for this level of insensitive cruelty.[4]

Even in this world of violent revenge and cruelty, Shakespeare takes care to make Richard of Gloucester a special case, one in whom revenge awakens untold evil. When news of York's death reaches his family, for example, Edward, whose main fault is sensuality, is crushed by the news: "O, speak no more, for I have heard too much" (*3 Henry VI*, 2.1.48). His father's death poisons his existence:

> Now my soul's palace is become a prison;
> Ah, would she break from hence, that this my body
> Might in the ground be closed up in rest!
> For never henceforth shall I joy again,
> Never, O never, shall I see more joy. (74–78)

Richard, on the other hand, is energized by the news: "Say how he died, for I will hear it all" (49):

> I cannot weep; for all my body's moisture
> Scarce serves to quench my furnace-burning heart;
> Nor can my tongue unload my heart's great burthen,
> For self-same wind that I would speak withal
> Is kindling coals that fires all my breast,
> And burns me up with flames that tears would quench.
> To weep is to make less the depth of grief:
> Tears then for babes; blows and revenge for me.
> Richard, I bear thy name, I'll venge thy death,
> Or die renowned by attempting it. (79–88)

What crushes Edward pushes Richard forward to express a vindictive nature that looks for occasions to be violent under the pretext of avenging family honor. But even as he pursues that goal, Richard moves in another direction altogether: to be rid of his inferior brothers—Clarence and the "lustful Edward" (3.2.129)—and make himself king.

Shakespeare might have been led to see the events surrounding the Wars of the Roses in this light by Edward Hall. Speaking of the murder of Henry VI, but unsure whether Richard or Edward did the deed, he marks it as a moral disaster and a harbinger of worse to come:

> Whosoever was the manqueller of this holy man it shall appere, that bothe the murtherer and the consenter, had condigne and not undeserved punishment, for their bloudy stroke, and butcherly act: and because they had now no enemies risen, on whom they might revenge themselves, as you shall hereafter perceive, they exercised their crueltie, against their awne selfes: and with their proper bloud, embrued and polluted their awne handes and membres.[5]

Having defeated their rivals, the Yorkists turned against each other; and in the end, Richard of Gloucester, shaken by dreams that prophecy his doom, turns against himself:

> Is there a murtherer here? No. Yes, I am.
> Then fly. What, from myself? Great reason why—
> Lest I revenge. What, myself upon myself?
> Alack, I love myself. Wherefore? For any good
> That I myself have done unto myself?
> O no! Alas, I rather hate myself
> For hateful deeds committed by myself. (*Richard III*, 5.3.184–190)

The vindictive revenger becomes the victim of a just patriotic revenge, and the destructive cycle is finally broken.

Shakespeare's ideological scheme is evident: it is to trace the consequences of social disorder and to identify its cure with the royal dynasty in power. But in the process, he offers a series of character studies through which we can identify mental processes connected to victimization and its consequences. It is the latter aspect that makes the plays memorable.

NOTES

[1] For a fuller discussion, see Keyishian, *The Shapes of Revenge.*

[2] Foucault, *Discipline and Punish,* 51, 55.

[3] Urkowitz points out that this courteous exchange between York and Old Clifford is a Folio addition. In the quarto version, the two men are "mutually vituperative, politically simplistic, and unrelievedly bitter." "Good News About 'Bad' Quartos," 198.

[4] For a view of this exchange that is more sympathetic to Margaret's position, see Dash, *Wooing, Wedding, and Power,* 180–187.

[5] Bullough, 3, 207.

SHAKESPEARE'S QUEEN MARGARET
UNRULY OR UNRULED?

Naomi C. Liebler and Lisa Scancella Shea

As one of only two Shakespearean characters who survive through four plays,[1] Margaret of Anjou, Henry VI's queen, is much underrated by critics who have written about the figures of the First Tetralogy. They variously describe her as "an archvillainess . . . epitomiz[ing] the worst qualities of her own sex" (Lee 216), "monstrous" (Howard and Rackin 96), and "conniving" (Bevington 57). Indeed, as Nina Levine has recently pointed out, York's characterization of her as "a tiger's heart wrapped in a woman's hide" has "come to dominate discussions of Margaret in the years since" (*Women's Matters* 68). Generally missing from discussions of Margaret is a recognition of her amazing endurance despite the pervasive corruption, duplicity, and political intrigue of which she is sometimes the agent and at other times the intended victim. In this regard she evolves into a most worthy opponent to the chameleon king, Richard III. She warms up for this, her apotheosis, by first taking on Suffolk in *1 Henry VI*, Eleanor and Gloucester in *2 Henry VI*, and York in *3 Henry VI,* at each turn honing her confrontational skills, working toward her ultimate challenge to the king in *Richard III*. What is at stake in each of these contests is, above all other considerations, her personal and political autonomy—as a woman and a queen.[2] At each successive stage of her career she takes on one of the archetypal roles Jung was later to describe for the life cycle of a woman—Virgin, Wife, Mother, and the "Wise Old Woman" or Crone (Jung 5–21; 41–53). Margaret sustains a feminine autonomy by resisting patriarchal definitions of femininity; she will not be subjugated or silenced, or defined by those around her, despite their persistent attempts to do so.

In each play, Margaret shares a specific archetypal role with a parallel female representation: Joan la Pucelle, the maiden warrior in *1 Henry VI*; Gloucester's ambitious wife, Eleanor Cobham, in *2 Henry VI*; Lady Grey, later Queen Elizabeth and the mother of the heir to the throne, in *3 Henry VI*; and the Duchess of York, the cursing crone in *Richard III*. Shakespeare draws each of these women as a complementary foil to Margaret, consistent with her successive archetypal stages. Three of these—the maid Joan, the wife Eleanor, and the mother Elizabeth—either lose or fail to gain the power they seek. Only the crone figures, Margaret and her counterpart, the Duchess of York, maintain their strength even when their political power has dissolved.

1 HENRY VI: A TALE OF TWO FRENCH MAIDS

In *1 Henry VI*, Joan la Pucelle rises from the peasant ranks to fight by the Dauphin's side. Joan represents herself as divinely ordained, sent by heaven to save the French (1.2.51–54).[3] Joan promises the Dauphin that she will "exceed her sex" (90) if she can become his "warlike mate" (92), but before she is allowed to join the ranks of his men, the Dauphin requires that Joan prove herself. He challenges Joan to single combat and finds himself sexually attracted to her when she defeats him:

Whoe'er helps thee, 'tis thou that must help me:
Impatiently I burn with thy desire;
My heart and hands thou hast at once subdued.
Excellent Pucelle, if thy name be so,
Let me thy servant and not sovereign be;
'Tis the French Dolphin sueth to thee thus. (107–112)

Immediately, Joan exerts a form of sexual power. She reminds her suitor that she cannot give in to physical temptations until she has defeated France's enemy, but suggests that she will consider his offer at a later date:

I must not yield to any rites of love,
For my profession's sacred from above;
When I have chased all thy foes from hence,
Then will I think upon a recompense. (113–116)

Joan uses the Dauphin's interest in her as a means of securing her position within his army; by making herself unavailable sexually, she hopes to ensure his continued interest.

Gabriele Jackson has argued that Joan's display of freedom as a warrior woman dictates that she must be "more completely feminized at the end of the play" (60). Moreover, since Joan was "subversively powerful," she must be both "feminized and demonized" (64). Jackson's comments imply that Joan's prowess in battle is unfeminine, but in fact Joan draws her strength from her feminine roles, of which she has several. She is preeminently the archetypal Virgin, and the impression of a woman as a desirable maid has immense power as something irresistible and divine (Jung 10). But she is more than that. Lorraine Helms underscores Joan's sequence of roles as a series of theatrical masks, aptly suited to her treatment at various masculine hands in the play:

> She is first a numinous presence whose powers of divination are revealed on stage. She is then a shrewdly pragmatic military leader, and those skills too are represented. Finally, she is a witch, resorting ignominiously [*sic*] to feminine evasions and deceptions, enduring sexual humiliations. These discontinuous images suit a script in which all the *dramatis personae* are emphatically *personae* rather than persons. They insist that the player work through mask and gesture rather than motive and emotion. (116)

In this regard, Joan appears to be a "shape-shifter" at need, prefiguring the several incarnations later required of Margaret.

In Act 5, Joan is defrocked, stripped of her aura of "divinity," literally demonized when, just before she is captured by the English, she is seen conjuring devils in an attempt to turn the course of the battle in favor of the French (5.3.1–29). At this point Shakespeare introduces Margaret to take up the role of Maid of France, the role Joan vacates in the next scene by claiming, to save herself from execution, that she is pregnant, thereby negating her virginal representation.

Margaret first appears on stage as Joan is led off as captive to the Duke of York. Like Joan, Margaret is held prisoner by an Englishman, here the Earl of Suffolk (5.3.45). Like the Dauphin before Joan, Suffolk is smitten with his prisoner, wanting her for himself even though he is married, and plans to bring Margaret to England as Henry's bride so that he can make her his mistress. The only potential impediment to Suffolk's plan is Margaret's lack of dowry: the king, her father, is penniless (5.3.93–99), but Suffolk is determined to marry Margaret to Henry, despite Margaret's own diffidence in claiming that she is "not worthy to be Henry's wife" (122). Finally Margaret yields: "And if my father please, I am content" (127). Suffolk negotiates what might be called Margaret's "purchase" by returning to her father Maine and Anjou, won during the preceding generation by Henry V. Once Suffolk and Reignier agree upon the exchange that will make Margaret England's queen, she sends her future husband "Such commendations as becomes a maid,/ A virgin, and his servant" (177–178), but favors Suffolk with a kiss, a gesture which she claims is a "peevish token" (186).

Although Margaret may be read as the object of commerce between men, she uses that commerce to her advantage in her first scenes and throughout the tetralogy. Margaret understands her own economic worth, or lack thereof, but she also understands the strength of her position in the negotiation with Suffolk. Margaret catches Suffolk's slip when he makes his suit on Henry's behalf:

> *Suffolk.*   I'll undertake to make thee Henry's queen,
>   To put a golden scepter in thy hand
>   And set a precious crown upon thy head,
>   If thou wilt condescend to be my—
> *Margaret.*   What?
> *Suffolk.*   *His* love. (5.3.117–121; emphasis added)

Although Suffolk never directly proposes that Margaret become his mistress, she subtly acknowledges his attraction to her when he kisses her: "That for thyself" (5.3.185). Suffolk's infatuation recalls that of the Dauphin for Joan: as Joan used her sexual appeal to ensure her place in the French army, Margaret uses hers to ensure her marriage to the king. She is first led on stage as England's prisoner, but by the end of the scene she is its next queen.

Suffolk is able to convince Henry that Margaret is a worthy match by extolling her noneconomic values and thus persuades him to breach his promise of marriage to the daughter of the wealthy Earl of Armagnac:

> Whom should we match with Henry, being a king,
> But Margaret, that is daughter to a king?
> Her peerless feature, joined with her birth,
> Approves her fit for none but for a king.
> Her valiant courage and undaunted spirit,
> More in woman than commonly is seen,
> Will answer our hope in issue of a king;
> For Henry, son unto a conqueror,
> Is likely to beget more conquerors,
> If with a lady of so high resolve
> As is fair Margaret he be linked in love. (5.5.66–76)

Suffolk's description of Margaret is telling: lacking the conventional dowry, she has instead other important qualifications: beauty, royal birth, and the potential to breed warriors who will inherit both Henry V's "conquering" capabilities and Margaret's own "high resolve." Here Margaret's role as the high-spirited maid is critical. The unspoiled virgin holds the promise of motherhood, and Margaret, the maiden princess, has the potential to be the mother of the next great king. Ironically, the same "high resolve" that recommends her to Henry is the stubborn spirit he will come to regret.

2 HENRY VI: ENGLAND'S COSTLY QUEEN

Gloucester and Exeter display their concern over the proposed marriage even before they meet Margaret in *Part 1*, and try to dissuade the King from marrying this dowryless bride, but Suffolk prevails, and Henry agrees to return Anjou and Maine to King Reignier. With this proclamation, Margaret is transformed from a bride who brings neither money nor land to England to one who costs the country dearly. The declaration so upsets Gloucester that he drops the document: "Pardon me, gracious lord;/ But some sudden qualm hath struck me at the heart,/ And dimmed mine eyes that I can read no further" (1.1.53–55). Gloucester expresses his outrage to the court:

> O peers of England, shameful is this league!
> Fatal this marriage, canceling your fame,
> Blotting your names from books of memory,
> Razing the characters of your renown,
> Defacing monuments of conquered France,
> Undoing all, as all had never been. (98–103)

Margaret has cost them their honor. Henry's failure to maintain the position his father won in France is blamed on his bride, and Margaret is immediately positioned as a potential scapegoat for all of Henry's subsequent difficulties.

The savvy Margaret, however, aims to establish herself firmly in her new position. She expresses her displeasure at Henry's reliance on Gloucester: "Am I a queen in title and in style,/ And must be made subject to a duke?" (1.3.50–51). She is most disturbed by "proud" (78) Eleanor Cobham, Gloucester's wife, whose elaborate dress (in direct violation of the Elizabethan sumptuary laws) and haughty bearing cause strangers to think she is the queen (77–81). Eleanor's appearance and conduct threaten Margaret's authority: Eleanor "displays her lack of respect for the queen, and signals the power of her own husband, by boasting about the lavishness of her own dress, and wearing it ostentatiously" (Jardine 141). Margaret's complaint reveals the underlying source of her anger with Eleanor: "And in her heart she scorns our poverty" (83). Margaret is keenly aware of the opposition facing her in Henry's court; those who disapproved of her marriage to Henry may challenge both her and her husband.

Margaret recognizes that she must remove those who pose a threat to her or her husband, but she cannot do it alone. She must develop a network of supporters, the "net-like organization" Foucault would later describe as the means by which power is "employed and exercised. . . . And not only do individuals circulate between its threads . . . . [T]hey are always also the elements of its articulation. In other words, individuals are the vehicles of power" (98).

Margaret recruits Suffolk as the first in her cadre of loyal supporters. Complaining about Gloucester's influence over her husband, Margaret shares with Suffolk her disappointment in Henry:

> I tell thee, Pole, when in the city Tours
> Thou ran'st a tilt in honor of my love
> And stol'st away the ladies' hearts of France,
> I thought King Henry had resembled thee
> In courage, courtship, and proportion. . . . (1.3.52–56)

As she did during the wooing scene in *1 Henry VI*, Margaret here flatters her admirer in order to secure his support, and Suffolk commits himself to making the queen happy: "Madam, be patient: as I was cause/ Your Highness came to England, so will I/ In England work your Grace's full content" (67–69). He assures Margaret that he has already taken steps towards removing both Gloucester and his troublesome wife (90–102).

While Gloucester's care is for his country and his king, Eleanor's thoughts are more subversive. She attempts to goad her husband into vying for the throne, but Gloucester bids his wife to "Banish the canker of ambitious thoughts" (1.2.18). Disregarding his pleas, Eleanor goes on to share her dreams of glory:

> Methought I sat in seat of majesty
> In the cathedral church of Westminster,
> And in that chair where kings and queens were crowned;
> Where Henry and Dame Margaret kneeled to me,
> And on my head did set the diadem. (36–40)

The horrified Gloucester reminds her that she should be satisfied with and proud of her place as the Lord Protector's wife. Once she is alone, however, Eleanor expresses her desire to the audience, prefiguring, as Nina Levine has noted ("The Case of Eleanor Cobham" 111), the later gender-challenging manipulations of Lady Macbeth:

> Follow I must; I cannot go before,
> While Gloucester bears this base and humble mind.
> Were I a man, a duke, and next of blood,
> I would remove these tedious stumbling-blocks
> And smooth my way upon their headless necks;
> And, being a woman, I will not be slack
> To play my part in Fortune's pageant. (61–67)

Eleanor is thus established as both a threat to the present monarchy and a woman whose ambition will ruin both herself and her husband. Unlike Margaret, she cannot find, even in her husband, the network of support her "part in Fortune's pageant" requires, and instead seeks guidance from the spirits. Like Joan in *1 Henry VI*, Eleanor turns to sorcery and witchcraft and is brought down by her involvement in the black arts.

Suffolk and the Cardinal suborn Hum, a priest, to "undermine the Duchess" (1.2.98) so that she can be caught at her conjuring and convicted of treason. By discrediting Eleanor, they can inculpate Gloucester and remove him from his office. Eleanor wants to see her husband become king, and in this unstable court Gloucester's adversaries use his wife's desires against him. The duchess is "the victim of what we might call political entrapment: her ambitions are exploited and even manipulated by her husband's enemies to further their own power over the Lancastrian state" (Levine, "The Case of Eleanor Cobham" 105). When Eleanor is captured, Margaret remarks pointedly: "Gloucester, see here the tainture of thy nest./ And look thyself be faultless, thou wert best" (2.1.187–188). After banishing Eleanor, Henry requests that Gloucester relinquish his position as Lord Protector, and Margaret proclaims her approval: "Why, now is Henry King, and Margaret Queen" (2.2.39–40).

Although Shakespeare draws Eleanor and Margaret as contemporaries, the historical Duchess of Gloucester was actually tried and convicted of treason in 1441, four years before Margaret came to England as Henry's bride (Hosley 169, 171; see also Levine, "Eleanor Cobham" 106, Lee 184). By extending Eleanor's "life" Shakespeare underscores Margaret's and Eleanor's comparable roles as wives. Instead of presenting conventionally subordinate women, Shakespeare adduces in both cases a paradigm of marital relationships that Jung would later describe as one in which one party is the container, the other the contained. Whereas the one who is contained lives entirely within the confines of the marriage and clings to it, the container seeks its own complexity in another and may break down into unfaithfulness (47–48).[4] In *2 Henry VI*, both Eleanor and Margaret are the more complex partners in their respective marriages. Never merely ornamental or dutiful wives, these women are the driving forces behind their husbands for better or for worse. Jung writes that in choosing a husband, "a woman can often pick on a man of real significance who is not recognized by the mass, and can actually help him to achieve his true destiny with her moral support. . . . But more often it turns out to be an illusion with destructive consequences, a failure because his faith was not sufficiently strong" (51). Both wives illustrate this archetypal pattern. Each woman wants more for her husband than he wants for himself; Eleanor dreams of the crown, while Margaret urges Henry to reclaim his monarchy, to assert the authority that is his birthright as well as his obligation. Eleanor's "unfaithfulness" leads her to seek her own complexity in the demonic arts; Margaret's drives her into an intimate alliance with Suffolk and leads her to conspire against Gloucester, her husband's uncle.

Margaret confers with her potential networkers: Suffolk, the Cardinal, and York; together they resolve that Gloucester must be killed. Margaret intends to solidify her husband's authority, and Suffolk intends to please Margaret. He enlists the Cardinal's support even though he does not completely trust him (1.3.95–100). York, who has his own plans to pursue the crown, happily signs on to assist the queen in dispatching Gloucester. York is under suspicion of treason due to the allegations of a servant; his participation in the plot against Gloucester serves as a mask of loyalty to his king even as he plans his rebellion against Henry. While the group succeeds in destroying Gloucester, his murder leads to the dissolution of Margaret's power network. Suffolk is accused of involvement in the murder, and despite Margaret's pleas, Henry banishes her most trusted ally (3.2.287–299). The Cardinal, overcome by madness, dies in his bed (3.3.1–33), while York gathers his army in Ireland to march against Henry and declare himself the rightful ruler of England (3.1.349–354).

The queen, still determined to protect her husband's claim to the crown but left without her male allies, assumes control of her situation; no longer subtly attempting to sway her husband, she directs Henry specifically as York's army threatens to overpower their own:

> *Queen.* Away, my lord! You are slow; for shame, away!
> *King.* Can we outrun the heavens? Good Margaret, stay.
> *Queen.* What are you made of? You'll nor fight nor fly:
>   Now is it manhood, wisdom, and defense,
>   To give the enemy way, and to secure us
>   By what we can, which can no more but fly.
>   If you be ta'en, we then should see the bottom
>   Of all our fortunes: but if we should haply scape—
>   As well we may, if not through your neglect—
>   We shall to London get, where you are loved
>   And where this breach now in our fortunes made
>   May readily be stopped. (5.2.72–83)

With this directive, Margaret begins to shift from her position as the strong woman behind Henry into a new role as the warrior standing in front of the Lancastrian throne, guarding it against challengers. The historical Henry was thought to be mentally ill (Hall, in Bullough 123), but Shakespeare eliminates this detail, making Henry's passivity a simple mark of character weakness and drawing the queen, by contrast, as an aggressive defender of the Lancastrian right, a woman who fulfills the political role that her husband abdicates not out of necessity (as Hall suggests) but by choice. With this move, Shakespeare ends *Part 2* with a clear signal of what we may expect to see in Margaret's effective "reign" in *Part 3*.

3 HENRY VI: MOTHER MARGARET, "SHE-WOLF OF FRANCE"

Margaret is not present in Parliament when York and his followers challenge Henry's title in the opening act of *3 Henry VI*. In an aside to the audience, the king expresses his lack of confidence in his own right to rule:

> *King Henry.* Henry the Fourth by conquest got the crown.
> *York.* 'Twas by rebellion against his king.
> *King Henry.* [Aside] I know not what to say; my title's weak—
> (1.1.132–34)

In an effort to protect himself, Henry strikes a bargain with York that will destroy not only his reign but also his relationship with his wife:

> *King Henry.* My Lord of Warwick, hear but one word:
> Let me for this my lifetime reign as king.
> *York.* Confirm the crown to me and to mine heirs,
> And thou shalt reign in quiet while thou liv'st.
> *King Henry.* I am content. Richard Plantagenet,
> Enjoy the kingdom after my decease. (169–175)

With these lines, Henry disinherits his son, Prince Edward, and irreparably damages his own rule. When Margaret is notified of her husband's promise to York, she descends angrily upon him:

> Thou hast undone thyself, thy son, and me. . . .
> Had I been there, which am a silly woman,
> The soldiers should have tossed me on their pikes
> Before I would have granted to that act.
> But thou preferr'st thy life before thine honor:
> And seeing thou dost, I here divorce myself
> Both from thy table, Henry, and thy bed,
> Until that act of parliament be repealed
> Whereby my son is disinherited.
> The Northern lords, that have forsworn thy colors,
> Will follow mine, if once they see them spread;
> And spread they shall be, to thy foul disgrace
> And utter ruin of the house of York.
> Thus do I leave thee. Come, son, let's away.
> Our army is ready; come, we'll after them. (1.1.232, 243–256)

With this, Margaret is no longer a wife protecting her husband but a mother vehemently defending her son's right to succeed to the English throne. Henry has given away everything that she sought to preserve for him, and Margaret's declaration of divorce reinforces the idea that she now perceives herself as queen, not as the king's wife. Margaret does not wait for York to exercise his claim; she plans a siege against him. Underestimating the queen as an opponent, the Yorkists head into battle, and the man who will later become Richard III mocks, "A woman's general. What should we fear?" (1.3.68).

Indeed, Margaret gives York and his supporters much to fear. In battle Margaret takes on the characteristics of the "loving and terrible mother" archetype, capable of maternal sympathy, wisdom, and authority but also harboring a dark side that devours and terrifies (Jung 110). The mother who gives life can also destroy life: Mother Margaret's destructive energy is directed against those who threaten her son's right to succeed to the throne.

In 1.4, the queen's forces bring York to his knees in battle. Margaret revels in telling York that his youngest son, Rutland, has been slain. She offers him a napkin soaked in the boy's blood to dry his tears. In a perversion of the coronation ceremony, Margaret sets a paper crown on York's head, creating a profane antiritual (Liebler 41). She taunts him, "Ay, marry, sir, now looks he like a king!/ Ay, this is he that took King Henry's chair/ And this is he was his adopted heir" (1.4.96–98); York retaliates by attacking Margaret's femininity (Dash 183). Now that he has been subdued by the same power that he supported in 2 *Henry VI*, York here tries to injure Margaret with insults:

> How ill-beseeming is it in thy sex
> To triumph like an Amazonian trull. . . .
> Women are soft, mild, pitiful, and flexible;
> Thou stern, obdurate, flinty, rough, remorseless. (113–114, 141–142)

Jung noted that all people comprise both masculine and feminine yet do not understand the unconscious element that is opposite to their exterior genders. Man is "compensated" within by a feminine element that he cannot comprehend: the unknown is feared; therefore woman is man's "greatest danger" (170). This "renders men incapable of perceiving the humanness of women" (Wehr 110). York cannot reconcile Margaret's actions with his definitions of appropriate feminine behavior. He attempts to paint Margaret as an animal, a "she-wolf of France" (1.4.111), "inhuman" (134), having a "tiger's heart wrapped in a woman's hide" (137). Northumberland feels sympathy for the weeping York, but the queen is relentless: "Think but upon the wrong he did us all,/ And that will quickly dry thy melting tears" (173–174). The resolve of the "terrible mother" is firm; the wrong done to her child outweighs any possible element of remorse in her punishment of her enemies.

This mock coronation of York and his subsequent reaction evoke images of the shaming rituals designed to punish unruly women, such as the cucking stools on which convicted scolds were placed to be dunked repeatedly under water. "Because scolds were seen as threats to male authority, their carnivalesque punishments of mocking enthronement partake of the invert-ed structure of 'world-upside-down' rites" (Boose 190). Margaret is a woman "out of her place" who is allowed only what Natalie Zemon Davis calls a "temporary period of dominion" (135).

Whereas York accuses Margaret of unruly and unseemly behavior for a woman, it is he who is humiliated. Margaret uses the image of "unruly woman" to her advantage: rather than allowing York to undermine her control of the situation, Margaret projects the qualities of a weak woman onto York, who is reduced to tears and cries for vengeance (1.4.147–179). York's attempts to attack Margaret by challenging her femininity are futile; he is silenced, killed by Clifford, and stabbed by the queen, who orders that his head be set upon the gates of York (179–180).

Henry is shaken by the incident, crying "Withhold revenge, dear God! 'Tis not my fault,/ Nor wittingly have I infringed my vow" (2.2.7–8). Henry's emotional reaction to York's death shows a second inversion of male and female stereotypes: he is wailing and lamenting, and Margaret has assumed complete control of the army. This is reinforced later in the same scene when Clifford says to his king; "I would your Highness would depart the field./ The Queen hath best success when you are absent" (73–74). Henry is feminized to the point where he is dismissed from the field, and Margaret is the "manly woman" who appears in the historical sources (Bullough 176), the mother who assumes the traditionally masculine roles of soldier and ruler.

Margaret is an effective leader for the Lancastrian forces because she shares their conviction that York is a usurper. Foucault's comments on the "theory of right" help us to better understand Margaret's forceful defense of her son: "The essential role of the theory of right, from medieval times onward, was to fix the legitimacy of power; that is the major problem around which the whole theory of right and sovereignty is organised" (95). The queen draws her power from her conceptions of the truth, and her strength serves to reinforce that truth. Foucault sees this as a triangle of "power, truth, [and] right. . . . We are subjected to the production of truth through power and we cannot exercise power except through the production of truth" (93). The issue of rightful succession dominates the First Tetralogy, and the ambiguity of "right" allows for the continual shifting of power and the subsequent waves of repression and rebellion. "Right" is determined situationally: alliances are made and broken, and loyalties are fragile. In this unstable environment, Margaret's intentions are to uphold the order which she believes is the true monarchy, not specifically to subvert the patriarchal authority except insofar as that authority is perceived to be "wrong," that is, illegitimate.

Despite her best efforts, however, Margaret loses the battle for the throne. After York is killed, his claim is taken up by his eldest son, Edward. In his quest for power Edward targets Margaret, again raising the issues of her poverty and the loss of France:

A wisp of straw were worth a thousand crowns,
To make this shameless callet know herself.
Helen of Greece was fairer far than thou,
Although thy husband may be Menelaus;
And ne'er was Agamemnon's brother wronged
By that false woman as this King by thee.
His father reveled in the heart of France,
And tamed the King, and made the Dolphin stoop;
And had he matched according to his state,
He might have kept that glory to this day;
But when he took a beggar to his bed,
And graced thy poor sire with his bridal-day,
Even then that sunshine brewed a show'r for him,
That washed his father's fortunes forth of France.
For what hath broached this tumult but thy pride?
Hadst thou been meek, our title still had slept;
And we, in pity of the gentle King,
Had slipped our claim until another age. (2.2.144–162)

Edward attacks Margaret not only because she represents the Lancastrian faction but because she is outspoken. Edward blames Margaret for the wars, citing her pride: had she only been "meek," that is to say, submissive as befits a king's wife, there would not have been any conflict.

When his forces overcome the queen's, Edward's first priority is to marry so that he can father an heir for his newly won throne. Like Henry's, Edward's marriage is controversial: his marriage to the widowed Lady Grey, who becomes the Queen Elizabeth of *Richard III*, brings no wealth to England. It also costs Edward the loyalty of Warwick, who has traveled to France to propose to the French king's sister-in-law on Edward's behalf, and the support of the French king, who takes up Margaret's cause after hearing of Edward's marriage to Elizabeth.

By Act 4 of *3 Henry VI* Elizabeth is pregnant with Edward's heir, providing a parallel for Margaret as queen and mother of the successor in the play. Unlike Margaret, Elizabeth is not a woman of action. She protects her offspring not by fight but by flight. When Margaret's army, supported by French troops, captures Edward, Elizabeth is driven by fear rather than anger:

And I the rather wean me from despair
For love of Edward's offspring in my womb.
This is it that makes me bridle passion
And bear with mildness my misfortune's cross.
Ay, ay, for this I draw in many a tear
And stop the rising of blood-sucking sighs,

Lest with my sighs or tears I blast or drown
King Edward's fruit, true heir to England's crown . . . .
Come, therefore, let us fly while we may fly.
If Warwick take us we are sure to die. (4.4.17–24, 34–35)

She will protect her unborn child, but Elizabeth is passive where Margaret
is aggressive: this mild woman presents the audience with a second and radically contrasting image of motherhood in the play.

Margaret and her son continue their fight until they are captured.
Margaret is forced to witness the murder of her son, without whom she
loses her role as mother. Distraught, she cries out, "O, kill me too!"
(5.5.41), and Richard offers to oblige her; only Edward's directions prevent
him. She is denied her death, and her father pays ransom to England for her
return to France (5.7.37–40). Margaret is a prisoner of England, as she was
when she was introduced in *1 Henry VI*, and only now are her captors
compensated: the costly queen finally brings a ransom payment to England.
Edward believes that Margaret's expulsion from England will heal society:

Away with her, and waft her hence to France!
And now what rests but that we spend the time
With stately triumphs, mirthful comic shows,
Such as befits the pleasure of the court?
Sound drums and trumpets! Farewell sour annoy!
For here, I hope, begins our lasting joy. (5.3.41–46)

Edward and his followers assume that they will hear no more of the
"defeated" and "disempowered" (Howard and Rackin 98–99) former
queen, but in her final line of the play Margaret, anticipating her role in
Richard III, curses her captors: "So come to you and yours, as to this
prince!" (5.5.82). In Nicole Loraux's articulate formulation, "whether triumphant or heartbroken queens, they are always wounded in their motherhood. From that moment when mothers obtain only the horrified sight of
the child's corpse to compensate for their loss, mourning that has already
been transformed into wrath becomes vengeance in deeds. And mothers
kill" (49). Margaret does not go quietly from the stage; the queen is not
silenced. "Defeated" she may be, but not "disempowered"; her damning
prophecy comes true in the next play.

RICHARD III: MARGARET'S LAST LAUGH

Margaret makes an ahistorical return in *Richard III*, appearing in
Edward IV's court as the king lies ill: in fact, she died in France in 1482,
the year before Edward IV's death (Bullough 241). Indeed, as Alexander

Leggatt notes, "She is there, in defiance of both history and probability, to do a job for the playwright" (43). Shakespeare draws the former queen as a crone: done now with her earlier roles as virgin, wife, and mother, Margaret lives to embody the wisdom of the old woman; as Richard puts it near the end of *3 Henry VI*, she "live[s] to fill the world with words" (5.5.44). Having outlived her childbearing years, the crone is beyond her familial responsibilities and therefore cannot be made subject to male domination. The crone is not desexualized; rather, she remains female but surpasses—is no longer limited to or by—her domestic and reproductive roles. Like *Macbeth*'s Weird Sisters, she is ambiguously gendered; neither masculine nor entirely feminine, she is freed from the constraints of behaviors designated for either sex and thus, as Jung contended, allows a focus on the social task (12), or in this case, the dramatic task. Margaret's curses are now her only weapon, but her words are what Richard fears and loathes most. Calling for the destruction and death of those who killed her husband and son, she foretells the bloodshed that Richard will inflict upon England. Margaret's position as the crone allows her to instigate the sacrifice which her expulsion from England could not satisfy.

The English community is fractured by civil war. To heal the break, England must sacrifice a member of the community who is different and dispensable enough to be eliminated without threatening the integrity of the society; Margaret the French-English-queen-crone becomes the "monstrous double" (Girard 164, 254), a sacrificial surrogate whose elimination will restore England's peace. Margaret was driven out of England by the Yorkists in a futile attempt to "purify" their society, but in fact the "sacrifice" proves ineffective; as a French woman, she was never truly a part of English society. Richard III must be offered instead as the *pharmakos*, both cause and cure for societal ills. Richard is wholly English, but his physical deformities (1.1.14–27) qualify him as the "other," the true "monstrous double."[7] In ancient sacrificial rituals, "[t]he purpose of the Crone's curse was to doom the sacrificial victim inevitably, so no guilt would accrue to those who actually shed his lifeblood. He was already 'dead' once the Mother pronounced his fate, so killing him was not real killing" (Walker 26). With her curses Margaret absolves the English of the guilt that would lie upon their heads for killing their king. The crone nominates the scapegoat, both identifying and cursing the victim, Richard III. Richard is ultimately defeated by Henry of Richmond, who becomes Henry VII, the redeemer of the English crown and founder of the Tudor dynasty. Margaret's curse on Richard is instrumental in removing the taint of national guilt from the deposition and killing of the king.

Words are useful to Margaret not only as weapons against others but as armor, a means of protecting herself once her political power has dissolved. Margaret relies on self-definition to maintain her strength: significantly, in *Richard III* Margaret continues to refer to herself as queen even though her husband is dead and Edward is king: "A little joy enjoys the queen there-of;/ For I am she, and altogether joyless" (1.3.154–155). When Margaret makes her presence known, she reiterates this position, understanding the shock her presence causes: "Which of you trembles not that looks on me?/ If not, that I am queen, you bow like subjects,/ Yet that, by you deposed, you quake like rebels" (159–161). Margaret's insistence on retaining the title of queen after her husband and son have been killed is telling. Her power is in her autonomy, her persuasive insistence on self-definition: whereas Margaret dissociates herself distinctly from the deceased Henry, Elizabeth relies wholly on Edward to validate her position. Where Margaret is strong, Elizabeth is weak. Elizabeth understands her precarious situation when Edward is on his deathbed; upon his demise, she fears that only the succession of her children will make her valuable:

> *Queen Elizabeth*. If he were dead, what would betide on me?
> *Grey*. No other harm but loss of such a lord.
> *Queen Elizabeth*. The loss of such a lord includes all harms.
> *Grey*. The heavens have blessed you with a goodly son
>   To be your comforter when he is gone.
> *Queen Elizabeth*. Ah, he is young, and his minority
>   Is put unto the trust of Richard Gloucester,
>   A man that loves not me, nor none of you. (1.3.6–13)

Elizabeth knows that if her son does not succeed to the throne, she will be cast out, if not executed. Aware of Margaret's power and her own misery, Elizabeth fears the fate with which the older woman curses her: "Die neither mother, wife, nor England's Queen!" (1.3.208).

Indeed, Richard does destroy Elizabeth's family, leaving her one of three women in the tetralogy who have suffered the loss of husband and child or children at his hand: Margaret, Elizabeth, and the old Duchess of York, Richard's own mother. The trio recount their losses in a scene which has been called a moment of female bonding (Miner 47–48), or, as Loraux puts it, the "scene of mothers" (2). This moment, however, passes quickly. As she had done in regard to her dead husband, the always singular Margaret dissociates herself from these women too; rather, this is her final triumph. When, in her sorrow, Elizabeth begs Margaret to teach her how to curse, the crone replies:

> Forbear to sleep the nights, and fast the days;
> Compare dead happiness with living woe;
> Think that thy babes were sweeter than they were
> And he that slew them fouler than he is.
> Bett'ring thy loss makes the bad causer worse;
> Revolving this will teach thee how to curse. (4.4.118–123)

"Mourning leads to cursing; this is the lesson given to the gentle Elizabeth" (Loraux 5), but the lesson is lost on her. She is powerless because she cannot speak; she calls her own words "dull" (124); she cannot "fill the world" with them. The elderly duchess, however, can, and curses Richard after her meeting with the former queen: "Bloody thou art, bloody will be thy end;/ Shame serves thy life and doth thy death attend" (195–96). Loraux notes that the duchess, among the three women, bears the greatest sorrow "because she hates her son. She hates him because he killed her other two sons [*sic*], and for her, as for Margaret, there is hate in mourning. . . . The mother's last word is to curse her son for all time" (5–6).[8] Learning from Margaret, moving beyond her function as Richard's mother, she becomes a crone-in-training; she takes on Margaret's position.

Margaret revels in the unhappiness of those who hurt her as she has done throughout the action of the plays, gaining some degree of satisfaction in seeing her displacers displaced. Margaret reminds the duchess that it is her son who has destroyed them: "From forth the kennel of thy womb hath crept/ A hellhound that doth hunt us all to death" (4.4.47–48). Her words for Elizabeth are even less sympathetic:

> Thou didst usurp my place, and dost thou not
> Usurp the just proportion of my sorrow?
> Now thy proud neck bears half my burdened yoke,
> From which even here I slip my wearied head
> And leave the burden of it all on thee.
> Farewell, York's wife, and queen of sad mischance!
> These English woes shall make me smile in France. (109–115)

For Margaret, the misfortunes of Elizabeth and the duchess are justice. Elizabeth is now the displaced queen, the Duchess of York is the cursing crone, and Margaret is satisfied. Her job is done. Although her death is never depicted or announced, the old queen does not appear on stage again after this scene. Her dramatic function has been performed; the words have been spoken, Richard is doomed, and the portraits of the weak and the strong have been drawn.

In each of the four plays Margaret fulfills a Jungian archetypal image, and as she moves through her roles she becomes an incrementally more complex character. Each play highlights one of these feminine roles for Margaret, and the specific archetype is sustained throughout the play: in *1 Henry VI*, Joan leaves the role of French maiden as Margaret appears. In *2 Henry VI*, Margaret must eliminate the wife who precedes her in power, Eleanor Cobham. As Margaret watches her son die in *3 Henry VI*, Edward reminds the audience that his wife Elizabeth is giving birth. Finally, once Margaret has performed the function of the crone in *Richard III*, she instructs the old Duchess of York in cursing and strides out of the play. The other female figures in the tetralogy reinforce Margaret's difference and her strength, showing how she overcomes adversity and asserts her unique power by refusing to submit to grief, transforming it instead to an active and effective wrath. Loraux's powerfully provocative conclusion to her brief chapter on *Richard III* is worth quoting here, for both its astonishing insight and its graceful articulation: the play, she says, "is about power and its monstrosity. . . . But it is also about mothers, mourning, and hatred, which awakens a Greek echo. With, nonetheless, its characteristically Shakespearean dimension: that the relationship of the wives and mothers to their husbands and sons is a relationship to power itself" (6). By performing archetypal feminine roles, the dramatic figure of Margaret—neither submissive nor necessarily subversive—directs our attention to the power inherent in those roles. Instead of exemplifying the gender-violating accommodations in which a queen may rule only by adopting—in the words of his Tudor monarch before her troops at Tilbury in 1588—"the heart and stomach of a king," Shakespeare's Queen Margaret demonstrates a specifically feminine capacity for effective leadership and formidable political force by performing the full range of incarnations available to a woman.

NOTES

[1] The other, equally long-lived, is Mistress Quickly from the Second Tetralogy. Shakespeare stretches the historical record in order to include Margaret in *Richard III*, whose opening scene is set in 1483; Margaret actually died in 1482 (Bullough 241).

[2] Levine notes that "The plays may criticize Margaret's misrule, but in doing so on the basis of policy rather than biology, they effect a subtle but provocative shift that allows for an alternative discourse of power, one based not on expectations about gender but on an appeal to the nation's welfare" (*Women's Matters* 70); in fact she continues that critical practice when she argues that Shakespeare "freely extends the play's critique of the queen to censure aggressive women in general" (79–80). Levine's project is grounded primarily in identifying the ways in which "Elizabethans, including the queen herself, would not automatically have dismissed an association between Elizabeth and Margaret, nor would they have seen the Lancastrian queen simply as a darker inversion of their own" (75), and sees Margaret's representation throughout the tetralogy as predominantly misogynistic. We are arguing here that an "alternative discourse of power"

is central and critical to understanding Margaret's multifaceted representation, and further, that Shakespeare, though not necessarily his masculine characters in these plays, valorizes rather than demonizes her "aggressive" qualities as regal manifestations of autonomy.

[3] Citations from the plays in this essay follow the Signet editions, New York: New American Library: *1 Henry VI* ed. Lawrence V. Ryan, 1967; *2 Henry VI* ed. Arthur Freeman, 1967; *3 Henry VI* ed. Milton Crane, 1968; *Richard III* ed. Mark Eccles, 1964.

[4] Howard and Rackin place great emphasis on Margaret's infidelity to Henry: "In Shakespeare's play, Margaret's adulterous association with Suffolk is not just a rumor or a surmise, as it was when mentioned in his historical sources; rather, the two lovers appear frequently on stage together, and when Suffolk is banished, their farewell is an impassioned aria punctuated with kisses and tears" (72). Although the text of the play suggests an adulterous liaison, for the purpose of this paper we concentrate on Margaret's relationship with Suffolk as a political alliance and not a love affair.

[5] Shakespearean critics have also called Margaret inhuman: Riggs refers to Margaret's "grotesque display of 'courage'" as "an inexplicable deviation from nature, a relinquishment of human identity" (133).

[6] Davis here notes that this image of the unruly woman is a comic treatment; however, here we see that the concept is effective as a noncomic, dramatic image of feminine power.

[7] Shakespeare emphasizes Richard's physical deformities in *2 Henry VI*, when Clifford calls him a "heap of wrath, foul indigested lump,/ As crooked in thy manners as thy shape!" (5.1.157–158), and twice again in *3 Henry VI*: Margaret refers to Richard as York's "valiant crookback prodigy" (1.4.75) and Richard speaks of himself as "crook'd" in both body and mind (5.6.79). Richard's "difference" is reinforced by his account of his own birth and disfigurement (5.6.70–83), and of his uniqueness: "I am myself alone" (5.6.83). Shakespeare's words recall Hall, who describes Richard as "litle of stature, eivill featured of limnes, croke backed . . . hard favoured of visage . . . malicious, wrothfull and envious" (Bullough 253).

[8] To be precise, Loraux mistakes Richard as the killer of Rutland, who was actually killed by Clifford, or of Edward IV, who dies of natural causes. But her point is no less valid for this elision of Richard's culpability, focusing as it does on the Duchess's maternal rage provoked by Richard's horrific violation of fraternal bonds.

THE PAPER TRAIL TO THE THRONE

Nina daVinci Nichols

Right, says the fledgling playwright as he carries the script of his national epic into the theater. Players know that speech is action, but the audience had better see speech referring to something substantive—a man, an army, a crown, something visible on stage. Of course, some of this speechifying is operative language: oaths, pledges, and ceremonies authorizing allegiance. Those passages ought to work well with an audience accustomed to ritualized occasions. But what to do about all these letters, bills, proclamations, edicts, writs, and verses from the beyond? Written words are false signifiers, attributable to no one and addressing only an educated elite; hence they are secret, "the devil's writ." Worse still, they are fixed and so pretend to be absolute. Writing, ergo, provides only the "shadow of a substance," or an army, or a crown. Words in that form are not worth the paper they're written on. Aha! About my brain! Paper!

So the new man-of-theater tackles the problem for his history plays not only of how language fares in a fallen world, but how the legacy of Babel may translate into stage business.[1] Precisely as it's utterly insignificant, destructible, and the physical medium for words, paper in all three plays performs as a theatrical device. Or perhaps metatheatrical device would be more apt since, in several instances discussed below, papers operate as props and visual images nearly independent from writing. In all cases, bills, books, and supplications passed back and forth as characters jockey for position literally *show* written language asserting itself as substantive instead of referential. Whereas every character must assert or be checked by the final authority of combat, papers pretend to derive from a world as signified. No one in the trilogy scrutinizes words like a Richard II, or divides them from substance like a Lear wanting to keep his title, though Shakespeare introduces that idea when both Charles of France in *Part 1*

and King Henry in *Part 3* of *Henry VI* symbolically divide their crowns.
Nor are the *Henry VI* plays anchored like the Second Tetralogy to a poetic structure independent of chronology.[2] Shakespeare instead pits signifier
against signified more playfully—if I may—through papers that initiate
action, serve a symbolic coherency, and reflect the individualized conception of the self which will wreck so many of his tragic heroes. Even though
actual power shifts either with battles won or plots laid and discovered, as
these are represented on and by paper, so paper ironically expresses a sem-
blance of orderly procedure in the face of encroaching chaos.

Shakespeare, in other words, dramatizes the perfect analogy, indeed the
near equivalence, of verbal, social, and moral orders, that becomes typical
of his and other Renaissance theaters: the stage is the world. Still more
specifically, the insignificance of written papers expresses the medieval
world as fallen: a golden age of heroes exemplified by Talbot passing into
an era of self-interest and *Realpolitik.* As sedition and betrayal become
everyday evils, so writing comes to be mistrusted not only by an ignorant
rabble. Papers then signify the stability of person, family, and state
destroyed by ambition, factionalism, and superstition, separately and
together. Henry's crown is hollow yet mysterious, desired yet mocked,
claimed by him as a divine right and "shadowed" by York until paper and
crown become inseparable at the latter's death. Indeed, most of the many
papers passed back and forth in the three plays function either as premo-
nitions or consequences of York's paper trail to the throne. To lay out all
the references would amount to annotating the plays line by line. Let me
instead summarize some relevant actions and examine in more detail four
emblematic episodes in which, as I suggested above, paper acquires a theatrical function almost separable from the writing it bears: in *Part 1*, the
response to Gloucester's bill; in *Part 2*, the "exorcisms" orchestrated by the
priest, Hume, for Eleanor of Gloucester; also in *Part 2*, Queen Margaret
with the severed head of her lover Suffolk; in *Part 3*, York's paper crown.

Part 1 suggests that papers, like "shadows" and "pictures," are equally
insubstantial signifiers—that is, figures and images—during the quarrels
between followers of Lancaster and York after the death of Henry V. The
testing of England, the plays' overall subject, begins obliquely with the
arrival of "letters full of bad mischance" reporting that the Dauphin has
been crowned king (1.1.88) Immediately the scene shifts to the French
court and a bit of action that serves as an ironic *leitmotif* throughout the
trilogy: only heaven authorizes a true king. Laying a trap for Joan la Pucelle
and her claim of divine guidance, the Dauphin assigns a "shadow" king,
Reignier, to receive her. She, however, sees through the counterfeit, proving
that she may indeed commune with heaven, whence the mystery of kingship once found its source. To recognize Joan's triumph, the Dauphin will
"divide his crown with her" (1.6.18), a scandalous idea to the English audience and proof that La Pucelle is a witch. The Devil rules the French. A

divided crown cannot be substantive, although Charles implies that his crown is God-given.

The scene between Talbot and the Countess (2.3), when she compares the hero to her picture of him, makes a similar point in reverse: he calls on his army to *show* his substance. And then the Temple Garden scene (2.4) elaborates the theme again as it pivots on a *show* of allegiance either to Henry Lancaster or Richard Plantagenet in the "dumb significants" of red and white roses, respectively; these, too, refer to an abstract idea of power while effectively dividing the country's substance. Henry, later taking up a red rose (4.1.145–154), says it signifies only the accident of his birth as Lancaster, not his identity as king; a rose is "a trifle," a "toy" referring to nothing but itself. Linguistically he is right; politically he is wrong. During the quarrel between factions in the Temple Garden scene, the unnamed lawyer, the one character in the play whose person substantiates legal writ, plucks a white rose, saying that his "study and his books" show the Red Rose faction to be in the wrong (2.4.56–58). The latter argue that Plantagenet should remain a "yeoman" because his blood is "attainted" and "corrupted" by his father's execution for treason under Henry V (90–95). Plantagenet counters that his father was arrested and summarily executed without a legal bill of attainder; therefore he may not be deprived of his heritage as York. Deeper sources of division notwithstanding, expert interpretation of the law, in other words, rests as fully on the "dumb significants" of paper ("books") as roses themselves in the political realm or inscrutable messages from elsewhere in the spiritual one. Earlier in the scene Suffolk, in his arrogance, had dismissed law as incomprehensible, saying he instead intended to "frame the law unto his will" (9). Plainly, both factions prepare to wage a shadow war which, Warwick prophesies, will either advance Plantagenet as heir to the house of Mortimer during the next Parliament or send "a thousand souls to death" in battle (116–127).

Shakespeare then makes theatrical capital out of paper in 3.1, during the Parliament nominally called to effect a truce between Gloucester, the Lord Protector, and Bishop Winchester, the dissident. According to stage directions at the beginning of the scene before any dialogue, "Gloucester offers to put up a bill, Winchester snatches it [and] tears it," instantly demonstrating the fragility of the king's power. Presumably Gloucester's paper spells out the charge he delivers moments later, that the dissidents are plotting to bring him down (3.1.21–24), but an infuriated Winchester seizes the advantage by preventing Gloucester from reading his bill aloud:

> Com'st thou with deep premeditated lines,
> With written pamphlets studiously devised?
> Humphrey of Gloucester, if thou canst accuse
> Or aught intend'st to lay unto my charge,
> Do it without invention, suddenly

As I with sudden and extemporal speech
Purpose to answer what thou canst object. (3.1.1–7)

On the offensive, Winchester articulates the very antithesis between spoken
and written words that will characterize the machinations of the White
Rose faction hereafter. Gloucester's answer, by comparison, sounds defensive as he takes up the theme. Don't think I've "forged" this list of your
crimes, he says, I can recite my bill "verbatim" while your treachery is
"manifest" in the traps you have laid for my life (8–24). The argument
between Church and State at the least makes "manifest" the split between
words substantiated by a man and worthless papers, the point immediately underscored by civil strife made equally manifest on stage. A distressed
mayor breaks in on the Parliament for help with maintaining order in the
city; he is followed by both Gloucester's and Winchester's "servingmen"
with "bloody pates" who have been pelting each other with stones—carrying weapons has been forbidden. As the "skirmish" spills over in the hall,
one servingman vows he will fight rather than be "disgraced" by the likes
of an "inkhorn mate" for a neighbor (101–103).

Instead of ending here, however, the scene then reaches a brilliant climax, for no sooner has the mob departed and Henry made peace between
his warring uncles than Warwick "proffers a scroll" in the right of Richard
Plantagenet "to his blood" as York (159–162). In theatrical effect, this
indeed is the deeply "premeditated" paper anticipated dramatically by
Winchester's tearing up of the Protector's "bill." Warwick the king-maker
has been waiting in the wings for his cue to present the scroll, thereby bal-
ancing the scene structurally: Gloucester, next in blood to the throne, has
been silenced. Alone then with the threat to him implicit in Warwick's
scroll, Henry the conciliator unwittingly begins to divide his substance; he
creates a "princely Duke of York" (173) who, from this moment on, wears
a shadow crown. Exeter in soliloquy after the Parliament says as much.

This late dissension grown betwixt the peers
Burns under feigned ashes of forged love
And will at last break out into a flame. (190–192)

Yet York, at this point in the saga, seems not to be angling for the throne
but biding his time until his faction gains strength (Ornstein 40).
Nevertheless, by the close of the play written papers and "dumb significants" have become equivalent symptoms of discord. More letters are carried to and from France in 4.1; from the Pope in 5.1; from Henry to France
by Winchester in 5.4., the latter offering to turn King Charles into a "shadow of himself" by having him swear fealty to England (5.4.133). Although
these papers advance plot, dramatically they simply punctuate the action.

In *Part 2*, to the contrary, papers serve a more intricate structure combining their functions as medium for writing and as separable theatrical devices. Again the play opens with papers pertaining to France, this time "articles of contracted peace" (1.1.40) relating to Henry's marriage to Margaret. Gloucester reads them aloud first, and stage directions say he "lets the paper fall" as he is overcome by tears (53–54). Then his enemy Winchester takes up the paper and reads aloud, much as if this brief fall and rise of paper foreshadowed in little the imminent decline of Henry and rise of York. The papers' import? Anjou and Maine "are given to the French,/ Paris is lost," the peers disaffected, Humphrey's fall forecast, and, by the close of the scene, York in soliloquy expresses his intention: "when I spy advantage, claim the crown" from Henry, "Whose bookish rule hath pulled fair England down" (240, 257). In sum, papers now line the path for York, who hereafter remains vigilant for "advantage."

Papers establish York's presence even when he is offstage. For instance, though he takes no part in the Peter-Horner argument, it hinges on the dissidents' claim. A man called Peter comes to court with a "petition" against his master Horner for declaring York the rightful king (1.3). As several other petitioners also appear in the scene, it is not clear which papers Queen Margaret destroys in the stage direction instructing her to "tear the supplication" (SD, 39). The very mode of appeal through papers provokes her raging to Suffolk about "the fashion in the court of England" where commoners can overthrow a king "by petition," while Henry's "weapons" for retaliating are "holy saws of sacred writ" (42–58). By the end of the scene, in the presence of the king and York, Gloucester delivers the law: Peter and Horner shall meet in single combat because the master has witnessed "his servant's malice" (209–210). Do the implications apply to Henry's servant York? The episode feels prophetic partly because while the nobility wait for Horner to answer the charge in person, a quarrel breaks out among them about York's appointment as regent of France; that is, about his suitability as official shadow of the throne.

Then in 1.4, two priests, Margery Jordan, and Bolingbroke conjure up the spirit world for the vain, superstitious Eleanor, Duchess of Gloucester. Either the priest Southwell or Bolingbroke reads out black magic spells from papers and presides over "ceremonies" eliciting thunder, lightning, and a Spirit that "riseth" (23). In other words, the mysterious papers and incantations bring about a *coup de théâtre*. Earlier, Eleanor, wanting her ambitions endorsed by the beyond, had instructed Hume to seek out the "cunning witch" Margery Jordan as an interpreter of dreams (1.2.74–75), a variation on pictures as dumb significants. In this scene, the haughty duchess watches "from aloft"—ironically perched as high as she will reach—as the priest Southwell writes out the message delivered by Jordan's familiar (SD 32). It all seems more marvelous than dangerous until York and Buckingham break into the "exorcism," seize the papers, and York reads out "the devil's writ." These "oracles," York declares, "are hardly attained and hardly understood" (71), that is, irrational gabble. Yet as they seem to demand the death of the king along with others of his party, York arrests Eleanor as a traitor in a show of respect for law. Who framed the "oracles" and how probably matters less than the fact that York unifies them dramatically (Cutts 117). Eleanor provides him with "A pretty plot, well chosen to build upon!" (57), as he does.

After her judgment (2.3), a barefoot Eleanor, carrying a taper, parades in a white sheet with written "verses" (papers of accusation?) pinned to her back (2.4, SD 17). Punishment fits the crime in a public show of England's suffering under the curse of witchcraft, a popular interpretation of the country's plight at the hands of the French and a source of resentment that York counts on. Eleanor's white sheet, the costume of a penitent, serves in turn as a visual reminder of her former luxurious dress and of earlier complaints about her expensive tastes. Still, none of Shakespeare's sources, either for her adventures in necromancy or her sentence, mentions writings to and from a spirit world, whether located above or below. Hall instead says that Eleanor asked the witch Jordan to fashion a wax effigy of the king, which through sorcery would consume and bring him to death (Bullough 102). Shakespeare, however, ignores this potential dumb significant. Much ado throughout the next act about the exorcism and paper rather seems to unify the latter's implications thus far. For one, Eleanor is as mad in her way as Joan la Pucelle in hers: both women believe in primitive signatories, each is motivated by an extreme self-conception referring to an elsewhere at the expense of their responsibility to communal order. For another, Eleanor's language describing the scene of her shame anticipates York's shame with the paper crown:

Methinks I should not thus be led along,
Mailed up in shame, with papers on my back,
And followed with a rabble that rejoice
To see my tears and hear my deep-fet groans. (2.4.30–34, emphasis mine)

As she departs for exile to the Isle of Man, Gloucester charges the herald escorting her to see that her penance does not "exceed the King's commission" (75–76). The phrase may foreshadow the style of York's death, which ironically does exceed a king's commission. More immediately, the entire episode motivates the murder of Gloucester, who blocks York's ascent to the throne.

In *Part 2*, this strong anti-intellectual strain reaches a crescendo with the Cade rebellion, fomented by York in Act 3 and darkening his shadow with malevolence:

I have seduced a headstrong Kentishman,
John Cade of Ashford,

To make commotion, as full well he can,
Under the title of John Mortimer. . .
This devil here shall be my substitute; . . .
Say that he thrive, as 'tis great like he will;
Why, then from Ireland come I with my strength
And reap the harvest which that rascal sowed. (3.1.356–369, 371, 379–381)

The "commotion" pivots on rejection by the illiterate of everything written, from letters to laws and everyone who writes: "scholars, lawyers," and
their ilk. An "honest, plain dealing man," says Cade, only "has his mark"
(4.2.98). So the man named "Emmanuel" (meaning lord, but also a heading for documents meaning "God with us") in effect signs his own death
warrant with Cade's mob when he thanks God that he has been "so well
brought up he can write his name" (101). He then is taken off to be
hanged, an ironic exemplar "with his pen and inkhorn about his neck"
(106). Cade in full glory even justifies his own absurd bid for the crown
with a garbled genealogy that mimics the recitals of noble claimants
(130–140). Not that Cade commands the slightest political credibility
(Pearlman 36). The insurrection, rather, expresses a deep hostility between
classes that York at once deplores and exploits like a true Machiavel.

Paper then becomes a brilliant emblem in 4.4 when a mad Queen
Margaret addresses the severed head of Suffolk, cradled in her arms, while
the king reads "a supplication" from Cade's rebel forces. Mad she must be,
else the scene loses half of its theatrical point as a macabre spectacle of
deranged queen on one side of the stage and pious king on the other, each
engaged in acts symbolizing their difference. Her emotional disorder is
analogous to the social disorder reported by the very paper Henry studies,
another shadow of York. She speaks first "to herself," communing with,
fondling, kissing the grisly remains of her lover: "Oft have I heard that grief
softens the mind/ . . . Think therefore on revenge" (1–3). Then glimmerings
of reason seem to return, and a sense of occasion prompts her to hide the
head inside her gown: "Here may his head lie on my throbbing breast" (5).
Both line and gesture echo Suffolk's romantic farewell to her, in which he
anticipated death. In her presence, he said, death would be "as mild and
gentle as the cradle-babe's/ Dying with mother's dug between its lips,"
whereas "out of her sight" he would "cry out" to have her "lips to stop
[his] mouth" (3.2.388–396). Once dead he is indeed out of her sight, and
both her lips and her dug do stop his mouth. The physical immediacy of
Margaret's action, her elemental attachment to the severed head as more
alive to her than her husband, expresses not only the lovers' former physical union but her scorn for the merely legal bond of marriage and her affinity to the realm of the dead. She is French. Suffolk married her in France
for Henry *in absentia*, and her stance between her actual lover and ineffec-
tual husband expresses their three-way relationship thereafter. Henry is a

negligible tool of her ambition, a stepping-stone for the woman who cost him France and caused dissension among his noblemen.

While Margaret attends to the hideous trophy, the king remains so absorbed in reading the supplication from Cade that Buckingham must rouse and urge him to answer the rebels immediately. Their exchange is heavily ironic. Henry says he will "send some holy bishop to entreat" with the rebels lest many "perish by the sword" (10–12), in theatrical effect commenting on Suffolk's having just perished by the sword. Further, to avoid "bloody war," he himself will "parley" with Cade—for all the good talk will do with the man who burns books. Henry then turns to Lord Saye with: "Jack Cade hath sworn to have thy head" (19), again reminding the audience of Suffolk's severed head at Margaret's breast. Eventually, twenty lines into the scene, Henry turns to the mad Queen with the bloody head and refers to *her* vacancy; that is to say, first he was abstracted while she muttered to her lover's head, then they switch postures so that she is abstracted while he converses with his court. "How now, madam?/ Still lamenting and mourning for Suffolk's death" (21–22). That "still" is provocative. It suggests that Henry only at that moment recognizes in her a continuing demeanor of lament, for even this weak and remote young man would have reacted more strongly to the sight of her clinging to the bloody remnant.

Be that as it may, the brief scene presents an astonishing tableau of paper or shadow versus substance. The scholarly Henry here becomes a shadow of himself, a believer in a lost unitary world of words and things: to him the supplication, like all papers, at once represents, symbolizes, and signifies. Put still differently, the supplication persuades Henry, an educated gentleman, to a meeting with his opposite, an outlaw incapable of entering a symbolic reality. Cade lives in his body and in fact fears the symbolic, as becomes still more apparent in the following scenes. In this sense, Margaret, the hated Frenchwoman gone mad, is as anarchic emotionally as Cade is politically. Or again, in Act I of *Part 3*, when Margaret berates Henry for disenfranchising her son by appointing York as successor, warning him that Lancastrians will be alienated, Henry amazingly enough says he will "write unto them and entreat them fair" (1.1.271). She, like Cade, pins her faith to material substance. The scene functions as a commentary not only on Henry's trust in dumb significants like paper but on woman's irrational resort either to the supernatural, like Eleanor and La Pucelle, or to the preternatural, like Margaret. And York's shadow hovers throughout.

Immediately a messenger comes from the rebels and tells the king to flee: "All scholars, lawyers, courtiers, gentlemen,/ They call false caterpillars and intend their death" (2 *Henry VI*, 4.4.36–37) The king replies as a Christ: "O graceless men! They know not what they do." Only when a second messenger and Buckingham urge Henry again does he say: "Come Margaret. God, our hope, will succor us." Margaret knows better than to trust in metaphysical aid: "My hope is gone, now Suffolk is deceased" (56). The threat of total anarchy then follows with Cade's edict to "pull down the Savoy . . . the Inns of Court . . . all records of the realm" (4.7.1–17). Law will originate only from Cade's mouth, "extempore." He condemns books, schools, and paper mills (!), and orders the death of Lord Saye, who has men around him talking of "a noun and a verb and such abominable words as no Christian ear can endure to hear" (37–38). "Kill all the lawyers," those middlemen interpreting abstract codes and other written arcana.

These and more implications of paper culminate in the scene of York's death in *Part 3*, perhaps the most overtly theatrical of the four episodes outlined here and one dense with allusions to events in the Christian tradition. To sketch out the relevant prior actions, York claims his right to the crown (*2 Henry VI*, 5.1.1–2), and then resists arrest by Somerset for "capital treason against the King" (106–108). Openly defiant, York several times during the scene says, "We are thy sovereign," and "I am thy king" (127, 143), while Clifford calls him mad to think so, tries to enforce the order of arrest, and threatens York with beheading (134–135). Several phrasings, too, seem particularly to anticipate his end. When York protests that his sons' "words" will be his "surety" or bail (120–121), Margaret complains to the king that York "will not obey" the law (136). In the critical scene later, Margaret and Young Clifford not only enforce obedience but luxuriate in their lawless revenge on York for disinheriting Margaret's son and killing Clifford's father.

The opening scene in *Part 3*, however, foreshadows York's ignominious end more specifically. York and Warwick at court urge York's claim with the threat of arms: "Will you we *show* our title to the crown?" (1.1.102, emphasis added). Henry, reminded of Bolingbroke's usurpation, admits in an aside that his title is weak and decides to "adopt" an heir (136); so again, as in *Part 1* when he created York, Henry advances his enemy, now as official successor. The two embrace to show themselves reconciled, and their pact, we learn later "is enrolled in the parliament" (2.1.173), that is, written into law. York's sons scorn the "vain and frivolous" pact as not sworn before a lawful magistrate (1.2.22–34), and so combat resumes. Retaliating for York's slaying of Old Clifford (*2 Henry VI*, 5.2), his son Young Clifford slays York's boy Rutland. He brings the body to Margaret, who dips a cloth in the blood on Clifford's sword to substantiate report of the boy's murder with visible evidence. Plainly this line of action in *Parts 2* and *3* modulates the themes of law, vengeance, and the sins of the fathers visited on their sons down generations since the reign of Richard II. The densely interwoven themes come to the forefront especially as the atmosphere of York's death recalls that of the Divine Son Christ; for Margaret and Clifford murder the man who would be king in a mock coronation resembling the Passion.[3]

The extraordinary play-within-a-play in 1.4 hints not only at analogues to the Corpus Christi plays but at both the anti-intellectualism earlier in the trilogy and the dynamic between sign and substance at the heart of Shakespeare's history. While no such borrowing can be proven by historical or textual study—indeed there is no absolute proof that Shakespeare ever saw the mystery cycles performed, much less which ones and where—Shakespeare at the least seems to be authenticating his own fifteenth-century chronicle by evoking the moods and actions typical of several climactic episodes.[4] Scholarly opinion about similarities among cycles and guesswork about their provenance goes so far as to suggest that the plays of the Wakefield Master provided a source for those seen at York and Coventry, or alternatively, that all playwrights involved at these and other locales drew on a common vernacular source now lost.[5] Nothing said here means to resolve these issues by simplifying them. I instead refer mainly to the Wakefield and York texts as their depictions of the trials, judgment, and death of Christ at the hands of officials and commoners alike recur with varying fullness in other cycles as well as in liturgical recitations, biblical passages, and prayers.

When Northumberland asks what should be done with the captive York, Margaret at exuberant length outlines the "game" or "sport" they will play to degrade the false king (1.4.66–86). To this end she proves a consummate stage manager. I take the sense of her instruction to "stand" him "on a molehill," followed immediately by her echoing of York's grandiose lines at the end of *Part 2* about his right to the crown, to be cues to the scene's staging as a crucifixion. He that "raught at mountains with outstretched arms" [i.e., reached for Henry's throne]/ Yet parted but the shadow with his hand" (68–69); that is, parted King Henry, a shadow, from his substance, her army. If York's arms are not outstretched, her line is purely metaphoric and its precise placement here more arbitrary than seems plausible. Either way, she alludes to York's regal claim in the earlier scene: "this hand was meant to handle naught but gold./ I cannot give due action to my words/ Except a sword or scepter balance it" (*2 Henry VI*, 5.1.7–9). He repeats the same magisterial image a few lines later in that scene, comparing Henry's hand, "made to grasp a palmer's staff," to his own, "to hold a scepter up" (97–103). Repeating images from play to play seems to exemplify Shakespeare's technique in building to this climax, for Margaret intends York to recognize himself in her taunting summary: "Was it you that would be England's king?" (70). At the same time, the wider context echoes Christ's indictment:

Sir Pilate, prince peerless, hear what is said,
That he escape not harmless but ye doom him dead:
He calls himself king in every place, thus has he misled
Our people for a space, and might our laws down tread.
                    (Wakefield Scourging, 380, emphasis mine)

Margaret berates York for his imposture, insults his "mess of sons" (70–79), then gives him the "napkin" stained with Rutland's blood. Through it all York makes no reply. Typically, the Christ refuses to reply either to Herod and Pilate during his trials or to his tormentors during the Buffeting, Scourging, and Crucifixion sequences of the plays. One or another figure in these episodes decides Jesus is "mad" not to defend himself against coming "doom," and initiates his mockery. So Margaret ridicules York: "I prithee, grieve, to make me merry, York. . . ."

> Why art thou patient, man? Thou should'st be mad;
> And I, to make thee mad, do mock thee thus.
> Stamp, rave, and fret, that I may sing and dance.
> Thou woulds't be fee'd, I see, to make me sport.
> York cannot speak, unless he wear a crown.—
> A crown for York! And, lords, bow low to him.
> Hold you his hands, whilst I do set it on. (1.4.86, 89–95)

In the York play by the "Shermen," soldiers decide Jesus must be "a foyl" to remain silent (l.28). In Wakefield's Buffeting, the torturers make good "cheer" of their task and "teche him . . . a new play of Yoyll" (yule?) at which they "dawnse" (l.497). One Torturer in the Wakefield Scourging promises the others great cheer by proposing to "lead [Christ] a dance unto Sir Pilate's hall" (l.376). The salient point is that game, violence, dance, and jest, sometimes by "soldiers" or "knights," or "a consultus," are elaborated only in these episodes of the mystery pageants and might be cited here at length to parallel Margaret's wish that York give her "sport" (Kolve 196–198). The vengeful queen extends her abuse of York almost as if reminding the audience that torturers in the plays traditionally "behave like raving madmen," in Kolve's phrase, to incite the Christ to react. Most tellingly, to further humiliate the man, Margaret addresses him as one of the actors hired especially to perform various "japes" around the cross, an action extended largely for its own sake (Kolve 181): "Thou woulds't be fee'd, I see, to make me sport," that is, to entertain me as would a player king.

Cutts believes the crown Margaret then bestows on York might have been fashioned on the spot out of the legal "pact" she somehow has been carrying (122). If so, York's paper trail may have been still more visible on Shakespeare's stage than I imagine. Margaret congratulates herself on her creation and pretends to recognize him suddenly as Henry's usurper:

> . . . Now looks he like a king! . . .
> But how is it that great Plantagenet
> Is crowned so soon, and broke his solemn oath
> As I bethink me, you should not be king

Till our King Henry had shook hands with death. . . .
O, 'tis a fault too, too unpardonable!
Off with the crown, and, with the crown, his head! (96–107)

She conferred kingship with a bit of paper and may depose him as easily.
Hall's Chronicle dispatches York in a phrase or two. Clifford discovers
York's dead body, cuts off the head, crowns it with paper, then presents it
to Margaret on a pole "in great despite." It is greeted with "much derision
. . . much joy . . . and rejoysing" (Bullough 178). Holinshed additionally
provides the version paralleling the crucifixion: "Some write that the duke
was taken alive,. . . ." mocked, crowned with a garland of "sedges or bul-
rushes," and was treated "as the Jewes did unto Christ" (Bullough 210).
Neither source, however, suggests why Shakespeare extends the action here
so that it deepens the theme of trial by law and intensifies the implications
of sign and substance. As Young Clifford starts to remove York's crown,
Margaret stops him, saying, "Nay, stay. Let's hear the orisons he makes,"
rather like Caiaphas urging a slower pace on the torturers so as to increase
the fun (Wakefield Buffeting, 467–470).

While Christ's words before he dies vary from play to play, the pattern
of his breaking his long silence at this juncture remains constant. And in
general, as liturgical drama becomes Shakespearean parody, so Christ's
prayer—"Eli, eli, eli."—becomes York's lengthy curse, beginning "She-wolf
of France" (111–149). Yet remarkably enough, part of his speech momentarily restores the play's fallen language to something like its ideal power to
signify, for York calls on the "napkin" with Rutland's blood as a testament:

See, ruthless Queen, a hapless father's tears?
This cloth thou dippedst in blood of my sweet boy,
And I with tears do wash the blood away.
Keep thou the napkin, and go boast of this;
And if thou tell'st the heavy story right
Upon my soul, the hearers will shed tears.
Yea even my foes will shed fast falling tears
And say, "Alas, it was a piteous deed." (156–163)

In rhetorical effect, he recalls the instant repeated in the York, Wakefield,
and other cycles when Jesus calls to those present to "behold" if "ever ye
sagh body/ Bufet and bett thus blody (York Crucifixion, 233–285).[6] With
that gesture, his sacred body substantiates the epiphanic word "behold"
and encapsulates the essence of liturgical drama's unity of signifier and signified. The context for so sacramental an event, however, has long since
become theater of the world and *its* imitation in Shakespeare's play. So
York, a parodic Christ, can only evoke the idea of "behold" as he envisions
some future audience who will see the bloody napkin that authenticates

Margaret's cruelty (156–169). In such a recital, joining word to material thing, language will regain its authority as sign, and the highest justice will exonerate York. In fact speech does retrieve some efficacy right then, for Northumberland is moved to tears (150–151; 169–171), while York plays out the significance of Christ's "gyltles thus am I put to pyne" (York Crucifixion, 176). He may indeed be a player king as he likens himself to the Divine Father who suffered his innocent son to be martyred. York himself then hands over the paper crown, deposing himself in a gesture Shakespeare was to repeat with historical consequence in *Richard II*. Structurally, York's surrendering the paper crown not only reverses Henry's inept pact elevating York; it anticipates Henry's later ceding the protectorship to Warwick and Clarence, another division of his crown. York's mood on returning the paper crown, however, is bitterly triumphant rather than abject; he has effected an ironic reversal of victim and victor while reinvesting language with an aura of its original, mythic power. Clifford and Margaret then stab York, who commends himself to heaven in a final echo of the Christ.

Shakespeare thus layers his evocation of the Corpus Christi Passion both dramatically and rhetorically. The report of York's death later to his sons, for instance, might be echoing the torturers' reports to Pilate in most of the cycle plays, or in the liturgical poem quoted below.[7] Shakespeare's messenger says

> Who crowned the gracious Duke in high despite
> Laughed in his face; and when with grief he wept,
> The ruthless Queen gave him to dry his cheeks
> A napkin steeped in the harmless blood
> Of sweet young Rutland, by rough Clifford slain.
> And after many scorns, many foul taunts,
> They took his head. . . . (2.1.59–65)

The narrative poem "Evangelie," reporting to Pilate, reads

> While ihesu crist thus hanged on the rode
> the wikke men that about stode/
> Scorning him did & shame—
> & of him made al her game/
> And shoke her hedes & lough & pleied. (quoted by Kolve 198)

The sheer abundance in the 1590s of both popular and religious references to the Passion tell that Shakespeare needed only to hint at this most theatrical event in the entire Christian tradition if he intended, say, to elaborate "Margaret's Revenge" for the wrongs done her, or to balance the scene's dramatic weight between the two adversaries (Keyishian 130). The scene's substrata in the mystery pageants, however, also implicate the trilogy's interweavings of emblematic paper, writing, law, and lawlessness, as I suggested earlier, while casting an eerie light on Margaret's characterization. The illiterate mob in the pageants always threatens legality, and Pilate, chief judge, always insists on a written tablet at the head of the cross. Torturers or soldiers, traditionally puzzled by the message, know the "scrawl" is Pilate's, for "there is no man alive/ But for Pilate . . . that dare write in our view" (Wakefield Crucifixion, 409–423). When one of them finally translates: "Yonder is written Jesus of Nazareth/ He is King of Jews," the others claim it is "written wrong"; as the Jew is not a king, the writing can be "nought but fable" originating with "the devil." Still, Pilate the "man of law must have his will." In the Chester cycle, Pilate insists on the written tablet as the "King of the Jews . . . must have recognition"; and in the York Passion II, lengthy stage directions for Pilate's writing are followed by protest at his results.[8] Pilate in most texts dismisses complaints imperiously: "That I have written, written it is,/ And so it shall be for me, iwis!" Judgment, in other words, is at once unilateral and according to the letter of the law.

As for the mad queen, crowning York with paper, whether or not made of the parliamentary pact, again proves her scorn for written petitions, supplications, and their roles in lawful procedure. Her chaotic scene with Suffolk's severed head dramatizes this same primitive aspect of her personality, opposed to the symbolic and perhaps anticipating her brutal sport with York. In her drum head court she, like Pilate, is on the right side of the law; yet Margaret's true court is rule by the body. York in fact expends his greatest rhetorical energy on excoriating her inhumanity: "O tiger's heart . . ."(111–142). The fierce warrior who, York says, bears no resemblance to woman ("Women are soft, mild, pitiful, and flexible," 141), exults in her power over material life. In the theatrical terms proposed here, she creates a spectacle that juxtaposes the physical reality of the here-and-now to spirit in the hereafter, thereby exploding an otherwise conventional division of male and female orientations. York, in contrast, genuinely believes by *Part 3* in both the temporal and divine justice of his claims. He even envisions heaven's response to the depredations wrought on his person (168). In short, beyond the idea of player-king in the paper-crown scene is Margaret's ironically doubled role: her fortuitous prosecution of the letter of the law and her unruly subversion of trial by law, the lynchpin of all the passion plays. She literally enacts Suffolk's arrogant promise to "frame the law unto his will" (*1 Henry VI*, 2.4.9).

A wide circle of reference to liturgical and popular Christian traditions touches on more hints about what constitutes legality than are feasible to pursue here. Is York a sacrifice to an ultimate order in the future, in the sense that parody by definition retrieves the idea it mocks? The least that may be said about the paper-crown scene is that Shakespeare intensifies the contrast he will dramatize so often in later plays between a medieval world where shadow and substance are unified by a divinely anointed king (the model to which York and Henry subscribe), and the new world of political rapacity and willfulness that Margaret personifies. As only belief distinguishes between religion and superstition, so there can be no one true, uncontested monarch in these deeply skeptical plays. Henry too will sit on a molehill in a battlefield (*3 Henry VI*, 3.2.5) and contemplate the wreckage of his rule before he surrenders. By then he is a "quondam king" (3.1.23), in effect a shadow of York, as the Second Keeper implies with his question: "If thou be a king, where is thy crown?" (60)

> My crown is in my heart, not on my head;
> Not decked with diamonds and Indian stones
> Nor to be seen. My crown is called content;
> A crown it is that seldom kings enjoy (62–65)

All subsequent references to the crown—the one Richard of Gloucester sees "far off" (3.2.140); that Warwick turns his back on (4.1.200) and then removes from Edward's head, making him "the shadow" (4.3.50); the metaphoric "laurel crown" (4.6.34) of the Lord Protector that Warwick accepts with Clarence as "double shadows" (49); the continuing barrage of letters and proclamations about rule—these never regain their substance until Richmond ascends the throne at the end of *Richard III*.

NOTES

[1] I am endebted to Jonathan Hart's premise in Theater & World that the Christian idea of the world as "fallen" is germane to the problem of linguistic meaning in the history plays. He limits his examination to the Second Tetralogy.

[2] I suspect that the "paper trail" I am proposing indicates that Shakespeare revised *Part 1* to anticipate the theatrical capital he made of papers in *Part 2* and *Part 3*. My remarks, however, make no pretense of addressing the vexed issues of the trilogy's authorship and order of composition. I simply adopt Ornstein's position that the three plays are Shakespeare's and were written in chronological order (35). All quotations refer to David Bevington's fourth edition of the plays.

3 John Cutts says, "there is something of the atmosphere of Christ being scourged, ridiculously crowned and mocked, and this is sustained by

York's commending his soul to heaven" (122). Holinshed additionally provides a version of York's death paralleling the crucifixion (Bullough 210), discussed in the text.

⁴ I am relying on both the text and copious notes for the Wakefield Master's (Towneley) cycle of Corpus Christi plays, edited by A. C. Cawley and Martin Stevens. Cawley also produced a facsimile of the sole copy of the cycle housed at the Huntington Library in San Marino, California. For comparison's sake, I refer also to the York cycle, edited by Canon J. S. Purvis (London, 1957) and to the Chester cycle, edited by R. T. Davies (London, 1972).

⁵ The evidence for this argument is thoroughly reviewed by Cawley and Stevens, xii–xxii. Also see Cairncross's notes on the scene, *2 Henry IV* liii; and Cutts 119–122.

⁶ The Corpus Christi cycles celebrate a showing forth, Craig, 34. In the York *Crucifixio Christi*, Jesus says "All men that walkis by waye or strete . . . Byholdes myn heede, myn handis, and my feete. And fully feele nowe . . .yf any mourning may be meete / Or myscheve mesured unto myne" (252–259). In the N-Town Crucifixion, the call to "behold" is spoken to Mary: "Woman, woman, beheld there thy sone" (145–147). Or again in the York play XXXVI by the "Bocheres," Jesus addresses the thieves hung with him: "Man, see what bitter sorrow I suffer for thee; on me for to look" (183–189).

⁷ In the Wakefield Talents, for instance, the Torturers report to Pilate that their good time on Calvary was very like their fun at a new play in town, which the Second Torturer taught to the King of the Jews. We taught him, they say, ". . . *a new play . . . the play we lately had in town,/. . .* That *game* me thought was good/ *When we had played with him our fill/ Then led we him unto a hill,/* And there we wrought with him our will" (54–59, emphasis mine).

⁸ "Here shall Pilate ask pen and ink, and a table shall be take him, written before, '*Hic est Jesus Nazarenus rex judeorum.*' And he shall make him to write, and then go upon a ladder and set the table above Christ's head. And then Caiphas shall make him to read. 'Sir Pilate, we marveleth of this,/ That you write him to be King of Jewes./ Therefore we would that you should write thus, That he named himself King of Jewes'" (quoted in Davies 311).

FOLK MAGIC IN *HENRY VI, PARTS 1* AND 2:

TWO SCENES OF EMBEDDING

Frances K. Barasch

While problems of authorship, the use of sources, the authority of texts and, more recently, gender and politics, have been central in discussions of the three parts of *Henry VI*, the drama itself has received limited critical attention as an imaginative construct about war and disorder. Critics have recognized its disjointed, episodic qualities that play havoc with history and causation, and they have duly noted the shabby treatment of Joan of Arc, Lady Eleanor, and Queen Margaret.[1] Concern with these matters, however, has obscured the canonical importance of Shakespeare's first or very early group of plays and has overlooked the imaginative strategies Shakespeare developed for the encoding and production of meaning. Although the introduction of the demonic or magical scenes in *Parts 1* and *2* is often ignored or dismissed as extraneous, renewed interest in Renaissance magic, witchcraft, and women has urged a reexamination of these scenes and leads me to a very different assessment.

The texts of *Henry VI, Parts 1* and 2,[2] interrupt their diachronic schemes to introduce several embedded scenes, all highly reflective of the thematics of the outer play, which are *mises en abyme* of sorts. Two of the scenes are demonic interludes with misogynist subtexts, which engage the audience in vivid spectacle and produce synchronic "readings" or interpretations of the principal text. The contained scene of *Part 1* allows the appearance of fiends as familiars of Joan of Arc, thus presenting dramatic and "ocular proof" of English assertions that she employed witchcraft to defeat England's heroes; in *Part 2*, another contained scene introduces the conjurers who perform magic for Lady Eleanor, linking her to witchcraft, charges of treason, disgrace, and the ultimate downfall of the Lancasters. At the heart of the two scenes are subtextual signifiers of evil causation derived from popular beliefs about dangerous women, particularly those of "manly" disposition, which conformed with common folklore about women, witches, and conjurers.[3] These beliefs, reinforced in actuality by Church and State, fed into the political unrest and concern over Queen Elizabeth's rule in the troubled years near the century's end. While seemingly extraneous, Shakespeare's demonic scenes are, in fact, integral to the principal texts. They call up referential meanings validated by the historical fiction of the plays and, although dependent on the complicity of a superstitious and misognynist audience for their full impact, may be appreciated as strategic devices which strengthen the structure of the whole.

Structurally, these scenes—that is, the *mises en abyme*—constitute a microtext or microcosm of the principal texts, which may double or oppose or ambiguate the thematic concerns of the play. The *mise en abyme*, it will be recalled, is a structural device named by André Gide from heraldic imagery, in which a figure *en abyme* appears at the center of the shield and is a miniature replica of the shield itself. In *The Mirror in the Text*, Lucien Dällenbach describes the duplication *en abyme* as a kind of "reflexion" by "which a work turns back on itself" to give "meaning and form to the work" (1–2, 9). In drama, it is an "interior duplication," like the internal play in *Hamlet*, which holds a mirror up to Claudius's guilt (12). But the concept is not simply that of a reflecting mirror. Like the mirror or window of Renaissance art, which is "embedded" in the composition, the *mise en abyme* can deepen meaning by reflecting the world within the frame or by extending meaning beyond the canvas. It can also have a circular structure—implicit at the beginning, explicit at a later point, as in *Hamlet*, where the Ghost's story is later amplified and verified in "The Mousetrap." The device can also be a tale within the tale, a puppet show, festivities, or a song introduced to the larger structure, having symbolic, allegorical, or metatheatrical import. And its purpose can be ambivalent as well as definitive. In *Part 2* of *Henry VI*, the comic interlude of Simpcox's "miracle" in 2.1 exposes the beggar's fakery unequivocally, reflecting a common crime among charlatans of the time who exploited the superstitious with magical tricks for personal gain. It is followed in the same scene by grim certainties in the sentencing of "the witch" Margery, her cohorts, and Lady Eleanor. Next in the same scene is the trial by combat between the apprentice Peter and his master Horner. Although using different terms, Phyllis Rackin describes the *mise en abyme* and the ambivalent function of this trial:

A trial by combat constitutes a miniature plot that stages conflicting propositions about historical truth in the form of physical action, its outcome designed to ratify one proposition and discredit the other. As such, it exhibits in simplified microcosm the dynamics of the larger and more complicated plots of the plays. (54)

When Peter defeats Horner, disrupting the servant-master order of society, Shakespeare offers two views of the trial's surprising outcome to reflect major dichotomies in the play. On the one hand, King Henry believes providential justice has been accomplished by Horner's defeat and confession; on the other, York offers Peter an opposing interpretation: "Fellow, thank God, and the good wine in thy master's way" (2.3.92–93). Horner's drinking and not providence has brought the traitor to justice.

The *mise en abyme* often calls attention to itself by an announcement or a striking interruption in the main play and by startling closure. The cry "A miracle!" (2.1.SD 56) introduces the Simpcox interval, which ends when Simpcox is whipped and runs away (SD 150). Trumpets sound for Hamlet's play to begin (3.2.SD 135); it ends when Claudius interrupts with the cry, "Give me some light. Away" (269). At other times, the device may be introduced more ominously with the sound of thunder or show of lightning. Often the *abyme* creates "the illusion of mystery and depth," as C. E. Magny has written, a concept which aptly applies to the hellish shapes rising from the stage trap which signifies the *abyme*, literally the "abyss" with connotations of depth, infinity, vertigo, and falling. In *Henry VI*, two of the *mises en abyme* provide horrific associations with women and evoke demonic reflections on the historical or referential disorders of the so-called Hundred Years War, the contentions of cousins in the War of the Roses, and the witch-hunt hysteria of the fifteenth and sixteenth centuries. Together these embedded scenes emit strong signals for the reception of meanings: "low" magic tells truth; Elizabethan policy thrives in the knowledge that the Tudor regime has fulfilled God's providential plan for national harmony in the legitimate and virtuous body of the reigning queen. Yet opposing anxieties, encoded within both sub- and main texts and produced by disorders in the past, figured in terms of history's dangerous women, remain underlying threats in the uncertain Elizabethan present.

Shakespeare determined the reception of these embedded scenes by responding to popular interest in plays with Faustian themes which expressed a common belief in spirits and echoed the painful conflict within Renaissance society between traditional folk knowledge of witchcraft or "low magic" and humanist challenges to these inherited beliefs, advanced in learned theses on occult philosophy or "Neoplatonic magic." Church authorities believed in witch lore and persecuted its practitioners, while the learned "magi" claimed virtue in taming spirits and argued that occult practice gave mankind the creative power to conquer the unknown (Mebane 98ff.; Levack x). To the extent that the Renaissance stage bears witness to popular interest in magic, sorcery, and witchcraft, the period of attraction was relatively short, beginning in the 1570s, peaking in the 1590s, waning by 1614, and little more than an extended metaphor in the 1620s (Traister 33, 157, 179). The *Henry VI* plays were performed at the peak of theatrical interest, giving rise to modern assessments that the witches' scenes were mere crowd-pleasers, unnecessary to the plots. For many Elizabethans, however, the demonic shows reinforced belief and established providential causation, even as they may have provoked debate among the skeptical.

Witchcraft lore was based on a continuum of ancient magical practice of the people and Christian ideology; it was crystallized in the twelfth-century Church and culminated in the inquisitorial procedures of the fourteenth century. The advent of print made it possible to perpetuate these ancient superstitions in demonological literature, notably represented by Jakob Sprenger and Heinrich Kramer in *Malleus maleficarum* (1486ff.), which became "the standard manual for the persecution of witches for two centuries" (Mora lv, xlv). At least thirty-four editions of *Malleus maleficarum* appeared between 1486 and 1669, mainly during 1486–1520 and 1574–1621 when persecutions were at their height, the latter period coinciding with Shakespeare's career. In 1582 alone, 300 women were condemned on the Continent for causing calamities in the guise of werewolves (Mora xlv). Although aristocratic women such as the queen widow of Henry IV, Lady Eleanor, and Ann Boleyn were accused of witchcraft for political reasons, it was commonly held that wicked women and wizards were of the lower class, that they met with fiends at night, had sexual relations with demons, practiced pagan blood rituals, could bewitch neighbors, cause storms, change form, and injure livestock.

More skeptical views of witchcraft were also current. Besides stage satires of fake magicians which circulated widely in the last quarter of the century, there were serious discussions challenging witch belief. In *De praestigiis daemonum* (1563), which appeared in numerous editions before the end of the sixteenth century, the physician Johann Weyer declared outright that alleged witches were disturbed but innocent victims of superstition, that accusers were usually frightened or jealous neighbors, that pacts with the devil were impossible, and that the magistrates who tried and condemned witches were deluded. Weyer was supported in English publications by Reginald Scot (*The Discoverie of Witchcraft*, 1584) and Samuel Harsnett (*A Discovery of the Fradulent Practices of John Darrell*, 1599), but his work had been placed on the *Index Librorum Prohibitatorum* 1570 and was regularly discredited by both religious and political figures, such as Jean Bodin in *De la demonomanie des sorciers* (1580) and King James I in *Daemonologie* (1597, 1603). In short, witchcraft lore, reinforced by church and political authorities, continued to inform popular culture, even in distant Salem, until the end of the seventeenth century (Mora lxix–lxxi, lxxxiv; Mebane 98ff).

Today's scholars seek causation of the Renaissance witch-hunt from modern perspectives, some finding it in the overwhelming psychological stresses of simple people beset by religious wars, devastating storms, mysterious deaths of humans and animals, and ancient superstitions expressed in a "universal contempt toward women [which] must serve as a background for any understanding of the Renaissance witch-hunt" (Mora li). Other scholars add a political perspective, recognizing that for doctrinal and political reasons both Church and State defended witch-hunting, asserting power by exploiting common fears of eccentric women. Whether shepherd's daughter, duchess, or queen, a woman might be accused of witchcraft if a political scapegoat were needed, and for other political and doctrinal reasons opposing forces might defend her. As Constance Jordan points out, Joan's reputation in the sixteenth century often controverted English opinion "as the result of shifts in political power": Italian and French writers praise Joan's "successful liberation of France," note "that her fellow countrymen regarded her as divine," saw her deeds as the expression of God's will, and commended her virtuous constancy (75n, 204, 210). In contrast, the Tudor position on Joan and Eleanor was defensive. Edward Hall's account (1543) justifies Joan's prosecution for her great crimes against the English, and Raphael Holinshed (1587) "details contradictory accounts" of her death to mock her defenders (Levine 43–44). Eleanor's histories also became somewhat controversial. The certainty of her treasonous necromancy, advanced in the early Yorkist chronicles, is challenged on doctrinal grounds in Foxe's *Acts and Monuments* (1570). But, although hints of political animosity behind Eleanor's case entered Tudor accounts of her life, these later histories did not clear her of the charges brought against her (Levine 50–58; Howard 136).

In *Henry VI*, Shakespeare evoked traditional beliefs in witchcraft and, through contradictory or circular structures of the *mises en abyme*, reaffirmed the misogynist histories condemning Joan and Eleanor, even as opposing histories attempted to defend them. Shakespeare's strategy for producing meaning in *Part 1* is signaled by the *mise en abyme* located near the end of the text (5.3), after the French flee in defeat. To the noises of "Alarum" and "Excursions," Joan enters alone to work her witchcraft. The *mise en abyme* which ensues calls attention to itself by Joan's magical chant and the sounding of thunder: "Now help, ye charming spells and periapts [amulets],/ And you choice spirits that admonish me" (5.3.2–3). Thus, with blasphemous invocation, Joan leaves the historical frame of the play and enters the *mise en abyme* to perform as a witch, inducing thunder and uttering conjurations to summon the "speedy helpers" that serve "the lordly Monarch of the North" (that is, the Devil) to her aid. The Fiends (perhaps with monstrous heads and hairy suits) appear promptly from "under earth," for the the stage trap has opened Hell's *abyme*, introducing "internal space . . . into the very heart of the work" and suggesting an infinite series of parallels with the surrounding text (Magny 271). To the spirits Joan declares:

This speedy and quick appearance argues proof
Of your accustom'd diligence to me.
Now, ye familiar spirits, that are cull'd
Out of the powerful regions under earth,
Help me this once, that France may get the field. (5.3.9–12.)

Joan's voice has been altered in this speech, for the voice heard here is inap-
propriate to this speaker. It is not Joan who needs to "argue proof," but
the author who, probably in a forgetful moment, usurps Joan's voice to
have her accuse herself of "accustom'd" demonic practice. The English
have so charged her throughout the play. At the same time she pleads for
"help . . . this once," apparently a fracture in the text which refers to the
Fiends' first appearance on stage, although it also seems to argue that Joan
has had no prior assistance from the lower world.

The position of the *mise en abyme* near the end of *Part 1* has an important bearing on its reception, for it "argues proof" for the first time and
forces the reader/viewer to readjust earlier receptions of Joan's character.
Whereas some of Shakespeare's audience would accept English assessments
of her victories as witchcraft from the start, skeptics must now replace
doubt for certainty. In Dällenbach's theoretical system of analysis, the *mise
en abyme* may be placed at the center or end of a text and made suddenly
to "appear as the opposite of the dominant reception and as such is unsur-
passed as a means for bringing contradiction into the heart of reading [or
viewing] activity" (1979–1980:445). By usurping Joan's voice in the self-
condemnation of Act 5, the author brings into play a competing "reading"
or interpretation which challenges the foregrounded text and calls for a
second or recursive "reading" of the entire play that resolves earlier ambiguities.

Initially, the reception of Joan is ambivalent, balanced between Pucelle
and Puzel (virgin and whore). However, the *mise en abyme* with its invert-
ed point of view dramatizes and subverts this initial balanced reception.
Joan la Pucelle arrives on the scene as a "holy maid . . . / Which by a vision
sent to her from heaven" will drive out the English (1.2.51–54). Although
she is a "shepherd's daughter" (1.2.72), the French accept her as a savior
sent by "God's Mother" (78), and she is praised as a "Bright star of Venus"
(144) by the Dauphin. To England's heroic Talbot, on the other hand, this
"woman clad in armor" (1.5.3) is a witch in service of the Devil, a "Devil,
or devil's dam" (5–7), and a "high-minded strumpet" (12). In four acts of
the play, Joan's promise of victory over the English is fulfilled and provides
seemingly sound evidence that "God's Mother" is on her side and she on
Hers. The *mise en abyme*, however, is so fashioned as to oppose and deconstruct the divine aura Joan has claimed for herself since the play's first act.

By dramatizing proof of her witchcraft, the embedded scene submits for
Elizabethan reception the "ocular proof" that was required in actual

inquisitorial procedures. As late as the Salem trials of 1692, magistrates required evidence of witchcraft that they could observe with their own eyes. They stationed the alleged victims in the courtroom to observe their reactions to the witch's testimony, and the accusers invariably obliged with hysterical performances. Doubtless for the same reasons, Othello demands "ocular proof" that Desdemona is a "whore" (3.3.359–360), the attribute commonly associated with witches and assigned to Joan by England's Talbot. At Salem, as in *Othello*, the evidence was manipulated by envious persons and later shown to be false, but Tudor propaganda did not permit Joan's vindication, and the *mise en abyme* proves the English case.

In the misogynist climate of Renaissance Europe, the vast majority of witches were, like Joan, unlearned women of "contemptible estate" (1.2.75) who allegedly made blood pacts with the Devil and caused harm to their enemies by supernatural means. In the *mise en abyme*, Joan heaps evidence against herself when the Fiends refuse to speak by reminding them that she has fed them with her blood (5.3.14). She offers to "lop a member off" (15) if they will help; however, they are silent still. Desperately she offers what witches must: "My body shall/ Pay recompense, if you will grant my suit" (18–19). And in her final self-condemnation, she pleads: "Then take my soul—my body, soul, and all,/ Before that England give the French the foil" (22–23). But silently the Fiends depart. There is no thunder to mark their exit in the First Folio text; perhaps its absence is an oversight, perhaps an intentional sign that Joan has lost her power, for her "ancient incantations are too weak,/ And hell too strong" (27–28). Joan must pay the Devil, and France must fall.

Through authorial usurpation and "ocular proof," Joan has been made to comply with the inquisitory system promoted by the Church through its demonologists in the course of the sixteenth century. Shakespeare has enacted her "confession" and thus "proved" her a witch. By blasphemous invocation of Fiends and allusion to her pact with the Devil sealed with her blood, Joan's balanced presentation is completely reversed in the *mise en abyme*. Because the *mise en abyme* is retro-prospective, that is, a flashback to first impressions of Joan and a flash-forward to her final image, it signifies that the chaste maiden has been "misrepresented" in the initial acts of the drama; at the same time, it forecasts her transformation into the "true" witch that emerges in her final appearance in the play. With the Fiends' departure in 5.3, the main text is resumed. Immediately, Joan is captured and accused of witchcraft, never mind that no one but the audience has had "ocular proof" of her conjuration.

When Joan is brought forward by her English captors in 5.4, having been condemned to burn, she is represented through York's eyes, completely transformed into an "ugly witch" with bended brow (5.3.34) who curses her English captor York and as well as the French Dauphin. The English accusations become unambiguous truth; the Dauphin has also readjusted his initial perception of Joan, holding to his words: "No prophet will I trust, if she prove false" (1.2.150). With the French defeat, Joan is the scapegoat he requires at this point. Thus ally and enemy alike are objects of Joan's demonic vengeance (5.3.39). Through the offices of the *mise en abyme* her transformation into a "fell banning hag, enchantress" (5.3.42), as York describes her, also becomes the fictive truth of the historical text. (The description may mean that Joan's stage appearance has been altered to seem an ugly hag's in this scene.) As accused witches were commonly women of peasant stock who practiced low magic, Joan's father is brought in to prove her base birth. Joan denies him and claims noble lineage in an attempt to prevent her execution under English law of her time but is mocked for her effort. (In *Part 2*, the noblewoman Eleanor will be banned, not burned.) Joan also denies that she has consorted with "wicked spirits" (5.3.42), but it is now clear to the audience that she lies.

Nor does Shakespeare ignore the deep contradictions which marked six-teenth-century debates over learned and low magic. These metatheatrical oppositions are incorporated in Joan's denials when she issues an eloquent defense of the learned magic she claims as her practice. This defense implic-itly contradicts her earlier claim to having "wit untrain'd in any kind of art" (1.2.73) and is introduced as further evidence that Joan lies. Renaissance Neoplatonic philosophy attempted to reconcile medieval Christian belief with ideas derived from the influential *Corpus Hermeticum* (mistakenly attributed to the ancient philosopher Hermes Trismegistus); this learned philosophy retained belief in demons and spirits but held that power in nature resided in "the spheres of heaven [which] were moved by spirits" and which could be dominated by inspired men (Garin 86). Joan argues hermetically that she was divinely chosen to "work exceeding mir-acles on earth" (5.3.41) and to "compass wonders" (48). It is a magic that would fulfill man's infinite possibilities in a boundless universe "by inspi-ration of celestial grace" (40). But it cannot be argued that Joan's Neoplatonist appeal is intended to mitigate her readjusted negative recep-tion. Just as official Church decrees treated Neoplatonism as heretical, so the embedded scene resolves the debate on the side of traditional misogy-ny and popular witchcraft belief. The more learned in the audience would believe the simple maid lacked the "wit" and "art" to reach so high. Joan's appeal is denied within the historical text, and the *mise en abyme* has con-vinced the audience, the superstitious and skeptical alike, that Joan's gold-en tongue is merely an instrument of the Devil. Joan's next plea for mercy, that she is with child, is consistent with the sexual degradation associated with witches. Naming a succession of fathers for her child, she proves her-self a "Strumpet" (5.3.84) as well as a witch, confirming Talbot's charges in 1.5. With her last words, Joan curses England and the lords who torment her; thus, with the sin of anger on her lips, she condemns her soul to Hell, neither forgiving her enemies nor seeking salvation in prayer.

In the final analysis, the *mise en abyme* has become a second-order signifier and a locus for readjustment in audience reception. Shakespeare's strategy for readjusting Joan's reception in the embedded show of Fiends is neither extraneous nor merely sensational, but rather a complex device for justifying England's persecution of Joan to her sixteenth-century defenders. Joan was exonerated by the Church in the seventeenth century. In Shakespeare's play, however, responsibility for the French war is deflected from England's heroes to the French "witch" and to the abstract forces of evil which rise from the *mise en abyme*.

In *Henry VI, Part 2* Shakespeare's strategy for introducing another demonic *mise en abyme* varies from *Part 1*. Although its subtext, as before, is the association of national disorder with the evil nature of a dangerous woman and her destructive powers, this association is not left for the final act but is programmed into the historical fiction at the outset, producing a circular structure in which outcomes reflect upon the *mise en abyme*. Placed in an initial position, the embedded scene elicits a double reception: to most Elizabethans its credibility would be implicit, but its skeptical reception within the play challenges the reader/viewer's interpretation. Either the witchcraft is actual and its prophecies providential, or it is fakery devised for evil purpose by the ambitious Duke of York. In the end, the fulfillment of prophecies makes the meaning of the embedded scene explicit, resolving initial ambiguities for the reader/viewer and establishing further expectations for *Henry VI, Part 3* and *Richard III*.

In *Part 2*, as early as 1.2 Eleanor and her husband exchange dreams, which are also instances of embedding reflecting themes of failed ambition in the main play. At the outset Eleanor enunciates her unlawful desire for the throne as told in her dream, and her "manly" ambition, marking her a dangerous woman like Joan before and Lady Macbeth after, is declared in the soliloquy that follows:

Were I a man, a duke, and next of blood,
I would remove these tedious stumbling blocks,
And smooth my way upon their headless necks;
And being a woman, I will not be slack
To play my part in Fortune's Pageant (1.2.63–67).

Thereupon she conspires with Sir John Hume to employ "Margery Jordan, the cunning witch" and "Roger Bolingbrook, the conjurer" to assist her plans. Eleanor's reception as a "manly" woman of evil ambition is thus established early in the principal text.

Eleanor's wicked nature is soon reinforced with the supernatural display of 1.4, signaled before and after by the lightning and thunder of disordered nature (SD 22; SD 40). These sensational effects bracket the embedded scene, separating it from the principal text yet serving as a mirror of things to come. Lady Eleanor, who observes from "aloft" (SD 13) with the villainous priest, Sir John Hume, is also separated from the conjuration that takes place below. At a functional level she serves as mediator between the embedded drama and the real audience. Hume's earlier soliloquy, however, reveals that he has been "hired . . . [by the Cardinal and Suffolk] to undermine the Duchess" (1.2.98). Therefore, in ushering Eleanor to her observation post and standing by her, Hume represents the conspiratorial presence that watches Eleanor watch the conjurers. Because York and Buckingham will soon "break in" (SD 40), they too probably stand by as silent witnesses who spy on Hume, Eleanor, and the conjurers. Structurally, then, the *mise en abyme* is at least triply embedded, suggesting the "infinite series of parallel mirrors" which C. E. Magny associates with *mises en abyme*: the audience sees the dukes who watch Hume who watches Eleanor as she watches the conjurers raise a spirit from the abyss. This multiple layering serves to convey and complement the complex of villainies within villainies of the principal text. Although the *mise en abyme* is distinguished structurally from the main play by lightning and thunder, it is centered within the image of spies upon spies and reflects the referential world of vanity, malice, and treachery that is King Henry's court.

The demonic scene itself is retrospective. The reenactment of conventional stage hocus-pocus recalls Joan's invocation of the Fiends in the final act of *Part 1*. As a subtext, it serves to mirror the ambitious Eleanor's spiritual degradation and to foretell murderous events in the principal text. Eleanor's public disgrace when she later appears disrobed and barefoot on flintstone (2.4), is prefigured in the embedded image of the witch Margery Jordan, who must "grovel on the earth" (1.4.11). The conjurer's invocation of "Deep night, dark night" (1.4.16) mirrors Eleanor's subsequent despair: "dark shall be my light, and night my day" (2.4.40). Dire omens of dramatic outcomes in the historical fiction are also conveyed. When the Spirit answers questions prepared beforehand by Eleanor, it poses three riddles which are integral to the principal text. Two of the riddles prophesy deaths that will occur before the close of *Part 2*: Suffolk's, "by water"; Somerset's, "where castles mounted stand." The third prophecy, of Henry's death, must await fulfillment in *Part 3*.

When the Spirit departs in thunder and lightning (1.4.SD 40) marking the end of the *mise en abyme*, the historical world is highlighted abruptly: Eleanor's enemies (here, York, Buckingham, Stafford, and Guards) "break in" (SD 40), seize the evidence, and arrest the lot. In this way the historical text resumes. As in *Part 1*, where York is an ominous presence at Joan's capture, so in *Part 2*, York's compelling vision is imposed upon Eleanor's arrest:

Lord Buckingham, methinks you watch'd her well.

A pretty plot, well chosen to build upon!
Now pray, my lord, let's see the devil's writ. (55–57.)

York repeats the prophetic riddles and dismisses them. His cynical reaction
to the conjurers' performance conflicts with the audience's reception of the
embedded text, for he suggests that the *mise en abyme* is merely the enact-
ment of "a pretty plot"—a scam by fake magicians hired by York's dubious allies to "undermine" the duchess. York's subversive voicing challenges
his credibility and produces a recursive reading of his relationship to the
misogynist subtext of *Part 1*. In *Part 1*, we recall, York's is the merciless
voice which transforms Joan to an "ugly witch" with bended brow and
which rejects all her appeals; in *Part 2*, York and his faction maliciously
exploit the ambitious Eleanor and instigate her disgrace. Thus York's skepticism ambiguates the meaning of the *mise en abyme* in *Part 2*. By suggesting that the conjuration is merely "a pretty plot . . . to build upon," he
implies that his witch-hunts are not exercises in piety or patriotism but
misogynist projects devised by an envious lord to achieve and maintain
political power.
    For the audience, however, Suffolk's capture and murder "by water"
(1.4.33) off the coast of Kent in 4.2 and Somerset's death in 5.2 "where
castles mounted stand" (1.4.37) fulfill two of the Spirit's promises conveyed in the *mise en abyme*. A readjusted response by reader/viewer to
York's ambiguation is forced by these events: witchcraft believers gain certainty in their faith, and skeptics must now realize the Spirit has spoken
truth. Still, York's skepticism is renewed by his son, the future King
Richard III. Having personally fulfilled the second prophecy by killing
Somerset in combat, York's son mocks the prophecy as coincidence:

>   So lie thou there;
>   For underneath and alehouse' paltry sign,
>   The Castle in Saint Albons, Somerset
>   Hath made the wizard famous in his death. (5.2.66–69).

Thus Richard's skepticism is circularized in a replay of the "pretty plot"
his skeptical father had devised. It spirals forward to *Henry VI, Part 3*,
where Richard will fulfill the third prophecy, for the King's fate awaits "the
duke [who] yet lives that Henry shall depose" (*Part 2* 1.4.30). The
ambiguation ends finally in *Richard III*, where the duke will "him out-live,
and die a violent death" (1.4.31). What the father and son believed was
accomplished by personal agency and was only coincidentally mirrored in
the *mise en abyme* is ultimately turned against the cynics who had scoffed
at black magic as a "pretty plot."
    Although critics have addressed Shakespeare's considerable power to
stage history as human events for all time, their assessments have often

excluded the *Henry VI* plays. Yet careful analysis of the early histories reveals imaginative structures embedded in the plays which give thematic order to the episodic material of the chronicle sources. Identified much later as *mise en abyme*, the Renaissance device of the embedded mirror encoded themes of its surrounding text or canvas, reinforced internal meanings, and extended them beyond the text or canvas itself. If this imaginative strategy is disregarded, if the demonic scenes are dismissed as unnecessary interruptions, the *Henry VI* plays may well be perceived as disjointed and their embedded structures irrelevant. However, the *mises en abyme* in *Henry VI, Parts 1* and *2* disrupt the diachronic scheme of the historical fiction to great advantage. They introduce meanings which are superimposed on prior or subsequent events and force reinterpretation and understanding in terms of the embedded scenes. These dramatic interpolations are thus converted into a demonic code which circularizes themes of dangerous women, English heroics, and political treacheries in the framing play. Through this structural device, Joan la Pucelle and Lady Eleanor are momentarily demarginalized and centered in the subtextual world of demonic magic, where they function as mirrors of misogynist belief at the heart of the principal plays. Although the demonic scenes reflect realities within the historical fiction, they also mirror the metatheatrical turbulence of contemporary politics, actual witch-hunts, and the patriarchal anxieties of Elizabethan life. As Dällenbach observed in another context (1989:55), the interventions of the *mise en abyme* serve as "internal repetition," generating "the means to reflect back [or forward] on the fiction," consequently giving the "work a strong structure." By underpinning the meaning of the primary texts, the *mises en abyme* strengthen the structure of the whole and provide "a means whereby the work can interpret itself." In this manner, through dark reflections of the referential world, the embedded structures of *Henry VI, Parts 1* and *2* give order to themes of disorder as they explore the deep anxieties of a superstitious and misogynist audience.

ACKNOWLEDGMENTS

An earlier version of this essay was presented at the Shakespeare Association of America, annual conference 1995. I am indebted to Professor Marshall Schneider, Chairman of Modern Languages and Comparative Literature, Baruch College/CUNY, for his editorial guidance throughout this project.

NOTES

[1] For summaries of these issues, see *The Complete Works*, ed. David Bevington, 496–498, 538–540; also *The Riverside Shakespeare*, gen. ed. G.B. Evans, 587–595; Andrew S. Cairncross, Introductions to Arden editions of *Henry VI, Parts 1* and *2*; Michael Hattaway, Introductions to New Cambridge editions of *The First Part* and *The Second Part of King Henry VI*. Phyllis Rackin observes that the disjointed qualities of *Henry VI* "frustrate any attempt to discover a clear principle of causality" (27). Also see discussions of *Henry VI* by Irene G. Dash 1981, Jean E. Howard 1994, and Nina S. Levine 1998.

[2] The magician of *2 Henry VI* and thus the scene are dismissed by Barbara Traister 62. For recent studies of magic, see Dympna Callaghan; also David Schalkwyk; John S. Mebane; Barbara Rosen (rpt 1991); Brian P. Levack; and Linda Woodbridge 1994.

[3] The association of women and witches in *Henry VI* is discussed in gender studies by Hodgdon 1991, Howard 1994, Levine 1998, among others.

Shakespeare's Medieval Devils and Joan La Pucelle in *1 Henry VI*

Semiotics, Iconography, and Feminist Criticism

James J. Paxson

All things considered, Shakespeare's plays avoid the representation of devils. In Shakespearean drama, a devil or a demon is about as welcome as the personified abstraction: although ornamental personifications may crowd spoken discourse, only a few personified characters lumber onto Shakespeare's stage—Time in *The Winter's Tale* or Rumour in *2 Henry IV*—and even then in very compromised ways. The same goes for devils, as John D. Cox once pointed out.[1] Very rare were characterizations of the devil on the Renaissance stage overall; at that, he would usually appear in programmatic incantation scenes of the sort witnessed in Greene's *Frier Bacon and Frier Bongay*. Shakespeare, in sum, seemed to have little use for stage fiends.

In accord with the aesthetically oriented drift in Shakespeare criticism— the drift monumentalized by E. K. Chambers and followed by virtually all of us—the personification character and the devil do not serve Shakespearean dramaturgy well. Although personifications or devils intrigue Marlowe (whose *Dr. Faustus* presents the pageant of the Seven Deadly Sins along with the most famous of Renaissance stage devils, Mephistopheles), Shakespeare's drama distinguishes itself as having gotten beyond the crude clutter of medieval devils, angels, and embodied abstractions. The stripping of the medieval in general, as customary wisdom has it, animates Shakespeare's early modern drama; dramatic modernity entails escape from the medieval. As a semiotic category, the medieval demonic must likewise be stripped away or avoided.

Although I support historicist or ideologically focused explanations about the evacuation of devils from the Tudor stage,[2] the aestheticist model—the bardolatrous model that fosters our view of a Shakespeare who was ever perfecting a modern form of art that needed to reject medieval materials—serves me as a mainstay in my teaching of Middle English and Tudor drama. I can adore postmodern theory; but I'm sometimes timorous about straying far from Chambers or Tillyard pedagogically.

However, alone among all of Shakespeare's plays, *1 Henry VI* presents devils in a manner drawn from the traditions of medieval theater, the preprofessional theater of miracle and mystery plays in the English tradition. Called "fiends" in the play's rubrics, they remind us of figures such as Tutivillus, Lucifer, or the blackened, raucous demons of the Fall and the Harrowing of Hell in cycles such as Chester or Wakefield. If Shakespeare's history plays contain an often-ignored reservoir of medieval dramatic or iconographic images, structures, and characterizations, then the fiends of *1 Henry VI*, as well as the sorciological figures Joan la Pucelle and Margery Jourdain, serve as the most direct and literal markers of residual medievalism.[3] The fiends and witches (or personifications) must not, I believe, be brushed aside as merely aesthetic detritus still cluttering the desk of a new and young playwright finding his way; linking a "witch" such as La Pucelle to the old personificational Vice, in fact, David Bevington, Robert Turner, and Bernard Spivack have emphasized the importance of Shakespearean characterizational hybridity and its concomitant regeneration of medieval dramatic principles.[4] (This is of course a still-popular treatment regarding Iago and Falstaff.) The devils and their allied witches of Shakespeare's First Tetralogy signify in unexpected ways.

But above all, I assert, we must visualize Shakespeare's scarce devils according to a tradition still popular in the sixteenth century: the carnivalesque fiends who graced stages as well as public pageants or festivities on the Continent and in England bore faces or heads on their crotches instead of genitals. The "nether-faced devil" can thus be understood as a version of the polyfaced devil well known throughout medieval and Renaissance Europe, and their purview, especially in manuscript illuminations and printed books, was so widespread that the tradition was in fact a cliché (see Figure 1 and Figure 2). To imagine a devil in the fifteenth or sixteenth century meant to envision a thing with a face on its crotch as readily as it meant envisioning a devil's horns, scales, and saucerlike eyes.

If several of the essays in this volume support the thesis that of all Shakespeare's texts, the First Tetralogy draws most heavily on medieval dramatical and cultural models, then I too seek to promote that thesis, specifically by showing that the imagery of *1 Henry VI*'s fiends depends upon a common iconographic tradition in the sixteenth century—the nether-faced devil. My method will be at times highly speculative; such is the cast of theory-driven projects. But I believe there is enough evidence to warrant articulation of an important symbolic connection between Joan la Pucelle's briefly conveyed characterization as a witch, a witch whom we actually see commercing with devils, and some traditional demonic iconography common to the Tudor era.

My argument will thus have three phases. First, I shall argue that the nether-faced devil proper "appears" not in person but at discursive levels in other Shakespeare plays, notably *1 Henry IV, King Lear,* and *Othello.* Yet the image of the nether-faced devil also surfaces as well during a key moment in the discourse of Joan la Pucelle at the end of *1 Henry VI.* Second, I provide a detailed and lengthy analysis of the nether-faced devil in medieval and Renaissance visual art, having already noted at the outset of this article's first phase, what I believe to have been its possible theatrical purview and material production in the English mystery plays. This iconographic segment, which delineates the heart of my project, will try to account for many meanings in the nether-faced devil, most of which descend from medieval theological and philosophical protocols formed largely in late-classical patristic thinking. My emphasis here, however, will be on gender, on the significance of embodied femininity in residual medieval imagery. Third, I shall conclude by trying to reconcile the demonic iconography of the nether-faced devil with the current stream of feminist and ideologically oriented criticism of La Pucelle as a demonic or negative feminine dramatic type central to the gender poetics of *1 Henry VI.* The nether-faced devil incorporates a variety of semiotic codes, as I will show, but I find that in the case of *1 Henry VI* the cartoonish La Pucelle can be better understood if we contextualize her appearance and her literal commerce with demons not just within our historicist sense of Tudor dramatic propaganda or according to insights from modern gender theory, but within the historically warranted medieval iconographic matrix centered on the demonization of female physiology. Medieval and early modern stage fiends who sport faces on their crotches and bellies represent a plausibly "feminized" notion of the demonic; in corollary terms, problematic or evil women equate to a demonization of the feminine.

I will come to this conclusion in order to give more depth and solidity to the now commonplace notion, made by feminist Shakespeareans including (especially) Phyllis Rackin, that Joan la Pucelle exhibits or signifies a broad but diffuse sense of "the demonic" that threatens masculine or paternal order, English national sensibility, vertical class structure, and even the philosophical stability afforded by a kind of Realism seen residually in the nostalgic project of the First Tetralogy.[5] No doubt the "demonic" has taken on the chic of terms including "power" or "subversion" or "subjectivity" in contemporary Shakespeare criticism: it has been inflated out of all useful proportion and lives, as Bardolph would say, out of all reasonable compass. I want to restore to the term the iconographic texture or edge evident in the semiotics of the medieval demonic, an edge evident, though often tacitly, through Shakespeare's characterization of Joan and her fiendish familiars in *1 Henry VI.*

At the defeat of the French in Act 5, La Pucelle—who is indisputably a sorceress in this play—calls on her familiars for protection and deliverance one last time. References to "fiends" are made by both the French and the English characters in the play as casual rhetorical flourishes; indeed, even Talbot is called a "fiend of hell" (2.1.46) well before he brands Joan a "fiend of France and hag of all despite" (3.2.52).⁶ But Shakespeare wants to materialize demons in this play directly:

> The regent conquers and the Frenchmen fly.
> Now help, ye charming spells and periapts,
> And ye choice spirits that admonish me,
> And give me signs of future accidents.
>   *Thunder.*
> You speedy helpers, that are substitutes
> Under the lordly monarch of the north,
> Appear, and aid me in this enterprise!
>   *Enter Fiends.*
> This speedy and quick appearance argues proof
> Of your accustomed diligence to me.
> Now, ye familiar spirits, that are culled
> Out of the powerful regions under earth,
> Help me this once, that France may get the field.
>   *They walk, and speak not.*
> O hold me not with silence over-long!
> Where I was wont to feed you with my blood
> I'll lop a member off and give it you,
> In earnest of a further benefit,
> So you do condescend to help me now.
>   *They hang their heads.*
> No hope to have redress? My body shall
> Pay recompense if you will grant my suit.
>   *They shake their heads.*
> Cannot my body or blood-sacrifice
> Entreat you to your wonted furtherance?
> Then take my soul—my body, soul, and all—
> Before that England give the French the foil.
>   *They depart.*
> See, they forsake me! Now the time is come,
> That France must vail her lofty-plumèd crest,
> And let her head fall into England's lap. (5.3.1–26)

Joan's speech and the scene's interlinear directions give us the fullest material expression of devils on Shakespeare's stage; the scene is remarkable if only for the specificity of the directional rubrics, rubrics that prompt precise choreographic or kinesic effect of a sort rarely witnessed in

Shakespeare even with his human characters. Only two other conjurations in the Shakespeare canon involving full demonic materialization can compare, though faintly: these include the witch Margery Jourdain's calling up of the demon Asmath, or Asmodeus, in *2 Henry VI,* 1.4.27–43; and *Macbeth*'s interpolated invocation of Hecate by the First Witch (3.5.1–36), along with the subsequent appearance of Hecate and the three spirits or apparitions (4.1.39–44, 71–94).

Several sorciological topoi find expression in the Act 5 conjuration: the spirits serve Joan by giving her foreknowledge (cueing her in on which battles to avoid or cut short—such as the curtailed single combat with Talbot in 1.5.19); they stand in as proxies for Satan, traditional "monarch of the north"; they are undoubtedly infernal or netherworldly yet astonishingly rapid at arriving here or there in this world (like all angels or devils known to St. Thomas Aquinas in his *Summa Theologica*—more on this below); and their commerce with witches works on the currency of (literally and figurally) traded "limbs," portions of flesh, body parts. Above all, the physical realness of La Pucelle's fiends is not to be disputed—thus insuring, as criticism has long noted, the character's guilt as a witch who enjoyed wrongful victory over the English all along. If the text leaves us unclear as to how she overcame Talbot in single combat, this final demonic materialization casts nothing in doubt about the fiends' reality, specifically their physicality which has to do with everything from kinesis to their commercial stake in portions of human anatomy.

What of the implicit imagery of these dramatized devils? What of their material production on the stage of the early 1590s? We do not have a costume description of the devils in *1 Henry VI,* but I am convinced that they would have been nether-faced. The best "journalistic" authority on the speculative visual rendering of the Shakespearean stage has been, for six decades, C. Walter Hodges. Though his own writings do not often record the historically iconographic details which might have prompted his ruminations and conjectural reconstructions, his choice of the nether-faced devil for the Act 5 conjuration scene—witness Figure 3—is decisive and powerful. His verbal explanation of Shakespeare's fiends also makes a tendentious connection between Shakespeare's stage and its medieval precursors:

> The fiendish costumes would have been made up in canvas or leather, cut into fish scales and painted black, red or green. The masks and headdresses would have been of leather or moulded parchment. A collection of all these would have been a permanent part of the playhouse wardrobe, and it may be imagined that some items may even have been bought in from the surplus stock of the ancient mystery plays. They were, after all, timeless in their use.[7]

"Timeless in their use." The phrase suggests what might be less kindly thought of as the "cliché" iconography constituting such "surplus stock" left hanging around after the 1570s—when the last of the mystery plays were mounted once they had been illegalized.

The sixteenth-century civic craft guild records also lack the preciseness of iconographic description regarding costumes and masks which one might wish for; but they provide what I believe is general reference to nether faces. Filling in the holes in Hodges' description, I adduce a typical payment record from the Coventry accounts:

> 1536, it. for mendyng the demones heed vj d; 1440, it. for peyntyng and makyng new ij damons heds (inter alia); 1556, payd for a demons face ij s . . . payd for makyng the ij devells facys x s.[8]

The summarized record covering the cost of demons indicates occasional payments for single faces or heads, but more interestingly, there seem to be customary indications for two faces at a pop. To be sure, these could be for two costumes (since demons in the Coventry plays often appear, as do many kinds of characters, in groups of two or three) or for one costume representing a Janus-type polyfaced devil. But of equal likelihood, the record could refer to a devil's costume that sports an upper face and a lower face, exactly as Hodges envisions regarding the remnant costumes possibly used in the staging of the *1 Henry VI* conjuration scene. But does such literal and staged manifestation of demonic physiology have as its counterpart a purely discursive vitality in Shakespearean drama?

Other Shakespeare plays indeed furnish leads. We might, for instance, read the nether-faced devil as a visual pun or rebus evident in the culmination of Falstaff and Bardolph's brief flyting match in *1 Henry IV*. After trading mutual insults on each other's "demonic" physiognomies—Falstaff has a swollen, Lord-of-Misrule physique while Bardolph has a fiery, fiendish face—the two thieves come to a curious conclusion:

> *Bardolph*: 'Sblood, I would my face were in your belly.
> *Falstaff*: God-a-mercy! So should I be sure to be heartburned. (3.3.55–58)

The rebus characterizes Shakespearean poetics at its best: what might have been a literal and actual image on the primary or outermost level of textual representation finds transformation—and really a kind of defusing—merely as an ornamental rhetorical trope rigged, in this case, purely for comic effect.

But the discursive rebus of the nether face can have more ghastly and terrifying ends while it can translate to a more direct figural form—a conscious metonymy. Shakespeare directly equates female nether anatomy with an imaginary face in Lear's famous conceit of the vagina as a "face between [woman's] forks" (4.6.121), an image which, within ten lines, takes on even fuller equation with the bodies of devils and the pit of hell ("Down from the waist they are Centaurs,/ Though women all above./ But to the girdle do the gods inherit;/ Beneath is all the fiends'./ There's hell, there's darkness, there's the sulphurous pit. . . ." (126–133). The misogynistic conflation or exchange of the feminine and the demonic constitutes the heart of the nether-faced devil's semiotic function—a matter which will completely occupy my discussion shortly.⁹ The conceit from *King Lear*, however, verges on the erasure of rebus and the movement virtually to pornography since little ambiguity is left regarding the theme and emotional pitch of the figural reference.

A far subtler instance of the nether-face rebus organizing the discourse of a character's speech occurs in *Othello*. Here is a figurative and fugitive image that has perplexed critics as to its actual significance. Discursively toying with the idea of the found-out Iago as a devil, Othello remarks:

I look down towards his feet; but that's a fable.
If that thou be'st a devil, I cannot kill thee.

> Wounds Iago.
> (5.2.287–288)

It would seem on first reading that Othello's conceit refers to the proverbial cloven hooves of the devil, though critics have argued that the passage indicates the disfigured lower limbs characteristic of criminal physiognomy as well as the well-known deformed anatomy of the classical hag.¹⁰ However, given the linguistic universe of *Othello*, a universe which does not seem to admit the rebus of the sort seen in the comical Shakespearean flyting match, the passage may suggest the anatomy of the nether-faced devil acknowledges demonic presence by latching onto certain fixed rhetorical formulas in Othello's discourse. The preposition "towards" in line 287 connotes the downward-moving gaze of the hypothetical viewer (the discursive "Othello") fixed upon an imagined devil standing before him. This involves an ocular dynamic that constitutes the rhetorical or phenomenological structure of the conventional blazon, the descriptive trope which signals "movement" of a viewer's eyes in head-to-toe or toe-to-head sequence. Othello does not say, "I look down *at* his feet," which would more emphatically indicate cloven hooves. The blazonic rhetoric of that single line, rather, only mutely suggests an anatomical feature—the crotchface—that is part and parcel of the demon's body; but apprehension of such anatomy would be unvoiceable in this play.

Given these plausible discursive appearances of the nether-faced devil in other Shakespeare plays, we should look for a rebus closer to the mimetic realization of the image made by C. Walter Hodges somewhere in the discursive armature of *1 Henry VI*. In Joan's admission that her demonic familiars have abandoned her, we might have a potential candidate:

See, they forsake me! Now the time is come
That France must vail her lofty-pluméd crest
And let her head fall into England's lap. (5.3.24–26)

Figure 1:
From *The Purgatory of Saint Patrick*. Paris, 1530.
Courtesy of Dover Books.

Perhaps it is no coincidence that Joan's metaphor of national capitulation (pun intended)—a severed head dropped into someone else's lap—comes exactly when the fiends have departed from the stage: Hodges's face-crotched fiends go down through the stage's trapdoor while a poetic line of soliloquy coming out of Joan's mouth contains an occulted, paranomastic reference to the fantastic beings we the audience have just been scrutinizing with our eyes. And if the word *periapt* (line 2), which means an amulet or fetish worn on the body to ward off spirits or to work magic, connotes the iconography of the polyfaced devil because it could be linked in Protestant thought to the multi-faced, papistical imagery of ubiquitously worn Catholic saints' medals or wax effigies,[11] then the mimetic appearance of the fiends on stage is cordoned off not just as a sort of dumb show but as an inset episode *framed* by a pair of very oblique, tacit images in the text's discursive field—the images of little faces displayed on the surface of the body in the wrong places. This pair of images, periapt and head-in-lap (5.3.2 and 26), might itself signify poly- or nether-faced humanoid anatomy, the imaginary anatomy par excellence of the medieval devil.

In medieval and Renaissance art and literature, devils or demons could appear in any form—human, humanoid, zoomorphic, theriomorphic, or chimaeric, even amorphous—though they usually sported cliché charred black skins, claws, hooves, horns, bat wings, and barbed tails.[12] The particulars of disfigurement, exaggeration, and monstrosity predominated with the intent of repelling and terrifying. Just as hagiographic icons inspired veneration, serenity, and sublime feeling, demonic icons provoked revulsion, disgust, and panic. The devil's prime social or ideological function in the Middle Ages and Renaissance, with English culture taking no exception, was the sowing of fear.[13]

But what of the equally cliché and widespread image of the nether-faced devil? To be sure, the phantasmagoric image could be as comic and absurd as it was surreal, alien, and scary. This is a fact long grasped not just in early modern but in medieval representation, well prior to any examples evident in the Renaissance English cultural setting.

For example, the nether-faced devil appears as a humorous literary rebus well before Shakespeare and as early as Dante's *Inferno*. Towards the end of the final canto, when Vergil and Dante arrive at the earth's core, at Hell's center, we get an extraordinary wordplay treating the actual crux or crotch of Satan's gigantic, icebound body:

When we had reached the point at which the thigh/
Revolves, just at the swelling of the hip,/
My guide, with heavy strain and rugged work,/
Reversed his head to where his legs had been/
And grappled on the hair .... (34.76–80)[14]

To exit Hell, Vergil and Dante must turn their own bodies' heads over heels (or "heads-for-hips," *testa* for *zanche* in the Italian) and climb up Satan's fur once they have passed through the gravitational center of the planet. Vergil and Dante must effect this vertical exchange of their heads and crotches at the moment they arrive at Satan's crotch, the physiological site that might as well bear an ugly visage as does the traditional image of the nether-faced devil.

But more importantly, the image's source as a serious and actual visualization might be Hildegard of Bingen's vision of the Antichrist in the twelfth-century *Scivias*:

> And I saw again the figure of a woman whom I had previously seen in front of the altar that stands before the eyes of God; she stood in the same place, but now I saw her from the waist down. And from her waist to the place that denotes the female, she had various scaly blemishes; and in that latter place was a black and monstrous head. It had fiery eyes, and ears like an ass's, and nostrils and mouth like a lion's; it opened wide its jowls and terribly clashed its horrible iron-colored teeth.[15]

As the world's final and apocalyptic "substitute" for the Devil, Hildegard's female Antichrist suitably proffers an anatomy which revitalizes what was probably, by the twelfth century, the insipid or hackneyed imagery of the Devil as humanoid monster—even though the crotch face itself would suffer to become a cliché and the association of the feminine with the demonic would take on still greater weight.

Nonetheless this intriguing and widespread nether-faced devil, prevalent from the thirteenth through the sixteenth centuries in European art, has so far provoked only minimal description or analysis among modern historians, iconographers, or literary and cultural critics.[16] Jeffrey Burton Russell flatly declares: "[t]he monstrous Devil, with horns on knees, calves, or ankles and with faces on chest, belly, and buttocks reflects Lucifer's inner moral monstrosity."[17] On this same note, Barbara D. Palmer writes that medieval devils are "multi-headed or multi-faced to suggest their duplicity."[18] "Monstrosity" and "duplicity" so stated underline the moral or ethical purpose of medieval demonology, a purpose well served by the affective or aesthetic impact of devils with nether faces. However, rarer in contemporary commentary is the direct connecting of the diabolical nether face to specific scriptural passages—as in the case of the Pauline condemnation of those sinners who "serve their *bellies*."[19] More often than not, the image of the nether-faced devil has been merely ignored in modern scholarship.

On a more promising note, the nether-faced devil has drawn the attention of folklorists and students of the grotesque. As the most comprehensive and up-to-date iconographic project of its sort, a 1995 essay collection in German included several lengthy essays treating fool figures (*Zanner* and

Blecher), drolleries, ass-baring contortionists (*Hinternentblösser*), acrobatic dancers, gargoyles, scatology, the polyfaced little monsters of ornamental manuscript *entrelacements*, and the malformed creatures from travel literature. Especially of importance in this last category are the infamous Blemmyae or Acephali—well known in Shakespearean discourse as Othello's mention of "men whose heads/ Do grow beneath their shoulders" attests (1.3.144–145)—who were thought to inhabit Asian and African hinterlands.[20] These imaginary humanoids, believed by ancient and medieval geographers to lack heads but to have big faces on their bellies or torsos, are the closest iconographic relatives to the nether-faced or polyfaced devils who likewise sprout faces from chests and bellies and from thighs, crotches, buttocks, knees, elbows, and ankles as well.[21] Yet the crotch-face predominates as a subspecies of the general diabolical polyface, with the belly-face and the rump-face following close behind in quantity— a summary fact well captured in Hodges's varied visualization of Joan's nether-faced fiends standing in their semicircle.

However, the programmatic consolidation of nether-faced devils with Blemmyae diminishes their demonic properties. Such demonic properties of course obsessed scholastic medieval discussion of the "bodies" possessed by angels and demons; they must also dominate contemporary semiological models that seek to articulate the rhetorical, structural, and gendered constitution of the medieval or early-modern nether-faced devil. The phenomenology of the grotesque with its subordinate (and diminished) category, the demonic, tends to underwrite an anthropology of premodern culture which we brand Bakhtinian; here we encounter the theorization of all cultural practices (artistic, literary, or festive) that are inversional, irreverent, disruptive, or vulgar. But such inversion of course reinscribes or fortifies the status quo of the "real" social world that maintains itself apart from or prior to art, literature, or festival.[22] Conversely, the realization that the grotesque cannot be extricated from the demonic (the view promoted by Wolfgang Kayser)[23] partakes of a more historically localized tradition in the understanding of bodily disfigurement or inversion. The first course (Bakhtinian) in the study of the nether-faced devil has reached, in my opinion, near-exhaustion; the second course (Kayserian) still holds great theoretical potential for the grotesque demonic.

Iconographers who assimilate the nether-faced devil to the polyfaced devil diminish or elide, as I have suggested, the image's own plenary semiotic potentials. Therefore, setting it aside as a specific object of inquiry in its own right should open the way for an expanded and enriched understanding of the image that can more fully draw on the resources of contemporary theory and that can illuminate fugitive images and symbolic relations in the plays of Shakespeare. I therefore propose a semiological treatment of the image that will show how it allegorizes the late medieval, polarized representation of gender and sexuality. As a widespread representation, the nether-faced devil builds itself out of the cultural poetics of misogyny drawn ultimately from late-classical and medieval sources.

I have speculated that the earliest description of the nether-faced devil appears in Hildegard of Bingen's *Scivias*. Some direction for understanding Hildegard's visionary image may come from near-contemporaneous, Thomistic theories about angelic or demonic beings. Many theological and philosophical writers up through the High Middle Ages took up the subject of devils, but St. Thomas Aquinas has provided the most incisive and authoritative conclusions. In line with prior opinion (St. Augustine, in the main), Thomas has it in the *Summa Theologica* that the angels are immaterial, incorruptible, and eternal.[24] As sempiternal beings, they could all be thought of as confined to one generation. Angels need not exist in large, self-regenerating numbers, as nature commands of naturally produced, mortal animals, and their populations could in effect be tiny in number (1.50.4). Not driven by the mandates of biological nature, they therefore have no need for reproduction and procreation. This conclusion suggests in turn that as living organisms, angels or demons would have no need for sexual organs (although in some circumstances they can imitate sexual behavior, as in the folkloric *incubus* or *succubus* and the biblical *nephilim*).[25] The transplanted face might therefore function as a humorous sign for the idea that angels or devils are monogenerational; not needing genitals to produce a generationally subsequent, replicant individual whose identity would be synecdochally signified by an individuated face, the devil possesses that already-present synecdochal face right on an imaginary, "parental" body at the presumed site of sexual or procreational potency. The supernumerary face stands in place of the entity's superfluous (and thus absent) genitals.

Furthermore, as Thomas would have it, the "bodily" features of angels who were believed to have appeared to humans had no structural or substantial essence in themselves anyway; the appearances of angels in humanoid form had always involved an "imaginary" process whereby their visible forms existed only as phantasmata in the minds of humans who had beheld them (1.51.2). So in lacking reproductive organs, the elaborate nether-faced devil, which presents phenomenal somatic features only in deference to human perception and cognition, first and foremost signifies what Thomas understood as the angel's or demon's ontic status as an "ever mobile intelligent substance" (1.50.1). This designation could produce, in the domain of visualization, the rampant theriomorphism so characteristic of all medieval and Renaissance devils. As a mental or psychic intelligence always "on the move," the devil aptly appears, via logical correspondence, as a body whose contours or features are fluid, mobile, plastic, chaotic, transformative. They come and go very rapidly too (making trapdoors in stages a histrionic necessity). Demonic duplicity and mobility are thus as much ontological categories as they are moral ones, according to Thomas.

The angelology in Thomas Aquinas's *Summa* goes on to provide supplemental explanatory models of this chaotic demonic "body." After all, Thomas (as well as Augustine) had emphasized that Satan and his angelic followers fell from the realm of heaven, from the unmediated presence of God to the lower realm of air or, still farther, to the subterrestrial region of infernal privation and punishment. The vertical *fall* found fitting expression as a spatial or somatic association of the evil angels with the lower or nether in general. Yet the vitality of the lower would manifest itself as desire or will to overcome the upper; devils desire, in the spirit of Milton's Moloch, to reascend the vertical cosmic ladder and retake their heavenly homeland. So they are nether creatures whose behavioral proclivity is the energetic and preemptive subversion or inversion of God's cosmos (as well as its corresponding microcosmos, the body).

It is fitting, then, that numerous images from medieval art and literature convey this set of ideas not only by representing devils lamenting their everlasting nether conditions at the earth's nadir, but also by picturing upside-down Lucifers about to crash into our planet. Dante, for example, follows this tradition by placing his icebound Satan feet toward Heaven inside the earth's geophysiology because the angel had fallen headlong from Heaven into the earth's southern hemisphere, causing an impact that formed the concave cone of Hell, the antipodean (in relation to Jerusalem) convex mountain of purgatory, and the aggregate mass of northern-hemisphere continents opposite the impact site (*Inferno* 34.121–126).

So in sum, the demonic body, sometimes upside down, sometimes nether-faced, signifies the concept of the inversional itself. The "demonic" means the switching of the upper for the lower, the top for the bottom: the Devil has fallen from the top of the macrocosm to its stratified bottom; he has also suffered the "fall" of his own microcosmic or bodily apex, his head or face, to the bottom of his torso as a signature of his desire to replace the uppermost level of the cosmos with his own secondariness, his own baseness. This condition resonates in metaphorical terms and, more to my purposes here, in literalized terms. Having an actual face instead of a backside, vulva, or penis, the demonic body exists as a sign of the fallen, twisted, upside-down mentality and spirituality of the rebellious Satan; it stands as microcosmic emblem of the whole macrocosmos Satan attempted to invert and contaminate.

The drift of modern criticism about devils adheres closely to Thomistic protocols. Following Maximilian Rudwin's conclusions, Barbara Palmer declares devils to be exemplary of "disintegration, fragmentation, incongruity, antithesis, exaggeration, adaptation, juxtaposition, and recombination"[26]—each term boiling down to both literal and figural senses of inversion. That is, demonic inversions are indeed purely symbolic in that they evoke the carnivalesque social dynamics articulated by Bakhtin;[27] but they are also less abstract, "intrasomatic" (the body itself has upside-down anatomy) and "extrasomatic" or "choreographic" (the demonic body inverts other physical things long after it has suffered its own vertical, downward trajectory through cosmic space and its attitudinal switching of its feet for its head). At the apocalyptic conclusion of *Piers Plowman*, for example, Antichrist "cam þanne, and al þe crop of truþe/ Torned it vp so doun and ouertilte þe roote" (B.20.53–54).[28]

However, let it also be said that the semiotics of inversion evident in the image of the nether-faced devil—that is, the interaction of fundamental binary oppositions like the upper and the lower exchanged—can be understood as the semiotic mechanism of structural self-reflection or self-reflexivity *par excellence*. The conceptual conflation of the demonic with the semiotic in medieval thought exists in this image, in the orthodox linkage between trope or rhetoric and the demonic, and in the conjoint symbolization of the feminine—a chain of associations this article will take up shortly. Physical reference and rhetorical trope neatly flip-flop in the conceptional realm of the demonic, as we have already seen regarding Shakespearean poetics. The demonic body serves as a sign of sign-making itself, for when the putatively fundamental binary constants of semiosis (such as upper and lower) can be highlighted and transposed, an element of vital self-reflexivity can be seen to inhabit the whole iconographic process at hand.

Apart from hypotheses about monogeneration and vertical inversion, a third semiotic moment—one not to be eclipsed in regards to the paradigm so far delineated—emerges from Thomas's findings: as I have already noted, Thomas stressed that any "forms" devils or angels supposedly possessed were imaginary, illusory, phantasmatic. Devils in particular would cultivate the dramatic powers needed for efficacious materialization; they are masterful at projecting themselves as shadows or images, as insubstantial and flattened but convincing *picturae*. This idea gained great vitality in the popular arena of later medieval demonology. Aron Gurevich summarizes the importance of this demonic quasi-body:

> It is impossible to see the devil in his actual form, as a spirit, with mortal eyes. . . . But to the living the devil and his servants appear in any form. . . . Their capability for metamorphosis is unlimited. However, a demon assuming human form cannot be seen from behind, *since demons do not have backs and always withdraw by walking backwards. They are hollow inside.*[29]

Gurevich draws this notion from Caesarius of Heisterbach's well-known *Dialogus miraculorum*, a rich collection of saints' lives and miracle tales composed in the twelfth century. And the formulation, when expounded a little further, reveals another conceptual play of logical oppositions central to medieval metaphysical thought: devils are surface-only "projections." (I suppose we could say that, in Euclidean terms, their optical manifestations are "two-dimensional" phenomena, despite Thomas's own claims that angels and demons are extra-Euclidean beings that would "contain" three-dimensional beings such as humans.)[30]

Everyone knows that the devil's "presence" in the material world is, as Thomas insisted, illusory. So those imaginary materializations of devils are masks, *prosopa*, facades or *faciae.* That is to say, if there is no actual, representable posterior opposite to an anterior, why should the demonic body have an anatomical posterior—a buttocks, a backside, a bottom, a fundament, a pudendum, genitals? Devils have no backs, no insides, no bottoms. As psychogenic illusions or *phantasmata,* they are tops, fronts, shells, heads, faces. What better sign to convey this ludic deconstruction of natural bodily physio-logic than a head or face put in the place of a bottom?

This explanation, however, further supports my idea that the nether-faced devil exists as an occulted sign of semiosis—not by signifying a symbolic manipulation of the upper/lower binarism but rather by the binarism of interiority/exteriority.

In turn, the conclusion that the devil serves as an occulted sign of semiosis collaborates with contemporary theoretical understanding of powerful but latent rhetorical tropes: the anatomical reassignment of the natural face's location incorporates the trope *anachorism* ("out of place")—the displacing of some object or element from a space in which it properly belongs. (The cliché "I have eyes in the back of head," which we grumble at unruly children, employs anachorism; yet Spenser's geographical juxtaposition of a low-altitude willow with a high-altitude pine in an epic tree catalog is equally anachoristic.) In addition, the descriptive designation that the multiplied visages of a polyfaced or nether-faced devil involve making faces, of course, broadens the denotation of the monumental rhetorical trope *prosopopeia* (Greek *prosopon poein,* "to make a face"). The making of a nether face enacts in occulted form the device championed by Paul de Man and allied deconstructionists as the "master trope of poetic discourse,"[31] the rhetorical figure or trope of troping. Virtually all the semiotic models of the nether-faced devil so far described enjoy structural parallelism with this rhetorical algorithm: nether faces self-reflexively signify the semiotics of binary semes disposed or exchanged (upper/lower and inner/outer); they also self-reflexively signify, and are mutually signified by, the trope prosopopeia, the trope taken by de Man and others to represent the very foundational semes (exteriors trying to contain or playing off interiors) of rhetoric or troping.[32] Moreover, increased self-reflexivity rests in the fact that the lexical label "prosopopeia," the culprit in a chain of so many *figurative* and occultational processes, appears in the image of the nether face as the *literalized* visual rebus of its own lexical or semantic constitution. To repeat, the devil's nether face visually echoes the poetic or pictorial move to "make a face," an anachoristic face which thus advertises its own faceness.

Figure 2:
From *Histories Prodigieusis*. Paris, 1560.
Courtesy of Dover Books.

Whereas de Man always located the main significance of such figural faceness in the register of voice, the demonological realization that nether faces could be the sites of actual speech further underlined such bodily ana-chorism in accordingly humorous ways. Ambroise Paré's 1575 *Des Monstres et prodiges* helped to get the modern medical subfield of teratol-ogy under way, particularly in its notable description of a man out of whose belly grew a human head—a description that might remind one of Blemmyae, but that makes an effort to usher in a new and empirical dis-course—medical teratology, the science of anatomical deformity. On the other hand, Paré's subsequent declaration concerning the bodies of persons suffering demonic possession puns wryly on the medieval stock image of the demonic body endowed with its nether, potentially loquacious mouth: "Those who are possessed of Demons speak—their tongues having been torn out of their mouths—through the belly, through the natural parts [gen-itals] and they speak various unknown languages."[33]

Nether faces imply nether speech; yet it is curious how Joan la Pucelle's familiars "speak" not vocally and aurally, but by *shaking their heads* alone! If mystery-play devils such as Lucifer and Tutivillus, as well as typical Renaissance stage devils such as Greene's oracular demon or the bombastic Mephistopheles of Marlowe, are known for their loquacity, then Shakespeare has gone another step in estranging only select cliché ideas about devils and voice in early modern theatricality. Nether-visaged dia-bolicality and monstrosity entail speech governed by those figures, so inventoried in Renaissance rhetoric, called *bomphiologia* and *cacophonia*.[34] But Shakespeare ironizes this custom, giving us instead diabolical mimes.

All of the foregoing semiotic descriptions of the nether-faced devil hold promise but they pull us away from the ends of this essay—a fuller illumi-nation of the femininity of Shakespeare's Joan and her fiends. As a witch, Joan enjoys the service of a demonic *familiar*—a term we need to put under more philological pressure since it captures the sense of maternality hinted at in Joan's characterization. The term, first used in English demonological writing by Shakespeare's contemporary Reginald Scot, connotes social, even biological kinship (*OED*, "familiar," B.3). Demonic familiars could take on the guises of pets, though equally often they would behave as if they were a witch's *children*, even to the point of nursing from their mis-tress's body, sucking blood from her supposed witches marks, as Gary Wills has emphasized in his analysis of Joan la Pucelle's authentic sorciological representation in *1 Henry VI*.[35]

This focus on the imagery of maternality takes us to the obvious, and to one of my best insights into this project's iconographical puzzle: the image of a head or face emerging from a groin might suggest human parturition. Note the particulars: the nether face looks forward; it is in line with the axis of the demon's body; and many times it replicates or suggests the contours or traits characterizing the demon's upper face (see again Figure 1). In the language of obstetrics (that is, the masculizcd, professional transformation of medieval and early modern midwifery),[36] the demonic nether face or nether head emerges from the demonic body according to the manner of a typical maternal labor which culminates in symmetrical *presentation*. By "typical," obstetrics means the delivery enjoyed by a newborn who has emerged in that preferred posture or position clinically termed "anterior-vertex presentation." Parturitional presentation is complete once the newborn achieves what is called "internal rotation" followed by "translabial extension."[37] Many devils with faced crotches display a variety of stylizations and scalings but they all allegorize, I want to theorize, this quotidian, universal, human experience, the experience of labor known by midwives especially. To be sure, the nether-faced devil conceived as a parturitional symbol and thus an allegory of human maternality captures a "timeless" experience, to use C. Walter Hodges's own word.

My argument at this juncture proceeds by the systematic recognition of innuendo. Yet the visual evidence at times pushes beyond mere innuendo. Perhaps in no other representation of the maternalized devil is there a more emphatic combination of all these clinical elements—anterior-vertex presentation, familial isomorphy between two faces, and the further feminization of the demonic body via the inclusion of pendant female breasts that seem ready for nursing—than in the intriguing image of enthroned Satan (Figure 2) from Pierre Boaistuau's treatise on demonology and teratology, *Histoires prodigieuses*, first published in 1560.[38] We could even interpret the diabolical throne as a medieval birthing chair, common up until the middle seventeenth century,[39] and the attendant *Bramines* as midwives; the one on the right even strokes the devil's cheek, perhaps in a gesture of comfort.

Whereas the visual representations of the nether-faced devil undergo such maternalization in early modern texts such as Boaistuau's popular *Histoires,* literary or dramatic analogs are less blatant but still unmistakably akin. For instance, the Middle English morality play *Wisdom* implies the disfigured, sin-marred female personification Soul to be a demonized parturitional body from whose loins emerge actual devils. A manuscript rubric reads, "Here rennyt owt from [v]ndyr þe horrybyll mantyll of þe SOULL seven small boys in þe lyknes of dewyllys and so retorne ageyn" (ll. 912 ff).[40] If the critical findings of Ribner or Spivack still hold water, the seminal morality play *Wisdom* furnishes a direction regarding the allegory of demonic maternality used in the characterization of Shakespeare's Joan.[41]

It is worth noting too that, what obstetrics construes as typical and healthy presentation resonates with the scholastic analysis I summarized concerning St. Thomas Aquinas's pronouncements. The fetus's final, prenatal placement in the womb, its subsequent descent through the birth canal, and its final emergence characterized by symmetrical alignment (that is, it finds itself quite upside down and backwards) adumbrate the orthodox cosmological narrative of the Devil's vertical drop through the cosmos compounded by direct bodily *inversion*. Devils are the upside-down-and-backward agents in the medieval universe, as are all neonatal humans when they enter their world. And because the *typological* relationship among everyday human birth, Christ's incarnation, and Lucifer's fall from Heaven would have been evident as a point of catechism (all three "descents" signify the intrusion of spirit into the subempyrean domain of materiality and the switching of what had been high for that which is low), I argue in turn that the conceptual mechanism governing the demonization of maternality or the maternalization of the demonic may well be traditional patristic typology.

In sum, the conflation or interchangeability of the demonic body and the female body bespeaks the tidy patristic equation built on the perceived biblical relationship between women and Satan the tempter. Tertullian provides the definitive version of this equation in his *De Cultu feminarum*:

You are the Devil's gateway: you are the unsealer of that (forbidden) tree: you are the first deserter of the divine law: you are she who persuaded him whom the Devil was not valiant enough to attack. You destroyed so easily God's image, man.[42]

The fact that the female body of Eve served as the cosmic entry point for the Devil into this world permitted the fathers' unrestrained analogical license in promulgating a mythology of the female demonic, the demonic feminine, one of the most permanent and powerful expressions of "medieval misogyny," as R. Howard Bloch has identified it.[43] As a figurative gateway for the Devil, Eve's body is opened to a subsequent tropological penetration: all women, in the phenomenology of their bodies and specific body parts, have inscribed or reified the *modus operandi* of the Devil. The chain of analogical essentializations thereby incorporates the parturitional body. What had probably always been the most essentialized representation of women—the convulsed and agonized female body at the moment of childbirth—could have become yet another occulted version of the demonized female or the feminized demon.[44]

Other versions of this demonic female, such as the ubiquitous image of the woman-headed serpent dramatized in the mystery plays (recall the serpent in the Chester play of Adam and Eve)[45] and reproduced in hundreds of manuscript illuminations and Renaissance paintings,[46] would have been more blunt than, though ultimately unequal to, the nether-faced devil in semiotic potency. Unlike the rouge-faced and often languorous-looking creature who leers at Adam while trying to hide its coils among the limbs of the Edenic Tree of Knowledge, the parturient devil signifies woman differentiated or alienated from man not in mythological but in everyday ways: none of the commonplace "feminine" markers comprising the sexual dimorphism of essentializing medieval gender aesthetics—cosmetic beauty, supple limbs, curvaceous anatomy, smaller stature, even the lack of the penis—compares to the parturient's body as a decisive marker of biological gender and sexual differentiation. Whereas gender finds construction as a social process, the sexed body of the parturient seeks to achieve a differential status from the male that is biologically essential and foundational. The moment at which the human neonate's head emerges from its mother's womb serves as the reductive sign of sexual differentiation *par excellence*; it is the moment that could not be faked even by a male body trying to "perform" gendered female roles or sexed female physiology.

Parturition names the site or scene experienced by just about every human (excluding caesarian-section newborns), though witnessed only by women, by premodern midwives, mothers, sisters, aunts. In medieval culture, it was a view inaccessible and "invisible" to the male gaze—as historians of obstetrics and medicine like Renaté Blumenfeld-Kosinski and others have demonstrated. Indeed the earliest and most prominent Middle English gynecological or obstetrical treatise, the *Trotula*, contains only stylized, cutaway views of the fetus *in utero*; never does the text illustrate actual parturition.[47]

So if residual patristic typology powers up even early modern, residual representations of the female as the demonic (and the demonic as the female), the parturitional body need not be altered or morphed very much in order to signify the demonic body—the body which itself already signifies all that is fallen, degenerate, unholy, invisible, unviewable, taboo (to males), toxic, and alien. Writing too on the important connections among early-modern sorciology, the hysterical fantasy of head-genital exchange (which fascinated Freud), and human maternality, Hélène Cixous and Catherine Clément have reached the same conclusion concerning our culture's long-standing symbolic representation of "women . . . the bearers of the greatest norm, that of reproduction, [who] embody *also* the anomaly."[48]

It is curious that in C. Walter Hodges's memorable illustration (Figure 3) of the Act 5 conjuration scene in *1 Henry VI* we count seven devils standing about Joan la Pucelle in a semicircle. They accordingly "hang their heads," while the first devil, who faces Joan, seems to replicate her posture. The choreography of Hodges's reconstruction summarizes the semiotic system I have so far articulated.

But the equation between demonic body and parturitional body arises one final time in another signal moment of dialogue when Joan pleads to her English captors, apostrophizing herself along the way:

Will nothing turn your unrelenting hearts?
Then, Joan, discover thine infirmity

That warranteth by law to be thy privilege:
I am with child, ye bloody homicides;
Murder not then the fruit within my womb,
Although ye hale me to a violent death. (5.4.59–64)

In a dialogue marked by turns, lies, evasions, confusions (in which Joan variably claims Alençon and Regnier as lovers), she proclaims her pregnancy and thus waiver (by law) from death. Aside from Joan's final curse on the English (86ff), this is the closing image, the ultimate claim of identity, that the text furnishes for her.

Figure 3:
The First Part of King Henry VI, 5.3 Joan La Pucelle deserted by the Fiends.
They hang their heads. From C. Walter Hodges, *Enter the Whole Army*
(Cambridge, 1999). By permission of Cambridge University Press.

The claim—perhaps false—frames the full representation of Joan begun many scenes ago; in her final moment she is a maternal body, while our initial reception of her, in her Act 1 first encounter with the Dauphin, disclosed her (diegetic) narrative of origin, a narrative marked by a sole physical detail. Here, Joan's claim that she was "black and swart" (1.2.84) prior to her spiritual and psychic transformation by Mary can be construed a number of ways. (Michael Hattaway's, for instance, glosses "black" to denote Joan's original "black hair," later disguised by a blonde wig, though I'm inclined to gloss the word merely as "filthy"; the term also denotes deep, peasant-grade suntan, a mark of ugliness in medieval cosmetics.) But the point connotes diabolical embodiment, for medieval and early modern stage fiends were, above all, black in appearance. As part of its semiotic framework, Shakespeare's text deploys iconic signs that demarcate Joan's diabolical agency in particular as well as the feminine status of the demonic and the demonic status of the feminine in general.

I argue, therefore, that the text's figural depictions of Joan's body designate that she herself is a kind of embodied demon or devil, though her unquestionable status as witch and her implicit commerce with the actual demons who appear on stage already configure her as a collage (and decollator, if you will) of human anatomy. When the Duke of York interrogates her as to her pastoral origins, she rejects her father, the old shepherd, who counters by declaring casually that Joan is a "collop of his flesh" (5.4.18), that is, a severed slice of his body. The metaphorical or literal (but programmatic) imagery of lopped limbs, clipped flesh, and spilled blood permeates the conjuration or staging of demons in Act 5. The devils conjured not only share the same ontological stage space with Joan alone, but they have been physiologically spliced, it is implied, onto her actual body during sorciological nursing. Joan promises her body as both food and nursing reservoir to the fiends, drawing on the characteristic imagery of sorciology thought to have been part of the witches' Sabbat and typically displayed in the literary depiction of demonic monsters (witness Errour's ghastly offspring who eat of and nurse from their mother's blood in the first book of Spenser's *Faerie Queene*). The consumption of (co)lopped limbs and spilled blood suggests a range of normative and abnormal practices, from parturition, with its sanguinous theatrics and extrusion of a new body from a maternal body—a "collop," one might imagine—to cannibalism, incestuous intercourse, and matricide:

> Where I was wont to feed you with my blood
> I'll lop a member off and give it you
> In earnest of a further benefit,
> So you do condescend to help me now.
>   They hang their heads.
> No hope to have redress? My body shall
> Pay recompense if you will grant my suit. (5.3.14–19)

The explicit evocation of maternal nursing, of course, lies in the image of blood-feeding habitually practiced by Shakespeare's witches, as Gary Wills has observed. Joan's subsequent offer that her "body shall Pay recompense" implies sexual union, taking the monstrous collage of demonology, sorciology, female sexuality, and maternality yet another horrid step. The text's demonic nether-faced iconography, occulted sign of inversion, chaos, and the maternal feminine, finds reinforcement through Joan's demonic discourse, a discourse inhabited by literal and figural references to the abnormal, monstrous, and maternal too.

My semiological, iconographical, and historical speculations, reinforced by some conventional close readings of Shakespeare's texts, provide what I hope is a larger historical platform on which to situate feminist critical inquiry into the characterization of Joan la Pucelle. The critical or theoretical treatments of the character range from broad ethical judgments to broad ideological claims involving political and social states of affairs in Elizabethan England. That is, major feminist critics have actually paid little attention to the iconographical basis of Shakespeare's dramatical diabology. Critical inquiry has underlined Joan la Pucelle's military prowess, her cunning, and her single-mindedness as she aids the Dauphin Charles against the invading English, embodied in the heroic Talbot. In short, the emphasis of feminist criticism—best summed up in Phyllis Rackin's work on Joan in *Stages of History* and *Engendering a Nation*—has been on the various "social imaginaries" that constitute Joan, from her depiction in the chronicles of Holinshed and Hall (and back further—to putatively more authoritative French sources such as Froissart or de Pizan) to the always-prioritized mimetic representation of her in the dynamic (and thus very seductive) action of *1 Henry VI*. Joan's actions, less so her language, tag her as an emblem of "antihistoricality," antiaristocracy, and a sixteenth-century anxiety about emergent feminine unruliness and dominance.[49] Rackin's summary work responds to or echoes a number of earlier critical projects adumbrating these themes.[50]

In some partial form or another, however, feminist discussions of Shakespeare's Joan key on versions of the deep structure of gender consciousness I have traced back to patristic topoi in this essay. Programmatically, these discussions rearticulate what had been identified by pioneering feminist theorists (such as Simone de Beauvoir or Sherry Ortner) as the motivating binarisms of patriarchal thought: women in general and powerful women in particular get depicted as saints or whores, pucelles or puzels, mothers or murderers, creators or destroyers, nourishers or parasites. Nonetheless, these structural binarisms get explored or situated overwhelmingly in the context of the historical tableau of Shakespeare's socially transitional England (an England remaking itself as an infrastructure of modernity) and far less so with a debt to medieval materials.[51]

All this has amounted to a stream of good and productive scholarship—frequently revolutionary though much of it actually redolent of long-standing and conservative critical views of Joan and women in Shakespeare's history plays.[52] But I maintain that such scholarship will make a greater impact when the further cultural underpinnings of the "demonic"—medieval iconographic and semiotic underpinnings—enjoy fuller exposure. Such readings gain greater impact, too, when the medial and rhetorical structures of Shakespearean histrionic representation are integrated into the iconographic and semiotic picture. C. Walter Hodges and Phyllis Rackin represent two poles of historical reconstructive speculation, but the two are seldom brought together in Shakespeare criticism. I insist that we must bring them together—we must splice them—if we are to understand how Shakespeare's Joan and the bard's employment of the medieval devil, a devil who wears a symbolically overdetermined nether face, energizes *1 Henry VI* in creative ways.

NOTES

[1] Cox, "Devils and Power in Marlowe and Shakespeare" 14. I add that in a parallel study I am treating the "diegetic quarantining" of personification characters in Shakespeare's plays among discrete narrative levels such as framing inductions or embedded stories and plays-within-plays.

[2] See my article, "Theorizing the Mysteries' End," for a discussion of the ideological need to rid the sixteenth-century English public of the common idea that devils were predominantly the stuff of play and theater. As a directive coming from both Church and State, this evacuation of the "artificial demonic," which was never realized or theorized consciously, stemmed from the witch craze—a cultural exercise that was all about making devils more real and serious because they were invisible. I add that the inspiration for this 1997 article came from Stephen Greenblatt's work on witches and devils in Shakespeare; my 1997 article owes a debt to his "Shakespeare Bewitched." I am dismayed at present, therefore, that Greenblatt's article, which focuses on *Macbeth* and Reginald Scot's 1584 *The Discoverie of Witchcraft*, completely avoids discussion of Shakespeare's Joan, though it alludes to *1 Henry VI* but once (111).

[3] See Stevens, *Four Middle English Mystery Cycles*, 6, 203. Stevens champions the idea that the mystery plays were the main contributors of tradition to Shakespeare's history plays; for an earlier and pioneering glimpse of this thesis, see Kastan, "The Shape of Time." But see below, Note 41, for the parallel argument that the morality plays contributed materials more decisively to Shakespeare's histories.

[4] Bevington, "The Domineering Female in *1 Henry VI*"; Turner,

"Characterization in Shakespeare's Early History Plays"; Spivack, *Shakespeare and the Allegory of Evil* 253–254.

[5] Rackin, *Stages of History* 156.

[6] All citations to the text of the play are taken from Hattaway, ed., *The First Part of King Henry VI*.

[7] Hodges, *Enter the Whole Army* 116.

[8] Craig, *Two Coventry Corpus Christi Plays* 100. See also Ingram, ed., *Coventry* 247.

[9]. The exchange of upper and nether anatomy, the casting of genitals as heads or faces, and the linking of the demonic to the feminine, have held special prominence in Freudian psychoanalytical criticism of *Lear*. For the most complete treatment of this critical tradition and its fruits, see Rudnytsky, "'The Darke and Vicious Place,'" 291–311.

[10] Citing texts such as Helkiah Crooke's seventeenth-century *Microcosmographia*, Otten, "What's Wrong with His Feet?" 87–88, argues for reference to criminal physiognomy in *Othello*'s conceit; countering Otten's study by adducing seventeenth-century sorciological literature such as Richard Head's *The Life and Death of Mother Shipton* is Levin, "What's Wrong with His Feet ?" 28-29.

[11] On the Protestant anxiety over Catholic charms and amulets worn on the body, see Thomas, *Religion and the Decline of Magic* 30–31. Displayed animal forms or faces matched human ones in number, for, as Thomas writes: "The most common amulet was the agnus dei, a small wax cake, originally made out of paschal candles and blessed by the Pope, bearing the image of the lamb and flag" (30).

[12] See Russell, *Lucifer: The Devil in the Middle Ages* 209–212, for a good summary of the devil's physical representation in art of the later Middle Ages. An equally succinct summary can be found in Palmer, "The Inhabitants of Hell: Devils" 22–27. Link, *The Devil: The Archfiend in Art from the Sixth to the Sixteenth Century* 35–79, provides a comprehensive but nontechnical summary of diabolical iconography throughout the Middle Ages mainly in terms of pagan source images. But see Russell 129–133, for description of early medieval pictorializations of the devil which tended to be minimally grotesque and more human. For this second section of the present essay, I draw material from my article, "The Nether-Faced Devil and the Allegory of Parturition." I am grateful to the editors for permission to reprint parts of that article in revised form here.

[13] Vatter, *The Devil in English Literature* 44. This also seems to be Russell's view regarding the general utility of diabolical images; see 210 n. 4.

[14] *The Divine Comedy of Dante Alighieri*, trans. Mandelbaum 298–299.

[15] Hildegard von Bingen, *Scivias*, trans. Hart and Bishop, 493. For original text, Führkötter and Carlevaris, eds., *Hildegardis Scivias, Corpus Christianorum Continuatio Mediaevalis* 576–577. I thank Rick Emmerson

for bringing to my attention Hildegard's Antichrist image. See also his "Introduction: The Apocalypse in Medieval Culture," *The Apocalypse in the Middle Ages* 298, for discussion of the Scivias image. For more general discussion of medieval Antichrist iconography, see Emmerson's *Antichrist in the Middle Ages*.

[16] In his elaborate summary of demonic iconography, for instance, Link mentions the devil's nether face only once (71). But following the lead of Russell, I have surveyed photographic reproductions (in the Princeton Index of Christian Art) of over a thousand manuscript illuminations, paintings, and sculptures containing devils that were completed between the twelfth and fourteenth centuries. I concur with Russell that pre-twelfth-century images of devils tend to be minimal and more human, and that the elaborate bestial devil proliferates only in the High Middle Ages. I thus found Anglo-Saxon and Carolingian manuscripts to contain devils that were nothing more than the "small black imp" (see Russell 130) so common to illuminational miniatures. Moreover, images in Greek manuscripts tended to maintain the same minimalistic human devil through the late fourteenth century. If, as Russell asserts, no images of the devil predate the sixth century (129), neither does the nether-faced devil predate the late twelfth-century or postdate the early seventeenth century.

[17] Russell 210.

[18] Palmer 24.

[19] Link 71.

[20] Kröll and Steger, eds., *Mein ganzer Körper ist Gesicht*.

[21] Friedman, *The Monstrous Races in Medieval Art and Thought*, *passim*, provides one of the fullest accounts of the Blemmyae by tracing their Plinian conceptual roots and their eventual centrality in travel tales from the East.

[22] Bakhtin, *Rabelais and His World* 303–367.

[23] Kayser, *The Grotesque in Art and Literature* 19–23.

[24] *Summa Theologica* 1.50.5, ed. Gilby. All subsequent citations from this edition of the *Summa* will be made parenthetically in the text to part, question, and article numbers.

[25] The *incubi*, whose sexual powers would not have been doubted, invoke the rare images of medieval pictorial devils who in fact do have penises, although the depiction of devils with genitals becomes more pronounced in the illustrations to printed books on demonology in the sixteenth and seventeenth centuries. On the masculine sexuality or penile emphasis of the devil's body, see Robbins, *The Encyclopedia of Witchcraft and Demonology* 466–468.

[26] Palmer 27. See also Rudwin, *The Devil in Legend and Literature* 35–53.

[27] See Jonassen, "The Morality Play and the World Upside Down" 19–42, for comparison of (Bakhtinian) symbolic and actual manifestations

of inversion in the English morality plays.

[28] *Piers Plowman: The B Version*, ed. Kane and Donaldson 662–663. For general discussion of Langland's agri-allegory, see Aers, *"Piers Plowman" and Christian Allegory.*

[29] Gurevich, *Medieval Popular Culture* 188; my emphasis.

[30] See *Summa Theologica* 1.50.2 for Thomas's claim that angels, demons, or spirits would in fact "contain" a dimensive and material object with which they came into spatial contact, just as the human soul should be said to contain a person. This idea supersedes the Euclidean idea that three-dimensional objects and beings contain two-dimensional ones.

[31] de Man, *The Resistance to Theory* 48.

[32] See Paxson, *The Poetics of Personification* 68–70, 152–156, 162–164, *et passim.*

[33] See Paré, *On Monsters and Marvels* 21, for the illustration of a sixteenth-century man who had a head growing out of his belly; see 88 for the point regarding nether-speech produced by possessed persons from their *parties naturelles* ("genitals," translator's English interpolation). For French original of the possession passage, see Paré, *Des Monstres et prodiges*, trans. Pallister 83.

[34] Sonnino, *A Handbook to Sixteenth-Century Rhetoric* 197. The former is the figure of bombast or overblown language; the latter is the general cultivation of ugliness or viciousness in speech.

[35] Wills, *Witches and Jesuits* 45.

[36] Donegan, *Women and Men Midwives,* makes the case that early modern midwifery competed with the obstetrical practices institutionalized in the emerging arena of male-controlled professional medicine. She in fact attributes the early-modern witch craze to this competition—one in which midwives were often accused of witchcraft by default and linked to the demonic.

[37] Olds, London, and Ladewig, *Maternal-Newborn Nursing* 399–420.

[38] See Boaistuau, *Histoires prodigieuses* 1; the source I have used for this figure as well as Figure 1 is Lehner and Lehner, *Picture Book of Devils, Demons and Witchcraft* 18 and 14, respectively. Note that the image of Satan enthroned—the first-page image in Boaistuau's popular treatise on teratology and monsters—presages the image-text mismatch in Hodges's illustration of Joan and her fiends in Act 5 of *1 Henry VI*. Because Satan's body serves, for Boaistuau, as the genealogical beginning of all deformed bodies, monsters, and wonders that would follow chronologically (1–2), the maternal allegory is implicit. However, Boaistuau's terse description does not identify an actual crotch-face, although it does make an ambiguous point, using an indefinite article, about "an open mouth" of great size: Satan possesses "quatre dens avec une grand bouche ouverte, le nez & les yeulx de mesme, les mains comme un Singe, les pieds comme un Coc. . . ." (4). As the illustration shows, the upper face's feline-looking mouth is

closed, while the mouth in the identical nether face is "open"; nor does Boaistuau mention the pendant female breasts in the illustration, despite the on-target mention of the rooster "feet" and the ape "hands."

[39] See Weigle, *Creation and Procreation* 128.

[40] Eccles, ed., *The Macro Plays* 144.

[41] The important early studies arguing for continuity between the English moralities and the Shakespearean history play include Ribner, *The English History Play in the Age of Shakespeare* and Talbert, *Elizabethan Drama and Shakespeare's Early Plays*.

[42] Tertullian, "On the Apparel of Women" 14.

[43] Bloch, *Medieval Misogyny and the Invention of Western Romantic Love*.

[44] My argument at this point therefore downplays the bestial attributes of the late medieval devil, hastening to the semiotic features which reveal the Devil always allegorized as a human form. I thus play out here another version of the orientation exhibited in Stevens and Paxson, "The Fool in the Wakefield Plays" 49–80, an article in which we explored the English mystery-play devil as "the demonic fool, the insipient demon." See also my article, "Personification's Gender," 169–174, for a fuller unpacking of Tertullian in relation to the feminized demon/demonic feminine and the master trope prosopopeia.

[45] A rubric reads, "Upper part of the body with feather of a bird; serpent, by shape in the foot; in figure, a girl" (ll. 208ff); Mills, ed., *The Chester Mystery Cycle* 33.

[46] Images of the woman-headed serpent are so prevalent in medieval and Renaissance art that survey would escape the scope of this essay; widespread knowledge of the Edenic serpent's womanlike face goes back to Peter Comestor's influential *Historia scholastica*. For the earliest full study of the woman-headed serpent, see Bonnell, "The Serpent with a Human Head in Art and in Mystery Play" 255–291.

[47] See text of the Middle English *Trotula* (British Library Sloane 24648... 3) in Rowland, ed., *Medieval Woman's Guide to Health*.

[48] Cixous and Clément, *The Newly Born Woman* 7–8.

[49] Rackin, *Stages of History* 197–200, 209–10. See also Howard and Rackin, *Engendering a Nation* 50–57, *et passim*, for a rehash of the discussion of Joan from Rackin's earlier book.

[50] Silber, "The Unnatural Woman and the Disordered State in Shakespeare's Histories," 87–96, like French, *Shakespeare's Division of Experience* 46–48, zeroes in on Joan's depiction as a violator of natural order; Pitt, *Shakespeare's Women* 148–150, studies her status as whore; Kahn, *Man's Estate*, and Bamber, *Comic Women, Tragic Men*, investigate how Joan bends gender categories; Sundelson, *Shakespeare's Restorations of the Father* 20–23, employs the Freudian picture, arguing that Joan is a castrator and infantilizer of the men around her; and Bassnett, "Sexuality

and Power in the Three Parts of *King Henry VI*," reads Joan as a negative version of Elizabeth I.

[51] Linda Woodbridge, *Women and the English Renaissance* 160, and Williamson, "'When Men Are rul'd by Women'," give Joan better mythographical density: she is the most vital embodiment of the medieval Amazon topos on Shakespeare's stage.

[52] See Bevington, "Domineering Female" 51–58; Tillyard, *Shakespeare's History Plays* 194, for whom Joan is an instrument of "theodicy," a "scourge" of God against the reprehensible English; Fiedler, *The Stranger in Shakespeare* 150, for an existentialist analysis of Joan as a liminal figure marking off the human.

CLIMBING FOR PLACE
IN SHAKESPEARE'S *2 HENRY VI*

Maurice Hunt

> Such is in man the greedy mind to reign,
> So great is his desire to climb aloft,
> In worldly stage the stateliest parts to bear,
> That faith and justice and all kingly love
> Do yield unto desire of sovereignty.
> —*Gorboduc* 1.2. 262–266

I abstract my thesis about the consistent dramatic method of Shakespeare's early history play *2 Henry VI* by exploring its emblematic representation in the Sander Simpcox episode (2.1.57–162).[1] In this scene, Humphrey, Duke of Gloucester, unmasks beggarly Simpcox as a fraud. Supposedly blind, Simpcox (his name a compound of simpleton and cox-comb) claims to have recovered his sight at St. Alban's shrine. But Humphrey, suspecting a hoax, traps him by getting him to give correct names to various colors that he sees supposedly for the first time. "Sight may distinguish of colors," Humphrey concludes, "but suddenly to nominate them all, it is impossible" (132–134). Simpcox has also claimed to be lame. When Suffolk asks him how he became crippled, Shakespeare crafts this significant dialogue:

> *Simpcox* A fall off of a tree.
> *Wife* A plum tree, master.
> *Gloucester* How long hast thou been blind?
> *Simpcox* O, born so, master.
> *Gloucester* What, and wouldst climb a tree?
> *Simpcox* But that in all my life, when I was a youth.
> *Wife* Too true, and bought his climbing very dear.
> *Gloucester* Mass, thou lov'dst plums well, that wouldst venture so.
> *Simpcox* Alas, good master, my wife desired some damsons and
>   made me climb, with danger of my life.
> *Gloucester* A subtle knave! But yet it shall not serve. Let me see
>   thine eyes. Wink now. Now open them.
>   In my opinion yet thou seest not well. (97–110)

Simpcox's claim that, while blind, he was able to climb a tree makes Gloucester doubly suspect him, a doubt expressed by his attributing figurative blindness to Simpcox in the final verse of the quoted dialogue.[2] Gloucester's allusion identifies Simpcox's sin as a blinding pride that his hoax will remain undetected while he boasts of his ability to satisfy a woman by climbing high. His fabrication transparently reveals the aspiration and fall of Original Sin, of the garden and the tree and plucked fruit that cost humankind residence in paradise. Simpcox has a wife, a beggarly Eve who supposedly incited him to pluck plums for her, at the price of presumably crippling him. David Bevington glosses the plum tree as "a slang phrase for the female pudenda that sets up an elaborate ribald joke here about a husband risking his life to try to satisfy his wife's craving."[3] So interpreted, Simpcox and his wife's dialogue becomes a little allegory about the original sin of climbing for place, its origins in sexual appetite, and its consequence of a laming fall. Simpcox's aspiring pride appears in playgoers' first view of him, carried by the mayor of St. Albans and his brethren aloft *"between two in a chair."* Whipped progressively back to Berwick, Simpcox and his wife will eventually sink to their ordained, "proper" station—a low place among people who have always known them for the sturdy rogues they are.[4]

The Sander Simpcox episode emblematically condenses the manifold experience of major characters of *2 Henry VI*. The variations that Shakespeare orchestrates upon the motif of high climbing establish it throughout the initial acts of this history play as the catalyst for political conflict and impending civil war. One after another, figures such as Eleanor, Duchess of Gloucester; Queen Margaret; the Duke of Suffolk, William de la Pole; and Cardinal Beaufort succumb to the fatal temptation to rise above their prescribed station in life. In the latter part of *2 Henry VI*, Shakespeare depicts a nemesis of the courtly high climbing repeatedly represented in early acts. A principle of crude earthly justice emerges as this nemesis, involving the naval lieutenant and the rebel Jack Cade, brings down de la Pole and other malicious climbers to their ruin. A degree of poetic justice attaches to this process because, in their aspiring pride, would-be high climbers have killed relatively innocent men such as Humphrey, Duke of Gloucester. Finally, aptly named Alexander Iden in a garden kills Jack Cade, disposing of a nemesis grown diabolic after serving a providential purpose. This deed provides closure to a neat symmetry of dramatic design in a play that analysts have sometimes described as either episodic or partly (or poorly) organized.[5] The title of the present essay derives from a phrase uttered during the opening dialogue of Act 2, scene 1 of *2 Henry VI*, a conversation that uses the metaphor of hawking to convey humankind's radical flaw:

Queen Believe me, lords, for flying at the brook

> I saw not better sport these seven years' day.
> Yet, by your leave, the wind was very high,
> And ten to one old Joan had not gone out.
> *King [to Gloucester]* But what a point, my lord, your falcon made,
> And what a pitch she flew above the rest!
> To see how God in all his creatures works!
> Yea, man and birds are fain of climbing high.
> *Suffolk* No marvel, an it like Your Majesty,
> My Lord Protector's hawks do tower so well;
> They know their master loves to be aloft
> And bears his thoughts above his falcon's pitch.
> *Gloucester* My lord, 'tis but a base ignoble mind
> That mounts no higher than a bird can soar. (2.1.1–14)

Hawking here becomes a symbol for the social-climbing instinct of humankind moralized by pious King Henry VI (7–8). This generic instinct locates itself in the apparently humble Duke of Gloucester, who confesses to a mounting mind (3–14). The modest benevolence of this mind immediately comes into question when Gloucester and his enemy Cardinal Beaufort exchange nasty asides about dueling later in a grove of trees. Overhearing their savage threats, King Henry underscores the scene's vertical imagery by exclaiming, "The winds grow high; so do your stomachs, lords./ How irksome is this music to my heart!" (53–54). The intrusion of Simpcox borne aloft in his chair, however, prevents playgoers from immediately knowing whether angry Gloucester and Beaufort reconcile their differences.

The symbolic import of the Simpcox episode thus seems in Act 2, scene 1 to apply to Humphrey, Duke of Gloucester. Like self-fashioned Simpcox, he has a wife who threatens his ruin by her desire to see her husband and herself climb beyond their prescribed sociopolitical place.[6] Eleanor, Duchess of Gloucester's first speech in the play moves along an axis from low melancholy to a forbidden seat on high. "Why droops my lord," she asks Humphrey,

>   like overripened corn,
> Hanging the head at Ceres' plenteous load?
> Why doth the great Duke Humphrey knit his brows,
> As frowning at the favors of the world?
> Why are thine eyes fixed to the sullen earth,
> Gazing on that which seems to dim thy sight?
> What seest thou there? King Henry's diadem,
> Enchased with all the honors of the world?
> If so, gaze on, and grovel on thy face,
> Until thy head be circled with the same.

Put forth thy hand; reach at the glorious gold.
What, is't too short? I'll lengthen it with mine;
And having both together heaved it up,
We'll both together lift our heads to heaven
And nevermore abase our sight so low
As to vouchsafe one glance unto the ground. (1.2.1–16)

Even though, as King Henry's uncle, Humphrey would inherit the crown
should the boy die, as Lord Protector he has no legal pretext for presently
claiming "King Henry's diadem" (7). Eleanor elaborately articulates the
traitorous sin of pride, of desiring to climb beyond one's ordained place in
a traditional political hierarchy. When Eleanor tells Humphrey that she
dreamed that she sat

> in seat of majesty
In the cathedral church of Westminster,
And in that chair where kings and queens arc crowned,
Where Henry and Dame Margaret kneeled to me
And on my head did set the diadem,

her horrified husband interrupts to identify the original nature of her sin:

Nay, Eleanor, then must I chide outright.
Presumptuous dame, ill-nurtured Eleanor,
Art thou not second woman in the realm,
And the Protector's wife, beloved of him?
Hast thou not worldly pleasure at command
Above the reach or compass of thy thought?
And wilt thou still be hammering treachery,
To tumble down thy husband and thyself
From top of honor to disgrace's feet?
Away from me, and let me hear no more! (1.2.36–50)

Eleanor's sin reflects Lucifer's; like him she enjoys blessed status yet presumptuously wishes to usurp the divinely, prescribed pinnacle not meant
for her. Like his competitor Marlowe, Shakespeare represents overreaching, a devilish climbing for place, as humankind's radical flaw. When
Somerset and his other enemies conspire to ruin Humphrey, one accusation
made against the Duke involves his "wife's attire [which has] cost a mass
of public treasury" (1.3.130–131). Shakespeare implies that, like Adam in
some Augustinian narrations of the Fall, Duke Humphrey—despite his
condemnation of her ambition—may very likely be undone by his acquies-
cence in his Eve's vain longing to climb beyond her ordained sphere.

Dame Eleanor's employment of a witch and conjuror to raise through black magic a spirit from underground not only reinforces the satanic nature of her sin but also threatens to become the prime means of her husband's undoing. Humphrey's enemies, Cardinal Beaufort and the Duke of Suffolk, have corrupted Eleanor's priest, Sir John Hume, both to encourage her tendency to learn from an earth spirit what the future holds politically for her and her husband and to report to them the moment when Dame Eleanor joins the witch and conjuror so that they can arrest her for the crime of participating in black arts. By this means Beaufort and Suffolk hope to attaint Humphrey through his wife. The "spirit raised from depth of underground" in this scenario corresponds in its movement to Eleanor's "aspiring humor" (1.2.79, 97).[7] The apparition thus symbolizes the devilishness of Eleanor's proud aspiration.[8] Appropriately, in the conjuring scene (1.4), Shakespeare stages her aloft, watching the conjuror Roger Bolingbroke and the witch Margery Jordan raise the spirit Asnath (an anagram for Sat[h]an) from beneath the earth (presumably through the stage's trapdoor). After delivering several equivocal political prophecies, the spirit sinks down again, its motion coinciding with the intrusion of the Dukes of York and Buckingham to arrest Eleanor and bring her aspiring spirit of ambition down from its lofty position.

Stripped of her rank—King Henry calls forth "Dame Eleanor Cobham, Gloucester's wife" (2.3.1)—the former Duchess receives the punishment of "three days' open penance" followed by lifetime banishment to the Isle of Man (2.3.11–13), a fallen oasis the antithesis of the figurative paradisiacal garden her ambition has cost her.[9] While her accomplices are condemned to being burnt or strangled on the gallows, Eleanor receives this lighter sentence because she was "nobly born" (2.3.9). Punished for wanting to climb beyond her place, she paradoxically survives because of her inherited high rank. Still, her final appearance in the play reveals a genuine new humility, acquired through severe mortification of the flesh. In Act 2, scene 4, she enters *"barefoot, in a white sheet, with verses pinned upon her back, and a taper burning in her hand."* Eleanor can hardly bear the humiliations of the jeering rabble, but she has come to understand her crime. Even though Sir John Stanley promises to treat her in exile "like to a duchess and Duke Humphrey's lady" (2.4.99), Eleanor exits London humbly realizing that

My shame will not be shifted with my sheet.
No, it will hang upon my richest robes
And show itself, attire me how I can. (2.4.108–110)

"Go, lead the way," she murmurs, "I long to see my prison" (111).[10]

Nevertheless, Shakespeare takes elaborate pains to show how Eleanor's sin indirectly ruins Queen Margaret and King Henry and directly undoes Duke Humphrey and herself. In this respect, the Sander Simpcox episode definitively becomes the play's emblematic episode of tragic origin: Original Sin derives from a woman's forbidden desires.[11] An orthodox dramaturgy resembling that of a morality play rather than an early modern Machiavellian methodology of *Realpolitik* grounds sociopolitical change in the first half of *2 Henry VI*. Competition with Dame Eleanor has fueled the aspiring spirit of Queen Margaret, who finds in the vying compensation for her sense of her father's low aristocratic status. Honorific King of Naples, Sicilia, and Jerusalem, Reignier, Margaret's French father, must give away his daughter dowerless, so impoverished is his estate. This shameful fact torments proud Margaret inwardly, especially since she is aware that King Henry in essence bought her by giving Reignier the French duchies of Anjou and Maine. By relinquishing English territory won by the blood of Henry V's troops, Henry VI foolishly predisposes his courtiers to dislike Margaret and her father, who have gained higher places than Englishmen believe that they deserve. "And our King Henry gives away his own," York sadly concludes, "to match with her that brings no vantages" (1.1.128–129). "She should have stayed in France," Duke Humphrey asserts, "and starved in France. . . ." (1.1.132).

The chilly English reception of Margaret exacerbates her desire to climb beyond the Protector Duke Humphrey's station to a place equal to Henry's. "What, shall King Henry be a pupil still," she angrily asks Suffolk,

> Under the surly Gloucester's governance?
> Am I a queen in title and in style,
> And must be made a subject to a duke? (1.3.46–49)

Because, to use her words, King Henry's "mind is *bent* to holiness" (1.3.55, my italics), Margaret considers herself her husband's superior. Her radical sense of social inferiority, of her status as a purchasable commodity, coalesces in the presence of Dame Eleanor. Both women negatively act upon each other by mutually activating the social climber within each. Margaret confesses,

> Not all these lords do vex me half so much,
> As that proud dame, the Lord Protector's wife.
> She sweeps it through the court with troops of ladies,
> More like an empress than Duke Humphrey's wife.
> Strangers in court do take her for the Queen.
> She bears a duke's revenues on her back,
> And in her heart she scorns our poverty.
> Shall I not live to be avenged on her?
> Contemptuous baseborn callet as she is,
> She vaunted 'mongst her minions t'other day
> The very train of her worst wearing gown

Was better worth than all my father's lands,
Till Suffolk gave two dukedoms for his daughter. (1.3.75–87)

Dame Eleanor's royal pretensions and airs precipitate Margaret's hatred for her own origins and sense of obligation to her husband Henry, becoming the object of her deflected malice. These unpleasant feelings encourage Margaret to think that she needs to climb beyond her place as the king's consort. When her admirer Suffolk says that one day, once the two of them have weeded the isle of their competitors, Margaret herself "shall steer the happy helm" (1.3.100), his traitorous remark receives silent assent from the queen. Rebelliously aspiring Margaret becomes the immediate catalyst of Eleanor's ruin, of the proud woman whose mere presence originally fueled the queen's ambition. Turn-about roles of victim and victimizer ironically work their own unintended justice. When Humphrey's adversaries begin blaming him for England's military demise, he, resolved not to bicker, exits, and Margaret drops her fan before Eleanor: "Give me my fan. What, minion, can ye not?" (1.3.138). Pretending that she momentarily mistakes Eleanor for one of her ladies in waiting, she *gives the Duchess a box on the ear* and falsely says, "I cry you mercy, madam. Was it you?" (1.3.139). "Was't I? Yea, I it was, proud Frenchwoman," Eleanor snarls, "Could I come near your beauty with my nails,/ I'd set my ten commandments in your face" (140–142). Significantly, Eleanor appears more aware than anyone of Margaret's desire to climb beyond her affixed place. In Margaret's hearing she tells King Henry that someday Margaret will "hamper [him] and dandle [him] like a baby" (145). Eleanor realizes that already "in this place most master wear no breeches" (146)—that in the court the person most in charge (the queen) wears no pants yet usurps rule with masculine authority. When Eleanor, her cheek smarting, exits determined to learn of Margaret's (presumably bad) future through her witch and conjuror, Buckingham correctly judges that "She's tickled now; her fume needs no spurs./ She'll gallop far enough to her destruction" (150–151). Margaret's own climbing for place indirectly prompts a corresponding, suicidal inclination in Eleanor.

Shakespeare thus suggests that a corrupt courtly environment of social climbing can attaint and destroy characters vulnerable to this proud fault. The spiteful ambition to be more than one's rank drives Suffolk, Cardinal Beaufort, and the Duke of York to focus their envy on the Lord Protector Humphrey and work to remove him from his office. Their climbing for place becomes the *leitmotif* of their characterizations. Twice in the opening sixty-five lines of *2 Henry VI*, William de la Pole "humbly" (but actually hypocritically) kneels and rises before his king, the second time as the first Duke of Suffolk—a title de la Pole crassly gains by purchasing Margaret for Henry at the price of two French duchies heroically won by Henry V. Humphrey draws Suffolk's hatred by courageously voicing this truth—that

Suffolk's new promotion basely derives from the struck deal of artificially elevating Reignier's French place. Beaufort hates Humphrey simply because as Protector he stands in the way of the churchman's desire to fill this influential role. Beaufort's blood runs close to the throne. Or so the Cardinal, Humphrey's uncle, thinks. Finally, the Duke of York hates Humphrey because he has restricted York's climbing for the crown. Humphrey, in his own words, refers to "dogged York, that reaches at the moon,/ Whose overweening arm I have plucked back" (3.1.158–159). In retaliation, York, Humphrey realizes, "by false accuse doth level at my life" (160).

It comes as no surprise that the many social climbers about Humphrey, plotting to destroy him, projectively imagine him to be darkly ambitious. For example, when Humphrey tells Suffolk, "England knows thine insolence," Queen Margaret retorts "and thy ambition, Gloucester" (2.1.31–32). So aspirant is she and the upward-looking others that they disingenuously impose their own climbing pretensions onto Humphrey, assuming that he possesses them. But the modest Duke, with the one possible exception of the hawking metaphor previously described,[12] never reveals a shred of personal ambition; his words and deeds reflect contentment with his dukedom, loyalty to his king and England, and a willingness to resign his protectorship whenever asked to do so, even though he knows that England will suffer from the misgovernment of his adversaries.[13] "Madam, I am Protector of the realm," he tells Margaret with dignity, "and at [the king's] pleasure will resign my place" (1.3.120–121). Among the major characters of this early history play, only King Henry VI and Duke Humphrey show no vain signs of wishing to climb from one earthly station to another worldly one. As much as he loves Dame Eleanor, Humphrey rebukes her proud ambition and with great pain dissociates himself from her after her conviction for participating in the practice of black arts. Duke Humphrey remains so opposed to the climbing humor that twice he even exits the stage when taunted by his enemies so as to avoid expressing a "high" temper (and recall his attempt to express his hostility to Beaufort in careful asides).[14]

Granted sustained images of Humphrey's modest integrity, many playgoers and literary critics do not believe that the duke's adversaries succeed in bringing him down through the contrived tainture of his wife, Dame Eleanor.[15] Duke Humphrey falls, this camp argues, not because of his association with Eleanor, but because his enemies successfully imprison him in the Tower, where he is strangled on vague charges of treason connected with the losing of France (3.1.93–194).[16] His adversaries' success depends upon Humphrey's loss of the office of Protector, a loss which makes him more vulnerable and Henry VI, now unguided, more weak and malleable. Ironically Henry rises from his royal seat as arrested Humphrey exits (staging suggestive of the monarch's sudden potential for ascension), and yet the spineless words the king utters—"My lords, what to your wisdoms seemeth

best/ Do or undo, as if ourself were here" (3.1.195–196)—predict the
beginning of his personal descent to an early death at Richard Crookback's
hands (*3 Henry VI* 5.6.56–57).

Humphrey's fatal loss of the empowering protectorship, despite a major
critical argument, directly results from his becoming attainted by Dame
Eleanor's sin of high climbing. Immediately after King Henry formally banishes Eleanor, he turns to Humphrey, ominously commanding

> Stay, Humphrey, Duke of Gloucester. Ere thou go,
> Give up thy staff. Henry will to himself
> Protector be. . . . (2.3.22–24)

This rash and eventually fatal decision for both men clearly derives from
the monarch's loss of confidence in a counselor tragically wived. Through
his wife the archetypal crime of high climbing touches Humphrey[17] as
though it were the original, hereditary guiltiness figured by the complex of
overweening climbing/ tree/ fruit/ complicit female of the Sander Simpcox
allegorical scene.

The nemesis of high climbing in *2 Henry VI* chiefly depends upon the
aggression of representatives of lower social classes galvanized by the
oppression of callous, aspirant nobility. The naval lieutenant and Jack
Cade become fatal agents in this retributive dynamic, and Suffolk's ruin
symbolically stands for the punishment of aristocratic high climbing in this
history play. Throughout *2 Henry VI* Shakespeare periodically alludes to
noble privilege detrimental to poorer, marginalized people.[18] For example,
Sir John Hume and John Southwell, priest accomplices of the witch Jordan
and conjurer Bolingbroke, are executed terribly along with the latter two
characters, while Dame Eleanor, their instigator, receives only three day's
public humiliation and an aristocratic life of exile on the Isle of Man, "for,"
to use King Henry's words in sentencing her, "you are more nobly born"
(2.3.9).

More to the point, Queen Margaret and especially Suffolk sarcastically
dismiss the petitions of socially abused citizens, injured partly by Suffolk
himself. The First Petitioner mistakes Suffolk for good Lord Humphrey and
thus loses his petition to a joking Queen Margaret and Suffolk (1.3.1–41).
When the pleader anxiously tells the aristocrats that his complaint is
"against John Goodman, my Lord Cardinal's man, for keeping my house,
and lands, and wife and all, from me," Suffolk, whose dalliance with
Margaret has made him notorious, cruelly jests: "Thy wife too? That's
some wrong, indeed" (21). And when he grabs another petitioner's paper
and reads aloud: "What's here? . . . 'Against the Duke of Suffolk, for
enclosing the commons of Medford'" (22–24), Suffolk ironically pro-
nounces an indictment against the unjust consequences of his own high
climbing. Angry, he denounces this petitioner as a "knave" and immedi-

ately becomes absorbed in the more interesting case of Peter Thump against his master Thomas Horner "for saying that the Duke of York was rightful heir to the crown" (28–29). Aspirant nobility's oppression of justly complaining commoners condenses in haughty Margaret's tearing of the petitions and her disdainful command: "Away, base cullions! Suffolk, let them go" (40). Her snobbish contempt for "cullions"—low fellows—extends to her question: "My lord of Suffolk, say, is this the guise,/ Is this the fashions in the court of England?" (42–43). Queen Margaret's question reveals that her ignorance of the most basic human rights derives from her (unmonied) upper-class origins in France, where commoners lack even the few rights granted to them in fifteenth-century England.

Suffolk's contempt of commoners meets its fate when the English Lieutenant captures him, disguised in rags and ostensibly on secret embassy from Margaret to her friends in France. Apportioned to the common seaman Walter Whitmore for his ransom value, Suffolk understandably believes that he shall live. "Look on my [Saint] George," he exclaims, uncovering the insignia of nobility beneath his rags; "Rate me at what thou wilt, thou shalt be paid" (4.1.29–30). Learning to his horror of his captor's name, Walter (a seer has proclaimed that Suffolk one day will die by "water"), the disguised aristocrat comically tries to elevate Whitmore: "Thy name is Gualtier, being rightly sounded" (37). Whitmore, however, with poetic justice, rejects this skewed, pretentious etymology, articulating an uncoded nobility of the English commoner:

> Gualtier or Walter, which it is, I care not.
> Never yet did base dishonor blur our name
> But with our sword we wiped away the blot.
> Therefore, when merchantlike I sell revenge,
> Broke be my sword, my arms torn and defaced,
> And I proclaimed a coward through the world![19] (38–43)

Ironically, "noble" Suffolk has been the commoner when, tradesmanlike, he made his rank material and attempted to sell it in exchange for his life ("Rate me at what thou wilt, thou shalt be paid"). When he finally uncovers his face, proclaiming himself a "prince,/ The Duke of Suffolk, William de la Pole" (44–45), he also haughtily announces that "these rags are no part of the Duke" (47). And when the Lieutenant threatens nevertheless to kill him, he erupts:

> Obscure and lousy swain, King Henry's blood,
> The honorable blood of Lancaster,
> Must not be shed by such a jaded groom.
> Hast thou not kissed thy hand and held my stirrup?
> Bareheaded plodded by my footcloth mule

And thought thee happy when I shook my head?
How often hast thou waited at my cup,
Fed from my trencher, kneeled down at the board,
When I have feasted with Queen Margaret?
Remember it, and let it make thee crestfall'n,
Ay, and allay this thy abortive pride.
How in our voiding lobby hast thou stood
And duly waited for my coming forth?
This hand of mine hath writ in thy behalf,
And therefore shall it charm thy riotous tongue. (50–64)

Suffolk's contemptuous attitude toward his rags contrasts sharply with
Dame Eleanor's humble wearing of the penitent's sheet, suggesting that he
most likely is incapable of learning modesty.[20] And the foolishness of his
"noble" opinion that the Lieutenant, simply because he was once "privileged" to be Suffolk's self-abasing servant, ought to spare his life, by its
audacity becomes his death warrant. The Lieutenant's "abortive pride"
rises upon hearing this disdainful portrait of his previously slavish life,
becoming the fateful antidote to Suffolk's climbing arrogance.[21] Crudely the
enraged Lieutenant strips Suffolk of his nobility, calling him only "Pole"
(70). His lengthy and remarkably prescient summary of the crimes that
Suffolk's aspiring pride has led him to commit against the commonwealth
(71–104) recasts his victim as the symbolic source of England's troubles—
the "filth and dirt" which "troubles the silver spring where England
drinks" (71–72). In the Lieutenant's words, "reproach and beggary/ Is
crept into the palace of our King,/ And *all* by thee" (101–103, my italics).
Thus destroying this high climber represents metaphorically the ruin of
other haughty aristocrats in the play, those unnamed nobles whose upward
gaze and demeanor lead Jack Cade and his rebels to kill them.
    True to the end to his self-destructive climbing spirit, Suffolk never real-
izes that it is his "noble" disdain that enrages his captors. "O, that I were
a god," he shouts:

                    to shoot forth thunder
Upon these paltry, servile, abject drudges!
Small things make base men proud. . . .

Drones suck not eagles' blood, but rob beehives.
It is impossible that I should die
By such a lowly vassal as thyself. (104–106, 109–111)

Shakespeare emphasizes the vertical trajectory of Suffolk's character to the
end by depicting him resisting Whitmore's command that he stoop (120)
with the words: "No, rather let my head/ Stoop to the block than these

knees bow to any/ Save to the God of heaven and to my king" (125–127). But Suffolk's stooping to God and Henry VI has always been hypocritical, subservient to Machiavellian schemes of higher climbing. He would have his head "sooner dance upon a bloody pole/ Than stand uncovered to the vulgar groom" (128–129). His last wish grimly comes true. Severed by the pirates from his body, Suffolk's head eventually comes into Margaret's possession. There it becomes a *memento mori* punishing her for her pride (for her lover Suffolk figured in her plans of self-aggrandizement). "My hope is gone," she sadly concludes, "now Suffolk is deceased" (4.4.56). As certain scenes of *Hamlet, Measure for Measure,* and *Pericles* indicate, pirates throughout the Shakespeare canon regularly implement unintentionally a design of Providence. Duke Humphrey in Act 1 told Dame Eleanor he dreamed that his badge of office, the Protector's staff, was broken by Cardinal Beaufort and that on the ends of the broken wand were placed the severed heads of Edmund, Duke of Somerset, and the Duke of Suffolk, William de la Pole (1.2.23–31). Suffolk's vision of his head dancing "upon a bloody pole" creates an uncanny pun and fulfills Humphrey's dream. Shakespeare thus suggests that a supernatural design calls for Suffolk's death, presumably as punishment for his role in killing the humble Lord Protector Humphrey. More generally, the playwright implies that God, as he did with Lucifer, abhors unwarranted attempts to climb beyond one's prescribed place and punishes the aspirant harshly.

Shakespeare orchestrates Jack Cade's rebellion to make the same point. Like Dame Eleanor, the Duke of York determines to raise a spirit, in this case John Cade of Ashford, a charismatic soldier who can foment rebellion in England on York's behalf. York resolves that Cade shall "make commotion . . . under the title of John Mortimer" (3.1.358–359), a member of "a powerful family claiming descent from Lionel, Duke of Clarence, and hence entitled to the crown."[22] This scheme depends upon Cade's uncanny resemblance to Mortimer—"For that John Mortimer, which now is dead,/ In face, in gait, in speech, he doth resemble" (3.1.372–373). When York calls Cade a "devil" (371), Elizabethan playgoers most likely recalled the popular doctrine of devil possession—that when a wicked man died, a devil might inhabit his body afterwards, by all appearances causing mortals to believe the man's soul had not died and gone to hell but that he lived as he always had. Cade's dancing after battle "like a wild Morisco," shaking "as he his bells" the bloody darts stuck in his thighs, does seem more (or perhaps less) than human (360–366). York's calling Cade a "devil" closely links his spirit raising with Dame Eleanor's. As a raised spirit, Jack Cade embodies the Luciferan ambition of his master, York, who ruthlessly lusts for the crown.[23] But Cade actually believes that he is descended from the genteel Mortimers (4.2.38–51). In this sense, Shakespeare makes him a presumptuously climbing spirit mirroring the social aspirations of the nobles he quells during his rebellion. In other words, he becomes a providential retributive incarnation of the fault that his revolt punishes. As providential scourge, he attacks a fault he personifies (despite his democratic proclamations), only at last to be destroyed himself (as cleansing scourges always are in this early modern paradigm).[24]

John Holland, a commoner, emphasizes at the beginning of the Jack Cade episode that Cade's rebellion will chastise (lower) climbing gentlemen: "Well I say," he facetiously exclaims, "it was never merry world in England since gentlemen *came up*" (4.2.7–9, my italics). Andrew McRae has recently demonstrated that both the English social and literary impulses to a communistic leveling of social classes during medieval and early-modern centuries were stronger and more widespread than previous historians had supposed.[25] John Holland's above-quoted pronouncement could constitute a reply to one of the most popular heretical questions of the fourteenth, fifteenth, and sixteenth centuries: "When Adam delved and Eve span/ Who was then the gentleman?"[26] The rebels leading the Peasants Revolt of 1381 used the gnomic query to muster supporters, and its implied answer of "no one" provided a rationale for the generally subversive arguments for social leveling put forth by (among others) the Edwardian pamphleteer Robert Crowley, Ralphe Robynson (in his 1551 translation of More's *Utopia*), Peter Chamberlen (1547), and Francis Trigge (1604).[27] Levellers of every philosophical stripe, however, often revealed their own social pretensions, a fact which did not escape Shakespeare's notice.

In *2 Henry VI*, Holland and George Bevis characterize the nobility's aversion to physical labor, concluding that the adage to "'labor in thy vocation'" must apply to commoners alone (4.2.10–16). By punchy logic, the laborer Holland then translates the adage to mean "'Let the magistrates be laboring men.' And therefore should we be magistrates" (17–18). So construed, the adage reveals the rebels' unwarranted climbing for place. This pretension implies that, after they have pulled down gentlemen who came up, they will put themselves in their places. The implication includes Jack Cade. When he enters, Cade professes to be "inspired with the spirit of putting down kings and princes" (34–35). Jack Cade's personal motive to revolt derives from his belief that he and English commoners "live in slavery to the nobility" (4.8.27); this conviction of enslavement fuels Cade's supposed (but actually bogus) aim of helping the oppressed English to recover their "ancient freedom" (25–26).

When Cade depicts his utopian England where money shall be abolished, bread and ale cheap, enclosure illegal, and all citizens brothers and sisters wearing one livery, he voices the contradiction that Gonzalo will express in *The Tempest*: that the promoter of a leveled utopia apparently remains unaware of his own lust for rule, for kingship.[28] Cade's unadmitted rising spirit surfaces in his remark that utopian England will materialize "when I am king, as king I will be—" (4.2.68). Cade's mockery of the climbing spirit of Suffolk and other villains in the play appears in his attempt to make himself Sir John Mortimer and thus equal to his adversary, Sir Humphrey Stafford: "To equal him, I will make myself a knight presently. *[He kneels.]* Rise up Sir John Mortimer. *[He rises.]* Now have at him!" (4.2.115–117). Cade's comic self-dubbing parodies the crass self-promotion of aristocrats such as Suffolk and York. Cade's foolish claim that, as John Mortimer, he is "rightful heir unto the crown" (127) burlesques the claim of York, for Cade is actually no more than a "shearman" (129). The gap between shearman and king simply exaggerates the differences between the crown and the lesser noble place of York, who aspires to it.

As a nemesis Cade acts inexorably, cutting through appearances and falsehoods. Despite Lord Saye's plea that he has not aspired beyond his place (4.7.93–100), he nevertheless, like Suffolk, conspired to give back to the French the English territories of Anjou and Maine and unjustly inflated the taxation on the commoners, forcing them to pay the exorbitant rate of "one-and-twenty fifteens, and one shilling to the pound" (4.7.18–21).[29] Moreover, Saye has promoted the widespread early-modern abuse of justice deriving from "neck-verses" (exemption from execution through the demonstration of literacy in Latin).[30] Because jailed poor men "could not read thou hast hanged them" (41–42), Cade tells Lord Saye. Thus Saye's execution curtails several kinds of abuse. Cade stresses his role of scourge in this action by acknowledging the "besom [broom] that must sweep the court clean of such filth as [Lord Saye]" (28–30). When Saye admits that he covers his horse with an expensive cloth, Cade pointedly says: "Marry, thou oughtst not to let thy horse wear a cloak, when honester men than thou go in their hose and doublets" (46–48). Nevertheless, Saye claims never to have aspired to more than his place:

Tell me wherein have I offended most?
Have I affected wealth or honor? Speak.
Are my chests filled up with extorted gold?
Is my apparel sumptuous to behold?
Whom have I injured, that ye seek my death? (93–97)

Apparently the answers to all these questions are in the negative. While punishing some vices of Lord Saye (this victim is hardly "filth"), Cade's Rebellion falters as providential purge when the nemesis Cade starts killing nobles who have not fallen victim to Luciferan ambition. This injustice signals that Cade has transgressed the providential scheme for thwarting the evil of proud social climbing and his scourge role in it, and that it is time the "besom" be destroyed.[31]

Lord Clifford quells Jack Cade's Rebellion by appealing to the rebels' tacit antiutopian, socially pretentious desires and by using these yearnings against Cade himself (in a poetically just way, since Cade as "Mortimer" possesses the same "noble" wishes). In effect, the nemesis principle and figure are applied against themselves. As part of his argument that Cade is not a true aristocratic warrior like Henry V and that he will not (or cannot) lead English soldiers through France to win back lost English territories, Clifford asks the rebels if Cade can "make the meanest of you earls and dukes?" (4.8.36). Since the rebels have known all along that Cade is no more than a poor bricklayer's son, they by silence answer Clifford's rhetorical question negatively and begin to abandon Cade, partly to fight new, supposedly heroic wars in France under a certifiably noble captain's proper leadership.

Abandoned and alone, fleeing arrest, Jack Cade realizes the deathly wages of his vain aspiration. "Fie on ambitions! Fie on myself" (4.10.1), he exclaims. Shakespeare stresses the Luciferan dimension of Cade's ambition by showing him, famished, climbing over the garden wall of Alexander Iden (Eden) in search of food.[32] By aspiring to climb higher than he should, Jack Cade has sunk below his previous place in society, in fact near the condition of a hungry animal. In the "Idenic" garden, fallen Cade wants "to see if [he] can eat grass or pick a sallet another while" (7–8). Shortly, he will exclaim, "here's the lord of the soil come to seize me for a stray, for entering his fee simple without leave" (24–25).

Shakespeare stresses in Alexander Iden's first speech his status as one of the play's two exemplary characters (Duke Humphrey is the other) with regard to their place in the commonwealth. The likely doubling of Duke Humphrey's and Iden's parts by the same actor in the repertory company performing *2 Henry VI* would have visually reinforced this point. "Lord," Iden says to himself,

> who would live turmoilèd in the court,
> And may enjoy such quiet walks as these?
> This small inheritance my father left me
> Contenteth me, and worth a monarchy.
> I seek not to wax great by others' waning,
> Or gather wealth, I care not with what envy.
> Sufficeth that I have maintains my state
> And sends the poor well pleasèd from my gate. (4.10.16–23)

Iden's surname suggests the consummate value of these modest ideas about place in the world of *2 Henry VI*. Unlike Cade, York, or Suffolk, Iden does not aspire to a monarchy; his little wealth buys a pastoral kingdom. Unlike King Henry VI, who as king belongs in the court, the country squire Iden rightfully belongs in a garden. King Henry VI's downward yearning represents a counterpoint to Cade's and various noblemen's criminal wish to be king. "Was never subject longed to be a king," Henry, afflicted by rebellion, laments, "As I do long and wish to be a subject" (4.9.5–6). But even as the nobles' and especially Cade's wishes are wrong for England's health, so Henry's pining to be a commoner, eventually a shepherd, remains equally pernicious, for it also would disrupt an established order crucial for relative peace. Shakespeare's prejudice for the private ownership of property (rather than for a utopian common ground) registers in Iden's accusation that Cade, breaking into his garden, comes "like a thief to . . . rob my grounds,/ Climbing my walls in spite of me the owner" (4.10.33–34). Not aware that the intruder is the notorious traitor Jack Cade, Iden kills him in a struggle chiefly to preserve his rights in his private property.[33] In keeping with his sociopolitical modesty, Iden announces that he will let Cade's blood dry on his sword so that his weapon might "wear it as a herald's coat/ To emblazen the honor that thy master got" (68–70). In Alexander Iden's opinion, true honor derives from deeds loyal to the crown, those that preserve a private (and the public) commonwealth, rather than from inherited scutcheons or aristocratic titles, especially those acquired by upward climbing men like William de la Pole.

Alexander Iden becomes the focus of the only worthy elevation portrayed in *2 Henry VI*. When Henry joyously asks the man who has brought him Cade's head to identify himself, Iden responds, "A poor esquire of Kent that loves his king" (5.1.75). Buckingham then advises Henry, "So please it you, my lord, 'twere not amiss/ He were created knight for his good service" (76–77). "Iden, kneel down," Henry commands; when his loyal subject obliges, the king tells him to

> Rise up a knight.
> We give thee for reward a thousand marks,
> And will that thou henceforth attend on us. (78–80)

The note of humble service heard in risen Iden's last words in the play confirms the appropriateness of this concluding promotion in rank: "May Iden live to merit such a bounty,/ And never live but true unto his liege!" (81–82). Alexander Iden symbolically identified himself with Adam—not simply through his surname but when he referred to his garden as "this small inheritance my father left me" (4.10.18). His merited promotion to knight fulfills without overtones of envy or social revolution the old poetic tag about Adam representing true gentility. Adam was a gardener, and his fifteenth-century Kentish avatar literally becomes a knight.

Nevertheless, Shakespeare does not end his play with this uplifting episode. Enraged to see his adversary Somerset at liberty, York angrily lets fall the mask concealing his fierce ambition and commands the stunned Henry to "give place" to himself: "By heaven, thou shalt rule no more/ O'er him whom heaven created for thy ruler" (5.1.104–105). Moreover, Queen Margaret's splenetic accusations against York provoke him, once he hears her call his sons bastards, again to remind her of her low place. Terming her the "Outcast of Naples" (an insult based on the titular nature

of her poor father's claim to Naples), York insists that his sons are "thy bet-
ters in their birth" (117–119). Quickly England again becomes a house
sharply divided against itself, with Clifford and his son joining the king,
queen, and Somerset against York, his three sons, and the Earls of Warwick
and Salisbury. This division results in the Battle of Saint Albans (1455). In
this fight York kills Clifford (5.2.28), prompting Young Clifford to depict
the scene as one of self-wounding disorder and Apocalypse (32–33, 40–45);
Richard Crookback kills Somerset; Henry, Margaret, and their allies flee to
London; and York and his supporters pursue them to foment civil war that
the playwright would stage in *3 Henry VI*.

Thus the final scenes of *2 Henry VI* suggest that the play's pervasive
motif of an almost-always-wrongful climbing for place will continue to rip
apart the English court and commonwealth. Despite this fact, Shakespeare
in the present play gives audiences, in the memorable representations of
Humphrey, Duke of Gloucester, and especially Alexander Iden, a wise perspective on humankind's presumptuous natural instinct to climb beyond
one's rank or place in society. This early history play reflects its author's
generally conservative political assumptions mainly by showing the havoc
wrought by Luciferan ambition that never acknowledges hereditary right
or orderly process. Queen Elizabeth created relatively few knights during
her reign (the number nothing like the horde James I would coin to fill his
empty treasury). While Shakespeare in Alexander Iden's knighting plausibly sets for his queen and society an ideal criterion for conferring knight-
hoods, he does not appear by his implicit criticism of the motif of climbing
for place in *2 Henry VI* to be defining a phenomenon especially notewor-
thy between 1589–1594, the time span within which a date of composition
is usually fixed for this play. This possibility seems unlikely because overweening courtiers and lords appear to have been no more numerous in
London in this five-year period than they were in the 1570s and early
1580s and than they would be in the later 1590s and early 1600s.

Shakespeare's intense competition with Christopher Marlowe suggests a
more likely source for his interest in making climbing for place an inform-
ing motif of *2 Henry VI*. If Shakespeare's play postdates Marlowe's *Dr.
Faustus*, talk of sorcery and devils and the staging of the hocus pocus of
black magic in *Henry VI, Parts 1* and *2* testify to Shakespeare's (probably
uneasy) awareness of the popularity of this tragedy of Marlowe's. Harry
Levin some time ago showed just how thoroughly the Marlovian protagonist is an overreacher, a man like Faustus or Tamburlaine bent on aspiring—Lucifer-like—to much more than the place allotted to him by orthodox theology and politics.[34] The motif of high climbing in *2 Henry VI* may
amount to Shakespeare's response to Marlowe's latent intermittent admi-
ration for the overreacher,[35] in that his treatment essentially never glorifies
or makes attractive instinctive presumption but roots it in Original Sin,
with all its cataclysmic consequences.

NOTES

[1] References to 2 *Henry VI* are to *The Complete Works*, Bevington.
[2] The relevance of this figurative blindness for the various but related strengths and deficiencies of political and moral vision among noble characters of 2 *Henry VI* is suggested by Calderwood, "Shakespeare's Evolving Imagery," esp. 485–489.
[3] *Complete Works*, 551.
[4] For alternative readings of the importance of the Simpcox episode for 2 *Henry VI* as a whole, see Berry, *Patterns of Decay*, 36–37; Jones, *The Origins of Shakespeare*, 172–175; Knowles, "The Farce of History," esp. 169-70; and Dessen, "Stagecraft and Imagery," esp. 78–79.
[5] The relative formlessness of 2 *Henry VI* has been remarked by, among others, Kay, "Traps, Slaughter, and Chaos," esp. 1, 12; Ornstein, *A Kingdom for a Stage*, 42, 52; A.L. French, "The Mills of God," esp. 314; Fly, "'Dumb Significants,'" esp. 186–188; and Dessen, 65–66.
[6] This parallel is also noted by Williamson, "'When Men Are Rul'd by Women,'" esp. 48.
[7] Cox, "Devils and Power in Marlowe and Shakespeare," analyzes the role of the fiend Asnath and its implications (62–63) and concludes that the focus in typically Shakespearean fashion in the *Henry VI* plays remains "not . . . on the cosmic frame of human action but on human action itself" (61), on, that is to say, the "devilish" motives of Dame Eleanor that prompt her to employ a witch and a conjuror.
[8] My interpretation receives support from Kelly's assertion that the conjured spirit of 2 *Henry VI* appears to be "a real denizen of the underworld, though hardly characterized in terms of a traditional devil or damned soul. . . . As far as theological doctrine is concerned, it was universally accepted by Christians in Shakespeare's day that only God had certain knowledge of the future, and that evil spirits could only conjecture future events from already existing causes" (254).
[9] The Morality-play-like features of the spectacle of Dame Eleanor's public punishment have been described by Martin, "Elizabethan Civic Pageantry," esp. 249.
[10] Eleanor's penitent attitude appears to be evidence contradicting Turner's generalization that "the major figures in the *Henry VI* plays undergo no moral change of character" ("Characterization," 241). The pathos of the lamentation has been focused and described in detail by Clemen, "Some Aspects of Style," 9–11.
[11] In this respect, my argument denies Turner's claim that "Duke Humphrey's exposure of Simpcox's pretenses" is an episode "which

stand[s] outside the main line of action, neither arising from what precedes [it] nor leading to further events" (246).

[12] In fact, Berry interprets Gloucester's words and behavior in the hawking episode as indicators of virtue: judged within the popular context of the Earl of Oxford's famous affront to Sir Philip Sidney, "Winchester's direct challenge and added insults cannot be honorably ignored. . . . Throughout the play Gloucester's passion is righteous, open, honestly eccentric, an endearing contrast to the wily self-control of his opponents" (37).

[13] Duke Humphrey is described as "a new type of ideal ruler, the Ciceronian governor" by Riggs in *Shakespeare's Heroical Histories*, 115, 119–120; as a "good governor" modeled upon the ideals of Sir Thomas Elyot's *Book Named the Governor* (1531) by Berry 1975, 38–40 and by Jones 161–166; and as an exemplary Christian humanist by Manheim, *The Weak King Dilemma*, 90–95.

[14] Blanpied, *Time and the Artist*, 51–52. But cf. Reed, Jr., who argues in *Crime and God's Judgment* that: "at times cantankerous, especially when crossed by Cardinal Beaufort, and openly disdainful of the oily self-interest of Suffolk, Duke Humphrey is no paragon of diplomacy. His strength is his iron-minded presence . . ."(106).

[15] See, for example, Smidt, *Unconformities*, 26; and Lee, "Reflections of Power," esp. 201, 205.

[16] Champion, "'Prologue to Their Play,'" esp. 296–301.

[17] This is also the conclusion of Pratt, "Shakespeare and Humphrey," esp. 205–206; and of Hodgdon, *The End Crowns All*, 61.

[18] See, for example, Helgerson, *Forms of Nationhood*, 195–210; and Hodgdon, 63–64.

[19] The details of the play focused thus far in this paragraph do not appear in Shakespeare's sources but constitute his invention (Williams, "Suffolk and Margaret," esp. 315–316).

[20] In his analysis of this episode, Candido in "Getting Loose," 398–400, accentuates Suffolk's craven bartering attitude in captivity with Talbot's refusal to do so in *1 Henry VI* when he finds himself in a similar situation.

[21] Jones concludes that in Suffolk's and the naval Lieutenant's dialogue, "a startling degree of class hatred is given vent" (168).

[22] *Complete Works*, 561.

[23] Berman in "Fathers and Sons" judges that "[i]n defense of his 'honorable house,' Cade resorts to the same cunning savagery as does York in defense of his 'honorable house.' The two are linked not only by conspiracy, but by an identical obsession which brings chaos to the realm" (493). In this respect, see also Riggs, 124–125 and Berry, 45–47. In "'More Than History Can Pattern,'" Pugliatti remarks that in *2 Henry VI* Shakespeare "suggests a leveling to the lowest plane of those who intrigue at court for their own advancement and profit and of those who rebel out of material need and hunger" (456).

²⁴ At some point prior to the late sixteenth century, the idea of God's scourge as apocalyptic deluge (Isaiah 28: 14–29) was translated into the notion of a bad man who punishes equal or greater evil. For specific references to the human scourge, see Marlowe's *Tamburlaine, Part One* , 3.3.44–60; 4.2.31–32; 4.3.1–14; *Tamburlaine, Part Two,* 2.4.78–80; 4.1.148–169; 5.1.181–183; and of course *Hamlet,* 3.4.173–177. Cf. Elliott, *Scourge and Minister,* 122–125.

²⁵ McRae, "Agrarian Communism," esp. 110–121.

²⁶ Quoted by McRae, 112, who notes that the pithy couplet "surfaces," among other places, "in both Henrican and Elizabethan drama; it is confronted in a sixteenth-century conduct manual for the gentry, and its currency after 1640 suggests an unabated popular vitality within aural and local cultures" (112). Also see Hill, "From Lollards to Levellers," esp. 100; and Patterson, *Shakespeare and the Popular Voice,* 46.

²⁷ See McRae 110–115. "In 1549, 'men were saying "there are too many gentlemen in England by 500"'" (118).

²⁸ In this respect, see Hattaway, "Rebellion, Class Consciousness," esp. 19.

²⁹ Caldwell, in "Jack Cade," notes that a satirical poem circa 1450 blames "a Lord Say for the financial burdens borne by the populace" (37). "If in reading or viewing the play one sees Saye and his son-in-law as innocent men brutally murdered by an urban mob, one must remember the sometimes brutal role they themselves played in the historical changes in Henry's government" (57). Also see Cartelli, "Jack Cade in the Garden," esp. 58–59. But cf. Brockbank, "The Frame of Disorder," esp. 88–89; and Manheim, "Duke Humphrey and the Machiavels," esp. 256.

³⁰ Hill, in "The Many-Headed Monster," 303, maintains that in this period one-third of those individuals adjudged to die "escaped by pleading Benefit of Clergy."

³¹ Extended analyses of Jack Cade's rebellion as depicted in *2 Henry VI*—ones which generally emphasize Cade's viciousness—appear in Wilson, "'A Mingled Yarn,'" esp. 167–177; Pugliatti 471–478; Caldwell 49–62, 67–70; Sterling 228–240; Helgerson 206–210, 212–216; Knowles 175–185; Rackin, *Stages of History,* 207–221; Hattaway 17–20; Cartelli 53–67; Bevington, *Tudor Drama and Politics,* 238–240; and Patterson 47–51.

³² The emblematic symbolism of this scene has been identified and described by Pierce, *The Family and the State,* 56–57.

³³ See Rackin, 211–217 and Greenblatt, "Murdering Peasants," esp. 24–25. Both critics downplay Iden's positive characterization in this episode by stressing Cade's words that he dies by famine as much as by Iden's sword and by identifying Iden with Elizabethan propertied men antagonistic to the rights of the masses for food and land. In this vein, also see Cartelli 48–52.

³⁴ H. Levin, *The Overreacher;* Ornstein concludes that the Duke of York in *2 Henry VI* possesses "the mythic largeness of the Marlovian superman" (50).

³⁵ Cf., however, Reese, *The Cease of Majesty* 181.

HENRY VI, PART 2
COMMODIFYING AND RECOMMODIFYING THE PAST
IN LATE-MEDIEVAL AND EARLY-MODERN ENGLAND

M. *Rick Smith*

What we used to call "source study" was clearly an enterprise doomed one day to pursue itself to exhaustion, yet it would be impossible to analyze the status of the narrative contents of the Elizabethan history play as somehow originating in previously commodified forms without undertaking work on sources, analogues, and their relationships. I intend here, however, not to investigate sources and analogues of Shakespeare's *Henry VI, Part 2* for their own sake but to provide a—necessarily preliminary—account of these narrative contents insofar as they had a history as published commodities in the century and a half that separated Shakespeare's play from the historical events it dramatizes. Any such "commodifying of the past" must have occurred most extensively only after the advent of printing. However, much of the material in Shakespeare's principal source for the First Tetralogy, Edward Hall's *The Union of the Two Noble and Illustre Families of Lancastre and Yorke* (1548), itself enjoyed no small measure of clapper-clawing, having been circulated and recycled in many forms from the *Brut*, the *Polychronicon,* and John Hardyng's verse chronicle of events down to 1436, to Robert Fabyan's *New Chronicles of England and of France* (published in multiple manuscript copies during the fifteenth century and printed in 1516), and Sir Thomas More's *Historie of Kyng Rycharde the Thirde* (printed 1543) to Polydore Vergil's *Anglica Historia* (commissioned by Henry VII, but not printed until 1534). Subsequently, Richard Grafton continued Hardyng's chronicle in *The Chronicle of John Harding in Metre . . . with a Continuation in Prose to this our Time* (1543), incorporating More's *Historie,* and also published Hall's *Union.* Finally, Grafton printed his own *Abridgement of the Chronicles of England* (1562). By the time of Grafton's *Abridgement,* which went through five editions by 1572, an English appetite for the matter of history had been whetted that would consume multiple editions of John Foxe's *Actes and Monuments* (1563; nine editions by 1610), John Stowe's *A Summarie of Englyshe Chronicles* (1565; ten editions by 1610), and Raphael Holinshed's *Chronicles of England, Scotlande and Irelande* (1577; five editions within ten years). Certainly, even beyond considerations about how these titles were related to one another and the works of Shakespeare that were based upon them, the list makes up an impressive record for publication about the past in the first one hundred years of printing in England. It illustrates how much history-book publishing in England contributed to the "printing revolution" in early-modern Europe.

Indeed, a vast literature about this "printing revolution" has accumulated over the past fifty years, and Elizabeth Eisenstein's magnum opus, *The Printing Press as an Agent of Change*, and the subsequent work that gave us this tag have inevitably made all but commonplace the idea that printing brought in a revolution. But thinking about this momentous transformation in such terms has tended to obscure the complex and long-term economic and social processes that supported it. I would like to begin here from the standpoint that printing was as much an effect of a revolution as it was revolutionary itself, indeed, that printing emerged in the course of the commodity—and the consequent finance—revolution that was ongoing throughout the first two thirds of the fifteenth century. The pressures for transformation of the European economy in the late Middle Ages were many, but one of the most insistent and intense was what John Day has referred to as the "great bullion famine" of the fifteenth century. The old money economy had weakened, accelerated by the shortage of labor and insufficient production of suitable commodities for trade, and the effects of both processes were aggravated by the prodigious export of silver and gold, mostly to the Levant. The metals' status both as currency and commodity, in the context of an overall scarcity of goods and labor, led readily to their wholesale conversion from currency to commodity and to the "famine" Day described (1–71). One consequence was a crisis in credit—hitherto based almost entirely on the supply of hard cash ("merchant's capital," in Marx's terms) at both the point of sale and the point of delivery—brought on by a pervasive uncertainty about how to calculate liquidity. A new mode of creating exchangeable value, one no longer dependent on the availability of gold or silver, had to be devised. Commerce itself now had to assume the role of creating wealth.

While the basic details of the commodity revolution that resulted are well known—a population recovering a century after the Black Death gradually put an end to upward pressure on wages, and increased production of goods and services combined with increased demand stimulated circulation, allowing for the beginnings of "primitive accumulation" of capital—the nascent commodification of information about this time (a process of commodification that significantly predates the establishment of printing) continues to receive little study.[1] The past, and specifically the historical or legendary past of England, became one of the most important of these cultural commodities between 1440 and the accession of Elizabeth I in 1558. While the very events of the First Tetralogy were taking place, conditions were developing that would favor not merely the record of these events but the transformation of such records of whatever form—whether memoir, biography, history, chronicle, or matyrology—into salable multiple identical copies, whether manuscript or print. This essay examines Shakespeare's *Henry VI, Part 2* as an instance of how the public theater was launched at least in part by the theatrical recommodification of a segment of the English past that had already been extensively commodified as a part of the change in the circulation of economic energy occurring between about 1450 and 1550.

COMMODIFYING THE PAST

The development of a mechanism for the commercial circulation of texts—and by extension, of texts about the past—began well before the establishment of a printing industry in early-modern Europe. Transformations in the conditions of manuscript commissioning and production began in the late fourteenth century. Authors such as Gower and Chaucer achieved a hitherto unknown level of recognition and marketability, assisted by both poets' instinct for self-promotion; and their successes encouraged the commercial ambitions of hacks such as Lydgate, the earliest known English poet able to boast of making a living from writing. Meanwhile, an unprecedented degree of popular interest in religious questions centered around the growth of early reform movements, particularly Lollardry, created a steadily growing demand for copies of sermons, scriptures, and controversies.[2] Anne Hudson and Vincent Gillespie have demonstrated the breadth of demand for both manuscript production of dissenting religious texts as well as vernacular books of religion in general (Hudson 125–126, Gillespie 317–344). Both tendencies worked gradually to move the production of manuscripts out of religious or cathedral-collegiate-based scriptoria and into the commercial workshop, and although the production of bespoken manuscripts for aristocratic patrons remained important, workshops began to acquire and to copy manuscripts on the expectation of being able to sell multiple copies.

It is uncertain, however, whether we can speak of this early circulation of texts in market terms, and scholars for some time have disputed the extent of the commercial trade in manuscripts in the late fourteenth and fifteenth centuries. In 1979, A. I. Doyle and M. B. Parkes argued convincingly against the early existence of anything like large commercial scriptoria (163–210). On the strength of Doyle and Parkes's strong skepticism about a medieval manuscript-publishing industry, A. S. G. Edwards and Derek Pearsall conclude that the production of significant numbers of copies depended on an infrastructure that was not yet industrial, "a group of professional scribes, used to working independently, perhaps in adjacent premises, brought together to execute a specific commission" (262). Nevertheless, Edwards and Pearsall note that certain commercially adaptable practices of mass production—notably "dictation for simultaneous multiple copying"—were common on the Continent (and in England "in legal and notarial circles"), and they somewhat nervously acknowledge that the practice "seems, on the face of it, an obvious means of making several copies quickly" (262).

Whether we assume conservatively, with Doyle and Parkes, that "commercial" scriptoria remained tied to a strictly bespoke trade or take heart from Edwards and Pearsall's suggestion that the logistical means for "mass production" could have been assembled, it is clear that improving economic and logistical resources could have responded readily to a period of growing demand. We must also not forget that the period saw a dramatic growth in vernacular literacy. All three forces—the growing recognition of public literary personalities and their reputations, intense interest in religious controversy, and an increasing rate of literacy—worked together to ensure that commercial publication would continue to look more and more like a lucrative prospect, and well before the advent of printing. In any case, the concept that a book could be a profitable commodity was well established even before any commercialization of scriptoria. As Rudolf Hirsch observed, "bookshops had existed, especially in connection with writing centers [that is, 'scriptoria' in the usually understood sense of the term, not commercial writing centers], but their number was small. The trading in manuscripts was frequently a part of the operation of a merchant who also dealt generally in a number of other commodities" (11). Certainly, however, demand for and consequently the pressure to commodify certain kinds of texts was strengthening at the same time that mechanisms for the efficient production of multiple copies were coming into place.

We have already noted that the work of laureate, or notorious, or opportunistic poets was likely to have been extensively commodified during the beginnings of significant manuscript publication. We have also suggested that vernacular works of religion and all kinds of texts associated with the progress of Lollardry made for sound commodities. Although saints' lives and chronicles are respectably represented among the manuscripts prepared under all auspices, still, as F. J. Levy states, "by the fifteenth century the art of writing chronicles had nearly vanished" (9). While pessimistic about the scope of fifteenth century demand for chronicles, Levy nevertheless characterizes the necessary dynamics for a revival of chronicle writing in terms that complement the conclusions outlined above:

History writing in fifteenth-century England held no official position, and its haven in the monasteries was gradually closing.

The result was the decline and termination of the classic medieval Latin chronicle. Its readership had always been limited to the educated, and whatever view one takes of the extent of literacy in the Middle Ages, this group can never have been a very large one. A revival of chronicling depended upon the demands of a new audience, and this turned out to be an audience of laymen with some education and with interests only in certain specific aspects of the past. For them the chronicles had to be written in English. The groups involved were the wealthier merchants, mostly but not exclusively in London, and some members of the wealthier landed class, and what they wanted to read was a kind of general history slanted in the one case toward city history and in the other toward heroic legendry. The works that they read were the *Polychronicon* of Ranulph Higden, as Englished by John of Trevisa, and the chronicle of the *Brut*. (10)

One may presume, however, considering the work on the growth of demand cited earlier, that the potential market for writing about the past was significantly more extensive than Levy suggests throughout the period of manuscript publication. From an early date, indeed, Lollard writers (as well as those with reforming sympathies) knew well the power of appealing to the past as a way of not just commenting on the abuses of the present. Ecclesiastical history was cited frequently and provided the basis of many a polemic against those practices which the reformers considered the most corrupt: monastic establishments and the celibate clergy, the doctrine of the real presence in the mass, the veneration of the host, the delivery of communion to the faithful only in one kind, and the material establishment of the church hierarchy and its claim to separate sovereignty. Given the kinds of evidence cited by Anne Hudson—possession of many Lollard texts in English by members of the artisanal classes, Lollard circuit preachers handing out carefully annotated copies of their sermons for study in *conventiculae*, identical copies from several sites of meticulously documented and cross-referenced tractates, theological discussions, and polemics (125–27, 131–134)—a lay readership with considerable interest in the uses of the past and its significance for how its members were to conduct themselves in the present seems likely.

Levy also tends to undervalue the content of the two kinds of such literature he acknowledges—the "general history" "slanted in the one case toward city history and in the other toward heroic legendry." Levy dismisses the former as "mere record," the concern of men who, "even more than the monks . . . saw the world with blinkers" (17). Indeed, even the laureled Polydore Vergil drew on Richard Arnold, Robert Fabyan, and the Calais Chronicle for judgment as well as detail, while contemporary writ-

ers on fifteenth-century literature and culture, from David Bevington to
Sheila Lindenbaum, have demonstrated the value of consulting Henry
Machyn, whose diary, Levy flatly declares, "is best ignored" (24).
Meanwhile, the vernacular historical literature Levy describes as "heroic
legendry"—*videlicit*, Geoffrey of Monmouth, William of Malmesbury,
Ranulf Higden, Froissart—was copied and recopied throughout the fifteenth century, a proliferation that not only contributed to its value as a
staple of the book trade before printing, but one that also worked together with the tendencies discussed above to establish the past itself as a cultural commodity well in advance of the composition of more "scientifical-
ly" historical works expressly intended for the press.

When printing did arrive, late-medieval and early-Renaissance historiography—especially chronicle literature and what Arthur B. Furguson
called *res gestae* history, ecclesiastical history, and the biographies of notorious figures typified by Sir Thomas More's unfinished life of Richard III[3]—
would make up, along with popularized medical and legal tracts and, especially after 1517, religious polemics, a significant proportion of print commodities. And although this voluminous cultural commodification could
not have occurred without the invention of moveable type, the dynamics
that produced the quantities of these materials so eagerly sought out and
promoted by early print entrepreneurs had their roots in the previous nine-
ty or so years of manuscript marketing.

They were also assisted by the arrival of Continental humanists and of
a dynasty with a particular interest in augmenting its claims to legitimacy
with appeals to the past. Alistair Fox points out that the very stylistic properties of humanist historiography contributed to its usefulness under the
new Tudor regime:

> Rulers quickly grasped the fact that the new historiography could
> serve their practical ambitions, and seized the opportunities it held
> out to them. The humanist habit of partitioning experience into a
> binary opposition between good and bad, and then of depicting the
> contrasting qualities of rhetorical stereotypes, held immense implica-
> tions for the interpretation of history. A present reign, for example,
> could be favorably contrasted with one in the past simply by invok-
> ing a rhetorical contrast between the two. Humanist style, with its
> propensity to classify experience by division and opposition, would
> take care of the rest according to the decorum of its own laws.

Among the shrewdest of those monarchs who exploited the potential of the new historiography was Henry VII. From soon after he
ascended the throne, he employed historians to celebrate his merit
and achievements, so as to justify his tenure of it. By 1500 he had
appointed a royal historiographer in the person of Bernard André,
whom he had commissioned to write a *Vita Henrici Septimi* (in imi-

tation of Tito Livio da Forli's *Vita Henrici Quinti*, written half a century earlier), and a series of annals. . . .

When Polydore Vergil arrived in England in 1502, fully versed in
the new Italianate historical doctrines, Henry was quick to commission him to prepare a humanist history of England written in the new
vogue. (109–110)

The first Tudor monarch shrewdly exploited the coincidence of
Continental talent, economic moment, and the possibilities of the new
invention; in doing so he also helped release a flood of historiographical
and controversial publication that neither he nor his successors could ever
completely control.

Henry VII may have seen the political value of historiography that supported his regime, but both he and Henry VIII strenuously sought to control the contents of publications which made use of the past in whatever
mode. If Henry VII's pursuit of censorship and sanction of the press looks
a little lax, it is only because neither the volume of publication, the number of imports, nor, in general, the content of English or imported impressions was sufficiently threatening during his reign to warrant anything like
the severe measures to which his son increasingly resorted. Humanism
reached high tide during the first decade of Henry VIII's reign, with the
works of More, Erasmus, Colet and the humanist translations of Livy,
Suetonius, Tacitus, Valla, and Vives. Soon homegrown reformers such as
William Tyndale and Robert Barnes were fiercely struggling to revive and
build upon the remnants of Lollardry, particularly through numerous and
relatively cheap printings of Tyndale's updating of the Wycliffite Bible as
well as of reforming sermons, commentary, and anti-Catholic polemics. As
with the texts that had driven the earlier movement, such materials made
much use of historical exempla, historical standards of proof, and historical comparison.

After 1517, the advance of the Reformation on the Continent led to
aggressive campaigns of publication by Lutherans, Hussites, Calvinists,
and exiled English reformers, and to the importation of large quantities of
contraband books into England. The burning of heretics was preceded by
the burning of their heretical books, and, as with the followers of Wycliff
in the late fourteenth century, the broad appeal of these materials is illustrated by the variety of persons from whom they were seized. Archbishop
Cuthbert Tunstal's and Sir Thomas More's campaigns in the 1520s to
detect and destroy heretical books uncovered surprising numbers in the
possession of persons whom Louis A. Schuster (not disinterestedly?)
described as "a ragman's roll of heretics: bakers, bricklayers, haberdashers,
leathersellers, pointmakers, saddlers, tallowchandlers, curates, grocers, and
the inevitable tailors and weavers" (1138). The book-burning campaigns
culminated in the great auto-da-fé of heretical texts that celebrated the

abjuration of Robert Barnes on Shrove Sunday, February 11, 1526 (Lusardi 1382–1383). But despite all Henry's efforts to regulate both Catholic and Protestant publication, demand escalated, the flood of printed matter increased in volume, and with it came a the proliferation of historical exempla, citation, and comparison. The king's death unleashed what John N. King called "the explosion of radical reformist publication during Edward's reign" (20), contributing not only to the dissemination of the details of religious controversy but also to a mass of historiographical citation that further commodified many fundamental details about Britain's late-medieval and early-Renaissance political as well as its ecclesiastical past. King also points out the far-reaching effects of Seymour's protectorate on the publishing industry, for Seymour

> permitted an unprecedented degree of religious toleration and freedom of speech, reading, and publication. . . . Printers turned out a huge volume of Protestant pamphlet literature, which had been forbidden so long as Henry VIII lived. Seymour's *de facto* relaxation of censorship brought him into direct confrontation with Gardiner, whose Winchester diocese was disturbed by outbursts of iconoclasm. Lutheran writings and inflammatory Protestant tracts went openly on sale in the Winchester market, including Bale's account of the persecution of Anne Askew which singled out the bishop as the bête noire of English reformers. (26)

When Mary Tudor drove multitudes of reformers abroad, she only moved the sites of English language publication of suspect materials offshore again, and although she was able to burn hundreds of the reformers who stayed behind, her regime was too weak to stem either the importation of books or even their clandestine presence on her own soil. Her reign had almost no effect on the processes which, by the accession of Elizabeth, had commodified hundreds of narratives about the past and how they related to the momentous events of reform and counter-reform.

COMMODIFYING THE ALREADY-COMMODIFIED: "VIRTUAL DELIRIUM"

What I referred to earlier as the "matter of history" (following Irving Ribner [63] and on the analogy of the Arthurian "matter of Britain") thus comes to Elizabethan playwrights in the last quarter of the sixteenth century having been, in a sense, already "consumed" in the lengthy but inexorable process that turned the first tentative attempts at organized manuscript publication in the late fourteenth century into the thriving publishing industry of the mid-sixteenth. The rise of a recognizably federal, embryonically modern, if embattled, English state coincided with the occasional irruption of truly modern instances of jingoism and nationalism and accounted in part for the strong demand for history. Print warfare between Protestants and Catholics throughout the period of reform and counter-reform—originally confined to the Continent but establishing itself on English soil whenever dynastic politics allowed, and always a prolific source of imports—led to the development of a fiercely polemical histori-ography aimed alternately at undermining and shoring up the accounts of the origins and privileges of nations and national churches, augmenting the demand for the matter of history by deploying it in religious struggles throughout Europe, and helping to transform it from intellectual ordinance to cultural commodity.

As already noted, this kind of demand appeared as early as the late four-teenth century, driven by the Lollard controversy and served by the earliest attempts at commercial publication. The rapid spread of printing presses on the Continent and in England alike between the 1480s and the reign of Edward VI, coupled after 1517 with the advance of the Reformation and the growth of nationalism, meant that the publication of any materials whatever could be made more commercially successful by incorporating material with intellectual, religious, or political application or topicality. Notorious events and identities[4] were consumed, recycled, and circulated by a fiercely partisan public in a variety of entertaining and narrative forms stimulated in the first instance by nation-building and national projects of reform and counterreform, but later sustained by an affect resembling the "virtual delirium" of the "consumption of consumption" described by Frederic Jameson in *Postmodernism* (269). As anachronistic as it may seem to attempt to apply aspects of Jameson's theory of late capitalist "cultural logic" to the stage of "primitive accumulation" in the fifteenth and six-teenth centuries (if both Marx's and Richard Halperin's analyses have enti-tled us to use the term),[5] I believe there are good reasons for doing so. Jameson sees postmodernism, used as a descriptive term for the character-istic culture of Western-style market economies since the mid-1950s, as peculiar to "late capitalism," an era that has seen "the disappearance of the individual subject," conceived as the human resource unit especially required for sustaining the modes of capitalist production.[6] In the field of cultural production, pastiche reigns:

> If the ideas of a ruling class were once the dominant (or hegemonic) ideology of bourgeois society, the advanced capitalist countries today are now a field of stylistic and discursive heterogeneity without a norm. . . . In this situation parody finds itself without a vocation; it has lived, and that strange new thing pastiche slowly comes to take its place . . . the producers of culture have nowhere to turn but to the past: the imitation of dead styles, speech through all the masks and

voices stored up in the imaginary museum of a now global culture. This situation evidently determines what the architecture historians call "historicism," namely, the random cannibalization of all the styles of the past, the play of random stylistic allusion, and in general what Henri Lefebvre has called the increasing primacy of the "neo." This ominipresence of pastiche is not incompatible with a certain humor, however, nor is it innocent of all passion: it is at the least compatible with addiction—with a whole historically original consumers' appetite for a world transformed into sheer images of itself and for pseudoevents and "spectacles." . . . . It is for such objects that we may reserve Plato's conception of the "simulacrum," the identical copy for which no original has ever existed. Appropriately enough, the culture of the simulacrum comes to life in a society where exchange value has been generalized to the point at which very memory of use value is effaced, a society of which Guy Debord has observed, in an extraordinary phrase, that in it "the image has become the final form of commodity reification." (17–18)

I would argue at least provisionally that, during a period of similar transitional instability, when the bourgeois subject was under construction during the process of "primitive accumulation," similar conditions of cultural production may have prevailed. In transforming his sources into *Henry VI, Part 2*, Shakespeare's procedures recall aspects of Jameson's notion of postmodern "pastiche."[7] This is not to reduce Shakespeare's dramaturgy to "mere" pastiche but to seek a term now grounded in Jameson's theoretical system for some of the most familiar peculiarites of Shakespeare's use of the matter of history: the frequent anachronistic juxtaposition of lives and portions of lives known historically to have been lived outside of the requirements the plot, a dramatic chronology that shifts back and forth from a historical to a fictional sequence of events, and the amalgamation of incidental details from the records of analogous events, particularly the Great Rising of 1381 (Wat Tyler's rebellion) and Jack Cade's rebellion, but also the Pilgrimage of Grace and various disturbances of the 1560s to 1580s. The legendarily popular Henry VI plays (*Henry VI, Part 1* was especially popular, but the *Part 2* was probably little less so) exploit the market history of all the "entertainment and narrative processes" (Jameson 269) of its matter of history.

For Jack Cade's rebellion in *Henry VI, Part 2*, as is well known, Shakespeare conflated sources for both the 1450 rebellion and the Great Rising of 1381. As Michael Hattaway (1988, 13–22) and Ellen C. Caldwell (49–62) have argued, Shakespeare in part "carnivalizes" his source material, using details taken from Hall and Holinshed (among others), to create *mises en scène* of misrule that parody the corruption, dishonor, rapaciousness, and injustice of the ruling elites. Caldwell's work further allows us to see in detail how Shakespeare's immediate sources for the rebellion—Hall, Foxe, Grafton, Holinshed—participate in a dense "intertexture," a veritable "textual system" in the Kristevan sense (although Caldwell uses neither term, and never cites Kristeva).[8] Within such a system manuscript sources, including records of interrogations, indictments, negotiations, pardon rolls for both 1381 and 1450, historical memoranda about the 1450 event in the hand of John Stowe, manuscript chronicles, verse and prose chronicles, and printed histories and martyrologies by Polydore Vergil, Hall, Grafton, Stowe, Crespin, and Foxe, circulate and entrain one another in an evolving "tropics of discourse."[9]

Where Arthur B. Furguson would have characterized this kind of recycling and circulation of accounts as "innocently plagiaristic" (7), I want to argue that the narrative processes of recording, narrating, appropriating, communicating, and circulating the events of 1381 and 1450 are embedded in a larger, historical process of *moyenne durée* that would eventually convert historical narratives into marketable commodities and finally "already consumed" commodities which bore an enhanced value conferred by their history of previous consumption. Driven initially by the twin engines of ideological consolidation that attended the formation of the modern state and the religious print warfare that raged alongside the armed struggle between reform and counterreform,[10] a flood of historiography broke from the printing presses with the publication, all before 1550, of works such as Sir Thomas More's *Historie of Kyng Rycharde the Thirde*, the epistolary animadversions of Erasmus and Luther, Polydore Vergil's *Anglica Historia*, the earliest Protestant martyrologies, works of historically revisionist theology and polemic by Calvin, Melancthon, and Reuchlin, and Hall's *Union of the Two Noble and Illustre Families of Lancastre and Yorke*.

The flood reached biblical proportions with the Marian reaction in England, the formation of the Guisard leagues, the outbreak of open religious warfare in France, and the mounting reports of Spanish conquest and atrocities in the Indies accompanied by the denunciations of Bartolomé de las Casas and the infamous justifications of Juan Ginés de Sepúlveda (who termed the 1527 sack of Rome by imperial troops, as well as the genocide in the Indies, instances of just warfare).[11] All the major genres of Renaissance religious polemic—martyrology, apology, tracts on apostolic succession and the origins of national churches, manifestos on church governance and on obedience to ecclesiastical and civil authorities—as well as the great institutes, kerygmas, christologies, ecclesiastical polities, soteriologies, eucharistic treatises and theological works drew authority and rhetorical effectiveness from the whole range of historiographical sources. Renaissance historians as such engaged in their own intense and prolific controversies, battling foreign historians as well as one another; and as Caldwell (21–23) discovered through a study of memoranda in Stowe's hand recorded in Lambeth Library MS. 306 and Harleian MSS. 543 and 545, a historian like Stowe could at various stages of the writing, publication, and reissuing of his *Chronicles of England*, nuance his own treatment of an event like Jack Cade's rebellion.

A large, hungry, and committed continent-wide market for historical narrative was in place by the accession of Elizabeth in 1558, and the restoration of Protestantism led to the establishment of a proportionally immense English market for the same materials, which was sustained as much by translation as it was by the efforts of English historians and polemicists. By the time of the earliest Elizabethan history plays, John Bale's *King John* (written before 1536; revised in 1538, and rewritten and presented before Queen Elizabeth at Ipswich in 1561) Norton and Sackville's *Gorboduc* (1561), Thomas Preston's *Cambises* (1560s), and *Apius and Virginia* (1567), the matter of history had become an established cultural commodity as well as an ideological one (cf. Ribner 33, 49).

Irving Ribner's enduring work on the English history play, even though it remains a little too philological or formalistic for new historicist or cultural materialist tastes, nevertheless impressively demonstrates that Shakespeare's history plays emerge toward the end of a lengthy process of dramaturgical development. "[A]ll of the writers of history plays in the 1580s," he concluded in his chapter on the early English history plays, "whether or not Shakespeare was among them, were extending and developing a dramatic tradition already in existence some half century before their time" (91). Indeed, drama about the past—whether the legendary or the historical past—was the genre that launched the Elizabethan theater in the 1580s as a paying proposition. A parallel process to the commodification of the past in manuscript and print publication seems to have been ongoing as the history play was born as a genre, following Ribner's argument, on the one hand out of the morality play transformed to a genre increasingly applied to secular politics and the problems of reform (32), and on the other out of a tradition of popular or folk-hero plays, such as *Chinon of England, Godfrey of Bouloigne, Richard Whittington, Robin Hood and Little John* (59–62).

As Joseph Loewenstein argues, dramatic representation itself should be seen as a distinct form of publication quite apart from the printing of dramatic texts (265–278), although one must be careful to distinguish the degree to which such publication could be considered "commercial" before the opening of the public theaters. Once the theaters were opened, however, drama about the past—whether that past was legendary, British, Continental, Mediterranean or Asian, classical, medieval, or recent—contributed greatly to their commercial success. Fifty or so years of dramatic experimentation with subject matter about the past had also contributed to the further commodification of history, whatever the auspices of the plays that represented it. Plays such as Norton and Sackville's *Gorboduc*, based on an episode of legendary British history and first performed at the Inner Temple in December 1561 and subsequently before Queen Elizabeth at Whitehall in January, and Thomas Preston's *Cambises*, based on two accounts in Herodotus and probably performed at court about the same time, and hence both acted under private auspices, were nevertheless dramatic publications in Loewenstein's sense. Plays about the past performed at court or the Inns of Court, from John Bale's *King John* to Preston's *Cambises*, assisted the economic processes that had been commodifying the past since the late fourteenth century, helping to transform the market for dramatic representation of the past in ways that made possible the sensational success of Marlowe's *Tamburlaine*.

Historical subject matter as it appears in plays like *King John, Gorboduc, Cambises*, and *Apius and Virginia* nevertheless continued to assert its three humanist historiographical prerogatives to be taken as authority, exemplum, and *speculum principium*. It took a Christopher Marlowe to notice that the real money was to be made by exploiting the energy of *affect* implicit in the market for exempla. His travesty of humanist normative historiography and narrative process, particularly in the first and second *Tamburlaine* (1587–1588) and *The Massacre at Paris* (before 1590?), proved that playgoers craved the staged *consumption* of the historiographic commodity rather than the didactic edification and timely admonition it might inspire as represented history. Indeed, with Shakespeare's First Tetralogy, the dramaturgic consumption of historical narrative commodities that had *already* been consumed (sometimes many times over) in the historiographic intertext or textual system emerged as the key to the cultural logic of the Shakespearean history play.

Shakespeare's First Tetralogy amounts to a case study in the theatrical recommodification of subject matter about the past that had already been circulated extensively in various antecedent commodified forms; further, the conditions which made possible such recommodification resemble in many ways conditions described in Frederic Jameson's account of "the consumption of the very idea of consumption" and serve a "cultural logic" parallel to Jameson's sense of the term. It is as though during the transition from the stage of "primitive accumulation" conditions amounted to a "mirror image" of certain key conditions of late capitalism as analyzed by Jameson. One feature Jameson remarks upon that was certainly prevalent in the 1580s and 1590s—both on stage and off—was spectacle. Where Jameson argues that "the very entertainment and narrative processes of commercial television . . . are, in turn, reified and turned into so many commodities" (269), I argue that the matter of history amounts, by the time of Shakespeare's First Tetralogy, to "entertainment and narrative processes" turned not only into commodities but into previously consumed commodities or acts of consumption themselves which Shakespeare's dramatic spectacle stages as consumption. The "entertainment and narrative processes" of Shakespeare's history plays are rooted in the prior cultural consumption of entertainment and narrative commodities. Such commodities were formed from the matter of history as it was published and republished in manuscript, print, and oral tradition. Concentrating on two figures among Shakespeare's dramatis personae whose stories were extensively commodified in the process outlined above—Humphrey of Gloucester and Jack Cade—the next section examines theatrical "consumption of consumption" in practice.

RECOMMODIFYING THE PAST IN HENRY VI, PART 2

The character of "the Good Duke" Humphrey in *Henry VI, Part 2* draws on the long process that commodified, circulated, and recommodified his identity in its various public and private contexts as it traveled through several media markets from the historical time of his protectorate to his appearance in Shakespeare's First Tetralogy. It is this "spectacular" Humphrey who commands the trust and affection of Shakespeare's equally "spectacular" commons, and whom Cardinal Beauford decries:

> What though the common people favor him,
> Calling him "Humphrey, the good Duke of Gloucester,"
> Clapping their hands, and crying with loud voice,
> "Jesu maintain your royal Excellence!"
> With "God preserve the good Duke Humphrey!"
> I fear me my lords, for all this flattering gloss,
> He will be found a dangerous Protector. (1.1.158–164)[12]

The Cardinal's speech cites expressions of popular acclamation for Duke Humphrey made thoroughly familiar by more than a century of publication in chronicle, history, matyrology, and ballad, in manuscript, print, and word-of-mouth forms alike, from Fabyan and More to Hall and the *Mirror for Magistrates*, and from Grafton and Foxe to Holinshed and Stowe. Shakespeare's Cardinal must denounce his enemy in terms taken from a tradition of texts consistently favorable to him (including even the account of Humphrey and Saunder Simpcox from Sir Thomas More's great defense of Catholic doctrine, the 1529 *Dialogue Concerning Heresies*). The unruliness of the commons, their unfitness for judgment, seems to be the target, except that the ideological critique originates in a particularly distasteful prelate. Ideologically speaking, however, Beauford remains a mere "simulacrum" of an anticlerical portrait, his character the dramaturgic "materialization" of a pastiche of already-commodified narrative contents. In a passage that literally enacts the very kind of spectacle that Beauford finds so repugnant, Suffolk and Queen Margaret confront the reputation of the same Duke Humphrey and the same commons in the famous Petitioners scene:

> *Enter three or four* PETITIONERS, [PETER], *the Armorer's*
>   *man being one.*
> 1. *Petit.* My masters, let's stand close. My Lord
>   Protector will come this way by and by, and then
>   we may deliver our supplications in the quill.
> 2. *Petit.* Marry, the Lord protect him, for he's a
>   good man! Jesu bless him!
> *Enter* SUFFOLK *and* QUEEN.
> *Peter.* Here 'a comes, methinks, and the Queen
>   with him. I'll be the first, sure.
> 2. *Petit.* Come back, fool. This is the Duke of
>   Suffolk and not my Lord Protector.
> *Suf.* How now, fellow? wouldst any thing with me?
> *Queen.* [*Reading.*] "To my Lord Protector"? Are
>   your supplications to his lordship? Let me see
>   them. What is thine?
> 1. *Petit.* Mine is, and't please your Grace, against
>   John Goodman, my Lord Cardinal's man, for keeping
>   my house, my lands, and wife and all, from me.
> *Suf.* Thy wife, too? that's some wrong indeed.
>   What's yours? What's here? [*Reads.*] "Against
>   the Duke of Suffolk, for enclosing the commons
>   of Melford." How now, sir knave?
> 2. *Petit.* Alas, sir, I am but a poor petitioner of our
>   whole township.
> *Peter.* [*Giving his petition.*] Against my master,
>   Thomas Horner, for saying that the Duke of York
>   was rightful heir to the crown.
> *Queen.* What say'st thou? Did the Duke of York
>   say he was rightful heir to the crown?
> *Peter.* That my [master] was? No, forsooth; my
>   master said that he was, and that the King was
>   an usurper.
> *Suf.* Who is there? (*Enter Servant.*) Take his fellow
>   in, and send for his master with a pursuivant
>   presently. We'll hear more of your master before the
>   King.
>   *Exit [Servant with Peter].*
> *Queen.* And as for you, that love to be protected

Under the wings of our Protector's grace,
Begin your suits anew, and sue to him.
                Tear the supplication.
Away, base cullions! Suffolk, let them go. (1.3.1–40)

Punctuated with the stage business of torn petitions made famous by
Kyd's *Spanish Tragedy* and spiced with the scandalous figures of Margaret
and Suffolk, the episode also prepares for the grotesque duel of armorer
and apprentice in Act 2, scene 3, based on one of the most familiar and
often cited incidents of Henry VI's reign. Although the outcome of the trial-
by-combat between Horner and Peter appears to accord with Providence,
the triumph of the social inferior raises questions. As a foreshadowing of
the combat between Iden and Cade in Act 4, scene 10, it is almost a travesty, with the defeat of Cade then functioning to restore order, but in ret-
rospect the two scenes seem to travesty one another and together they may
function like the Platonic "simulacra" cited by Jameson. In any case,
Shakespeare invokes both combats in the course of dramaturgically con-
suming the already-commodified textual trace of Suffolk's and Margaret's
appetite for both York's and Gloucester's destruction.

Humphrey's fate, however, has already been predicated much earlier by
a technique similar to the one employed for the Cardinal in 1.1.158–164,
but with quite an opposite effect. The first words the duke speaks are not
his own but words introduced by Suffolk as the "articles of contracted
peace / Between our sovereign and the French King Charles" (1.1.40–41).
These articles entail the marriage contract between Henry VI and Reignier,
King of Naples, and they conclude with the symbolic canceling of the
duke's specific court role charged with the oversight and approval of all
such agreements during the king's dependency:

Glou. (Reads.) "Inprimis, It is agreed between the French
        King Charles, and William de la Pole, Marquess of
        Suffolk, ambassador for Henry King of England,
        that the said Henry shall espouse the Lady Margaret,
        daughter unto Reignier King of Naples, Sicilia
        and Jerusalem, and crown her Queen of England,
        ere the thirtieth of May next ensuing. Item, [It
        is further agreed between them,] that the duchy of Anjou
        and the county of Maine shall be releas'd and
        deliver'd [over] to the King her father"—
                        [Duke Humphrey lets it fall.]
King. Uncle, how now!
Glou.   Pardon me, gracious lord;
        Some sudden qualm hath struck me at the heart,
        And dimm'd mine eyes, that I can read no further.
                                        (1.1.43–55)

The stage articles mimic the legalese of state papers; the details likely derive, however—by what intermediary processes of circulation is unclear—from contemporary hostile manuscript animadversions about the marriage and the peace that began to appear as early as February, 1445. Ralph A. Griffiths, in his massive history of the reign of Henry VI, points out that Suffolk is unlikely to have agreed to such terms and took care to repudiate them, "on more than one occasion [asserting] that he had not exceeded his instructions and certainly had not promised on behalf of Henry VI that Anjou and Maine would be ceded." He attributes the early appearance of popular "intelligence" about the counties' imminent cession to "the arch-rumour-monger of Lancastrian England, Dr. Thomas Gascoigne" (487). In any case, the verses John Lydgate composed to accompany the city pageants at Margaret's coronation on May 30, 1445, had already caught the drift:

Undir fals pees ther may be covert ffraude;
Good cheer outward, with face of innocence;
Ffeyned fllaterye, with language of greet laude;
But what is wers than shynyng apparence,
Whan it is prevydd ffals in existence?

The sentiments were taken up again in the 1450s "more offensively and directly" by Gascoigne and several chroniclers, and the popular campaign against the Angevin match culminated in the circulation of "a bitter satirical proclamation" about Reignier's pretensions entitled "The Constable of Jerusalem" (Griffiths 488–490). Shakespeare crystallizes the sentiments that had circulated in the popular manuscript campaign against the marriage and the peace into an extract from an ersatz diplomatic dispatch. The hostile popular reaction is used to reconstruct the obnoxious content of the supposed official protocols, which stimulated it as a way of emphasizing Gloucester's sympathetic relationship with the commons.

Historically, Gloucester's protectorship had officially ended with the king's coronation at the age of eight in 1429. Shakespeare has projected an *ex officio* protectorship sustained by a weakening "popular party" up to the moment of the precipitating crisis in domestic and foreign affairs. Gloucester's dropping of the dispatch symbolizes the *de facto* end of his power within the theatrical spectacle of Margaret's coronation and focuses the energy of the scene on a figurative pastiche of historical documentation. Dropping the paper, Humphrey is reestablished as the commons' Gloucester, the "Good Duke" who cannot preserve his subjectivity and survive the immediate business entrusted to him. But the impression of this subjectivity resides in an energy of affect immanent as a resource amid Shakespeare's audience itself and derived from the wide circulation over three or four generations of Humphrey as an indispensable element of a past lucratively commodified in several media, from published manuscripts to *de casibus* verse tragedy to printed chronicle, martyrology, and history. The history of Humphrey of Gloucester as an item of print commodity begins as early as Thomas More's *Dialogue Concerning Heresies* (London: 1529; 1531).[13] More's sources for the story of the false miracle of Simpcox are generally the same as those he used for *The History of King Richard III*; that is, most directly Polydore Vergil's *Anglica Historia*, but More doubtless had access to as much or more of the same material as Vergil used: "the continuations of the *Polychronicon* and the *Brut*, from Fabyan and Tito Livio, from foreign accounts such as those of Monstrelet, Froissart, and Gaguin. Besides the chroniclers, Polydore could make use of the statutes and of other documents; of direct observation, of legend and oral tradition; and of the reports of survivors of great affairs" (Levy 57). Thus More's Humphrey of Gloucester already exists as an identity within a dense intertexture of widely dispersed and variously circulated materials, some consisting of items long current in the commercial manuscript trade, others already familiar staples of the trade in printed books. Foxe recirculates the same story in *Acts and Monuments*, one of the most frequently reprinted and well-known works of the age. And although Bullough cites Foxe as possibly Shakespeare's own most immediate source for the Simpcox episode, he makes clear how the story inhabits three of the most popular print sources in a way that recalls the concept of the "textual system":

> J. D. Wilson has suggested that Grafton was used because the false miracle of Simpcox, originally told in Sir Thomas More's *Dialogue of the Veneration and Worship of Images* (1529) was not in Hall but was added by Grafton, who concluded his account with a reference to Gloucester's being 'loved by the commons', and called 'the good Duke of Gloucester' (cf. I.i.156–7). Shakespeare may indeed have got Simpcox from Grafton, but he could have found it in John Foxe's *Acts and Monuments*, which he certainly knew. If he dipped into Holinshed, as he almost certainly did, he would find himself directed to Foxe by the editors of the second edition who end the account of Duke Humphrey:

> 'But sith the praise of this noble man deserveth a large discourse . . . I refer the readers unto maister Foxe's booke of Acts and Monuments.' (627/2/16–26).(Bullough 91)

We can add the reinforcement of Gloucester's reputation as it became assimilated to that of another "Good Duke" of more recent memory, the Edwardian reformation's popular hero and martyr, Protector Seymour, Duke of Somerset (King 113-121).

Shakespeare's final treatment of the Duke and Duchess of Gloucester, however, is not consistent with any coherent ideological description of historical events, Protestant or Catholic. The Protestant sources, particularly Foxe, are ambiguous at best about the genuineness of Eleanor Cobham's necromantic practices. On the one hand there was pressure to see her as similar to Joan of Arc and Mistress Shore—that is, as an exemplum of Catholic depravity incarnate in disorderly women. On the other hand, the sources are anxious to portray the insidiousness of the conspiracy against Humphrey by showing the historical Thomas Southwell, John Hume, Roger Bolingbrook, and Margery Jordan as impostors and their conjuring to be as fraudulent as the mass. Shakespeare preserves the anticlerical, anti-Catholic flavor of Hall's "Thomas Southwel, prieste and chanon of saincte Stephens in Westmynster, John Hum priest," but the sources' tawdry waxen figure of the king, on which Eleanor was supposed to have practiced with the assistance of a Jordan and a Bolingbrook conceived of more or less as mere charlatans, has become the spirit Asmath:

Here do the ceremonies belonging, and make the
circle; *Bolingbrook or Southwell reads, "Conjuro
te, etc." It thunders and lightens terribly; then
the Spirit riseth.*

Spir. Adsum.
M. Jord. Asmath,
 By the eternal God, whose name and power
 Thou tremblest at, answer that I shall ask;
 For, till thou speak, thou shalt not pass from hence.
Spir. Ask what thou wilt. That I had said, and done!
Boling. "First of the King: what shall of him become?"
                         [Reading out of a paper.]
Spir. The duke yet lives that Henry shall depose;
 But him out-live, and die a violent death.
                         *[As the Spirit speaks, Bolingbrook
                           writes the answer.]*
Boling. "[Tell me] what [fate awaits] the Duke of Suffolk?"
Spir. By water shall he die, and take his end.
Boling. "What shall [betide] the Duke of Somerset?"
Spir. Let him shun castles.
 Safer shall he be upon the sandy plains
 Than where castles mounted stand.
 Have done, for more I hardly can endure.
Boling. Descend to darkness and the burning lake!
 False fiend, avoid!
                         Thunder and lightning. Exit Spirit
                         [sinking down again].

Enter the DUKE OF YORK and the DUKE OF BUCKINGHAM
with their GUARD [SIR HUMPHREY STAFFORD as
Captain,] and break in.

(1.4.SD 23–SD 40)

The moment cannot fail to recall *The First Part of King Henry VI*, Act 5,
where York's parting imprecations to Joan, "Break thou in pieces and consume to ashes,/ Thou foul accursed minister of hell!" cue Winchester's
entry: "*Enter [Winchester, now]* CARDINAL [BEAUFORD, *attended*]"
(54.92–93, SD 93). Bolingbrook's anathema serves here to invoke the
Dukes of York and Buckingham with a startling irony dependent on the
audience's familiarity with the previous theatrical *public*ation of similar
material in *Part 1*. Shakespeare's transmutation of the waxen figure to a
manifest conjured spirit seems to validate the witch-hunt against Eleanor as
well as Gloucester, but the conspiratorial context has undercut the ducal
witch detectors' integrity as well as reinforced the impression that the conjurers are mere charlatans:

> *Hume.* Hume must make merry with the Duchess' gold;
>   Marry, and shall. But how now, Sir John Hume?
>   Seal up your lips, and give no words but mum;
>   The business asketh silent secrecy.
>   Dame Eleanor gives gold to bring the witch;
>   Gold cannot come amiss, were she a devil.
>   Yet have I gold flies from another coast—
>   I dare not say from the rich Cardinal
>   And from the great and new-made Duke of Suffolk;
>   Yet I do find it so; for, to be plain,
>   They, knowing Dame Eleanor's aspiring humor,
>   Have hired me to undermine the Duchess,
>   And buzz these conjurations in her brain.
>   They say, "A crafty knave does need no broker,"
>   Yet am I Suffolk and the Cardinal's broker.
>   Hume, if you take not heed, you shall go near
>   To call them both a pair of crafty knaves,
>   Well, so it stands; and thus, I fear, at last
>   Hume's knavery will be the Duchess' wrack,
>   And her attainture will be Humphrey's fall.
>   Sort how it will, I shall have gold for all.
>   *Exit.*
>   (1.2.87–107)

It is the ideological instability itself which helps this scene function as the "consumption of consumption." Finally, Humphrey of Gloucester, as well as his antagonists and the details of the narrative processes whose dramatically engineered intersections will seal his fate in Shakespeare's play, consists almost entirely of textual commodities that have already been consumed in a variety of forms, including that of dramatic "publication."

The Jack Cade episode from *Henry VI, Part 2* similarly shows how Shakespeare's dramaturgy stages the consumption of an already-consumed commodity. Earlier I noted Michael Hattaway's and Ellen C. Caldwell's important observations that Act 4 of Shakespeare's play effectively "carnivalizes" the matter of history. Such carnivalization and parody depend upon the prolific knowledge of an audience familiar with notorious identities and events. Such an audience must have possessed a high degree of both oral and written cultural literacy that included considerable historiographical literacy (as well as sound knowledge of the grounds and the progress of contemporary religious disputation), the result in part of the market in history and religious polemic discussed earlier but also of the constant exemplary and admonitory iterations of pulpit and school room. Such an audience had also advanced as consumers to the point that narrative and entertainment processes had themselves become the commodities which they sought to purchase with their admission price to the theater. Hence the scenes of misrule, inversion, and travesty so prominent in Act 4 go beyond parody or carnival (which still focus on the ideological pressure of exemplum, admonition, and *speculum principium* as part of the apparatus of repression) to the delirium of the consumption of the already consumed.

The grand guignol of Suffolk's destruction which opens Act 4 recalls traditions about the judicial murder of Thomas of Woodstock, some of which have him beheaded on ship en route to Calais. As narrative process, the judicial murder (whether on ship or off) occurs dozens of times in the early-modern matter of history and features recurring motifs such as aristocratic expressions of contempt for the base-born murderer or murderers and the fulfillment of long-forgotten prophecies about the circumstances of death. Woodstock's death in *Thomas of Woodstock* preserves these features of narrative process, and the motifs recur throughout Shakespeare's histories but especially in the First Tetralogy. In *The Second Part of Henry VI*, Shakespeare names the murderer deictically, as the last item in a self-blocking series:

> *Lieu.* Master, this prisoner freely give I thee;
>   And thou that art his mate, make boot of this;
>   The other, Walter Whitmore, is thy share. (4.1.12–14)

Significant portions of the audience can be expected to know the name and to know what's coming from their familiarity with the historical sources;

but even if they do not know the precise factual reference, they certainly
know that this foregrounding of the ominous name is part of what they
came to the theater to enjoy, a narrative moment long commodified within the textual system of the matter of history and consumed here dramaturgically for their delectation more than their edification. So, too, with
Suffolk's recognition of "Gualtier":

> *Whit.* . . . my name is Walter Whitmore.
> How now? Why starts thou? What, doth death affright?
> *Suf.* Thy name affrights me, in whose sound is death.
> A cunning man did calculate my birth
> And told me that by water I should die:
> Yet let not this make thee be bloody-minded,
> Thy name is Gualtier, being rightly sounded. (31–37)

The name is iterated and discussed not to validate the claims of calculation
and prophecy nor to certify that the scene has historical authority, but to
prolong enjoyment. So, too, does the Lieutenant's prounouncement of a
sentence, the facts of which comprise a particularly memorable element
within the circulation of textual commodities about the events of the play
that extends back to their historical moment: "Convey him hence, and on
our longboat's side / Strike off his head" (68–69).

Suffolk's obligatory speeches of aristocratic defiance work in a similar
way, as does the Lieutenant's lengthy indictment, with its historical *senten-
tiae* and *loci communes*:

> *Lieu.*   Poole! Sir Poole! lord!
> Ay, kennel, puddle, sink, whose filth and dirt
> Troubles the silver spring where England drinks.
> Now will I dam up this thy yawning mouth
> For swallowing the treasure of the realm.
> Thy lips that kiss'd the Queen shall sweep the ground,
> And thou that smil'dst at good Duke Humphrey's death
> Against the senseless winds shall grin in vain,
> Who in contempt shall hiss at thee again;
> And wedded be thou to the hags of hell,
> For daring to affy a mighty lord
> Unto the daughter of a worthless king,
> Having neither subject, wealth, nor diadem.
> By devilish policy art thou grown great,
> And like ambitious Sylla, overgorg'd
> With gobbets of thy [mother's] bleeding heart.
> By thee Anjou and Maine were sold to France.
> The false revolting Normans thorough thee

Disdain to call us lord, and Picardy
Hath slain their governors, surpris'd our forts,
And sent the ragged soldiers wounded home.
The princely Warwick, and the Nevils all,
Whose dreadful swords were never drawn in vain,
As hating thee, [are] rising up in arms;
And now the house of York, thrust from the crown
By shameful murther of a guiltless king
And lofty, proud, encroaching tyranny,
Burns with revenging fire, whose hopeful colors
Advance our half-fac'd sun, striving to shine,
Under which is writ, *"Invitis nubibus."*
The commons here in Kent are up in arms,
And to conclude, reproach and beggary
Is crept into the palace of the king,
And all by thee. Away, convey him hence. (70–103)

A similar "discourse of indictment," moreover, was used against
Gloucester by Suffolk, York, and the Cardinal in Act 3, Scene 1. Its details
can further be traced to materials roughly contemporary with both
Suffolk's murder and the rising of 1450, for both the language of the
Lieutenant's indictment as well as the charges leveled by Jack Cade, his
confederates, and their followers resemble very closely the language of
numerous "bills" composed, copied, and distributed by the rebels during
the course of the revolt. I. M. W. Harvey, in his indispensable history of the
rebellion, summarizes the most important themes:

The bill with the most strongly Kentish concerns may date from the
earliest stages of events, perhaps circulating during May, its purpose
being to galvanize the men of Kent into action. Not only were the
compilers of this bill concerned about the rumour that Kent should
by destroyed by royal power and made into a wild forest, but they
wanted something done about the inconvenience and nuisance caused
to the tax collectors in Kent by the requirement that they sue out
writs of exemption for the Barons of the Cinque Ports (the Cinque
Ports having to provide properly manned vessels were exempt from
such subsidies but the people of Kent thought that the ports should
claim such exemptions at their own cost). Another issue was the way
in which the officials of the court of Dover outstepped their jurisdic-
tion; others, the rigging of the elections of the knights of the shire in
Kent and the need for the holding of the sessions of the peace in two
separate ends of the county so as to save the inordinately long jour-
neys some men were obliged at present to make. Alongside these
county issues they were complaining that the king should restore to

himself the Crown revenues he had granted away, that his natural counsellors among the aristocracy should be restored to their proper ascendancy in the king's council, and that inquiry should be made throughout the land to find out who the traitors were who caused the French possessions to be lost so that they might be punished without pardon. The remaining complaints concerned the extortions and grave abuses of office of royal household men and their colleagues holding positions in the county administration. Such grievances were comprehensive enough in scope to affect at some level every man and woman in the county. (80)

And although the Lieutenant's speech sums up the action of the first three acts and functions to introduce the remainder of Act 4, it does so not merely to shore up narrative logic but in order to remind the audience of the entertaining spectacle they have witnessed already and to promise that even better will follow, all the while exploiting the audience's status as more or less experienced consumers of various antecedent commodified forms of the very same material being represented on Shakespeare's stage.

When the rebels finally appear, they have been long prepared for, both within the play and without, their words and actions wrought out of the entire complex intertexture wherein their historical antecedents were gradually transformed into narrative commodities. The following speeches depend for their peculiar effect—neither pastiche nor parody seem to describe it appropriately—on the audience's "genealogy" as an audience within the processes which commodified the past events they refer to:

> *Bevis.* I tell thee, Jack Cade the clothier means to dress the common
>   wealth, and turn it, and set a new nap upon it.
> *Holl.* So he had need, for 'tis threadbare. Well, I say, it was never merry
>   world in England since gentlemen came up.
> *Bevis.* O miserable age! virtue is not regarded in handicrafts-men.
> *Holl.* The nobility think scorn to go in leather aprons.
> *Bevis.* Nay more, the King's Council are no good workmen.
> *Holl.* True; and yet it is said, labour in thy vocation; which is as much
>   to say as, let the magistrates be labouring men; and therefore
>   should we be magistrates.
> *Bevis.* Thou hast hit it: for there's no better sign of a brave mind than a
>   hard hand. (4.2.4–20)

The details of this dramatic exchange originate in an intricate substrate of intertextual exchange. Actual words and some phrases can be traced to petitions of grievance and pardon rolls, but many (if not most) of these may well have been familiar from frequent anthologizing, incorporation into broadsides and ballads, and publication and republication in the chronicle and historical literature from the early days of commercial manuscript production. Snatches of proverbs and homilies (e.g., "Labour in thy vocation"), even Latin tags (e.g., "O miserable age!" recalling Horace, "O vires! O mores!"), evoke the contexts in which proverbs and tags were used—alongside cautionary and admonitory narratives illustrating just the kind of social inversion, decay, and upheaval which is unfolding on stage. Jack Cade's own biblical reverberations evoke a similar panoply of familiar associations tied to narrative exempla. Thus he resonates, "For our enemies shall [fall] before us, inspir'd with the spirit of putting down kings and princes" (4.2.35–36), and commends Dick the butcher in the language of Joshua at Jericho, "They fell before thee like sheep and oxen" (4.3.3). The episode of the Clerk of Chartham repackages the petitions and the anticlerical murders of 1381; the audience, however, experiences not chastening and admonition, nor so much the sadistic pleasure of the mob itself in its detection and lynching of an ally of the lawyers, as the anticipation of that detection and lynching.

Cade's summation of his title, as has always been recognized, parodies York's (2.2.9–52), and his tyranny, capriciousness, and rapacity exaggeratedly reflect the back-stabbing, pretensions, self-righteousness, and depravity of the peers. York's title, as all sources except Polydore acknowledge more or less obliquely, is sound, but his pursuit of it in Shakespeare's dramatic spectacle ignites the all-but-Brechtian progress of Cade's rebellion. The rebellion proceeds in a kind of magniloquent pastiche from the confrontation with and defeat of the Staffords (4.2; 4.3), to the taking of Bridge and Tower (4.4; 4.5), to Jack Cade's striking his staff on London Stone (4.6), to the slaying of Matthew Gough and the parlay with and beheading of Lord Say (4.7; Say's speech recalls many a Roman patrician address to an unruly plebeian mob), the burning of the Savoy and the taking and beheading of Lord Say and his son-in-law, to the rebellion's final collapse and Iden's butchering of the starved and exhausted Cade. In the midst of all this, York's unimpeachable title is parodied by Cade's, and Iden's unequal defeat of Cade completes the parodic, ideologically ambivalent movement begun with the introduction of Peter and Horner in the Petitioners' scene.

Such details, seen, as I believe they must be, as commercial artifacts within a process of commodifying and recommodifying the past since the fourteenth- and fifteenth-century events on which they are based, appear as narrative and dramatic elements in the First Tetralogy whose value as saleable spectacle is conferred by their prior history of consumption. There is almost a sense in which such commercial artifacts in effect consume themselves once they are represented dramatically.[14] Their realization in a performance of Shakespeare's *Second Part of King Henry VI* staged the consumption of consumption, perhaps allowing the *premodern* subjects of the Elizabethan theater audience to experience, under the conditions of "primitive accumulation," something resembling the "virtual delirium" Frederic Jameson described as one of the characteristics of postmodern cultural production.

NOTES

[1] Significant work on the relationship between structural economic change, the market, literary production, and the theater as a market phenomenon has emphasized the Tudor and early Stuart periods. For example, Richard Halperin's *The Poetics of Primitive Accumulation* covers the (cultural) sixteenth century from just before 1500 up through the era of King Lear (1605–1610), while Douglas Bruster's *Drama and the Market in the Age of Shakespeare* concentrates on conditions from the 1570s to the 1590s. Halperin never really coordinates his economic analysis, mostly an account of how enclosure, disestablishment of manors and monasteries, dispossession of freeholders, and the decline of guilds led to the beginnings of a class of persons who owned nothing but their labor power, with his account of a parallel "poetics," except in his analysis of Sir Thomas More's *Utopia*, a text which responds directly to the crises of "primitive accumulation" (136–175). Walter Cohen, *Drama of a Nation,* includes a chapter on "Medieval Theater and the Structure of Feudalism" (33–81), but it contains no detailed economic or financial analysis of the developing trade in cultural commodities (by cultural commodities I mean physical objects—manuscripts, codices, printed books—and their representational or discursive contents, or such "performance articles" as a play text, preserved, as at York or Wakefield, in a manuscript collection of "originals" and used as the basis of memorial reconstruction or dramatic representation, as well as the contents of ballads and gestes, among other "commodities" realized in performance).

[2] For the medieval English manuscript book trade, see C. Paul Christianson, "Evidence for the Study of London's Late Medieval Manuscript-Book Trade," in Griffiths and Pearsall, *Book Production and Publishing in Britain, 1375–1475,* and Kate Harris, "Patrons, Buyers and Owners," *op. cit.* In the same volume Anne Hudson, "Lollard Book Production," cites evidence for the commissioning of multiple copies of Lollard texts by ordinary artisans, Lollard circuit preachers, and other commons (125–142). For the emergence of Chaucer as an eminently marketable writer and one of Caxton's most lucrative properties, see David R. Carlson, "Chaucer, Humanism, and Printing."

[3] Other examples include Cavendish's *Life of Wolsey* and the *de casibus*

tragedies in the *Mirror for Magistrates*. *De casibus* tragedies from the *Mirror* relevant to *Henry VI Part 2* include those of William de la Pole, Duke of Suffolk, and Jack Cade, printed in the 1559 edition, and the tragedies of Eleanor Cobham, Duchess of Gloucester, and of Humphrey Plantagenet, Duke of Gloucester, printed in the edition of 1578. See L. B. Campbell, ed., *The Mirror for Magistrates* 161–181; 428–460.

⁴ The embedded term is of course borrowed from Linda Charnes, *Notorious Identities*.

⁵ Marx formed the term, "primitive accumulation," out of a response to Adam Smith's speculations about a stage of "prior accumulation" (see *Capital*, vol. 1, trans. Ben Fowkes 280, 873–875, and for the fully elaborated argument, 873–940). Richard Halperin places the formation of the term in the context of Marx's exaggeratedly satirical account of Smith's version of the origins of political economy, attributing to him a crude myth of the origins of capital-owning and capital-deprived classes in virtuous and nonvirtuous primeval tribes of the naturally industrious and frugal on the one hand—whose descendents would evolve into capitalists—and the lethargic, spendthrift, and imbecilic on the other—whose descendents would evolve into the proletariat (*The Poetics of Primitive Accumulation* 63–100).

⁶ Jameson, 16. Although with David Aers, "A Whisper in the Ear of Early Modernists," in his *Culture and History, 1350–1600* 177–202, I agree that new historicists and cultural materialists play fast and loose with such concepts as the "history of the subject," nevertheless I believe that such a concept is useful. Cultures require different kinds of subjects at different stages of their evolution, and ideological apparatuses for producing and reproducing the required subjects have arisen at all stages of history. Aers is primarily concerned to correct the airy claims of critics led by Catherine Belsey that there simply were no subjects before the sixteenth century.

⁷ Bullough, Vol. 3, reprints the places in Hall, Foxe, and Holinshed, and analogues in Nelson's *Device for Lord Mayor's Pageant, The Life and Death of Jack Straw*, and the tragedy of Suffolk from *A Mirror for Magistrates*, but Shakespeare may well have used Grafton as well as other parts of the *Mirror* (the tragedies of the Duke and Duchess of Gloucester printed in the 1578 edition) besides the tragedies of Suffolk and Cade.

⁸ Julia Kristeva has developed these concepts in several works, including *The System and the Speaking Subject, Desire in Language*, and *Revolution in Poetic Language*.

⁹ The term is Hayden V. White's, *Tropics of Discourse*.

¹⁰ For a detailed (and definitive) account of the role of drama in this process of early modern state formation and nation building, see Cohen, *Drama of a Nation*.

¹¹ See las Casas, *Short Account* xiv, xxvii–xxx, xxxix–xl.

[12] All quotations come from *The Riverside Shakespeare*.

[13] 1531 ed., chap. 14. The 1529 edition is described in the Yale edition of the complete works as "a rare book of considerable interest from a bibliographical standpoint alone," *Complete Works*, Vol. 6, part 2, 548. Note that Bullough, Vol. 3, 90, cites the material under a separate title, *Dialogue of the Veneration and Worship of Images*. This appears to be paraphrased from the full title of the 1529 *Dialogue Concerning Heresies*: "A dyaloge of syr Thomas/ More knyghte: one of the/ counsayll of our souerayne lorde the kyng and chaun/ celloure of hys duchy of Lancaster. Whereyn be/ treatyd dyuers maters/ as of the Veneracy-/ on & Worshyp of ymagys & relyques/ prayng to sayntis/ & goynge on pyl/ grymage, With many other/ thyngys touchyng the pes-/ tylent secte of Luther/ & Tyndale/ by the/ tone bygone in/ Saxony/ &/ by the/ tother laboryd/ to be brought in to England." The episode appears in *Complete Works*, Vol. 6, part 1, 85–88.

[14] Cf. Stanley Fish, *Self-Consuming Artifacts*.

THEME AND DESIGN IN RECENT PRODUCTIONS OF *HENRY VI*

H. R. Coursen

These plays are very "unified" for apprentice work. Even if "unity" is an outmoded and sneered-upon concept these days, it is something a director has to consider, particularly in condensing the sequence, and even if he or she wishes to "deconstruct" the script toward the goal of "multiple signification." That is often an excuse, of course, for sheer incoherence. It is easy enough to say, Blackstone on evidence to the contrary, "There's just too much going on—too many speeches, too many battles, too many subplots—for Shakespeare's early trilogy to ever truly succeed onstage. . . . [T]hese [are] misshapen plays" (Shapiro 8). Shapiro seems to have forgotten or perhaps did not see Jane Howell's superb version of the plays for the BBC (see Coursen 1992)

In *Part 1*, two French women are captured. One is burned at the stake; the other becomes queen of England. Joan's spirits desert her (5.3); she is condemned as an "enchantress" (5.3.42). Then Suffolk captures Margaret, is enchanted by her into stunned asides (as Joan had earlier "bewitch[ed]" Burgundy: 3.3.58) and woos her for Henry. The "witch" (1.5.21 and 3.2.38) and "sorceress" (3.2.38 and 5.4.1), Joan, is sent to the stake but not before denying her father, claiming a Virgin-like status, then assigning her unborn child to a squadron of French noblemen. Joan's attributes—"A maid? And be so martial?/ Pray God she prove not masculine ere long" (2.1.22–3)—flow from her ashes into Margaret's marrow. This sequence emerges from the theme of desertion and betrayal already working through the plays. Another woman, Eleanor, will employ witchcraft and be betrayed. Another king, Edward, will abandon one match for another marriage and again foment political disruption. The "foul fiend of France" (3.2.52), Joan, can be dispatched, but a "She-wolf of France" (as York will call Margaret much later: *Part 3* 1.4.111) survives to go to England.

The transitions in the statuses of Joan and Margaret echo Falstolfe's treason, Cambridge's fall as narrated, Mortimer's long denouement and Plantagenet's rise, the betrayal of Talbot by Somerset, the shifting allegiances of Burgundy, Clarence, and "wind-changing Warwick" (*3 Henry VI* 5.1.57), the fall of Dame Eleanor, the mob's desertion of Cade, and the burning of another witch (Margery Jourdain). The kingdom, of course, suffers a general topsy-turviness in which York is at first a "yeoman" (*1 Henry VI* 2.4.81), Joan a "high-minded strumpet" (1.5.12) who claims to have been "issued from the progeny of kings" (5.4.38), where Cade can claim his midwife mother was a "Plantagenet" (*2 Henry VI* 4.2.44), where haughty Suffolk falls to an "obscure and lousy swain" (4.1.50), and a king takes "a beggar to his bed" (*3 Henry VI* 2.2.154), a "base-born" (2.2.143) woman to boot, and subsequently denies his own son his inheritance. Suffolk, standing in for Henry (and deluding Margaret as to the "proportion" of Englishmen: *2 Henry VI* 1.3.52), predicts Cade standing in for York and the facile interchangability of allegiances and of kings to whom oaths are transitorily sworn.

Underlying this confusion, of course, is a world without premises, the ad hoc situation that Richard II and Bolingbroke ushered in with their uneasy cooperation. They shifted paradigms from sacramental premises to mere expediency where, as Hastings says, "Now arms must rule" (*3 Henry VI* 4.7.61). This is a world of nightmare where the dreamers stand helpless in the presence of atrocity. It is the world of emergency, where reflection cannot occur in the midst of constant alarums and excursions. York's decision to go after the crown even after ceding it to Henry again is interrupted by Margaret's invasion, so that her accusation that he has broken his "holy oath" (1.4.105) is irrelevant by dint of circumstances, even if it would be accurate in a world where time had an opportunity to discover meanings within its sequential segments and where oaths were more than fleeting phrases. The product of this disorder and the beneficiary of the further turbulence that he foments is Richard, "a foul indigested lump" (*2 Henry VI* 5.1.157), "an indigested and deformed lump" (*3 Henry VI* 5.6.51), "Like to a chaos," as he himself says, "or an unlick'd bear-whelp" (3.2.161). He makes "the evil of Henry's disastrous reign concretely visible" (Fergusson 14). Shakespeare is already clear about the results of the *causes* he will explore later in *Richard II*.

The mid-90s productions of *Henry VI* in Washington and New York—as different as they were—removed the sense of what Peter Brook calls "deadly theatre" (11–46) and gave us more of the noisy, jostling feel of Shakespeare's theater than does the Royal Shakespeare model. Admittedly, the productions did so without inflicting discomfort or offense upon the spectator. It did not completely invalidate the productions that they were not competing with "bear-baiting, brothels, the stocks, the pillory, the exhibition of the mentally disturbed, public beheading and evisceration, and

royal processions" (Hawkes 13). While some people in the streets conducted their dialogue with memories of distant hope, and while the stretch
limos slid past like hearses with their invisible occupants, the audience for
each production got a sense of going to a play. These were events that
called for response and not the isolation attendant on reading a novel.

To "unify" the dramatic experience, Michael Kahn of the Shakespeare
Theater tended toward a thematic editing of the inherited script, while
Karin Coonrod of the Public Theater relied more on the physical design of
the stage. Both approaches proved remarkably effective in conveying the
complications of the scripts.

Kahn's conflation of ten hours of running time into four emphasized the
rhythm of generations, particularly of fathers and sons. We began with
Henry V's catafalque and "Hung be the heavens with black," though I
missed the "crystal tresses" of those ominous comets and their introduction
of the "malignant and ill-boding stars" (*1 Henry VI* 4.5.3–6) that brood
over an England bereft of the skillful Henry V. Talbot and his son died
together ("Now my old arms are young John Talbot's grave" 4.32).
Rutland was introduced suddenly at Sandal Castle (*3 Henry VI* 1.2) with
his tutor, when in the text he appears only in 1.3, where he is dispatched
by Young Clifford. The earlier entrance was an effort to show York's affection for the lad and perhaps York's wish to live out his old age in peace,
but it undercut York's change of heart about the kingship and the urgency
of Margaret's approach. Young Clifford is also introduced without any
introduction in the text as a foil to Richard Gloucester or perhaps as the
Lancastrian version of the Crookback. The Cliffords are the first to make
metaphors out of the deformity that we, the audience, notice as Richard
enters. Young Clifford's mourning over his father (*2 Henry VI* 5.2), a parallel to York's grief about Rutland at Wakefield (*3 Henry VI* 1.4.111ff.)
and Margaret's for Prince Edward at Tewksbury (5.5.51ff.), is one of the
unprepared-for moments that makes these plays occasionally resemble a
"chronicle" as opposed to superbly wrought drama. Henry's lines about his
father's "deeds" (2.2.49)—perhaps the only negative allusion to Henry V
in the canon—and Prince Edward's anger at Henry's deal with York
("Father, you cannot disinherit me": 1.1.226) came through clearly here
because Kahn shaped the material around the issue of fathers and sons.

Henry had been forced to resign at rifle-point in a scene that hearkened
back to Richard II's surrender to Bolingbroke's army at Barkloughly Castle.
The conflict between Henry and Prince Edward was energized by Michael
Barry's doubling of young Henry in *Part 1* and Prince Edward. The prince,
however, doffed the gray garments that matched the upstage wall and signaled his father's unwillingness to "stand out," and donned the soldier's
outfit worn by the rest of the kingdom. Henry was left alone in what
seemed a self-imposed exile, even in that madness which the person who is
a majority of one can feel (as *early* opponents of the war in Vietnam and

opponents of Desert Storm discovered). Henry seemed to wish to become another figure of the fifteenth century, DaVinci, and was ultimately stabbed with the point of his compass. It was appropriate, of course, that *Margaret* mourn for Prince Edward, since the kingdom's stereotypic masculine energy has flowed to her. The son/father, father/son sequence at Towton (*3 Henry VI* 2.5), with Henry's mournful commentary, usually a mawkish allegory, drew remarkable power from Kahn's emphasis on the generational contexts of these plays. Young Clifford's final speech ("The foe is merciless and will not pity;/ For at their hands I have deserv'd no pity" 2.6.25–26), a prelude to Richard III's soliloquy as he awakens on the morning of Bosworth Field, was cut. Also gone was the postmortem punishment inflicted on him by Richard, Warwick, and the others. That wonderfully macabre episode was a victim of Kahn's clear intention to show that nothing of value can be handed on from father to son when values themselves are merely personal.

Kahn brought the variation on the theme of father and son, the Thump-Horner combat, forward in this production, so that Horner became a precursor of Jack Cade, another "stand-in" for York. Horner had become an embarrassment, it seems, because of Thump's allegations. After Horner had been dispatched, York paid off one of the men who had gotten Horner too drunk to fight. This interpretation nicely undercut Henry's pious belief that "God in justice" has revealed the truth (*2 Henry VI* 2.3.105). The episode linked up with Hume's profitable manipulation of Eleanor and, of course, with her dreams of glory. The only father-son scenes missing were those between the Master Gunner and Boy (*1 Henry VI* 1.4.1ff.) and the "triple sun" sequence in which York's sons learn of the death of their father some ten days earlier at Wakefield (*3 Henry VI* 2.1). (In the history plays, we sense sweaty messengers riding the moors and spurring under the rising moon, but this horseman is the slowest in the canon.)

At the end of Hands's 1977 *Henry VI, Part 3,* during a historical moment when "irony" was still a permissible word, the drums and trumpets for which Edward (Alfred Lynch) had called caused Clarence (Jack Klaff) and Gloucester (Anton Lesser) to pull their swords. Edward then emphasized "*farewell* sour annoy," but his brothers had got it right. "Joy" was to be short-lived. Here the word did not have a chance to find an echo.

Kahn's soldiery carried carbines—the play's movement forward in time could be calibrated by the advance in weaponry and by Margaret's pregnancy and motherhood. But Kahn avoided the percussive anachronisms that tend to drown out Bogdanov's productions and the fatuous mixing of historical moments that marred Ron Daniels's recent Second Henriad at Cambridge, which insisted that we unsuspend our disbelief at the service of whatever multiple responses Daniels was attempting to invite (see my critique, 1996, 239–245). Kahn has always tried to make his plays "relevant," as in his famous antiwar *Henry V* at Stratford, Connecticut, in

1969. Here, with a "character issue" floating at the edges of an American presidential campaign, the play made the point quietly. Character was as irrelevant in this vicious fifteenth century as it seems to be to the American electorate here at the end of the twentieth. As Prince Edward says, "If that be right which Warwick says is right,/ There is no wrong, but every thing is right" (*3 Henry VI* 2.2.131–132). The program quoted Yeats's "Second Coming," but the play makes its own point about its historical moment. In the *Henry VI* plays principal is more important than any principle can be, and thus efforts to make things "right" become further wrongs that then cry to be redressed. While Kahn's editing necessarily simplified and at times hollowed out the inherited scripts, the narratives of Margaret, Henry, and Richard Gloucester were powerfully delivered. For an audience that had probably neither read nor seen these plays before, this production served very well indeed.

Kahn's cutting to a "theme" was well served by Riccardo Hernandez's design. Avoiding the "set" that the Landsburgh stage can invite, Hernandez kept the downstage virtually clear except for two towers of brick painted black that moved in and out according to inside or outside locations, and a brick wall that could drop down and foreshorten the sequence's few intimate scenes. A rose trellis came down for the Temple Garden. A balcony stood upstage. From there authority spoke. Clifford debated with the mob from there, while Cade stood downstage. From there, Edward declared his hopes for "lasting joy" (*3 Henry VI* 5.7.46) as Richard and his blackshirts came downstage with rifles pointed at us. Part of Richard's soliloquy had been delivered as Wallace Acton stepped out from under the lump of his upstage shadow and invaded our space. His mad-eyed Richard stomped up the left aisle ("Change shapes with Proteus for advantages": *3 Henry VI* 3.2.192). That moment signalled that, as E. Pearlman says, "The cracking of the bond between father and son . . . once the primary theme . . . is now exhausted. After Richard's transitional soliloquy, the remainder of the play turns its attention to cooperation and division among the three brothers" (425). We learned in advance of the characters on stage that we were to be Richard's victims even as we were pulled into that uneasy alliance that he, Iago, and Iachimo demand of us. The placement of anarchy and madness *closest* to the audience removed the comfortable "fourth wall" assumptions that the Lansburgh encourages if inhabited by an explicit set.

When I heard that Coonrod's was to be a "postmodernist" production, I grew fearful. The mishmash of the Daniels's *Henry V* for the American Repertory Theatre or of George Wolfe's *Tempest* for the Public sprang to mind. In those productions the tenet of "multiple signification" seemed to be an excuse for a mixture of periods, cultures, and concepts unloaded on the script by trucks that should have continued on to the dump. *The Tempest* fought free due to Patrick Stewart's superb Prospero. The *Henry V* sank into a puddle of hubris. Shakespeare's anachronisms are not resolved merely by creating a new set of anachronisms designed to puzzle us, conditioned as we are by media that insist on "historical accuracy." For the postmodernist attack on "thematic unity" to succeed, it must prove what cannot be proved, that is, that Shakespeare's plays are not thematically unified (even if different directors will discern and develop different themes in the same scripts).

Coonrod's production emerged from design. As Shakespeare explored his stage with these early scripts, Coonrod *used* her stage as the basis for a cohesive and understandable production in which the staging and the words were organically related, part of a whole. Hers was a minimalist, metadramatic approach similar to that of Deborah Warner or Jane Howell. We are asked to piece out imperfections with our own imaginations. Productions in this style explore the scripts as scripts, that is, as self-conscious plays that know they are on a stage and that recognize the presence of an audience. The approach permits us to infer more about the form and pressure of our own age than do productions which make a specific modern analogy—the Loncraine *Richard III*, for example. In that film everything is done for us. In Coonrod's production we had to bring ourselves forward and thus we learned what these plays have to say about us by our being forced to say something to them. We often do not know what we mean, after all, until we try to put it into words. Shakespeare was doing that in these plays—beginning to find out what he intended to mean. What he intended to mean was to excite his audience into a discovery of what *they* meant. The process still works.

History begins with the stage. The ways in which it is presented dictate the ways in which it is perceived. Richard Gloucester knows that and places his opportunism between two clergymen. "O, do not *swear*, my lord of Buckingham," he remonstrates. Richard Nixon gave one of his waterside chats on television in front of a dusted bust of Lincoln to remind us of the great tradition of which Nixon was an inheritor. Coonrod's stage showed, as did Kahn's editing, "the ways in which the anachronisms and temporal circularities of so many of Shakespeare's plays [can] effectively be realized on the contemporary stage" (King 299).

Coonrod's space mimed a seventeenth-century room of state or the main chamber of a great art museum—columns rose at intervals to suggest the stately symmetry of an ornamental ceiling. But across the center of the room, moving from southeast to north-west, was the slash of stage, raked—and I doubt this has ever been done before—*towards* the upstage area. The audience sat on either side of the stage. A long ramp stage right became a site for observation and meditation. A downstage platform became a place for Cade's incitement of his mob into a Bakhtinian carnival and for the Cliffords' melting of Cade's rebellion with the threat of Henry V's arm. That the latter was long gone did not matter. The lines represent the only successful invocation of Henry V in these plays.

The format resembled one of the disasters staged by Rich Kotite or Dan Reeves in the mid-1990s at nearby colossea, and the material was divided into four quarters. In the first quarter everyone was on stage, still responding to the echo of a world made coherent by the presence and power of Henry V. The English, falling apart into bickering factions, were contrasted nicely with the French, coming together into an effective polity. The second quarter—after the first intermission—provided exits and entrances downstage for the characters. A private world was developing. What we heard on stage was often the result of secret meetings or personal agendas. The use of exits neatly set up Salisbury's line "Pride went before, ambition follows him" (*2 Henry VI* 1.1.180), as Somerset and the Cardinal exited. The third quarter—the beginning of the second night's performance—began with Cade's rebellion. Space was used confrontationally, Cade shinnying up a column to a platform from which to command his rebels. The Cliffords dispersed them from the same dominating area. By the fourth quarter—after the intermission on the second evening—all distinctions *in* space were gone. The backstage area was in full view. Its graffiti was made up of lines scrawled on the walls from these plays and a crude painting of the upside-down crown that had been rendered right side up on the useful genealogy that came with the program. Killing was no longer killing in battle, but assassination—as it was often enough during and after these battles. The battles themselves were not individually described but stylized into a surreal flow of headless brutality. Jack Cade's rebels carried dummies with them—emblems of the mob—that became the corpses generated by the battles. This was a borrowing from Kahn's *Henry V*, in which the dead of Agincourt became those who cheered Henry V's triumphant return to London. At Saint Albans, Somerset's body—a red rose stuffed into his mouth—was dumped on to the pile of scarecrows. Suffolk's wrapped head, which Margaret carried, was blank like those of the dummies. Confrontations occurred as characters stood in line facing forward—Warwick, Edward, Gloucester, and then Clarence at Coventry (*3 Henry VI* 5.1), for example. The scene calls for Warwick to "Enter above" and, of course, debate with the Yorkists across the fictional space between the city walls and the besieging army. We had been educated to the issues and the characters by then, so that the lack of spatial contrast and definition did not matter. Loyalties could be neither graphed nor physically represented. We recognized that even the vanishing point from which perspective is defined had vanished.

The production established its style immediately. The black coffin of Henry V clumped down on rough ropes from the flies. The "heavens" were "hung . . . with black" in more than one sense. Mourners stepped forward from downstage to deliver eulogies and grim presagings. Messengers rushed from upstage with bad news from France. At the end of the scene Winchester sat on the coffin to ponder his stake in this dividing world ("long I will not be Jack out of office"). The modern point being made here was a point the play also makes: if responsibility to a public good is abandoned for personal gain, then everyone loses. The *New York Times* for that date—December 6, 1996—had in it an article about the return of the attitudes of the eighties. Thick steaks, public cigars, and formerly lived-in furs are back—just in time for Christmas! The paper subsequently reported that "luxury products are now selling at a rate reminiscent of the late 1980s" (Canedy 1). The stretch limos block entire intersections. French drifts among the cigarettes in the lobbies of the hotels and Spanish rides the hallways as maids patrol to clean the rooms. While drama never changes anything—regardless of what its most radical advocates may say—these plays said something to their city and to us tourists down from the farm.

The staging defined the action and our response to it throughout the production. Early on, Warwick, Winchester, and Humphrey stood downstage, backing Henry on his throne as he confronted upstaging Yorkist and Lancastrian factions. The tableau suggested that the competitors would overpower any support Henry had, particularly Humphrey, of course, and make Warwick a kingmaker. We already knew that Winchester was pursuing his own agenda and not the King's. York and Somerset debated up and down one side of the stage, so that we were cast momentarily as the supporters of Red or White Rose. Those on the right were Yorkists. I found myself a Lancastrian. For the second quarter, the English sat in a circle of chairs that had come down on blood-red lines. The circle picked up from Joan's "Glory is like a circle in the water . . . the English circle ends" (*1 Henry VI* 1.2.133, 136). Duke Humphrey was inside the circle to be accused of the various charges that Somerset and Winchester trumped up, but exited the circle, emphasizing its central emptiness. Later, his body was brought in in a chair and placed in that center again. This was what came of his "studying good for England" (*2 Henry VI* 3.1.111). Henry's silly pieties as he looked at Humphrey's corpse ("What stronger breastplate than a heart untainted!" etc., 3.2.232ff.) showed that he was desperately intent on missing the point. We were reminded much later of Humphrey's death when Warwick, who was Humphrey's more opportunistic alter ego here, died in the circle of a spot. A splendid bit of blocking showed the mad and dying Beaufort seeing the well-meaning Henry as "death" and the torturer (3.3). In a perverse way, of course, this *is* the way to view an inept king. In the confrontation after Cade's death (5.1), the Yorkists were down center, which was a superior position relative to the height of the raked stage. The Lancastrians were up center, with the throne between the factions. Henry's party was in a superior position relative to power relations on stage. The juxtapositioning neatly canceled out any sense of superiority at this point.

The front center space often signalled vulnerability, as when Henry descended from his elevated chair in the fourth quarter to be murdered by

Richard, who placed the knife in Henry's hand. The king *had* been a kind of suicide. Henry sat on his molehill there during the Battle of Towton. York lamented the death of Rutland there. Joan was taunted there by the upstage English in a brutal interpretation of that scene, made more so by Warwick's being depicted by a woman. But Joan had been captured by York up center against a column. York removed her sword—it was also the removal of a cross—as she slumped back, as if against the post on which she would be burned. The burning occurred in a metal framework up left—in effigy. The scent of burning was still in the air after the intermission.

Louis XI and Lady Bona were up left, one of the most obscure areas of tonality/meaning on any stage, but came down to join Margaret and Warwick once they had been reunited on the news of Edward's sudden marriage. This was an ironic reminder of the unity depicted in first quarter. Here, however, the audience laughed. They recognized a world in which free agency had run amuck.

At the end, as blood from Henry drained down the raked stage, the royal family cavorted to "Tea for Two." The absolute banality of the Irving Caesar/Vincent Youmans tune was just right for this auspicating moment of union and reconciliation. The song is unique in that the dummy lyrics—composed so that the song could be sung in rehearsals—became the "real" lyrics and in that few jazz musicians try to make anything of it (compare similarly silly songs of the mid-twenties like "Love Nest," "In a Little Spanish Town," or "My Blue Heaven," which converted well to Bix, Bunny, and Max Kaminsky). The blood stained the white gown of Elizabeth Grey, cradling her prince. He, in swaddling clothes, looked like the blank-faced puppets the mob had carried in and the similarly cloth-wrapped head of Suffolk that Margaret had toted around. Elizabeth's prince, though guiltless of his country's blood, would die a few years later in the Tower. In this world, on which the blood-dimmed tide is loosed, innocents escape not the thunderbolt.

The backstage area was exposed—the scrawled lines from the plays, the upside-down red crown, the bloodlines that had held the chairs for the previous production. All pretense was stripped away. Patrick Stewart had wafted away the special lighting and set of *Tempest* as he spoke Prospero's Epilogue. *Hamlet* in 1964 at the Lunt-Fontanne had been spoken against bare bricks as a rehearsal. Here, the final unveiling of a stage we had glimpsed all along in its various guises made its modern and postmodern point about politics and its staginess. Polonius was stabbed behind a costume rack in the Gielgud-Burton production. Here, characters were killed to rise again as other characters in a secular sequence of power hunger that did not pause to consider the fate of other power seekers: Somerset, ascendant at the end of *Part 1*, York, on the rise at the end of *Part 2*, now Richard.

In an interview, Coonrod said; "What fascinates me is the spatial quality of the medieval world." She cited the Unicorn tapestry at the Cloisters in New York, which, in its "crowdedness reflect[s] an aesthetic entirely different from that of the twentieth-century" (Shapiro 10). Perspective does not become mathematically precise until Brunelleschi and Uccello in the fifteenth century. Masaccio revolutionizes painting with the techniques born of science. These events occur at the time of many of the events depicted in the *Henry VI* plays, but in another country.

The tapestries at the Cloisters, woven in about 1500 in Brussels, are allegorical and partake of the several levels of medieval interpretation; therefore they represent a different use of "space." They show the hunt on one level, courtly love on another, and the agony and redemptive power of Christ on another. It is space as concept, not as reality, space to be interpreted beyond and beneath the surface experience. The vanishing point is the mind of God. The plays themselves provide immediate allegory, of course, and more subtle levels, like the many ways in which white and red intermingle in these plays (blushing, blood staining white skin, the blood settled in Humphrey's face, "pale as primrose with blood-drinking sighs,"2 *Henry VI* 3.2.63, etc., many of which Coonrod effectively retained). Beyond the script, of course, is the allegory these plays inevitably complete with our moment and our individual lives. That allegory is particularly strong if the plays are not coerced into those meanings. We are left to discover them. Coonrod respects her audience sufficiently to permit it to make the discoveries. That is where "multiple signification" comes into play.

The editing, of course, was a huge factor here. The play is "notoriously shapeless," James Shapiro argues (10). No. The plays are *long* but marked by constant parallels—the rise and the fall of individuals (the plays follow hard upon the extremely successful series, *A Mirrour for Magistrates*), the capture of women, the burning of women as witches, discovery (of Horner's treason, Simcox's original sight, the cause of Duke Humphrey's death), myriad desertions and treasons, a constant shifting of allegiances, and a consistent concealing of motive with rhetoric.

Coonrod's grasp of the plays' parallels came through in the public insults inflicted on Margaret, arriving dowerless at Henry's court, and on Lady Elizabeth Grey, having gotten her husband's lands back and become queen in the process. Each, of course, has blocked a more advantageous match and sown political dissension, so the parallel is meant. Here it was perceived and delivered. Richard's "that yoke so well together" (*3 Henry VI* 4.1.23) was rendered with obscene relish. Eleanor's ambition ("Put forth thy hand, reach at the glorious gold. . . . We'll both together lift our heads to heaven,": *2 Henry VI* 1.2.11, 14) predicted Richard's and adumbrated her distant cousin, Lady Macbeth. A smaller instant occurred in Edward York's brief grimace after the murder of Prince Edward. It was the expression that had signaled the onset of Winchester's remorse much earlier after the strangling of Duke Humphrey. Since Walker Jones doubled the

Cardinal and Edward IV, the moments were brilliantly linked. One distant upshot of the death of Gloucester is the death of Prince Edward.

Few cared, I would guess, that the scene in which the Countess of Auvergne attempts to capture Talbot was gone here, or that young Talbot was excised. Joan got her speech about her spirits deserting her, but it was a soliloquy. I would have enjoyed seeing them depart, perhaps like the strawman citizens of Cade's rebellion. The scene with the dying Mortimer could be cut—York filled us in on all of the genealogy later and made a good dramatic shift with it—so that the Temple Garden scene fast-forwarded from Warwick's "a thousand souls to death and deadly night" (*1 Henry VI* 2.4.127) to Plantagenet's complaint about the "bitter injuries/ That Somerset hath offer'd to my house" (2.5.124–125). For the Temple Garden a rug tumbled onto the downstage wall with roses on it, white and red. Later the same space held the big sheet of paper on which York outlined his claim to the throne, to Warwick and Salisbury, circling "ME" as the culmination of the historical process. Warwick's line, "What plain proceedings is more plain than this?" (*2 Henry VI* 2.2.53) got a big laugh. We had all been somewhere at some time when we had copied a history lecture into our notebooks. That York used "we"—the royal plural—in public made clear his personal agenda in the justification scene (2.2). The use of the same space for garden and chart showed us that the latter—York's claim to kingship—is a function of the former—York's demand for the reinstatement of his dukedom.

Joan's attempt to deny her father (*1 Henry VI* 5.4.33) was gone. The religious undertones of rejecting "a father" and a humble origin were lost. Even if Joan's spirits desert *her,* the world is falling to the Devil. I find no positive Christian emphasis in these plays, with the exception perhaps of Henry's blessing of Richmond (*3 Henry VI* 4.6.68–76), which was excised here. These three plays are aimed at the moment when Richard III's soul confronts his body on the dark morning of Bosworth Field. He has forgotten that such a thing as "soul" exists, and we, watching the sequence in 1594 and similarly lulled, shared more than vicariously in Richard's sweaty awakening. Joan's fall contrasts with the rise of "yeoman" York (*1 Henry VI* 2.4.81). Her insistence on a phony nobility parallels Cade's fabricated pedigree. These plays are hardly "shapeless," but I do not quarrel with the fact that editing was necessary here to condense the material into its four segments. York did not surrender his troops to Henry (*2 Henry VI* 5.1.44), nor did Iden enter almost immediately with Cade's head. Cade had been shot down on Leather Lane, with York there to close his eyes. Thus the long scene before the battle of St. Alban's moved quickly into the wonderful exchanges between the Lancastrians, the "blood-bespotted Neopolitan" (*3 Henry VI* 5.1.117), Margaret and the Cliffords, and the Yorkists, where for the first time Richard is identified as a "foul, indigested lump" (157) and a "Foul stigmatic" (215) as Shakespeare begins to invent the negative mythology of Richard III.

Exeter's speech at the end of *1 Henry VI*, 3.1.195 ("that fatal prophecy") and some of Buckingham's generic and partisan speeches fit neatly
into Warwick's role early in the play, making him a major figure and eras-
ing some of the confusion that can arise between this saucy Worcester or
that fatty Salisbury. It was very important for us to keep the nobles straight,
because the production was conducted almost exclusively on the level of
power politics. Cade was there to lead his crowd in a brief rock-and-roll
orgy, but Dick the Butcher did not demand that "all the lawyers" be killed,
nor were Saye and Cromer beheaded. Mob rule was short-lived, relatively
benign, and easily dispersed. Nor was it allowed to develop its thesis that
the poor and illiterate are an exploited majority in the fifteenth century,
and in any century. We lost here the wonderful combat between Horner
and Peter, although the latter was mentioned as a reason for choosing
Suffolk, not York, as Regent in France. The trial by combat is a reversal of
fortune, of course, showing that the wheel is constantly turning, and is an
ironic revealer of truth in a world intent on manipulating truth into mere
perception. The Simcox family's inept imitation of upper-class greed, their
exploitation of lower-class superstition, and their attempt to use religion
for personal gain (*3 Henry VI* 2.1) were also excised. Margery Jourdain
was not condemned to be burned, so the parallel with Joan was missing.
While the parallel complaints of Eleanor and Margaret about their inferior
statuses were juxtaposed effectively, the episode of the fan (*2 Henry VI*
1.3.138–147), a wonderful scene which involves another public insult, captures the theme of reversal of fortunes, and where two *women* combat each
other, was missing here, as was the Petitioners' scene (1.3.1–44). The point
about Eleanor as penitent witch was missed here. She came out in a black
gown scrawled with words like "witch" and "traitor," so this was a merely modern penalty. She escaped burning because she was of the upper class.
Margaret's long complaint ("I am no loathsome leper"), which can be a
shrewd punishment of poor King Henry, as Julia Foster showed in the BBC-
TV production, was also gone (*2 Henry VI* 3.2.73 ff.). The scene I missed
most, however, was that in which Suffolk dies (4.1). The scorn of
Whitmore and the Lieutenant for a merely self-serving nobleman helps balance the plays' demonstration of almost absolute self-interest. To complicate that, however, are the seamen's interest in ransom for the other prisoners and Suffolk's magnificently fatal defiance. When the queen appeared
with Suffolk's wrapped head, we were left to assume that he had encountered a roving band of mummy-makers.

Suffolk's comparison of himself with "the youthful Paris" (*1 Henry VI*
5.5.104) "is apt," says Gwyn Williams, "for he intends to steal a king's
wife. He realizes the dangers implied in the comparison but hopes to be
luckier in the end than Paris was. We remember the disasters brought upon
Troy by Paris's exploit, and we are prepared for similar results in England"

(313). The Suffolk-Margaret sequence, Williams says, "is Shakespeare's first essay in tragic, destructive love, and there is something grand in this shameless affection between two passionate, ruthless, and physically splendid lovers. . . . Suffolk's brave death and the effects his deeds had, in Shakespeare's view, on English history raise him to tragic level" (318–319). As in the Kahn version, this one omitted the brutal results of Suffolk's effort to become a happy Paris. Each production robbed us of the last scene of a love story, one that, however perverse and "politically incorrect," can be moving and can serve as a contrast to the purely greedy agendas of so many of the other characters.

A production ending with the *Henry VI, Part 3* and concentrating on a movement into anarchy could not include Henry's blessing of Richmond. The issue, however, is not just hope for the future and the prelude for another play that Shakespeare likes to build into his previous play (as in Bolingbroke's questions about his "unthrifty son" at the end of *Richard II*). The prediction can clarify Henry's "detachment from political reality [which is seen by critics as] culpable weakness or saintly wisdom" and show that he has been "a theatrically effective spokesman for reasonableness and common sense who does not realize that in the world he inhabits such values have ceased to operate" (Leggatt 491)—and will not be restored until the next generation. The three suns episode (*3 Henry VI* 2.1) was also missing here. A problem arises, though, if Prince Edward gets Northumberland's lines of pity for York (1.4). They muffle Edward's martial character: "Hardly can I check my eyes from tears" (1.4.151). The script does not invite us to believe that Edward has inherited some segment of his father's tenderheartedness. What he does say is "If that be right which Warwick says is right,/ There is no wrong, but every thing is right" (2.2. 131–132). That draws Richard's sneering "Whoever got thee, there thy mother stands,/ For well I wot thou hast thy mother's tongue" (133–134). Richard is implying, of course, that the prince looks more like Suffolk than King Henry.

If prophecies are included—Asmath's cautions about Suffolk and water, accompanied by an undulation of the hand, and about Somerset's shunning castles—what are we to make of them when they are not fulfilled? They become *ex post facto* nonsense syllables, "typical of Shakespeare" or of plays that "are notoriously shapeless," as Shapiro says (10). The plays are there to be shaped. The shaping here left some things to be desired.

That major companies in significant eastern cities have undertaken these plays argues for a spin-off of more productions in other places. The plays are no longer "*terra incognita* for playgoers," as director James Sandoe called them in the early 1960s (21). Kahn and Coonrod have provided brilliant models against which other directors can place their own productions. Beyond that, of course, our response educates us to the issues in these wonderful plays and lets their pressure exert itself within our historical moment, showing us what it is and is not. If productions do not issue the challenge to our response, "our relationship to our own culture becomes quaint and drained of energy," as Jane Smiley says (30). What we are discovering, of course, is that, in the hands of skillful directors, Shakespeare *is* our culture.

NOTE

[1] The text used for *Henry VI* is C. J. Sisson's 1963 version, published by Dell and based on the folios. For further comments see my review of the American Repertory Theatre production in *Marlowe Society of America Newsletter* XV/2 (Fall 1995): 5–8, and my chapter on the RSC *Henry V* in *Shakespeare in Production: Whose History?*, which also deals with the ART production. This essay is a revision of a chapter that appears in *Shakespeare: The Two Traditions* (Madison, NJ: Fairleigh Dickinson University Press, 1999). I want to give special thanks to Bill Coyle and Susan Shuttleworth.

TALKING WITH YORK
A CONVERSATION WITH STEVEN SKYBELL

Thomas A. Pendleton

[The following is a transcript of an interview by the editor (**TP**) with Steven Skybell (**SS**), a young actor who appeared as the Duke of York in the 1996 New York Public Theater production of *Henry VI*, directed by Karin Coonrod. The production rearranged the three plays into two performances: the first, "The Edged Sword," began with the funeral of Henry V (*1 Henry VI*, 1.1), closed its first act with the death of Joan of Arc (*1 Henry VI*, 5.4), and ended with the death of Suffolk (*2 Henry VI*, 4.1); the second evening, "Black Storm," opened with the Jack Cade rebellion (*2 Henry VI*, 4.2), closed the first act with Henry and the father and son murderers at Towton (2.5), and continued to the apparent triumph of York that ends *Part 3*. Mr. Skybell's references to the first part, or evening, or to the first act relate to the divisions of this production. The transcript has been edited and somewhat regularized; as promised to Mr. Skybell, we both sound a little smarter and smoother than in fact we were.]

TP: Steven, tell me something about how the production began. From what I've read, Karin Coonrod seems to have been very good to work with.

SS: She really was. The whole process was very unusual in terms of the theater because we did a workshop of the first evening ["The Edged Sword"]—it must have been about a four-week workshop, which again is unusual, and we concentrated on her staging; just doing the first evening, not even with the knowledge that it was going to be us in the final production. It was just a workshop as actors often do. Then it was a year later that the same group, luckily, was reassembled to do a workshop of the second evening ["Black Storm"].

219

TP: It was 1996 when the production opened at the Public?

SS: Probably late fall 1996. So this would have been two years preceding when we did the first workshop; then a year later we did the second, and then about four months later, we started full eight-week rehearsal period. So the amazing thing was the luxury of having that much time to be thinking about the characters and familiarizing yourself with the material.

TP: Did you know the play as a text or from another production?

SS: No, never read it, never seen it. In fact it was my first history play. I'd done a fair amount of Shakespeare before that, but I'd never done a history play.

TP: I see that you did *Two Gentlemen* as well. You're becoming an expert in obscure Shakespeare.

SS: And *Troilus and Cressida* in the Park too; definitely some obscure ones. But it was a revelation to do a history play because there's a general perception that they're kind of dry, harder to get dramatically exciting, and I found actually the opposite to be true in terms of performing it.

TP: I was very much struck in reading some background on this by the sense that this was done by a company; there were very few of you—ten people.

SS: Right, ten people.

TP: Which means everybody is doubling like mad. But in going through the cast list, it seems that everybody got a chance to do a really fat role, everybody got a chance to hold the stage.

SS: Definitely, that was true. And in productions of Shakespeare I've been in where there was doubling, it makes everyone's evening a complete thing, and that's so rewarding for an actor. You realize that in Shakespeare's day, things were being written for the strengths of certain performers. There was a core of people that would take on the heft of the evening and that would be fulfilling to them.

TP: I think curiously these plays, where you don't have one big star role—no Henry V, no Richard III—you do have loads and loads of strong roles. Now, York was your big role; you got both of the soliloquies, right?

SS: Yeah, I did. You know, York's a great role, a great role.

TP: From what I could judge there was some cutting, but you didn't lose much as York.

SS: I don't think so. Talbot was cut back, and the Jack Cade rebellion as well, but we concentrated the main story—it's Henry and it's York. I'm not aware of much cutting within York's role.

TP: This I think you would have been aware of—if there was cutting within York's big speeches, your death speech with Margaret and your two big soliloquies.

SS: No, those were basically played as written.

TP: The cutting seems to have been of actions; Horner and Peter, for example, went away.

SS: Yes, they did. That's how we did it.

TP: Something also happened with you as Bedford: you got killed early on as Bedford.

SS: Well, there was also some taking one character and consolidating him with another, just to keep the storytelling as clean as possible.

TP: Did you get shot up on the balcony as Bedford?

SS: No, I got shot down on the main playing area, but I did get shot.

TP: And by the gunner's boy?

SS: Yeah, that's right.

TP: So you had to get killed as Bedford so that you could come back as York?

SS: That's right. I remember that Karin thought it was important to have that first death. It's the first death in the whole story, so we wanted that moment. But they just needed it to be that character—I forget why, but they wanted to have a through line for certain other characters.

TP: I think it can't be Salisbury [who is actually the character shot by the gunner's boy] because Salisbury comes back on later as one of your supporters.

SS: Right, right.

TP: Historically, they were two different Salisburys and Shakespeare keeps them apart, but it's different when you guys are putting it all together. But I wanted to get back to another aspect of this company thing. It seems that as York you had very strong interaction, a big scene that's actually a two scene, with, I'd guess, about five different people. With Joan, with Margaret. When we talked about this before, you spoke of York as down on women and the one I'd forgotten—you also arrest Eleanor, don't you?

SS: Right, yes, I do. That was Karin. It's interesting that the Public hired a woman to direct this play that has such strong women, and she was the one who highlighted that aspect of the character for me. York has these high confrontational scenes with women, and that's interesting, that might mean something, and yet since his wife is nowhere to be seen, you see him as the one caretaker for his sons. You get to see a love he has for his family as well as any strange feeling he might have about women.

TP: I remember reading in Coursen's book [*Shakespeare: The Two Traditions*]—and he's very impressed with your production—

SS: Good, good. I'm glad.

TP: I don't remember the actor's name, but Coursen found Somerset—

SS: That was a woman, Jan Leslie Harding, who also played Joan.

TP: So that was her big role.

SS: Yeah, it comes very early in the play.

TP: To get back to Coursen. He praised her playing of Somerset in a manner that explains why he (or she) continually drives you up the wall.

SS: Yes, for whatever reason, there's such antagonism between them that stays in the play through such a high arc until finally York has his head. There is this desire—

TP: Did you get to carry his head?

SS: Yeah, there's a bloody scene in which Richard brings it in, and we tossed it. He tossed it to me. Richard has deserved best of all my sons—

TP: I was interested because you end up killing Old Clifford at that first battle, but the fellow who all the way from the Temple Garden scene is your opposite number is Somerset. And he gets killed by your son, who seems to be plugging into Dad's animosity. Throwing the head.

SS: That's right. There definitely was a true antagonism, and—this is Karin—she hoped to have the same overtones from Joan of Arc. You know it was the same actor having that highly antagonistic relationship, so that it would have its own cumulative effect.

TP: And just as the door closed on Joan, Margaret appeared, so that the sense of woman as disruptive—

SS: And French women, the She-wolf of France—

TP: This is Coursen again, talking about these plays, and I think he says something that you seem to have been very much onto. "What Shakespeare was doing in these plays was beginning to find out what he intended to mean. What he intended to mean was to excite his audience into discovering they meant. The process still works" [*Two Traditions* 67]. That it's exploratory. There are things developing, going on, in what would be your Part 2, Act 2 that wouldn't make sense if you didn't have the three earlier pieces.

SS: That's right.

TP: There seems to be an enormous amount of matching or paralleling of scenes you were into with the women, but that seems to have been strong throughout Karin's staging For an obvious example, you stand on the same molehill as Henry.

SS: The staging was very inventive and not without its challenges, because some things were rearranged at the last minute. I remember the thing about the space that was wonderful was that it was so intimate; the audience was split on either side, and you didn't feel you had to reach too far in any direction. There was a scene in which all these chairs came down for the Parliament scene—

TP: When you all turn on Humphrey—

SS: That's right, and I respected Karin as a director because she had a sense of minimal staging; she wanted to let the language really *be* the action, and this one Parliament scene was all about looks. She wanted it to be very tense, but very still. I always think that's such a good thing, especially for Shakespeare. You know there are fight scenes, big physical movements, but so often if you just let the language be the action and be very simple about where things are placed—

Figure 4:
Jan Leslie Harding (Joan of Arc) and Steven Skybell (York) in the
New York Public Theater production of "The Edged Sword," part one of a
two-part adaptation of *Henry VI*. By courtesy of the New York Public Theater;
photo by Michael Daniel.

TP: You did the same staging with Warwick?

SS: That right, and she felt that one of the moving things about the plays' history is that things just happen again and again and on the same boards, and history in this way repeats itself.

TP: Yes, when we talked about this before—and no actor could miss this— one of your York soliloquies is Shakespeare clearly getting ready to create Richard III.

SS: Again, that's something I really responded to in the character, that although he's the father of Richard III, and definitely has all the makings of a Richard III, there is something about him that has not quite fallen over to that side. People always say that the strength of Shakespeare is that if you read the character, you see it from that character's point of view. I really feel that about York, because although he's called the rabble-rouser and the usurper, when I played him, it was so obvious that he was doing it from such a place of righteousness in himself.

TP: When he announces that he'd be a better king than Henry, he's really got a case.

SS: And that again is what I love about it, as opposed to a play, say the Scottish Play. I feel that the audience's sympathies and their sense of balance are always being questioned in the *Henry VI*'s. The characters all make good points, and you see them go from such places of innocence— just a fight in a garden that then becomes more and more menacing.

TP: You know, you could make the same point with the opposite argument, that there's nobody in the play—except for Henry, and even he does some things along the way—

SS: Yes, they're all cutthroats; they're all power-hungry.

TP: This is something I wanted to ask about, and not everyone reads it this way, but when you and Somerset fail Talbot, it seems to me that Shakespeare made Somerset more culpable than he made York.

SS: That was always a very hard scene, but he did, in my impression as well. It seemed as if Somerset was laying a trap, a trap for both Talbot and myself, and yet Lucy, who's there, says that both are guilty, that, you know, you could give in, you could do it too. It's sort of a Catch-22. That was a hard scene because at that point Talbot is the golden child, England's savior, and we're the ones who do him in.

TP: And if York fails at about the same level as Somerset, I'd guess you thought that was going to make trouble for things you'd do later on.

SS: Yes, but if you look at the sweep of all three plays, you really do encompass that wide arc of doing bad things and doing good things, noble things and ignoble, and hopefully you find a balance.

TP: Once Shakespeare gets through with *Henry VI* and gets to *Richard III*, he pretty much blows that off, and everybody is black and white, especially with Richmond at the end.

SS: I guess so. You know, I'm not sure what it would be like to go to the theater and just see *Part 3*. You feel as if his scope and desire to tell a story were more rambling and more long arching, and then he became a little more formulaic.

TP: That's one of the reasons I'm interested in these plays. How do you do these things in a commercial theater? They have no closure at all. When *Part 2* ends, you've just won the battle of St. Albans and Warwick has the last line— let's get to London before they do— and that's what happens to open *Part 3*—

SS: Yes, and it's very early in *Part 3* that I die, and I was so thankful we were doing it in a different dramatic structure, because to have your third evening begin with such a high, such an end point, I think that that would be very frustrating for the actor and a challenge to have to start the evening and hit that point so early in the evening. A really tough challenge; one that I'm glad I didn't have to take on.

TP: I think it would be tough for the audience too, to respond to the death of York.

SS: Yeah, I wonder, and this ties in a little with having played the Globe. At the Globe, the crowd really dictates how they want to perceive anything. It's so clear that the burning of Joan and the taunting of Joan would have been a great scene for cheering; they would have been so into the defeat of France.

TP: She did "Done like a Frenchman, turn and turn again" in your production?

SS: Yes.

TP: And got a rise from the audience. You can imagine what that rise would have been in the Globe.

SS: Absolutely.

TP: How did you burn Joan, by the way?

SS: Oh, it was amazing. Because Joan was in a simple, blue pinafore dress, and this was the end of the first act of the first evening, and they brought in at the end a raised case—her dress was encased and it was rigged to go up in flames—it was a paper dress, so it was sort of burning the emblem of the little girl. It was quite stirring.

TP: You also had some props coming down from above, didn't you?

SS: Yes, the coffin of Henry V came down at the very beginning, with a big thud.

TP: And Cardinal Beaufort sits on it.

SS: Right.

TP: That's something you apparently went for. You realized that at times when the conflict devolves into an absurdity that can get a laugh.

SS: I think Karin felt she had to have that too, in order to entertain but also to create tension and release, and it is true that there are lots of asides—there are times when you're in cahoots with the audience. There can be a kind of knowingness that gets a laugh.

TP: You had a very strange stage; raked downward as you go upstage.

SS: Yeah, it was odd. Well, on one side there was a raised high platform that sloped down, and that was where I died and fell down.

TP: You were standing on the platform?

SS: No, I was just standing on this area down, and then when she stabbed me, I went back against the wall and was able to just kind of slide down because this corner was raked all the way down. It was covered actually in real leather, sort of animal skins.

TP: Did you have a balcony area? I'm thinking especially for the sieges of the cities.

SS: There was. It was basically a playing area that was confined like a balcony. Toward the end, when Margaret was on one side and the two sons of York and Warwick were on the other, that was definitely a pitting of the two different camps on two different levels. But there's another scene when York and his sons are on one side and Henry and Margaret and Somerset on the other, and that was all played in the same area. And we did—this was an interesting staging of Karin's which illuminated what was going on in the text. No one entered the area until he spoke; so I entered, and then Henry entered, and so on. It was the gathering of forces, but all in the same playing space, facing off.

TP: I also wanted to ask about speaking the verse. This is very early and the verse seems very stiff, relatively little variation, not many run-over lines—

SS: Right.

TP: I think all your big speeches are this way.

SS: Pretty much all three plays are this way. It's very ordered, very regular meter, every thought is five feet long. It's very line by line. But it wasn't a problem for me. I mean, you recognize it, you see it, and it's simpler than other verse that you have to wrap your tongue and wrap your mind around to convey the meaning. And in that sense it's very easy to convey the meaning. There's some Shakespeare, later Shakespeare, where you fear that the audience really will not follow, and this is cruder in a way, but much more immediately accessible to the audience. I always relish it in Shakespeare when you can simply say the line and know it's understood for what it is. And York gets to say a lot of things that have that immediate impact that I was happy to have. When York is being sent to Ireland and says that that's exactly what he wants, that they're putting weapons in a madman's hand, I always heard the audience go "Oh." They understood exactly.

TP: How directly did you play that to the audience?

SS: Oh, pretty directly. It was such a challenge to talk to that audience; they were so present, on both sides [at the Public].

TP: And on three sides at the Globe?

SS: Sometimes even four; they sell seats in the gallery. I believe that in Shakespeare's day it was more important that they could hear rather than see. So as long as they could hear Juliet, they didn't necessarily have to see her on the balcony, because with the columns and with sitting up there [in the gallery], it wouldn't have been a beautiful stage picture, not from our perspective in the twentieth century, it would have been kind of cluttered, and what's going on?

TP: What's it like to play in the open air in the afternoon, where everyone can see you?

SS: It's amazing; it's amazing. I've never performed in a space quite like it, and after, I thought how am I going to go back to performing at night, in the dark, in covered rooms. It was a real revelation. I've done Shakespeare in the Park at the Delacorte, which is the antithesis to that, because you're here with a microphone, and the audience is way over there, and if it rains everybody goes home. Whereas at the Globe, you can see everybody, and even though it's a good-sized theater, it's intimate, and of course if it rains, you keep going because only the groundlings get wet. Anyone seated doesn't get wet, and the actors don't get wet. We had that with *Henry V*; at times there was rain, and when he talked about rain at the battle of Harfleur and it was coming down—it was really coming down—and that was a revelation for me as an actor, to think about all those references to weather. I played the French Constable and I had a line about their climate being so rotten and raw. It was great, especially at the Globe, because they just hated me; they just loved to hate the French.

TP: But aren't you the one person among the French for whom we're going to have any respect, because you're so down on the Dauphin?

SS: Yes, but there was a sense that I was the captain of the opposing team. You could respect the power I represent, but they loved to boo. It was quite a thing. But the references to weather, as I said, if it was a sunny day, that would get them going, or if it was a rainy day, that would get them going. And you realize that that was a big thing for outdoor theaters. I think of Hamlet pointing to the clouds; we might have no clouds to point to if we were outdoors.

TP: I'd like to know something about working with the posts. You'd think it's a God-awful idea because of what it does to the sight lines, but— Coursen again—you do have to remember that the audience was standing, and even those who were sitting weren't in seats but on benches, and they could move.

SS: As they do at the Globe. Mark Rylance, the artistic director of the Globe, always loved to refer to the alternate title of *Twelfth Night, What You Will*, because he really feels it's always what you the audience want, and so from the audience point of view, if you're not interested in what's going on here, then walk around, change your perspective, see it from a different point of view, and that's remarkable about the groundlings.

TP: In this context, when you get them to really stand still, that's when you've got them.

SS: That's right, that's right. And we did. With the Crispin's Day speech, after all the moving and cheering and booing, then that moment was so quiet—a hushed quietness so that the actor doesn't even have to project to be heard. It was really something.

TP: You would have been at the Globe about two years ago?

SS: Two years, right. I was asked back, but just because it's so long, it's six months over there—I'd like to go back; but it was a little too soon to go back for another half year, and also it was such a great experience that I would be afraid that it wouldn't match up, you know?

TP: To go back to the Public production, your back wall was very important to the production.

SS: There were two walls, so I don't know which one you mean. There was a sloping wall—

TP: Weren't there graffiti visible at some point?

SS: Yes, I guess there was. There was a sort of Tyvek material that went away for the latter part of the second evening and revealed the wall of the theater, on which was an upside down crown and words, and lines from the play just scrawled there.

TP: Was that where you did your genealogy chart?

SS: No, that would have been on another side. There was a little black-board where I wrote it.

TP: Oh, you actually wrote it?

SS: Oh, I wrote it, I wrote it all. I had to know it all, you know, the seven sons. I gave them sort of initials, but I wrote it all down. I showed how if you followed the third son, you get to me, and how if you followed the fourth son, you get to Henry. It's so clear. (Laughs) I mean, it is clear. Warwick says what could be plainer than this. It is plain, but it's also not plain at all. Another thing about the women—if you remember how *Henry V* starts, about the Salic law and whether you can inherit through the woman. And in this play, I have a claim through a woman, which is interesting since York has this issue with women. But without women, he wouldn't even have a claim to the throne. I know we spoke about this before. After York died, Karin Coonrod had me come back as Lady Bona, and that was a sort of coup de grace for York: he has to come back as a woman.

TP: This business of recognizing actors coming back in other roles was part of this production, wasn't it?

SS: That's right, there was no attempt to disguise that; we sort of celebrated that.

TP: Didn't you play Bona behind a scarf?

SS: No, I had a long veil, and I might have just played with it, but I didn't cover my face. I had a beard, as I do now, so we just played it like that. And also by that point in the evening, there was an attempt to make Lady Bona humorous. What would she be otherwise? She'd just be sincere. That was a directorial choice; let's make this fun as opposed to—

TP: I expect you get a laugh when the King and Lady Bona are sympathetic to Margaret until Warwick shows up with a better offer.

SS: Right, right.

TP: You have one good line as Lady Bona—"I'll wear the willow garland for his sake"—and having a guy with a beard say this—

SS: Yeah, it was fun.

TP: Steven, with Old Clifford at the first battle of St. Albans, you and Clifford have speeches in which each admires the other as a chivalric presence; to the effect that if you weren't my enemy—I wonder if this stuff survived?

SS: Yes, that was in the text. We may have trimmed it a little, but definitely I remember those lines. If you weren't my enemy—It's a deep line, and he also says something after he kills Clifford, wishing him peace, as opposed to the killing of Somerset, which was a vindictive, a tainting victory.

TP: Or when Margaret kills you.

SS: Yeah, but the Clifford killing is different; it's more complicated.

TP: Yes, and I think as you found out playing it, that it's good to have it here, before everything goes on a downward slope, as a point of reference when you're throwing Somerset's head around. Something else. You also played Stafford; you and your brother confront Cade, and you both get killed.

SS: That's right. I'm trying to remember because we went through so many variations. Stafford was still in, but it wasn't as we originally staged it. We were just voices from way up above calling down, and then we do get killed, but you don't get to see that.

TP: There's actually a lot of narrative in the Cade rebellion.

SS: Yes, the Cade rebellion was difficult for us to get and get right. It's tricky because the crowd comes in with such a presence. We wrestled with it, and Karin wrestled with how much to put in. The rebellion is important for Henry because that's where things really start to crumble for him.

TP: The play links Cade to York, but when he comes out on stage, he doesn't seem to be York's creature; he seems quite autonomous.

SS: Well, that's something Karin picked up on, that if York started a fire with Cade, it gets completely out of control. She even characterized Cade as a sort of the Green Man, a pagan element from the country that gets riled with the power and the fever of what he's doing against the power structure.

TP: And his pitch has an attraction to it: we common people are always suffering.

SS: Absolutely. In some ways the Cade rebellion is the most contemporary; it's almost like Brecht, the revolution of the common man, and it's fascinating because Jack Cade is so right in his cause and yet so wrong.

TP: I think that a production that used period costume would make it easier to establish what Cade is. But you apparently did this in stylized costume with a kind of color coding, with everyone in gold on the first evening—

SS: And in grey on the second night. But everyone wore the same thing— jodhpurs, boots, a T-shirt, and different sorts of overcoats, but that still wouldn't delineate class. With different costuming, it would have been easier to understand the Cade business in specific terms of that time, without laying on anything from the twentieth century, without any suggestions of the other revolutions that have occurred since that time. And you can't help but think of them when you see something that seems so recognizable in recent history.

TP: Alexander Iden killed Cade in your production, right?

SS: Yes, that's right.

TP: That gets talked about by critics nowadays in some odd ways, because Iden is a bourgeois, a property owner, not an aristocrat, and some critics want to see Iden as a representative of capitalism, as a bad guy.

SS: But I don't think he is. And that's how Walker Jones played him. He's just a burgher, a satisfied middle-class man who has done well by life, and then Public Enemy Number One comes into his backyard.

TP: Iden may be something of a problem for being so obviously a symbol of contentedness.

SS: Yes, there's something of a rough quality to these plays in terms of how things come in and out like that. Like the Margaret-Suffolk farewell, that's remarkable, that seems so developed—two people who are having such a fine tuned dialogue. And then you have Alexander Iden coming on and announcing I am Alexander Iden; it's a sort of roughshod dramaturgy.

TP: Margaret and Suffolk scene is surprising. Suddenly you're let into such heightened and romantic feelings that you had no idea these people possessed.

SS: It's amazing. But the role of Margaret, if you follow her journey all the way through *Richard III*—what other character has been so totally realized and by such a playwright? And to go from her innocence at the beginning through the arc of her role. As an actor, when you come to *Henry VI*, which is three plays, you have so much put before you, and when you do the historical research and find out what really happened and what Shakespeare did with it, and then you have the luxury of seeing what happens to your character and who the people are he affects. You know, I also played Bedford, who was Henry V's brother, and so that whole play became a background resource.

TP: Let me go back to York's thing with women. You arrested Eleanor Cobham, right?

SS: Yes.

TP: And alone, without Buckingham?

SS: Right, he was cut. And Karin of course wanted to heighten that animosity.

TP: Yes, that comes across. When I was going through your big scenes, you had one with Joan, one with Margaret, I had forgotten Eleanor, and then of course Somerset was played by a woman. Let me ask you about the Temple Garden scene. You had something like a grass carpet—

SS: That was something that rolled down this sloping wall, and in it were all the red and white flowers. So we went and picked our flowers.

TP: When you played that scene—I know you don't get to say specifically—but in terms of your own preparation, did you know what the argument was about ?

SS: We decided ultimately to make it something nonspecific in law. It was nothing dead on about attached versus arrested or anything like that. We all came on wearing glasses and carrying briefcases, as if we were in the last year of law school, and from an innocent but heated discussion about something unrelated, these old wounds opened, but it was something unrelated that we were asking people to say who's right.

TP: Some people who write about the play claim that what they're arguing about is of course York's claim to the throne.

SS: No, if you think of the scene where I lay it all out; we imagined that in a dark room, in emptiness. This isn't something you go around spouting. There would be no need to have that scene if this were being discussed among people.

HENRY VI
A TELEVISION HISTORY IN FOUR PARTS

Patricia Lennox

It comes as something of a surprise to learn there are four film versions of *Henry VI, Parts 1* to *3*, all of them made for television: two as original TV productions and two from stage versions. Furthermore, there is a curious pattern to their existence. Two were filmed within a few of years of each other—and the other two followed nearly twenty years later, but again only a few years apart. In 1960 Peter Dews put the first *Henry VI* on the "box" as part of his epic BBC-TV series *An Age of Kings*, Shakespeare's eight English histories from *Richard II* to *Richard III*. Five years later, Peter Hall and John Barton's Royal Shakespeare Company version of the First Tetralogy, *The Wars of the Roses*, was filmed, also for the BBC. Two decades passed before *Henry VI* was broadcast again. In 1982 Jane Howell directed the plays as part of the BBC Time-Life Shakespeare series. Finally, in 1989 Peter Bogdanov and Michael Pennington's English Shakespeare Company filmed a performance of their own *Wars of the Roses*, this time Shakespeare's double tetralogy.[1]

In each case *Henry VI* was part of a larger series of Shakespeare plays: a tetralogy, the English histories, or the complete works. The amount of critical attention paid to the productions varied—benign neglect in the sixties, careful scrutiny in the eighties.[2] Each of the four versions has a distinctive directorial approach, an individual production style, and its own abridgment of Shakespeare's text. Each director also offers a different political interpretation. The last three were summarized by Michael Manheim as Hall/Barton's 1960s "pop existentialism" emphasizing individual conflict, "secretiveness and rampant self-interest"; Howell's "post-Vietnam humanism" focusing on "a likable" youthful energy in the plays; Bogdanov/Pennington's "neo-Marxist" approach that finds that all the factions within systems "ultimately end with the plundering of the weak by

THE KINGS

as portrayed on the BBC television series,

AN AGE OF KINGS

(See inside back cover for photographs of actors playing other famous Shakespearean roles in this series.)

RICHARD II
David William

HENRY IV   HENRY V   HENRY VI
Tom Fleming   Robert Hardy   Terry Scully

EDWARD V   RICHARD III   HENRY VII
Hugh Janes   Paul Daneman   Jerome Willis

Figure 5:
Reprinted from *An Age of Kings: The Historical Plays of William Shakespeare* (Pyramid Books, 1961).

the strong" (134). In this regard, Peter Dews's 1960 approach could be described as a post–World War II celebration of national idealism moderated by knowledge of the human cost of war. These double pairs of *Henry VI*, one in black and white from the 1960s, the other in color from the 1980s, also demonstrate growing sophistication in television production and broadcast technology. *An Age of Kings* has the look and sound of early television: part theater, part film, and part radio. The RSC *Wars of the Roses*, though only a few years later, is technologically superior with its inventive camera shots and, on the whole, is far more sophisticated in its blend of theater and television. Twenty years later, BBC Shakespeare series director Jane Howell subverted perceptions of television's inherent naturalism to produce a *Henry VI* that brilliantly combines a full-stage theatrical set with intimate camera work. The ESC *Wars of the Roses* is the stepchild in the quartet, having been filmed and edited under difficult conditions that reduced it to being an inadequate record of a stage performance.

The earliest television version of *Henry VI, Parts 1* to *3* in *An Age of Kings* was the brainchild of Peter Dews, a former schoolmaster with an intense interest in Shakespeare, turned television producer.[3] Dews's *Kings* was an ambitious series that presented Shakespeare's English histories arranged in chronological order by monarch, broadcast in fifteen one-hour segments from April to November 1960. The inspiration for the series drew on Anthony Quayle's 1951 production of the Second Tetralogy at Stratford, the late Douglas Seale's 1953 direction of *Henry VI, Parts 1* to *3* for the Birmingham Repertory Theatre (later moved to the Old Vic in London), and Dews's own teaching experience. Although the BBC had been televising Shakespeare since the network's first experimentation with live drama in 1937, *Kings* was its first extended Shakespeare series. Today the *Kings* working budget seems modest for such an undertaking. For example, the total cost for all three parts of *Henry VI* was £9,000, with *Part 1* coming in at a mere £2,598 (Rothwell and Melzer 103). For the series Dews brought in Michael Hayes as the television director (later Hayes would fill the same position in the Barton/Hall RSC television production). Eric Crozier, who had adapted *A Midsummer Night's Dream* for TV in 1958, would handle the script. For *Kings,* Crozier cut and edited the three parts of *Henry VI* into five segments, each approximately an hour long: *The Red Rose and the White* (*1 Henry VI* acts 1–5), *The Fall of the Protector* (*2 Henry VI* acts 1, 2, and 3), *The Rabble from Kent* (*2 Henry VI* acts 4 and 5), *The Morning's War* (*3 Henry VI* acts 1, 2, and 3), and *The Sun in Splendor* (*3 Henry VI* acts 4 and 5). The problem of casting the histories' hundreds of characters was solved by forming a repertory company described by Dews as "twenty young men" who could "match the youth and vigor of Shakespeare's early writing." Many of them were Old Vic–trained but their origins represented "the range of Great Britain"

(Dews 1961). Major roles would be played by visiting actors, including Judi Dench as *Henry V*'s Katherine and Sean Connery as Hotspur, while the core company would double, treble, and quadruple roles.[4] In the end *Henry VI* was performed with a total of thirty-nine actors.

A series has special needs ranging from theme music to a "permanent" set. As befits a national canon, *Kings*' theme was composed by Sir Arthur Bliss and performed by the Royal Philharmonic Orchestra, while incidental music was composed by Christopher Whelen.[5] The multipurpose set, "unashamedly theatrical because the plays were" (Dews 1963, 18), consisted of generic units that could be reused throughout the series: a collection of steps, platforms, corridors, pillars, and window frames. The close-up shots of actors speaking out of these windows proved to be one of the series' most effective visuals. When Henry (Terry Scully) is in the windmill at the snowy winter battle at Towton, (*3 Henry VI*, 2.5.5–55), he looks through a broken windowpane. As he sadly ruminates about the odd fate that left him a king at nine months old, he traces concentric circles in mist on the remaining glass panes. Those circles in the mist provide an apt visual metaphor for Henry's own entangled state and his impotent compassion for his country torn by civil war. The frame is filled with his grief-stricken face, part saintly ascetic, part fool.

Nothing else in the set was as effective as the window frames. The basic component pieces, along with some nondescript rooms, offered sites that were vaguely medieval and not particularly realistic. When seen on the screen in medium and long shots, the rooms are flattened, bleached shadowless by the intense lights required for TV broadcast at this time. However, Dews's "watchword" for the production was "Great Men in Small Rooms," and each scene required its own "room." He could not have known then, as Jane Howell was to prove two decades later, that you can work on a large set and let the cameras and lighting create the illusion of small spaces. Back in 1960, Dews and director Hayes were struggling with live broadcasts and comparatively limited technology. Although the microphone liberated actors to whisper and freed them from the need to project to the back row, it could also be crippling. The recording engineer could work with sound only between a given range of decibels, which meant that "total noise and electric silences . . . two great weapons in a director's armoury" were prohibited. Dews found it equally disconcerting that black and white television meant that sets and costumes (stock medieval with lots of armor and heraldic devices) had to be "envisaged in discreet shades of battleship grey" (Dews 1963, 18).[6] One of the most impressive aspects of *Kings* is that every segment of the show was broadcast completely live. Other than the opening credits, no film was used. What the actors said and did at a particular moment was what the audience saw and what we now have recorded on video. Later, when Peter Hall and Jane Howell created their television *Henry VI*'s, they relied on film techniques, and although Michael Bogdanov's film is a recorded theater performance, the final print was created in the editing room. The Dews-Hayes shooting plan was simplicity itself: "When in doubt close in. Let the faces do the work." Close-ups effectively circumvented the technical limitations of lighting and sound to result in intensely dramatic screen images. In the series, however, these effective close-ups are often at odds with the (far too many) flat mid-shots that dilute the actors' impact and give the series a somewhat schizophrenic quality—part old-style television, part emerging cinematic new style. However, it is the head shots that one remembers, especially the way the taut skin and facial bones of Terry Scully's Henry VI and Mary Morris's Queen Margaret become sculpted with highlights and shadows, or the way Eileen Atkins's (Joan la Pucelle) demon-ridden eyes fill the entire screen.

Although initial reception of the series was cool, Dews remembers how "we found the public responded, as had my Barnsley [school] boys to the slow unfolding of the plays, and we ended in something like a triumph" (Dews 1963, 18). *Kings* went on to win the British Guild of Directors' award for Excellence in Directing and America's Peabody Award for broadcast excellence. Based on the sheer volume of *Kings'* audience, estimated at over three million viewers in Britain alone, Dews was dubbed "the most influential interpreter of Shakespeare in the English-speaking world" (Kitchin 70). By the time the first part of *Henry VI* was broadcast, entitled *The Red Rose and White*, it was *Kings'* ninth installment and critics and public had become enthusiastically loyal viewers. It was just as well that there was a ready-made audience for *Henry VI* because at that time the attitude toward Shakespeare's earliest plays was fairly dismissive. *Henry VI* was seen as his "'prentice work." Maurice Evans "compassionately" introduced it to U.S. viewers as "school boy writing."[7] American critic Milton Crane found it shocking to hear the "starched rhetoric" of *Henry VI* after the "supple verse and dazzling prose" of *Henry IV* (324). However, the London *Times* praised the company's ability to accommodate the shift in style from Shakespeare's mature to more youthful verse. It complimented the actors' adroit handling of *Henry VI*'s "thundering pentameters," sniffed a bit at Shakespeare's youthful indiscretion in writing a plot "packed with penny-dreadful batterings and blood,"[8] and, finally, pronounced the series a major success.

The prejudice against *Henry VI, Parts 1* to *3* was such that no one seems to have objected to the loss of the enormous amount of material Crozier removed in order to fit the three plays into a running time of a little less than five hours. The Barton/Hall version runs six hours, Bogdanov/Pennington's is nearly five and a half, and Jane Howell's unabridged plays total nine and three-quarter hours. Crozier's deepest cuts were in *Part 1*, where almost no speech is left unabridged, and the most sweeping deletion is the removal of every Talbot scene (2.2–3, 3.2, 4.1, and

4.5–7). Along with Talbot, who had traditionally been seen as *the* central character in *Part 1*, thirteen other characters were also dropped, including the Earl of Salisbury, Sir John Falstaff, and Edmund Mortimer. Scenes 1.4 and 2.1 also disappeared. What remains is basically background material for the four-hour *Henry VI, Parts 2* and *3* that followed. The cuts and abridgements here, as in the Barton/Hall version, focused critics' attention on a very visible Queen Margaret played by Mary Morris (and later by the RSC's Peggy Ashcroft). But the newly discovered Margaret was a product of the times and not the result of cuts alone. Julia Foster's fiercely energetic Margaret (BBC series) seems to dominate even in the full-text, full-character version. It is worth noting that in all four versions, no matter how deep the cuts, Joan la Pucelle and Jack Cade remain and, even when abridged, are always dynamic.

In addition to achieving critical and popular acclaim in Britain, *An Age of Kings* was financially successful and helped defray production costs with international sales of a "telerecording" (made by shooting a 16mm film off the television screen during the live broadcast[9]). In America the series was seen first on commercial channels in Washington and New York and then nationwide over educational networks. Dews complained about the "Procrustean chopping" (1963, 18) carried out to fit the segments into the standardized American broadcast hour. BBC flexibility had let them vary in ranging from sixty to seventy-five minutes, but American TV's rigid sixty minutes had to encompass not only the play but commercials and an introductory commentary by the sponsor's spokesman.[10] The NET version, where segments run closer to their original length,[11] begins each program with a lecture by Frank C. Baxter, a University of Southern California professor who made a specialty of popularizing "highbrow" material on television. Armed with genealogical charts and maps, Baxter introduces himself engagingly as "an inadequate footnote" to the history plays. At least one cut, and possibly more, were made by the NET editors to reduce violence. Missing are the Grand Guignol touches that Crane deplored in the commercial broadcast, where, for instance, "the audience was spared not a dying shriek" of the burning Joan la Pucelle (325). Here she is tied to the stake as soldiers pile up straw for the fire, but she neither burns nor shrieks.

Consistent with *An Age of Kings'* emphasis on general audience accessibility, this *Henry VI* presents a somewhat simplified picture of the rift between England and France and between the houses of York and Lancaster. Its real focus is on the triangular power struggle: Henry VI on one axis, Margaret/Suffolk on another, and York and his three sons on a third. Terry Scully, who resembles portraits of the historical Henry, plays the monarch as a poor weak thing, "a pious weakling more suited to the offices of parish priest than the stern task of a king" (O. Campbell). In the opening scene, this Henry sounds like an obedient child parroting the Lord Protector's pronouncements while later he is a fondly foolish lover in his meeting with his new queen. Mary Morris is a mature and glamorous Margaret (Dews would later cast her as Cleopatra), who understandably finds her peevish king a disappointment, especially when compared to the virile Suffolk. Eventually Scully's Henry develops a moderate degree of *gravitas*, but not the necessary political insight to save his nation or impress his queen. He never gains the simple majesty and saintly dignity that David Warner (RSC) or Peter Benson (BBC) were to bring to the role. In this production Henry's weakest moment as king is when he dithers his way into agreeing to make York his heir. Warner's Henry reached his decision after carefully weighing the arguments and then being menaced by guards with spears. Benson's Henry also agreed only at swordpoint.

Only a few months after the final segment of *An Age of Kings* was broadcast, another, more complex *Henry VI* appeared on the stage. In 1961 Peter Hall's Royal Shakespeare Company was in its second year, and its biggest triumph to date on the Stratford stage was John Barton's three-part adaptation of the First Tetralogy *The Wars of the Roses: Henry VI, Parts 1 to 3* (in two parts titled *Henry VI* and *Edward IV*) and *Richard III*. Four years after its stage premiere, *Roses* was televised to international acclaim. When *Roses* opened at Stratford, it generated a great deal of critical and popular excitement. It was a national cultural event—Shakespeare interpreted with a contemporary approach by the theater's newest and brightest director, Peter Hall. He described the production as "an expression of what we found meaningful in the 1960s in Shakespeare's view of history" (1970, ix). The playing text was John Barton's sensitive and energetic adaptation. To fit the three parts of *Henry VI* into two plays, Barton cut the original 12,350 lines in half and ended with a final version of 7,450 lines, of which a little over 6,000 came from the original. The remaining 24 percent of the dialogue was crafted by Barton himself, primarily from Shakespeare's own sources, Hall and Holinshed.[12] Above all there were the spectacular performances. Henry was played by an impressive newcomer, twenty-one-year-old David Warner. Star magnetism was provided Peggy Ashcroft as Queen Margaret and Donald Sinden as York. Ian Holm, still remembered by critics as a youthful Peter Pan, was cast unexpectedly as a villain, Richard of Gloucester, later to become Richard III. Presenting *Richard III* as the final installment in the tetralogy means the actor needs to begin his interpretation with the more moderately drawn Richard of *Henry VI*. Holm's Richard drew upon Paul Daneman's performance in *Kings* and later would help shape Ron Cook's interpretation in the BBC series. None of these Richards are physical or psychological monsters. Instead, the famous hump is small, even inconspicuous at times, though highlighted in the battle scenes ensconced in its own armor. These Richards have neither twisted bodies nor withered hands but are barely malformed, just enough to make them the butt of cruel jokes, just enough to make "Dicky boy" the outsider.

Initially Hall rejected suggestions to televise the plays, pointing out that the tetralogy had been broadcast recently in *An Age of Kings*. But only two years later in 1963, possibly as a result of the RSC's loss of £47,473 through government reductions in arts grants, he agreed to transfer the play to television. It was well that Hall had waited. Since the filming of the first *Henry VI*, the BBC had undergone a face-lift; "urgency, topicality, and professional glitter were required" (Dews 1963, 18). The growth in BBC's sophistication can be seen in the contrast between stage actors captured in the point-and-shoot camera work of *Kings'* live broadcasts and the more subtle, film-based *Wars of the Roses*.

Figure 6:
David Warner (Henry), Donald Sinden (York), and Brewster Mason (Warwick)
in the 1965 RSC *The Wars of the Roses* telecast.
By permission of the Shakespeare Birthplace Trust.

The RSC had previously broadcast plays in performance from the Stratford theater, but for *Roses* Hall wanted something that had never been done before. Instead of simply televising a stage performance, he was determined to reformulate it completely to recreate the excitement of the theatrical event on the TV screen. A team of fifty-two people from the BBC and eighty-four from the Royal Shakespeare Company worked for eight weeks to prepare the filming of a production that had already been performed extensively on the stage. Some of Hall's team had gained their Shakespeare broadcast experience working on *An Age of Kings*: Michael Barry, the TV producer for *Roses*, was the former head of BBC–1 Drama who had been instrumental in getting *Kings* on the air; Robin Midgely and Michael Hayes, who had won awards for his direction of *Kings*, were *Roses'* television directors. They would handle technical aspects, such as camera shots, while Hall worked with the actors. Everyone involved in the project worked to "recreate theatre production in television terms–not merely to observe it but to get to the heart of it" (Bakewell). Midgley and Hayes were credited with consistently employing the "techniques of the medium" in "the best interest of the play, never as an end in themselves" (Griffin). Hall insisted the filming be done at the theater in Stratford, where the actors would feel at home. The RSC's theater was reconfigured as a television studio with a larger acting area built over a space created by removing half the theater's seating. This allowed the twelve cameras (one of the them handheld for battle scenes) to maneuver through scenes ranging from scaling walls (a camera on a tower at the back of the stage) to the soliloquies of dying soldiers (a camera in a pit stage front).

Hall used the same actors, sets, and costumes from the stage production; in fact the images on the screen match the still photos from the play. The "heart of the [stage] production" was John Bury's iron cage set. The set for each scene was dominated by a background of linked metal in a variety of patterns. It was there even in the country scenes, when vines grew across and climbed up it. The sides of the stage, the wings, were solid plates of metal, designed by Bury to resemble "the steel of the plate armour" (Bury). On film the camera emphasizes the set's prison-like aspects by shooting through crisscross networks of grilles and bars. Many scenes start by peering through openings in these barriers. The stage is left bare, and the throne room, for example, contains only a series of grillework screens, the throne, and a council table whose covering changed with each reign—and during Henry VI's changed from a cloth of monastic austerity to one of embroidered velvet. The costumes from the stage production, designed by Bury to convey the medieval rather than trying to recreate it, adapted spectacularly well to the screen. Great attention to individual details keep the play's many characters distinguishable, even though most were dressed in variations of black leather or cloth textured with dabs of gold paint (even in black and white, you know that it is gold). Armor is a mix of metal pieces and leather that has been padded and quilted in the Japanese style. In contrast with other members of the court, Henry is dressed in a light colored monkish gown of rough weave. Small visual details show up well on the screen, such as switching the crucifix around Henry's neck for a miniature of Margaret for their first meeting, and then replacing it with the crucifix again after the Lord Protector's death.

In the theater, momentum had been created through movable set pieces: thrones that moved forward, grilles that flew up, tables that rose from below. For television, the same momentum is captured by starting scenes in full motion, avoiding the delays of exits and entrances, editing for quick cuts and mixed camera shots. Hall envisioned much of the play as head shots against a black background and used this technique to move the viewer crisply from scene to scene. Scenes start with the setting clearly visible, but end with the characters backed by black. As the actors absorbed the viewers' attention, everything else had literally, but imperceptibly melted away. The return of background details signals a new scene.

The RSC *Henry VI* cast transferred their performances from stage to the screen with skill and subtlety. David Warner's Henry VI starts as an overgrown adolescent with a shy smile. He is overly deferential and gawky to the point that his elbows stick out when he sits on the throne. By the end he has acquired a mature gravity and saintly demeanor that makes his Christ-like forgiveness of Richard's fatal blow his supreme moment. Warner's Henry is neither a pious fool nor a bumbler. Instead, blinded by his own goodness and innate pacifism, he is simply unable to understand the motives of the machinations that surround him. Warner thought Henry was "a bit dotty though he's quite sweet to begin with. But he is not *clever.*"[13] In contrast, Roy Dotrice's Edward IV is the new generation. Hot and bawdy, he sprawls on the throne with one leg cocked over its arm, and when rousted from his battlefield tent, he is in the arms of a naked prostitute. (Dotrice was equally effective as Cade.)

David Warner's strong performance as Henry is powerfully matched by Peggy Ashcroft's Queen Margaret. Only a few television critics were unchivalrous enough to point out the camera's highlighting of Ashcroft's maturity (she was in her mid-fifties at the time), though many more did complain about her "French" lisp. While the camera certainly revealed that the actress was neither eighteen nor even thirty, there were moments when she even managed to fool it into letting her appear so. It is a riveting performance that keeps you glued to the set. Her passion for Suffolk is palpable; her grief as she cradles his severed head is wrenching.

TV critics, using their own pop argot, signaled the show's achievements: "Howling Success" (*Oxford Mail*), "Still Top Scriptman – Mr. W. Shakespeare" (*Western Evening Herald*), "Bard Makes the Grade" (*Eastern Daily Press*). The theater critics had spent a great deal of space discussing Barton's adaptations, his scissors and paste Shakespeare. Television critics seem even more disturbed by the fact that you could not follow along with a script in hand, although one would have thought trimming and packing material into a smaller space was a normal part of the medium.

Another concern arose when audiences were faced with realistic spectacles of gore on the home screen[14]—the distorted corpse of Somerset; the chopping off of Suffolk's head; the way swords slowly entered bodies, painfully forcing their way through flesh and sinew. In Hall's production the synecdoche of war is a close-up of a bloody soldier's fallen body lying across a broken cartwheel. Perhaps because of television's increasing permissiveness or perhaps because of audience's changing taste, each version of *Henry VI* becomes progressively more bloody. Dews included Joan's dying shrieks, Hall went further with his bloody corpses, and Jane Howell would pile bodies up in ever-increasing numbers until Margaret straddles a human mountain of death at the end of *Richard III*.

Figure 7:
Ian Saynor (Dauphin), Michael Byrne (Alencon), Brenda Blethyn (Joan),
Brian Protheroe (Bastard of Orleans), and David Daker (Reignier) in the 1982
BBC/ Time Life Shakespeare Series production, directed by Jane Howell.
Copyright, BBC.

With the broadcast of *The Wars of the Roses*, three of Shakespeare's most ignored plays, *Parts 1* to *3 Henry VI*, had now, within the short period of five years, been seen in two separate productions by an audience of millions—and would not receive another TV production for seventeen years. The leap in sophistication between the first two versions was significant, but nothing could match the way Jane Howell's 1982 production for the BBC Shakespeare series burst upon the screen with innovative energy, directorial confidence, and verve. Howell, who had worked in theater for fifteen years, but never in film or television, successfully directed *A Winter's*

Tale, Henry VI, Parts 1 to *3, Richard III*, and *Titus Andronicus* for the series, prompting comments that Shakespeare was best served by the series in his more obscure plays. In her BBC productions Howell challenged the idea that television called for complete realism.[15] Her goal, instead, was to allow viewers the kind of freedom of imagination experienced by theater audiences; "what you need in television is a space which can be inside or outside and which leaves you free to create" (Howell quoted in Willis 165).[16] For *Henry VI, Parts 1* to *3* Howell worked with her actors as though preparing for a stage production. Seven months of solid work went into the production. There were long rehearsals with careful blocking that allowed camera work to be strategized before shooting, a sound artistic and economic practice.

For *Henry VI, Parts 1* to *3* and *Richard III*, Howell's limited budget meant a single all-purpose set for all four plays. Designer Oliver Bayldon's solution was to ignore the BBC series' restrictions requiring period settings, and instead to use scrap lumber to build a series of scaffoldings inspired by an adventure playground.[17] The set successfully links contemporary theater with the open Elizabethan stage, and even more important, stretched across a wide "stage" to fulfill Howell's requirement that it be large enough to fill the television screen. This highly praised construction became the heart of Howell's *Henry* in much the same way that John Bury's cage had been for the Hall/Barton production. It is an integral part of the plays and reflects their changing fortunes. Howell makes great use of color in the production (the two earlier *Henry VI*'s were in black and white), and as time passes the slick, bright red, blue, and yellow paint dulls, peels, and turns gray. The set established the tone of the production as nonnaturalistic "Brechtian metatheatricality" that expressed "both historical and contemporary meanings" (Holderness 1985). It "dared" the audience "to remember that the action is taking place in a studio" (S. Wells 1982). Howell's audience is never allowed to become passive TV viewers participating in "maimed rites" (Zitner) but is instead challenged to become a part of the theatrical experience.

The two previously broadcast *Henry VI* could count on abridged texts for speed and kept the action moving swiftly by beginning scenes with actors already in place. However, Howell, dealing with the BBC-mandated full text, decided to build momentum, the "wonderful flow to the plays" (Willems 1984, 81), by using the theatrical energy of entrances and exits. Movement in and out of the massive doorways on either end of the stage sets the rhythm of this carefully orchestrated and meticulously choreographed production. Howell has every piece in place: sets, costumes, lighting, camera work, and actors. And for once, the text is totally Shakespeare's. Like the set, the costumes belong to no particular period. Howell had no interest in using them to establish historical accuracy or symbolism (relatively little is made of red and white roses, for example). John Peacock designed a splendid collection of varied and unique costumes that evoke the medieval while communicating contemporary sensibilities that help define characters. *Part 1* starts with pageant-bright costumes in vivid colors, but by the end of *Part 3*, not only are the colors muted, but the padded leather armor has taken on a contemporary look.

Although all the action takes place on the big stage, intimate settings are effectively created through tightly focused shots. Howell has perfected the camera shot that became a hallmark of the Miller-produced plays. The frame is midway to a close-up but can accommodate a small group of people to create the illusion of an intimate meeting (compare with Dews's great men in small rooms). One of the keys to the success of these scenes—and the entire flexibility of the single set—is lighting designer Sam Barclay's skillful, nuanced lighting that consistently creates a sense of time and place, whether battlefield, royal chamber, or prison cell. Though the camera work is infinitely varied, Howell used only five cameras and generally worked with just three, in contrast to Peter Hall's less technically evolved dozen. Howell's most sophisticated visuals are in the battle scenes, each one unique, where the turmoil of war is created through the confusion of quick cuts, overlays, double exposures, slow motion, multiple reflections—all made more chaotic by a panoply of sounds, including trumpet blasts and drum rolls.

Strong as the technical aspects are, it is the actors who carry the plays forward. Howell brought together a repertory company where everyone, even the leads, doubled and trebled parts, sometimes with witty cross-references. Ron Cook appears as a messenger and a hunchbacked porter before he comes on as the crookbacked Richard. Peter Benson is seen as a priest singing a eulogy for the dead Henry V before reappearing as Henry VI. Benson, like Terry Scully, bears a strong resemblance to portraits of the thin, ascetic Henry VI. But unlike Scully, his Henry moves from weakling to a mature king, able to see what is happening but helpless to stop it. His grief at Somerset's death (an especially grim corpse) is overwhelming. Later he almost takes command when he banishes Suffolk, but the burst of authority goes no further. Benson makes us care about his Henry and ultimately is touchingly saintly in his forgiveness of his murderer Richard.

As Queen Margaret, Julia Foster is fascinating to watch. When she first meets Suffolk, she is dressed in an elaborate white satin dress and at a distance seems doll-like with her masses of long blonde hair. But in close-up her young Margaret is vapid, pudding-faced, certainly not someone to inflame Suffolk's passion. Dennis Bingham suggested that Howell was drawing on "a favorite Brechtian device to have a character say something which is contradicted by what the audiences sees" (226). Foster's Margaret is more bemused than inspired by Suffolk's kiss and is still innocent when she meets Henry. Anticipating his kiss, she turns her cheek to receive it, only to be disappointed by his chastely kissing her hand. The look she exchanges with Suffolk is the beginning of a new understanding. Her physical transformation is remarkable. In later scenes her face becomes thinner, the small body wiry and intense. Her pale lashes and brows disappear under the strong lights, and the denuded face is that of an alien, as though her France were another planet. Margaret's passion is thoroughly adult by the time she parts from Suffolk, and later she carries his head as though it were a newborn baby. When she tortures York she is horrifying, mad with revenge, her sharp face and teeth like those of a ferret tearing at its prey.

As the plays move from the beginning of *Part 1* to the end of *Part 3*, everything on the screen becomes despoiled and deteriorated: sets, costumes, people. Death becomes the connecting theme. *Part 2* ends with a pile of bodies from the battle of St. Albans and *Part 3* opens with a shot of another stack of bodies. Severed heads mounted on city gates are mummified. In *Parts 1* and *2* the name of the play appears in a banner over the double doors; in *Part 3* it is written on a shroud. At the beginning of the first play the mood is hopeful. This is still Henry V's chivalric England. There are a series of theatrical jokes: the cocky French soldiers rush off to battle like Keystone Cops, only to limp back a minute later. Winchester and Gloucester challenge each other in a jousting match fought on comically fake hobby horses. In Howell's view:

> It's a childish world, the world of chivalry which is smashed to pieces by Joan. Talbot is the representative of the old values. Once he is gone, then the door is open to political chicaneries. . . .
> It was a game at the beginning until the choosing of sides in the Temple Garden. (Willems 1989, 85)

In many ways Howell's is the most satisfactory of the filmed *Henry VI*'s and might seem the place to stop, at least for a while. However, there is one last film made seven years later by the English Shakespeare Company. Founded by Peter Bogdanov and Michael Pennington in 1986, the ESC toured Britain, Europe, and America with their experimental production of the double tetralogy, called (*pace* the RSC) *The Wars of the Roses*. Originally the repertory company mounted the major tetralogy, *Richard II*, *Henry IV*, and *Henry V*, and then, using the same repertory group of actors and the same simple sets, expanded to include the minor tetralogy, *Henry VI, Parts 1 to 3* (abridged to two plays) and *Richard III*. In the last weeks of the company's final tour, the ESC's version was filmed as the company performed at the Grand Theatre in Swansea with Paul Brennen (Henry VI), June Watson (Margaret), Michael Pennington (Suffolk), Barry Stanton (York), Philip Bowen (Edward IV), and Andrew Jarvis (Richard of Gloucester).

However, the filming was a rushed job done with very little preparation because, typical of the beleaguered history of the ESC, the funding came in at the very last minute, leaving little time to plan and coordinate the technical details. Bogdanov, whose broadcast experience consisted of three years' (1966 to 1969) production training at the BBC followed by two years with Radio Telfis Eireann, would fill in as television director for the hastily assembled film crew (chosen in part for their demonstrated ability to catch the quick action of sports events). Seven cameras were used in the hopes that enough footage would be available for a successful reconstruction in the editing room. Limits on time and budget meant that almost no scenes were to be reshot. Further, there was no attempt to adapt the plays for television other than replacing some worn out costumes. In fact, the actors were told to carry on as usual and ignore the cameras. Some who had film experience toned down their performances; others continued with the broader mannerisms needed for the stage. The result is particularly weak, especially when compared to any of the previous versions.

The ESC had reformatted *Henry VI, Parts 1* to *3* into *The House of Lancaster* and *The House of York*. However, unlike Crozier's or Barton's cuts, in this version not only are speeches deleted and abridged, they are also rearranged in ways that make the proceedings confusing. Further, there is such a sameness to actors' appearances that it is difficult to keep characters separate and remember who is who. The members of Howell's troupe, on the other hand, had highly individual faces, hair, and costumes. In the ESC production, not only are the men of similar stature (useful for theatrical repertory but difficult on camera), but costumes, hair, and even the beards tended to be similar, with the exception of thin-faced, completely bald Andrew Jarvis. In court scenes, everyone wears identical tuxedos or frock coats except Henry, a king without a crown. In battle scenes the mix of uniforms from various modern wars does little to relieve the confusion, although the French are in blue while the English wear khaki with either a red or white rose. Bogdanov admitted that many of the cast, exhausted from months of touring and uncomfortable with the confusion of the cameras, gave atypically flat performances. Certainly the result is a far cry from the excitement expressed by reviewers of ESC's earlier work. The one real glimpse of the company's theatrical power occurs in Jack Cade's scenes. Michael Pennington's dynamic Cade is a punk rebel dressed in a Union Jack T-shirt.[18] Unfortunately nothing else quite matches it. The heroic stories behind the filming and editing of this film and the director's dedication in the face of countless obstacles make you wish they had had another chance, because very little of the creative energy that drew such praise for the company transferred to this film.

It is not likely that the current rage for Shakespeare movies will extend to a big-screen *Henry VI*. If in another decade or two, a new version of *Henry VI, Parts 1* to *3* is filmed, my guess is that it will once again be made for television. TV's intimacy and, even more, its ability to serialize make it an excellent medium for these plays. Perhaps now that the work is more firmly placed in the canon, each generation will want its own version. The directors Dews, Barton/Hall, Howell, and Bogdanov/Pennington have demonstrated the play's political flexibility. David Warner and Peter Benson have proved that Henry can be an enormously challenging and varied part. Finally, though, it may be Queen Margaret, possibly Shakespeare's most diverse woman's role, that inspires the next production. In the meantime we can only hope that the BBC will make all of its three versions of *Henry VI, Parts 1* to *3* more readily and economically available.

NOTES

[1] Researching early television often means piecing together information from many different sources, including the cultural flotsam and jetsam of clippings, posters, programs, and publicity releases. Many of my most serendipitous discoveries were the result of help by the splendid librarians at the Billy Rose Theatre Collection, the New York Public Library for the Performing Arts; the Shakespeare Centre Library, the Shakespeare Birth Place Trust, Stratford-upon-Avon; and the Museum of Television and Radio (New York). The Shakespeare Centre's meticulous clipping books on RSC productions were invaluable, as were the Museum of Television's videos of *An Age of Kings*.

[2] For *Kings,* see Crane; Dews 1961, 1963; Keats and Keats. For RSC *Roses,* Ashcroft, Barton, Hodgdon 1972, Potter; for Howell's *Henry,* see Bingham, S. Wells, Williams, Willis; for ESC *Roses,* see Bogdanov, Crowl.

[3] One of his earliest productions was "A Life of Henry the Fifth" for the BBC's *Television World Theatre* (1957).

[4] The roles played by Edgar Wreford (Gloucester in the Birmingham Rep's *Henry VI*) were typical: John of Gaunt (in program 1), Archbishop of York (3, 4, 5, 6), Duke of Burgundy (8), Earl of Suffolk (10, 11), Lord Stafford (13), Duke of Buckingham (14), Ghost of Buckingham (15).

[5] The theme was also transcribed for "concert band" and sold as sheet music.

[6] Laurence Olivier filmed *Richard III* in color for television in 1952. It was broadcast in color, but received in black and white on most sets, and later released in movie theaters.

[7] *New York Times,* February 14, 1966. n.p.

[8] "Shakespeare Serial Changes Style," *Times* August 26, 1960: 5b. Cited in Rothwell and Melzer, 103. "Nothing but Bonfires," *Times* September

23, 1960: 18gb. Cited in Rothwell and Melzer, 106.

[9] Technicians at the BBC archives confirmed that this was the BBC's standard method of recording live broadcasts at that time.

[10] Milton Crane was much taken by the sponsor's "amiable" spokesman and quality of the commercials (234).

[11] A version is in the archives of the Museum of Radio and Television in New York City.

[12] See Hodgdon, 1972 for a detailed discussion of the adaptation; and Barton's own discussion.

[13] *Evening Standard* Interview, London, August 16, 1963.

[14] Around the time Hall was filming *Wars of the Roses*, Peter Dews was producing Shakespeare's Roman histories for the BBC, *The Spread of the Eagle*. The network asked him to drop *Titus Andronicus* from the cycle because viewers would find its violence too unsettling.

[15] See Zitner for a discussion of this in relation to Shakespeare.

[16] This was due in great part to the work of Jonathan Miller, who, as producer of the series (1980–1982), jettisoned much of the original conservative baggage attached to the series, originally a necessity to lure corporate investors into underwriting the £7 million needed for the project. The success of Miller's innovations was confirmed. By 1982 the Shakespeare series had broken even and was making a profit on its international sales—a first for any BBC series (Willis, 8).

[17] Howell's scaffolding set seems almost cyclical. Dews wrote that his 1960 set was designed in homage to "Tanya Moiseiwitsch's brilliant scaffold that Stratford used in 1951" (1963, 18).

[18] For a more extensive comparison of the Cade scene in the RSC, BBC, and ESC productions, see Manheim, 1994.

APPENDIX: FILMOGRAPHY*

An Age of Kings: Parts 9–13 (*Henry VI, Parts 1* to *3*). The Red Rose and White (*Part 1*, Acts 1–5); The Fall of the Protector (*Part 2*, Acts 1–3); The Rabble from Kent (*Part 2*, Acts 4–5); The Morning's War (*Part 3*, Acts 1–3); The Sun in Splendor (*Part 3*, Acts 4–5). 1960, Peter Dews, BBC TV. Each program is approximately 60 minutes long. Producer/Director: Peter Dews; TV Director, Michael Hayes; Adapter, Eric Crozier; Composers, Christopher Whelen, Arthur Bliss; Designer, Stanley Morris. Cast: Terry Scully (Henry VI); Mary Morris (Margaret); Jack May (York); Julian Glover (Edward IV); Paul Daneman (Richard of Gloucester); Edgar Wreford (Suffolk); Esmond Knight (Jack Cade); Eileen Atkins (Joan la Pucelle). Not available for purchase. May be viewed at in New York at the Museum of Television and in London through special arrangements with the BBC.

The Wars of the Roses. I: Henry VI (ends with *Part 2*, Act 4, Scene 4*); II: Edward IV* (the continuation of *Henry VI, Parts 2* and *3*). 1965, Peter Hall/John Barton, The Royal Shakespeare Company, BBC TV. Producers, Peter Hall (stage), Michael Barry (TV); Directors, Peter Hall (stage), Michael Hayes, Robin Midgeley (TV); Adapter, John Barton; Composers, Guy Woolfenden, Gordon Bennett; Designer, John Bury; Lighting Designer, Robert Wright. Cast: David Warner (Henry VI); Peggy Ashcroft (Margaret); Donald Sinden (York); Ian Holm (Richard of Gloucester); William Squire (Suffolk); Roy Dotrice (Edward IV and Jack Cade); Janet Suzman, (Joan la Pucelle). Not available for purchase. May be viewed in London at the National Film and Television Archives and in Stratford-upon-Avon at the Shakespeare Centre Library, The Shakespeare Birthplace Trust.

1–3 Henry VI. 1982, Jonathan Miller/Jane Howell, The BBC/Time-Life Shakespeare Series. Each of the three parts of *Henry VI* is a separate video. Producer, Jonathan Miller; Director, Jane Howell; Adapter, David Snodin; Composer, Dudley Simpson; Designer, Oliver Bayldon; Costume Designer, John Peacock; Lighting Designer, Sam Barclay. Cast: Peter Benson (Henry VI); Julia Foster (Margaret); Bernard Hill (York); Paul Chapman (Suffolk); Ron Cook (Richard of Gloucester); Brian Protheroe (Edward IV); Trevor Peacock (Jack Cade); Brenda Blethyn (Joan la Pucelle). Available for purchase: Ambrose Video 28 West 44 St. Suite 2100, New York, New York 10036; www.ambrosevideo.com; and The Writing Company, 10200 Jefferson Blvd., Box 802, Culver City, CA 90232; www.writingco.com. Cost: all 37 plays $2,500, individual plays $99.95. If and when the series is released at a lower, general-market price, they will become part of the extensive Shakespeare video collection available through Poor Yorick, 89a Downie Street, Stratford, Ontario Canada N5A 1W8. 519–282–1999; yorick@bardcentral.com.

The Wars of the Roses: Henry VI, House of Lancaster; Henry VI, House of York. 1989, Bogdanov/Pennington, English Shakespeare Company. Director, Michael Bogdanov; Designer, Chris Dyer; Costume Designer, Stephanie Howard; Lighting, Mark Henderson; Composer, Terry Mortimer. Cast: Paul Brennen (Henry VI); June Watson (Margaret); Barry Stanton (York); Michael Pennington (Suffolk and Jack Cade); Andrew Jarvis (Richard of Gloucester); Francesca Ryan (Joan la Pucelle). Available for purchase: Films for the Humanities & Sciences, PO Box 2053, Princeton, NJ, 08543–2053. Cost: seven-part series $595, individual plays $89.95.

*See Rothwell and Melzer; for *Wars of the Roses: House of Lancaster and House of York*, see Bogdanov.

HENRY VI AND THE ART OF ILLUSTRATION

Irene G. Dash

Before the advent of film and television, illustrations for Shakespeare's plays drew on two major sources: staged productions and the literary text—or some version of it. Plays like *Hamlet, Macbeth, As You Like It,* and *A Midsummer Night's Dream*, for example, offered a broad range for illustrators. The *Henry VI* plays, on the other hand, belonged in another category. Popular with Shakespeare's audience because of their relationship, even if obliquely, with the times, they fell further and further into obscurity during later centuries.[1] And so illustrators, responding to the rage for Shakespeare, especially illustrated editions, turned to the text for inspiration. Or did they?

A study of the illustrations for the three *Henry VI* plays quickly suggests that while artists for *Parts 1* and *3* may have relied primarily on Shakespeare's text, those for *Part 2* extended beyond Shakespeare to two loosely related versions: John Crowne's Restoration *Henry VI The First Part With the Murder of Humphrey Duke of Gloster* (1681), and Ambrose Philips's eighteenth-century *Humfrey, Duke of Gloucester. A Tragedy* (1723). Both focus on the scenes surrounding the murder of Gloucester and both have an anti-Catholic slant. Crowne explains his aim in his dedication to Sir Charles Sidley, Baronet:

> [T]his Play is no indifferent Satyre upon the most pompous fortunate and potent Folly, that ever reigned over the minds of men, called Popery. . . . I use your [Sidley's] Name to guide that share of it is in this Play through the Press, as I did Shakespear's to support it on the Stage. I called it in the Prologue Shakespear's Play, though he has no Title to the 40th part of it. The Text I took out of his Second Part of Henry the Sixth, but as most Texts are serv'd, I left it as soon as I could.

The dramatist continues, comparing his play with Shakespeare's, where:

The Trees are all Shrubs, and the Men Pigmies, nothing has any Spirit, or shape; the Cardinal is duller then ever Priest was. And he has hudled up the Murder of Duke Humphry, as if he had been guilty of himself, and was afraid to shew how it was done: But I have been more bold, to the great displeasure of some, who are it seems ashamed of their own mysteries, for there is not a Tool us'd in the murder of Duke Humphry in this Play but what is taken out of their own Church Armory, nor a word put into the mouth of the Cardinal and his foolish Instruments, but what first dropt from the Heads that adorn their own Church Battlements.

Theatrically too, this work differs from Shakespeare's since here "The Ghost of Duke Humphry appears and goes out," sending the Cardinal "into a swoon" (63). However, Shakespeare does enter tangentially. Borrowing from the banquet scene in *Macbeth*, Crowne's Cardinal exclaims to the ghost: "Alive again, do you say? Ha! shew him me!" (64).

Anti-Rome attitudes also color Philips's version, where Gloucester— unlike Shakespeare's Duke—strongly supports his wife Eleanor and explodes against the Church:

Audacious Prelates!—Ministers of Rome!—
Most wicked Agents to the infernal Foe!—
Could I have suspected you of such Presumption,
You never should have judg'd Her Innocence.— (I.viii; p.12)

Illustrators, too, may have responded to the anti-Rome attitudes of the time through choice of subject matter, through decisions on elements to include, or even through preference for a particular text or acting version. When, for example, we see a group of priests at the foot of the dying Cardinal's bed, as occurs in Fuseli's drawings, we may wonder whether either of those acting versions had an influence on the artist. While illustrators theoretically looked at the text of Shakespeare's *Part 2*, they may also have been familiar with or remembered seeing Crowne's and Philips's versions, although no extant performance records of productions beyond the dates of the plays themselves have as yet been found.

How else did artists approach these plays? What motivated some of the illustrations? Did the tendency to search for broad subjects providing an epic feel influence the designers? In illustrating the history plays, did the artists glorify war or show its more negative face? How often did the illustrators concentrate on the individual characters and how often did they seem to work on a vast canvas? In addition, to what extent do artistic stereotypes enter certain illustrations? And how often do artists rely on their predecessors for choice of subject matter? Before the advent of

Figure 8:
First Part of King Henry VI. Act 5. Scene 4. Joan la Pucelle & Fiends.
Painted by William Hamilton, engraved by Anker Smith. Published by Boydell.
By permission of the Folger Shakespeare Library.

photography, did the desire to replicate reality drive some artists to record dramatic moments in a particular performance or scene? In other cases, how far did the artists' own visions, techniques, and philosophic points of view determine the direction of their illustrations? Here I include men like Henry Fuseli, George Romney, Sir Joshua Reynolds, and Francis Hayman.

Turning to the first of the *Henry VI* plays, we find that illustrations drew mainly on the dramatic figure of Joan la Pucelle for subject matter, whether as victorious warrior or prisoner calling on the fiends for help. Whereas most prefer her with the fiends, occasionally an artist has chosen her as hero. This was true of the illustration for Nicholas Rowe's edition (1709) where the frontispiece presents a heroic Joan rescuing Orleans.[2] Did the illustrator stop at the first dramatic scene he found? We do not know. In this vertical illustration, Joan, against a background of brick city walls leads her troops through the archway marked "Orleans" to the cheering of citizens hanging over the wall. A nobleman bows to her on the right front, while the larger panorama of the city peeps above the walls at the back. The design of the illustration relies on the darks and lights of bricks in light and shadow, the archway defined by the contrast with the dark bricks that enclose it. The dominant motif here is enclosing walls. The figures themselves are small and comparatively unimportant and undefined. Only the glimpsing soldiers and people peeping over a wall hint at the momentousness of the occasion. The scene is probably 1.6, where La Pucelle returns victorious and the Dauphin hails her as "Divinest creature" (4).

Later illustrations of Joan are far more dynamic and direct. Two, both presented at the close of the eighteenth century, offer differing perceptions of her, although both show her haunted by fiends. What an opportunity for artists to tap their imaginations for the size and shape and look of such creatures! William Hamilton's illustration [Figure 8] presents a very feminine La Pucelle at the end of her life (5.4). Facing front with one bare arm raised, her upper garment, a coat of mail ending above the elbow, reveals her beautiful white skin. Her lower body is covered modestly with a long skirt. Wearing sandals on her feet, she seems to be waving to people in the distance, beyond the picture frame at the right. But filling the space below the uplifted arm and creating a circular movement with the right side of her outlined figure, several fiends appear, beginning with a full figure in front and then continuing, with a series of faces and shoulders, moving in a subsidiary circle seeming to diminish into the mist—an endless series of fiends resembling the endless series of Banquo's descendents who sear Macbeth's eyeballs in the apparitions' scene (4.1). The fiends in this illustration occupy the space on the right. Only one of them is fully designed: a single dark figure with his back to us who fills the lower right corner. This figure, given dimension, seems to be sitting on a rock but also, because of the design of his legs silhouetted against a bright space, seems to be existing in space. The turn of his head to the right also indicates a hint of horns. La Pucelle, however, beautiful and heroic-looking, a feather blowing from her helmet,

Figure 9:
Joan of Arc. Enter Fiends. 1 Henry VI, 5.3. Henry Fuseli, artist, engraved by
[John] Lee after Fuseli's lost drawing. London: C. & E. Rivington. London, 1803.
By permission of the Folger Shakespeare Library.

dominates the illustration. Light concentrates on her upper torso and waving arm, her mantle blowing in the wind and the wind above and behind her. Clouds further reinforce the circular movement of the whole, enclosing the figures of Joan and the fiends in one unit. At her feet a sword in the form of a cross lies on the ground below her opened fingers, suggesting that the fiends' influence has forced her to relinquish both sword and cross. Once again the artist uses strong contrast; the sword, a light, is delineated against the black shadow of her body on the ground. Finally, borrowing from the pattern of Renaissance portraits, where a diminished landscape may be viewed far in the distance, Hamilton inserts a speck of a battlefield where figures are no more than dots on the horizon. Were it not for the fiends, this might be a painting of a glorious warrior rallying her troops. Here, of course, it suggests the close correlation between good and evil.

No ambiguity haunts Henry Fuseli's illustration for La Pucelle and the fiends [Figure 9]. Below the illustration are the words: "Enter Fiends" followed by her line, "See: they forsake me." Nor do we see here a young woman with bare arms dressed in a skirt. Fuseli's La Pucelle, shown to us on a side view, could be a man or a woman. Head covered with armor and arms also enclosed in armor, raised as if in prayer so that her face, deep in the shadow, is undiscernable, she appears, even in her posture, to resemble a warrior, while her legs covered in mail also hide her identity as a woman. Close examination, however, reveals the brilliantly integrated design of her long braided hair hanging down her back with the swirling cape thrown over one shoulder.

Despite the dominance of Joan's figure in the overall composition, the fiends, their eyes popping out of their darkly shrouded faces, horns ever so subtly growing from the head, and a third face—or is it a mask?—peeping from behind a cloak, invest the atmosphere with mystery and evil. Like so much of Fuseli's work, ambiguity shrouds their exact dimensions. Most easily apparent is Fuseli's love of anatomy as he concentrates on La Pucelle's legs, defining them in sharply contrasting tones. On the darker one, closer to the observer, the artist details the specifics of the armor or mail as he contrasts that darkness against an even darker background. The further leg, bathed in light, loses all specificity but in its larger design creates a triangle with the other leg. In fact, triangles provide part of the pattern of the entire illustration. Forming an open triangle, La Pucelle's two raised arms shoot into the black background space, while below, the two groups of two fiends are each separated by another open triangular space. Even the scallops on her armor are open triangles, while the flowing short cape, in its negative spaces, falls into triangular shapes even as the upper lines of the cape seem to continue past the helmet into the raised left arm. As an illustrator, Fuseli captured the mystery, terror, and otherworldliness of the fiends while his design took us deep into space suggesting cracks in the earth. It is a magnificent, eerie and creative design.

While Joan predominates—as does her story in *Part 1*—other scenes also stimulated artists to create illustrations. From Act 2 comes William Hamilton's (1751–1801) painting of Mortimer, Jailers, and Richard Plantagenet, for example, which tries to arouse sympathy for the jailed older man. Several versions of this scene exist in illustrations, some with chains hanging on the floor, suggesting a momentary respite for Mortimer. Others indicate a closeness between uncle and nephew that would logically lead the latter to seek revenge. The subject was part of the Boydell Shakespeare Gallery published in 1795. An eeriness and dank, dark quality inhabits the illustrations, with jailers standing on the sidelines and the vaulted arches of the prison entranceways suggesting Mortimer's endless imprisonment no matter how feeble he appears.

In a different vein, men are plucking the red rose and the white in illustrations deriving from 2.4, the garden scene. Interestingly, by 1744 Hanmer's edition replaced Joan as subject with a politically volatile one dramatizing the sources of civil war. An idyllic scene, Francis Hayman's illustration challenges the harshness of the moment. In comparison, a late-nineteenth-century work by Watson captures the antagonisms and the scene's explosiveness through the expression on the faces of Plantagenet and Somerset as well as the tone of the whole composition. In Hayman's work an elegantly dressed group of men in the garden occupies the lower third of the vertical space; in Watson's, two and a half figures are squeezed into a limited space. In Hayman's, a long garden path leads to the river's edge, where boats sail and houses of a town beyond may be glimpsed in the distance against a clouded sky. In Watson's, the figures of the two major players appear hemmed in by the garden wall, its horizontal edge cutting behind their heads and emphasizing the jutting thrust of their jaws as their fiery eyes seem to challenge one another. Below the illustration are the lines from Act 2, scene 4 : *"Plantagenet*: Hath not thy rose a canker Somerset?/ Somerset: Hath not thy rose a thorn Plantagenet?" Unlike many of the other illustrations so far cited, this one lacks a clear sense of design and seems primarily dedicated to telling the story in the text.

Finally, also from act 2, scene 3, the engraving by R. Thew from the painting by J. Opie (1761–1807) of the Countess, the Porter, and Talbot wonderfully captures the drama of the moment [Figure 10]. It presents the artist's interpretation of the action—an action that could not have happened onstage although Talbot does have the appearance of a man who might have played the role. In organization there is the sweep of curved lines as the Countess, surprised by the sudden appearance of Talbot's men—of an armored soldier and of the spears and flag of the troops below—angrily reacts, haughty but aware of being overcome. The painting has the quality of an epic with its sweep, the smoke outside the castle, the varied dress of the troops, and the bare-backed figure turning to look at her. His posture carries the design of lights across the canvas to the sweeping flag on the left and directs our eyes back to the Countess, whose elegant satin gown is bathed in light.

During the nineteeth century, when illustrated editions abounded, visually capturing many moments in the play, they frequently lacked design features that distinguish the best of illustrative art. Among such examples was the moment when Suffolk, bewitched by Margaret, assures her "O fairest beauty, do not fear," as he plans her betrothal to Henry. Wearing armor and a helmet with a feather flying from it, he addresses a modest Margaret standing by in a white dress, her head coyly turned away and down from him. Other such examples feature favorable portraits of Joan la Pucelle. One presents a beautiful young girl in armor leading the troops, her lustrous black, wavy hair flying in the wind; another offers a less beautiful Joan wearing a long skirt, her upper body covered with armor, and accompanied by Charles, who marvels at her success. Visually, he reminds us of Suffolk described in the previous illustration. Again the male character wears a helmet with a large feather flying from it, but Charles is also endowed with a mustache. Below the illustration the lines read: "Advance

Figure 10:
The Countess of Auvergne's Castle—Countess, Porter, Talbot, & c.
1 Henry VI, 2.3. Painted by John Opie, engraved by Robert Thew.
Published by Boydell. By permission of the Folger Shakespeare Library.

our waving colors on the walls. . . . Thus Joan la Pucelle hath performed her word," followed by Charles's: "Divinest creature, Astraea's daughter, How shall I honor thee for this success?"

Unlike illustrations for *Part 1*, those for *Part 2* do not reflect the major emphasis of the play but seem to be preoccupied with the political implications of the death of Cardinal Beaufort. His death and events leading up to it prevail despite the richness and panoramic diversity of the play's subject matter, which includes the marriage of Henry VI and Margaret of Anjou; the devoted exchange between Suffolk and Margaret before their parting; Margaret holding Suffolk's head; Cade's rebellion; his murder; the bringing of his head to the authorities; and the alternation of victory between Henry and Edward. Instead illustrations show us Bolingbroke, a conjuror, raising the spirit of the devil; the conjuring scene with Mother Jordan; the Duchess of Gloucester cloaked in a sheet and walking barefoot through the city doing penance; the death of Humphrey; and the report of that death by Warwick. Although scattered examples of the other subjects exist, the Cardinal's death and the machinations of those around him predominate.

Writing of Sir Joshua Reynolds's "Death of Cardinal Beaufort" in 1996, editors of *The Boydell Shakespeare Gallery* noted this seemingly skewed emphasis:

> This was not a play often performed in London, and when it was played it was usually in the altered versions of Cibber or Crowne. But even those among the Gallery visitors familiar with the play would have thought of this scene only as a *brief interlude* in the drama. (260, emphasis added)

"A brief interlude" it is in Shakespeare, but not in the works of Crowne and Philips. Devoted solely to events leading to the death of Cardinal Beaufort, both versions end with his death. The former consists of the first three acts of Shakespeare's *Henry VI, Part 2*. The latter revolves around the trials of the Duke and Duchess of Gloucester and the plotting by the Cardinal, the queen, and Suffolk to bring about Gloucester's fall and eventual death. Moreover, although according to London performance records, these plays did not appear during the second half of the eighteenth century,[3] by 1817 still another version appeared: *Richard, Duke of York; or the Contention of York and Lancaster (As altered from Shakespeare's Three Parts of Henry VI)*, which selectively includes scenes from Shakespeare and capitalizes on Beaufort's death.[4] Identified only as "Edmund Kean's version," it concentrates on the life of Richard Plantagenet, Duke of York, from the time of his claim "to the crown of England, . . . to his assumption of royal dignity, and short-lived conquest of the throne, and terminating . . . in his downfall and destruction" ("Preface," vi–vii). Kean played the role of Richard York. Once again a stripped-down version retains the Cardinal's death and his sinister plot leading to Humphrey's murder.

It is as if two hundred years from now, someone coming across an illustration for *West Side Story*, perhaps of the two lovers skipping down the street, would identify it as *Romeo and Juliet*. Although the twentieth-century musical is supposedly based on Shakespeare's play, not one word of his text remains. Arthur Laurents, who wrote the book, Leonard Bernstein, who composed the music, Stephen Sondheim, who composed the lyrics, and Jerome Robbins, its choreographer, felt they were basing their musical on Shakespeare's play. They sought to capture what they believed was the essence of that Renaissance work: the intensity of the hostility between two groups inhabiting the same space, the tragedy of two young people who fall in love and idealistically hope to bridge that gap of hatred, and the sense of waste brought about by their deaths. But this is a mid-twentieth-century reading of Shakespeare's tragedy. It would be a mistake if subsequent generations were to believe that the illustrations for *West Side Story* were illustrations for *Romeo and Juliet*. Similarly, illustrations for eighteenth-century versions, with perhaps a few lines from Shakespeare, should not be mistaken for illustrations for a *Henry VI* play.

I cite the illustration for *West Side Story* because of the problem critics have had identifying the specifics in the first two—of the four—illustrations Fuseli did of the death of Cardinal Beaufort. Not only were both early works but both seem to depart from Shakespeare's text. For example, editors, this time of *Füssli Pittore di Shakespeare*, in 1997, note the curious choice of the "Death of Cardinal Beaufort" as a subject for his many illustrations since the play was not performed during the second half of the century. They write:

> Paradoxically, the frequency with which in this period such a subject appears in paintings, designs, and book illustrations is completely out of proportion with respect to the popularity, which was not great, of the piece itself. This is testified to by the fact that there is no documentation recording a performance of one of the three parts of *Henry VI* in London theatres during the 2nd half of the 18th century. (See *The London Stage 1660–1800*, parte 4, ed. G. W. Stone; part 5, ed. C. B. Hogan.) (136)[5]

If, however, these illustrations were unrelated to Shakespeare's play except as the versions of Crowne and Philips are indebted to it, then there may be more textual relationship between the illustrations and text. Moreover, if we consider the early dates attributed to the illustrations, we may also consider the possibility that Fuseli saw adaptations, or some form of them, on the Continent—in Germany, or Switzerland, or Austria—before he ever came to England.

The first drawing is an extraordinary work in pen and sepia wash [Figure 11]. Here the figures are almost divided into two groups: on the right, the Cardinal leaning off his bed and facing right looks front while a crouching priest beside the bed turns and looks out. At the foot of the bed kneeling priests pray, while tenderly hovering over the Cardinal and pointing above and to the rear a character with a crown, probably the King, seems to be asking the Cardinal to repent. The highlighted pointing finger along with lights from two candles held by the kneeling priests carry our eyes across the dark background to the next highlighted whispering and astonished figures on the left—possibly Salisbury, Warwick, and others. The overall design is of sharp diagonals beginning in the right corner and moving up to the pointed finger. Paralleling that are the lines of the drapes at the top right and the heads of the figures in the left-hand group. But the composition is far more complex because the artist creates an isosceles triangle of the huddled priests at the bottom, their heads supplying one side of the triangle, their bent backs the other.

In marked contrast to the sketch, the finished drawing is based on a series of horizontals, only the sharply lighted diagonal line of the outstretched arm and pointed finger breaks the pattern [Figure 12].[6] Fuseli's development of this work is masterful. The central figure now wears a flowing cape that in an undulating movement sweeps across the scene, while the drapes, a series of curved lines at the top of the page broken by vertical hangings, reinforce the flowing line of the cape or train. Three fearful figures hold its end, their grouping horizontally extending to two troubled whispering characters at the far left. Are they Warwick and Salisbury, as some critics suggest, or could they possibly be the Queen (although not wearing a crown) and Buckingham who are united in the moments before the death of the Cardinal in Philips' version? The triangular group of priests has been modified to a horizontal row, their candles no longer major design elements. Beaufort's face reflects his turmoil while on the far right a figure turns facing outward. Is it the ghost of Gloucester? Here again conflicting interpretations exist. On the one hand, the bare feet seem to suggest a monk; on the other, critics suggest the apothecary who provided the poison. This seems a particularly extreme interpretation to me.

Rather, I believe that the text of Philips's version comes closest to being the basis for this illustration because just as the Duchess of Gloucester is central to that version, the major sweeping figure in the center of this illustration seems to be a woman. Her bare outstretched arm, the way the clothing hangs on her frame, and her facial contours—all hint at the feminine. While we know that Fuseli often altered or distorted representations of the body and often tended to present characters who are almost androgynous, the concentration on this scene, the closing scene in Philips's version, suggests rather that the figure is a woman, specifically Eleanor of Gloucester. Moreover in Philips's version, Eleanor speaks the lines: "Pray; pray, for Mercy!" while the Cardinal pleads, "Oh, my Niece;/ The Gates of Heaven are shut!——O, save me; save me!/ I shudder, on the Margin of the Gulph," (V.xviii). And then Philips, again adopting Shakespeare's text and again giving the lines to Eleanor, has her pray, "O, Thou eternal Mover of the Heavens;/ Look, with a gentle Eye, upon this Wretch!" Thus Shakespeare's lines belonging to the king in *Henry VI, Part 2* (3.3.19–20, 27–28) become those of the Duchess of Gloucester. Later, she instructs: "Lord Cardinal;—If thou think'st on Heaven's Bliss;/ Hold up thy Hand:— Make Signal of thy Hope" (*Humfrey, Duke of Gloucester*, 5.18).

Furthermore, other factors hint at Philips's work rather than Shakespeare's as having been the inspiration for this illustration. Discussing another of the artist's works, Tomory notes that a friend of Fuseli's thought he: "was being intentionally critical of the Catholic Church. . . . If so, he [the friend] was probably right. These aspects of organized religion were always repugnant to Fuseli, as they were to all adherents of the Enlightenment" (87). Certainly the versions of Crowne and Philips express

Figure 11:
The Death of Cardinal Beaufort. 2 Henry VI, 3.3.
Pen and sepia wash drawing by Henry Fuseli (1772).
By permission of the Huntington Library, San Marino, California.

that same hostility to organized religion, an attitude not particularly apparent in Shakespeare's play. Moreover, when Fuseli returned to the subject of the death of Cardinal Beaufort thirty years later, his approach had altered. He clearly defined the king and Cardinal. Designed as a vertical for the Rivington *Shakespeare* (1803), the illustration resembles other works on the subject: the frontispiece in Rowe's edition (1709); Hayman's illustration for Hanmer's edition (1744); and Reynold's illustration for the Boydell Shakespeare Gallery. In fact, there was some dispute as to the debt of one man to the other. Fuseli believed that Reynolds had borrowed the horror-stricken appearance of the dying Cardinal from the former's 1772 illustration. On the other hand, Fuseli, in his 1803 illustration for the Rivington edition, seems to have borrowed his format from Reynolds's Boydell

Figure 12:
The Death of Cardinal Beaufort. 2 Henry VI, 3.3
Pen and ink wash over pencil, sepia beneath, by Henry Fuseli (1772).
By permission of the Walker Art Gallery, Liverpool.

Shakespeare illustration (Tomory 208).[7]

Another subject related to the death of the Cardinal, the penance of the Duchess of Gloucester, also figures in Philips's version. Two interesting engravings, separated by a century, illustrate the scene: the earlier one, by Gravelot, appears in Theobald's edition (1740), where the duchess wears a sheet and carries a candle. The characters occupy the lower half of the picture. Behind them a series of buildings or a building with attachments rises almost like a prison. No trees or pastoral elements, so characteristic of Gravelot's work, exist here. Rather the artist has chosen to concentrate on the hard rocks of the street and the tall angular buildings that seem to enclose the scene. The second illustration, by Charles Green, a late-nineteenth-century artist, presents the figures in close-up. The duchess, carrying a candle, walks barefoot through the staring crowd, her husband standing behind her and partly hidden, wears the chain of office soon to be taken from him. The emphasis in this close-up is on the whiteness that seems to enshroud the duchess—the white that she is wearing in penance, her pale face, and her grey hair. Ironically in this scene of penance, the sharpest black is worn by her husband, black and white no longer symbolizing evil and good. Again the artist clearly delineates the stones on the street, emphasizing Eleanor's bare feet. Unlike the earlier illustration, where Gloucester's emotions are not expressed, here, the condemnatory look in Gloucester's eyes and his hand on his hip contribute to the distance he feels at this moment from his wife. "Be patient, gentle Nell; forget this grief," he counsels. "Ah, Gloucester, teach me to forget myself!" She responds, then astutely warns:

> But be thou mild and blush not at my shame,
> Nor stir at nothing, till the ax of death
> Hang over thee, as sure, it shortly will;
> . . . [for they]
> Have all limed bushes to betray thy wings;
> And fly thou how thou canst, they'll tangle thee. (2.4.48–55)

And they do tangle him, providing rich source material not only for illustrators but for writers of versions of the play as well.

The ironies of war, symbolized by Hayman's moving illustration of the father who killed his son and the son who killed his father, provide the keynote of *Part 3* [Figure 13]. Other illustrations compound this emphasis, among them the crowning of York with a paper hat; Rutland's death; York's death; the capture of King Henry; his murder in the Tower by Richard; the death of Warwick; and the murder of Prince Edward. Ironies of another sort tinge the illustration of Lady Elizabeth Grey pleading before King Edward as his brothers scornfully watch from a distance.

Francis Hayman's sepia drawing from which Gravelot made the engraving gives us a sense of the breadth of the original compared with the limi-

Figure 13:
The Father Who Killed His Son and the Son Who Killed His Father. 3 Henry VI,
2.7 [in this edition]. Hammer edition (1743), vol. 4. Design by Francis Hayman,
engraved by Hubert Gravelot. By permission of the Folger Shakespeare Library.

tations on the engraver by his medium. Tones of sepia ink define the youth's face and the remorse of the father, while slightly further back in the landscape a son, recognizing his dead father, weeps. Despite the warmth of the engraving, these subtleties as well as the expression on the king's face as he observes the encounters seem lost in the transfer. For one thing, the youthfulness of the dead son and the maturity of the dead father are clearly visible in the original. The varied middle tones of the son's face distinguish that youthfulness as his pitying father turns his victim over, only to discover his identity. A lyrical landscape, with two intertwining tree trunks shooting up on the left and the hidden king observing the tragedy, the work has a sense of emptiness as well as pathos. The engraver, less skilled in his delineation of people than of trees and shrubs and broken stumps, organizes his composition so that the front group forms a semicircle taking us into the picture and across fields, till deep in the background we see the spears of both sides decorating the horizon, while above, the vast endless sky diminishes man and his tragedies.

In contrast, Fuseli's illustration of the murder of King Henry in the Tower brings us into an enclosed space [frontispiece]. Once again we see a talented imaginative man at work. Reworking a subject that had attracted artists from the time of the earliest illustrations in the Rowe edition, Fuseli captures the moments before the actual murder, the leering Richard coming through the door and the subtitle defining the moment: "Enter Gloster: 'Good day, my Lord! What at your books so hard?'" What is fascinating about the engraving is the brightly highlighted figure at the left. Were it not for the title under the engraving, "Henry, the Lieutenant of the Tower," we would be at a loss to identify this almost nude figure even as we are aware of Fuseli's tendency to undress his subjects so as to better draw the muscles of the body. Somehow, despite the identification of the lieutenant, the figure almost looks like an angel, an emissary from above, anticipating Henry's approaching death. Whereas earlier illustrations showed Richard plunging a knife into the king, here Fuseli has reduced the message to symbolism. The dark, silhouetted figure of Henry in robe and cap, his body merged with the dark curtain at the right and the table at which he seems to be kneeling, contrasts with that highlighted lieutenant or messenger, while the intense Richard, scornful, his humpback suggested by his bent body, rushes through the doors, anxious to perform the murder. Made up of a series of verticals broken by the opened book Henry reads, the design moves our eyes quickly from one element to the next, including the lieutenant's open hand and the similarity of the caps worn by the two antagonists—Richard's sitting at a cocky angle and the king's resting quietly, floppily on his head.

The early illustrations for the *Henry VI* plays not only suggest the range of choices made by the artists or the publishers based on what they felt were dramatic or moving moments in the play, but also give us a glimpse of the political and social climate of the times. In the case of *2 Henry VI*, we also face another question. Why was the death of the Cardinal given primacy over other more pertinent topics in the play? Among these, certainly, were the Jack Cade rebellion, the death of Suffolk, the queen entering carrying his head, and the extraordinary scene of her mourning over his death while the king sits by. As of now, no performance records exist for this play nor for the two versions that emphasize the importance of the Cardinal's terrible death. However, new discoveries, particularly of productions on the Continent, are occurring. The fact that we have so many illustrations of the death of Cardinal Beaufort, a scene that occurs midway in Shakespeare's text but provides the culminating action of Crowne's and Philips's versions, suggests that rather than accepting these illustrations as tied to Shakespeare's play, we should recognize that they may provide important clues to productions seen by an artist, particularly Fuseli, before he ever reached England.

Artists do not live in a vacuum. This was particularly true of Henry Fuseli, a man involved in the intellectual movements of his time.[8] And while such involvement may partially explain his anti-Rome interpretation of the death of Cardinal Beaufort, it fails to explain other illustrators' concentration on the subject. Rather, the art related to the *Henry VI* plays reveals how illustration, beyond its intrinsic value, may open new avenues into the stage history of Shakespeare's plays and suggest the importance of distantly related versions.

FIGURES

8. *Joan La Pucelle & Fiends. 1 Henry VI*, 5.3. Painted by William Hamilton, Engraved by Anker Smith. Published for Boydell Gallery, 1795. From the Art Collection of the Folger Shakespeare Library.

9. *Joan of Arc, Enter Fiends. 1 Henry VI*, 5.3. Henry Fuseli, artist, engraved by [John] Lee after Fuseli's lost drawing. London: C. & F. Rivington, 1803. From the Art Collection of the Folger Shakespeare Library.

10. *The Countess of Auvergne's Castle—Countess, Porter, Talbot, & c. 1 Henry VI*, 2.3. Painted by John Opie, engraved by Robert Thew. Published by Boydell, June 1796. From the Art Collection of the Folger Shakespeare Library.

11. *The Death of Cardinal Beaufort. 2 Henry VI*, 3.3. Pen and sepia wash drawing by Henry Fuseli (1772). Huntington Library.

12. *The Death of Cardinal Beaufort.* 2 *Henry VI*, 3.3. Pen and ink wash over pencil, sepia beneath, by Henry Fuseli, 1772. Collection of Walker Art Gallery, Liverpool.
13. *The Father Who Killed his Son and the Son who Killed His Father.* 3 *Henry VI*, 2.7 [in this edition]. Hanmer edition (1743), vol. 4. Design by Francis Hayman, engraved by Hubert Gravelot. From the Art Collection of the Folger Shakespeare Library.
Frontispiece. *Henry, the Lieutenant of the Tower, and Gloucester.* 3 *Henry VI*, 5.6. Design by Henry Fuseli, engraved by James Neagle after Fuseli's lost drawing. London: C. & F. Rivington, 1803. From the Art Collection of the Folger Shakespeare Library.

NOTES

[1] According to Howard and Rackin: "In the case of *Henry VI, Part 1,* for instance, Thomas Nashe wrote in 1592 that 'ten thousand spectators (at least)' had wept at the spectacle of Talbot's death (Nashe 1592, in Chambers 1923: 4:239) and recent scholars report that Nashe actually underestimated the play's popularity by at least one half, for Henslowe's records of the receipts for its initial run suggest a figure closer to twenty thousand" (22).

[2] "Hanns Hammelmann believed that the illustrations were all produced by Francois Boitard (ca. 1670-1717)" and that the engraver was Kirkall (Ashton 58).

[3] According to Hogan, *Henry VI, Parts 1, 2,* and *3* were not acted during the second half of the eighteenth century. During the century's first half, *Part 1* was performed once, and Cibber's version, which was based on *Parts 2* and *3*, was performed once, in July 1723. Although nine performances are attributed to *Part 2*, all of these were actually Philips' version, and the performances all occurred during February of 1723 (I: 202–203; II: 719).

[4] This version has no author on the title page, but inside the book a slip of paper identifies him: "This adaptation was made by John Herman [Merivale], grandfather of H. C. Merivale, (see his 'Bar, Stage & Platform,' chapter VII) and contains additions from Heywood & Chapman & some comic passages from Croune [*sic*]."

[5] Translated by Barbara Kreps.

[6] It is described as "pen and ink washed over pencil. Highlights are in part scratched out of the paper. Specifically lower left hand corner (Roma

72) underneath that in Sepia (Fuseli)." According to Schiff, this was the first work that Fuseli sent to the Royal Academy. Moreover it was the first independently conceived work that was not linked to book illustration. To that extent it was a breakthrough. The death scene of the Cardinal was commended by English critics as a masterpiece (II: 449). [Translated by Patrick Lyon. Folger Shakespeare Library.] One wonders if its intensity as well as its bias was not influenced by the versions of the play that may have been circulating at the time in Germany or Switzerland or Austria.

    [7] Sir Joshua Reynolds's "Death of Cardinal Beaufort," engraved by Caroline Watson, was published on August 1, 1792. "Opposite the King, who stands at the bedside with raised hand, Reynolds painted in a fiend glowering from the curtains. . . . In response to criticism from Walpole and others, Boydell instructed Caroline Watson . . . to remove the figure of the demon. The first version of the engraving . . . was published in early 1790. The second state [was] published in 1792" (Pape 260).

    [8] According to Tomory, while at the Zurich Collegium (10) Fuseli came under the influence of J. J. Bodmer, a Swiss republican intellectual, who "was to provide the emotional stimulus of the *Sturm und Drang* movement." And again, while in Berlin, beginning in 1763, he "came into close contact with the three main streams of European thought" (11) the first was Sulzer—the leader of the German Enlightenment and author of *Allgemeine Theorie der schonen Kunste* (4 vols. 1771); the next was J. Spalding, "whome he met at Barth in Pomerania whose sermons and other texts were much influenced by Lord Shaftesbury and the Scot, Francis Hutcheson; and the third [was] Klopstock . . . a sort of founder father of romanticism" (11).

Bibliography

EDITIONS CITED

Alexander, Peter, ed. *The Complete Works of William Shakespeare.* London: Collins, 1951.

Bevington, David, ed. *The Complete Works of Shakespeare*, 4th ed. New York. Harper Collins, 1992.

Cairncross, Andrew S., ed. *The First Part of King Henry VI.* Arden ed. London: Methuen, 1962.

———. *The Second Part of King Henry VI.* Arden ed. London: Methuen, 1957.

———. *The Third Part of King Henry VI.* Arden ed. London: Methuen, 1964.

Crane, Milton, ed. *Henry VI, Part Three.* New York: Signet, 1968.

Eccles, Mark, ed. *Richard III.* New York: Signet, 1967.

Evans, G. Blakemore, gen. ed., *The Riverside Shakespeare*, 2nd ed. Boston: Houghton Mifflin, 1994.

Freeman, Arthur, ed. *Henry VI, Part Two.* New York: Signet, 1967.

Hammond, Antony, ed. *King Richard III.* Arden ed. London: Methuen, 1981.

Hattaway, Michael, ed. *The First Part of King Henry VI.* New Cambridge ed. Cambridge: Cambridge University Press, 1990.

———. *The Second Part of King Henry VI.* New Cambridge ed. Cambridge: Cambridge University Press, 1991.

———. *The Third Part of King Henry VI.* New Cambridge ed. Cambridge: Cambridge University Press, 1993.

Knowles, Ronald, ed. *King Henry VI, Part II.* New Arden ed. London: Thomas Nelson, 1999.

Levenson, Jill, ed. *Romeo and Juliet*. New York: Oxford University Press, 2000.

Ryan, Lawrence V., ed. *Henry VI, Part Three*. New York: Signet, 1967.

Sanders, Norman, ed. *Henry VI, Part One*. New Penguin ed. Harmondsworth: Penguin, 1981.

———. *Henry VI, Part Two*. New Penguin ed. Harmondsworth: Penguin, 1981.

———. *Henry VI, Part Three*. New Penguin ed. Harmondsworth: Penguin, 1981.

Wells, Stanley, and Gary Taylor with John Jowett and William Montgomery, eds. *William Shakespeare: The Complete Works*. Oxford ed. London: Oxford University Press, 1986.

Wilson, John Dover, ed. *The First Part of King Henry VI*. New Shakespeare. Cambridge: Cambridge University Press, 1951.

———. *The Second Part of King Henry VI*. New Shakespeare. Cambridge: Cambridge University Press, 1952.

———. *The Third Part of King Henry VI*. New Shakespeare. Cambridge: Cambridge University Press, 1952.

CRITICAL WORKS

Aers, David. *"Piers Plowman" and Christian Allegory*. New York: St. Martin's Press, 1975.

———. "A Whisper in the Ear of Early Modernists; or, Reflections on Literary Critics Writing the `History of the Subject.'" *In Culture and History, 1350–1600: Essays on English Communities, Identities, and Writing*. Detroit: Wayne State University Press, 1992. 177–202.

Alexander, Peter. *Shakespeare's Henry VI and Richard III*. Cambridge: Cambridge University Press, 1929.

Arthos, John. *Shakespeare: The Early Writings*. Totowa, NJ: Rowan and Littlefield, 1972.

Ashcroft, Dame Peggy. "Margaret of Anjou." *Deutsche Shakespeare-Gesellschaft West Jahrbuch* 109 (1973): 7–9.

Ashton, Geoffrey. *Shakespeare and British Art*. New Haven, CT: Yale Center for British Art, 1981.

Bains, Yashdip S. *The Contention and The True Tragedy: William Shakespeare's First Versions of 2 and 3 Henry VI*. Rashtrapati Nivas, Shimla (India): Indian Institute of Advanced Study, 1996.

Bakewell, Michael. "The Television Production." In Barton. 231–236.

Bakhtin, Mikhail. *Rabelais and His World*. Tr. Hélène Iswolsky. Bloomington, IN: Indiana University Press, 1984.

Bamber, Linda. *Comic Women, Tragic Men: A Study of Gender and Genre in Shakespeare*. Stanford: Stanford University Press, 1982.

Barber, C. L. *Shakespeare's Festive Comedy*. Princeton: Princeton University Press, 1959.

Barton, John, with Peter Hall. *The Wars of the Roses: Adapted for the Royal Shakespeare Company from William Shakespeare's* Henry VI, Parts I, II, III and Richard III. London: British Broadcasting Company, 1970.

Basho. *The Narrow Road to the Deep North and Other Travel Sketches*. Tr. Nobuyuki Yuasa. Baltimore, MD: Penguin, 1966.

Bassnett, Susan. "Sexuality and Power in the Three Parts of King Henry VI." *Shakespeare Jahrbuch* 124 (1988): 183–191.

Bergeron, David M. "Play Within Play in *Henry VI.*" *Tennessee Studies in Literature* 22 (1977): 37–45.

Berman, Ronald S. "Fathers and Sons in the *Henry VI* Plays." *Shakespeare Quarterly* 13 (1962): 487–497

Berry, Edward I. *Patterns of Decay: Shakespeare's Early Histories*. Charlottesville, VA: University Press of Virginia, 1975.

———. "Twentieth-Century Shakespeare Criticism: The Histories." In *The Cambridge Companion to Shakespeare Studies*. Ed. Stanley Wells. Cambridge: Cambridge University Press, 1986. 249–256.

Bevington, David M. *Action Is Eloquence: Shakespeare's Language of Gesture*. Cambridge, MA: Harvard University Press, 1984.

———. "The Domineering Female in *1 Henry VI.*" *Shakespeare Studies* 2 (1966): 51–58;

———. *Tudor Drama and Politics: A Critical Approach to Topical Meaning*. Cambridge, MA: Harvard University Press, 1968.

Bingham, Dennis. "Jane Howell's First Tetralogy: Brechtian Break-Out or Just Good Television?" Bulman and Coursen. 221–232.

Blanpied, John W. *Time and the Artist in Shakespeare's English Histories*. Newark, DE: University of Delaware Press, 1983.

Blayney, Peter W. M. "The Publication of Playbooks." In *A New History of Early English Drama*. Ed. John D. Cox and David Scott Kastan. New York: Columbia University Press, 1997. 383–422.

Bloch, R. Howard. *Medieval Misogyny and the Invention of Western Romantic Love*. Chicago: University of Chicago Press, 1991.

Boaistuau, Pierre. *Histoires prodigieuses*. Paris: 1560; Le Club Français du Livre, 1961.

Bogdanov, Michael, and Michael Pennington. *The English Shakespeare Company: The Story of* The Wars of the Roses 1986–1989. London: Nick Hern, 1990.

Bonnell, J. K. "The Serpent with a Human Head in Art and in Mystery Play." *American Journal of Archeology* 21 (1917): 255–291.

Boose, Lynda E. "Scolding Brides and Bridling Scolds: Taming the Woman's Unruly Member." *Shakespeare Quarterly* 42 (1991): 179–213.

Born, Hanspeter. "The Date of *2, 3 Henry VI.*" *Shakespeare Quarterly* 25 (1974): 323–334.

Boyer, Paul, and Stephen Nissenbaum. *Salem Possessed, The Social Origins of Witchcraft.* Cambridge, MA: Harvard University Press, 1974.

Britonin, Dorothy Guyver. *A Haiku Journey.* Tokyo: Kodansha International , 1974.

Brockbank, J. P. "The Frame of Disorder: *Henry VI.*" In *Early Shakespeare.* Ed. John Russell Brown and Bernard Harris 1961; rpt. New York: Schocken, 1966. 73–99.

Bromley, John. *The Shakepearean Kings.* Boulder, CO: Colorado Associates University Presses, 1971.

Brook, Peter. *The Empty Space.* London: Penguin, 1972.

Brownlow, F. W. *Two Shakespearean Sequences.* Pittsburgh: University of Pittsburgh Press, 1977.

Bruster, Douglas. *Drama and the Market in the Age of Shakespeare.* Cambridge, MA: Cambridge University Press, 1992.

Bullough, Geoffrey. *Narrative and Dramatic Sources of Shakespeare: Volume 3: The Early English History Plays.* London: Routledge and Kegan Paul, 1960.

Burckhardt, Sigurd. *Shakespearean Meanings.* Princeton, NJ: Princeton University Press, 1968.

Burden, Dennis. "Shakespeare's History Plays, 1952–1983." *Shakespeare Survey* 38 (1985): 1–18.

Bury, John. "The Set." In Barton. 237–238.

Calderwood, James L. *Metadrama in Shakespeare's Henriad.* Berkeley, CA: University of California Press, 1979.

———. *Shakespearean Metadrama.* Minneapolis: University of Minnesota Press, 1971.

———. "Shakespeare's Evolving Imagery: *2 Henry VI.*" *English Studies* 48 (1968): 481–493.

Caldwell, Ellen C. "Jack Cade and Shakespeare's *Henry VI, Part 2.*" *Studies in Philology* 92 (1995): 18–79.

Callaghan, Dympna. "Wicked Women in *Macbeth*: A Study of Power, Ideology, and the Production of Motherhood." In *Reconsidering the Renaissance*: Papers from the Twenty-First Annual Conference. Binghamton, NY: Medieval and Renaissance Texts and Studies, 1992.

Campbell, Lily B., ed. *The Mirror for Magistrates.* 1938; rpt. New York: Barnes & Noble, 1960.

———. *Shakespeare's "Histories"*: *Mirrors of Elizabethan Policy.* San Marino, CA: Huntington, 1947.

Campbell, Oscar J. Introduction. *An Age of Kings: The Historical Plays of William Shakespeare.* New York: Pyramid, 1961.

Candido, Joseph. "Getting Loose in the *Henry VI* Plays." *Shakespeare*

Quarterly 35 (1984): 392–406,
Canedy, Dana. "Quality, Not Flash, Marks New Gain in Luxury Sales." *New York Times*, December 12, 1996, p. 1.
Carlson, David R. "Chaucer, Humanism, and Printing: Conditions of Authorship in Fifteenth-Century England." *University of Toronto Quarterly* 64 (1995): 274-288.
Cartelli, Thomas "Jack Cade in the Garden: Class Consciousness and Class Conflict in *2 Henry VI.*" In *Enclosure Acts: Sexuality, Property, and Culture in Early Modern England.* Ed. Richard Burt and John M. Archer. Ithaca, NY: Cornell University Press, 1994. 48–67.
Cawley, A. C., and Martin Stevens, eds. *Wakefield Pageants in the Towneley Cycle.* 1958; Rpt. Oxford: Oxford University Press, EETS, 1994.
Champion, Larry S. *Perspective in Shakepeare's English Histories.* Athens: University of Georgia Press, 1980.
———."'Prologue to Their Play': Shakespeare's Structural Progress in *2 Henry VI.*" *Texas Studies in Literature and Language* 19 (1977): 294–312.
Charnes, Linda. *Notorious Identities: Materializing the Subject in Shakespeare.* Cambridge, MA: Harvard University Press, 1993.
Christianson, C. Paul. "Evidence for the Study of London's Late Medieval Manuscript-Book Trade." In *Book Production and Publishing in Britain, 1375–1475.* Ed. Jeremy Griffiths and Derek Pearsall. Cambridge: Cambridge University Press, 1989. 87–108.
Cixous, Hélène, and Catherine Clément. *The Newly Born Woman.* Tr. Betsy Wing. Minneapolis : University of Minnesota Press, 1986.
Clemen, Wolfgang. "Some Aspects of Style in the *Henry VI* Plays." In *Shakespeare's Styles: Essays in Honour of Kenneth Muir.* Ed. Philip Edwards, Inga-Stina Eubank, and G. K. Hunter. Cambridge: Cambridge University Press, 1980. 9–24.
Cohen, Walter. *Drama of a Nation: Public Theater in Renaissance England and Spain.* Ithaca, NY: Cornell University Press, 1985.
Cook, Hardy. "Jane Howell's BBC First Tetralogy: Theatrical and Televisual." *Literature/Film Quarterly*, 20:4 (1992): 326–331.
Coursen, H. R. *Reading Shakespeare on Stage.* Newark, DE: University of Delaware Press, 1995.
———. Review of American epertory Theater *Henry VI. Malone Society of America Newsletter*, 15.2 (Fall 1995): 5–8.
———. *Shakespeare: The Two Traditions.* Madison: Farleigh Dickinson University Press, 1999.
———. *Shakespeare in Production: Whose History?* Athens, OH: Ohio University Press, 1996.
———. *Shakespearean Production as Interpretation.* Newark, DE: University of Delaware Press, 1992.

————. *Watching Shakespeare on Television.* Rutherford, NJ: Associated University Press, 1993.

————. and J. C. Bulman, eds. *Shakespeare on Television.* Hanover, NH: University Press of New England, 1988.

Cox, John D. "Devils and Power in Marlowe and Shakespeare." *The Yearbook of English Studies* 23 (1993): 46–64.

Craig, Hardin. *English Religious Drama of the Middle Ages.* Oxford: Clarendon, 1955.

————, ed. *Two Coventry Corpus Christi Plays,* 2nd. ed. EETS e.s. 87 London: Oxford University Press, 1968.

Crane, Milton. "Shakespeare on Television." *Shakespeare Quarterly* 12 (1961) 323–327.

Crowl, Samuel. *Shakespeare Observed.* Athens, OH: Ohio University Press, 1992.

Cutts, John. *The Shattered Glass: A Dramatic Pattern in Shakespeare Early Plays.* Detroit: Wayne State University Press, 1968.

Crowne, John. *Henry the Sixth, The First Part. With the Murder of Humphrey Duke of Gloucester.* As it was Acted at the Dukes theatre. Written by Mr. Crown [sic]. Printed for R. Bentley and M. Magnus, in Russel-Street, in Covent-Garden, 1681.

Dällenbach, Lucien. *The Mirror in the Text.* Tr. Jeremy Whiteley with Emma Hughes. Chicago: University of Chicago Press, 1989. (Originally *Le récit spéculaire: essai sur la mise en abyme.* Éditions du Seuil, 1977.)

————. "Reflexivity and Reading." *New Literary History* 5 (1979–1980): 435–449.

Danby, John F. *Shakespeare's Doctrine of Nature: A Study of "King Lear."* London: Faber & Faber, 1949.

Dante. *The Divine Comedy of Dante Alighieri.* Tr. Allen Mandelbaum. Berkeley, CA: University of California Press, 1980.

Dash, Irene. *Wooing, Wedding, and Power: Women in Shakespeare's Plays.* New York: Columbia University Press, 1981.

Davies, R. T. *The Corpus Christi Play of the English Middle Ages.* London: Faber & Faber, 1972.

Davis, Natalie Zemon. "The Raw and the Cooked in *The Taming of the Shrew.*" *Journal of English and Germanic Philology* 88 (1989): 168–189.

Day, John. *The Medieval Market Economy.* London: Basil Blackwell, 1987.

de Man, Paul. *The Resistance to Theory.* Minneapolis: University of Minnesota Press, 1986.

Dessen, Alan C. "Stagecraft and Imagery in Shakespeare's *Henry VI.*" *Yearbook of English Studies* 23 (1993): 65–79.

Dews, Peter. Foreword. *An Age of Kings: The Historical Plays of William*

Shakespeare. New York: Pyramid, 1961.

———. "TV Shakespeare." *Plays and Players* 10 (July: 1963): 18–19.

Donegan, Jane B. *Women and Men Midwives: Medicine, Morality, and Misogyny in Early America*. Westport, CT: Greenwood Press, 1978.

Doran, Madeleine. *'Henry VI, Parts II and III': Their Relation to the 'Contention' and the 'True Tragedie'*. Iowa City: University of Iowa Press, 1928.

Doyle, A. I., and M. B. Parkes. "The Production of Copies of the *Canterbury Tales* and the *Confessio Amantis* in the Early Fifteenth Century." In *Medieval Scribes, Manuscripts and Libraries: Essays Presented to N. R. Ker*. Ed. M. B. Parkes and A. G. Watson. London: Scolar, 1979. 163–210.

Eccles, Mark, ed. *The Macro Plays*. EETS o.s. 262. London: Oxford University Press, 1969.

Edwards, S. G., and Derek Pearsall. "The Manuscripts of the Major English Poetic Texts." In *Book Production and Publishing in Britain, 1375–1475*. Ed. Jeremy Griffiths and Derek Pearsall. Cambridge: Cambridge University Press, 1989. 257–278.

Eisenstein, Elizabeth. *The Printing Press as an Agent of Change: Communications and Cultural Transformations in Early-Modern Europe*. 2 vols. Cambridge: Cambridge University Press, 1979.

———. *The Printing Revolution in Early Modern Europe*. Cambridge: Cambridge University Press, 1983.

Elliott. G. R. *Scourge and Minister: A Study of "Hamlet."* 1951. rpt. New York: AMS Press, 1965.

Emmerson, Richard K. *Antichrist in the Middle Ages: A Study in Medieval Apocalypticism, Art, and Literature*. Seattle: University of Washington Press, 1981.

———. "Introduction: The Apocalypse in Medieval Culture." In *The Apocalypse in the Middle Ages*. Ed. Emmerson and Bernard McGinn. Ithaca, NY: Cornell University Press, 1992.

Evans, Maurice. *The Wars of the Roses: John Bartons's Adaptation of William Shakespeare's "Henry VI" and "Richard III."* Television broadcast program prepared for WNEW-TV, New York, and WTTG, Washington. 1966.

Ferguson, Francis. "Introduction." *Henry VI*. Dell Laurel Shakespeare. New York: Dell, 1963.

Fiedler, Leslie A., *The Stranger in Shakespeare*. New York: Stein and Day, 1972.

Fish, Stanley. *Self-Consuming Artifacts: The Experience of Seventeenth-Century Literature*. Berkeley, CA: University of California Press, 1972.

Fly, Richard. "'Dumb Significants': The Poetics of Shakespeare's *Henry VI*

Trilogy." *Shakespeare: Text, Subtext, and Context.* Ed. Ronald
Dotterer. Selinsgrove, PA: Susquehanna University Press, 1989.
186–200,

Foakes, R. A. and R. T. Rickert, eds. *Henslowe's Diary.* Cambridge:
Cambridge University Press, 1961.

Foster, Donald W. "Reconstructing Shakespeare I: The Roles That
Shakespeare Performed." *Shakespeare Newsletter* 41 (1991):
16–17.

———. "SHAXICON 1995." *Shakespeare Newsletter* 45 (1995): 28, 30,
32.

Foucault, Michel. *Discipline and Punish: The Birth of the Prison.* Tr. Alan
Sheridan. New York: Pantheon, 1977.

———. *Power/Knowledge: Selected Interviews and Other Writings
1972–1977.* Tr. Colin Gordon. New York: Pantheon Books, 1980.

Fox, Alistair. *Politics and Literature in the Reigns of Henry VII and Henry
VIII.* London: Blackwell, 1989.

French, A. L. "The Mills of God and Shakespeare's Early History Plays."
English Studies 55 (1974): 313–324.

Frey, David L. *The First Tetralogy: Shakespeare's Scrutiny of the Tudor
Myth.* The Hague: Mouton, 1976.

French, Marilyn. *Shakespeare's Division of Experience.* New York:
Summit, 1981.

Friedman, John Block. *The Monstrous Races in Medieval Art and Thought.*
Cambridge: Harvard University Press, 1981.

Fuhrkotter, Adelgundis, O. S. B., and Angela Carlevaris, O. S. B., eds.
*Hildegardis Scivias, Corpus Christianorum Continuatio
Mediaevalis,* vol. 43a. Turnholt: Brepols, 1978.

Furguson, Arthur B. *Clio Unbound: Perception of the Social and Cultural
Past in Renaissance England.* Durham, NC: Duke University Press,
1979.

Garin, Eugenio, "Magic and Astrology in the Civilisation of the
Renaissance." In Levack, *Renaissance Magic.*

Gillespie, Vincent. "Vernacular Books of Religion." In Griffiths and
Pearsall. 317–344.

Granville-Barker, Harley, and G.B. Harrison, eds. *A Companion to
Shakespeare Studies.* Cambridge: Cambridge University Press,
1934.

Girard, René. *Violence and the Sacred.* 1977. Tr. Patrick Gregory.
Baltimore, MD: Johns Hopkins University Press, 1993.

Greenblatt, Stephen. "Shakespeare Bewitched." In *New Historical Literary
Study: Essays on Reproducing Texts, Representing History.* Ed.
Jeffrey N. Cox and Larry J. Reynolds. Princeton, NJ: Princeton
University Press, 1993. 108–135.

———. "Murdering Peasants: Status, Genre, and the Representation of

Rebellion." *Representing the English Renaissance*. Ed. Greenblatt. Berkeley, CA: University of California Press, 1988. 1–29.

Greg, W. W. *The Merry Wives of Windsor (1602)*. Oxford: Clarendon Press, 1910.

———. *Two Elizabethan Stage Abridgements: The Battle of Alcazar and Orlando Furioso*. Oxford: The Malone Society, 1923.

Greer, Clayton Alvis. "The York and Lancaster Quarto-Folio Sequence." *PMLA* 48 (1933): 655–704.

Griffiths, Jeremy, and Derek Pearsall, eds. *Book Production and Publishing in Britain, 1375–1475*. Cambridge: Cambridge University Press, 1989.

Griffiths, Ralph A. *The Reign of King Henry VI: The Exercise of Royal Authority, 1422–1461*. Berkeley, CA: University of California Press, 1981.

Griffin, Alice V. "Shakespeare through the Camera's Eye: IV." *Shakespeare Quarterly*, 17 (1966). Reprinted in Coursen and Bulman *Shakespeare on Television*. 242.

Gurevich, Aron. *Medieval Popular Culture: Problems of Belief and Perception*. Tr. János M. Bak and Paul A. Hollingsworth. Cambridge: Cambridge University Press, 1988.

Hall, Peter. *Peter Hall's Diaries*. Ed. John Goodwin. New York: Harper & Row, 1984.

———. Introduction. *Wars of the Roses*. In Barton. vii–xiv.

———. Interview in "Shakespeare in the Cinema: A Film Directors' Symposium." *Cineaste*. Shakespeare in the Cinema Supplement 24:1 (1999): 48–52.

Hamilton, A. C. *The Early Shakespeare*. San Marino, CA: Huntington Library, 1967.

Halperin, Richard. *The Poetics of Primitive Accumulation: English Renaissance Culture and the Genealogy of Capital*. Ithaca, NY: Cornell University Press, 1991.

Harris, Kate. "Patrons, Buyers and Owners: The Evidence for Ownership, and the Role of Book Owners in Book Production and the Book Trade." In Griffiths and Pearsall. 163–199.

Harris, Laurie Lanzen, and Mark W. Scott, eds. *Shakespeare Criticism: Volume 3*. New York: Gale 1983.

Hart, Jonathan. *Theater & World*. Boston: Northeastern University Press, 1992.

Harvey, I. M. W. *Jack Cade's Rebellion of 1450*. Oxford: Clarendon, 1991.

Hattaway, Michael. "Rebellion, Class Consciousness, and Shakespeare's 2 Henry VI." *Cahiers Élisabéthains* 33 (1988): 13–22.

———. "The First Tetralogy and King John." In *Shakespeare: A Bibliographical Guide*. Ed. Stanley Wells. Oxford: Clarendon, 1990.

Hawks, Terry. "Introduction." *Alternative Shakespeare 2.* London: Routledge, 1996.

Helgerson, Richard. *Forms of Nationhood: The Elizabethan Writing of England.* Chicago: University of Chicago Press, 1992.

Helms, Lorraine. "Acts of Resistance: The Feminist Player." *The Weyward Sisters: Shakespeare and Feminist Politics.* Ed. Dympna Callaghan, Jyotsna Singh, and Lorraine Helms. Oxford: Blackwell, 1994.

Helterman, Jeffrey. *Symbolic Action in the Plays of the Wakefield Master.* Athens, GA: University of Georgia Press, 1981.

Hibbard, G. L. *Thomas Nashe: A Critical Introduction.* Cambridge: Cambridge University Press, 1962

Hildegard von Bingen. *Scivias.* Tr. Mother Columba Hart and Jane Bishop. New York: Paulist Press, 1990.

Hill, Christopher. "From Lollards to Levellers." *The Collected Essays of Christopher Hill.* Amherst, MA: University of Massachusetts Press, 1986. 2: 89–116.

———. "The Many-Headed Monster in Late Tudor and Early Stuart Political Thinking." In *From the Renaissance to the Counter-Reformation: Essays in Honour of Garrett Mattingly.* Ed. Charles H. Carter. London: Jonathan Cape, 1966. 296–324.

Hinchcliffe, Judith. *King Henry VI, Parts 1, 2, and 3.* Garland Bibliography Series. New York: Garland, 1984.

Hirsch, Rudolf. *Printing, Selling and Reading, 1450–1550.* Weisbaden: Otto Harrassowitz, 1967.

Hobday, Chärles. "Clouted Shoon and Leather Aprons: Shakespeare and the Egalatarian Tradition." *Renaissance and Modern Studies,* 23 (1979): 63–78.

Hodgdon, Barbara. *The End Crowns All: Closure and Contradiction in Shakespeare's History.* Princeton: Princeton University Press, 1991.

———."The Wars of the Roses: Scholarship Speaks on Stage." *Deutsche Shakespeare Gesellschaft West Jahrbuch* 108 (1972): 170-84.

Hodges, C. Walter , *Enter the Whole Army: A Pictorial Study of Shakespearean Staging, 1576–1616.* Cambridge: Cambridge University Press, 1999.

Hogan, Charles Beecher. *Shakespeare in the Theatre, 1701–1800,* 2 vols. Oxford University Press, 1952–1957.

Holderness, Graham. "Radical Potentiality and Institutional Closure." In *Political Shakespeare.* Ed. Jonathan Dollimore and Alan Sinfield. Manchester: Manchester University Press, 1985. 181–201.

———. *Shakespeare: The Histories.* New York: St. Martin's Press, 2000.

Honigmann, E. A. J. "Shakespeare as a Reviser." In *Textual Criticism and Literary Interpretation.* Ed. Jerome J. McGann. Chicago: University of Chicago Press, 1985. 1–22.

Hosley, Richard. *Shakespeare's Holinshed: An Edition of Holinshed's Chronicles (1587)*. New York: Putnam's, 1968.

Howard, Jean E. *The Stage and Social Struggle in Early Modern England*. London: Routledge, 1994.

Howard, Jean E., and Phyllis Rackin. *Engendering a Nation: A Feminist Account of Shakespeare's English Histories*. London: Routledge, 1997.

Hudson, Anne. "Lollard Book Production." In Griffiths and Pearsall. 125–142.

Humphreys, A.R. "The English History Plays." In *Shakespeare: Select Bibliographical Guides*. Ed. Stanley Wells. Oxford: Oxford University Press, 1973. 39–83.

Hunter, G. K. "*Henry IV* and the Elizabethan Two-Part Plays." *Review of English Studies* 5 (1985): 236–248.

Ingram, R.W., ed. *Records of the Early English Drama: Coventry*. Toronto: University of Toronto Press, 1981.

Ioppolo, Grace. *Revising Shakespeare*. Cambridge, MA: Harvard University Press, 1991.

Irace, Kathleen O. *Reforming the "Bad" Quartos: Performance and Provenance of Six Shakespearean First Editions*. Newark, DE: University of Delaware Press, 1994.

Jackson, Sir Barry. "On Producing *Henry VI*." *Shakespeare Survey* 6 (1953): 49–52.

Jackson, Gabriele Bernhard. "Topical Ideology: Witches, Amazons, and Shakespeare's Joan of Arc." *English Literary Renaissance* 18 (1988): 40–65.

Jameson, Frederic. *Postmodernism, or, The Cultural Logic of Late Capitalism*. Durham, NC: Duke University Press, 1991.

Jardine, Lisa. *Still Harping on Daughters: Women and Drama in the Age of Shakespeare*. 2nd ed. New York: Columbia University Press, 1989.

Jenkins, Harold. "English History Plays, 1900–1950." *Shakespeare Survey* 6 (1953): 1–15.

Jonassen, Frederick B. "The Morality Play and the World Upside Down." *Mediaevalia* 18 (1995): 19–42.

Jones, Emrys. *The Origins of Shakespeare*. Oxford: Clarendon, 1977.

Jordan, Constance. *Renaissance Feminism, Literary Texts and Political Models*. Ithaca: Cornell University Press, 1990.

Jung, C. G. *Aspects of the Feminine*. Tr. R. F. C. Hull. Princeton, NJ: Princeteon University Press, 1982.

Kahn, Coppélia. *Man's Estate: Masculine Identity in Shakespeare*. Berkeley, CA: University of California Press, 1981.

Kastan, David Scott. "The Shape of Time: Form and Value in the Shakespeare History Play." *Comparative Drama* 7 (1973–1974):

259–277.

———. *Shakespeare and the Shapes of Time.* Hanover, NH: University Press of New England, 1982.

Kay, Carol McGinnis. "Traps, Slaughter, and Chaos: A Study of Shakespeare's *Henry VI* Plays." *Studies in the Literary Imagination* 5 (1972): 1–26.

Kayser, Wofgang. *The Grotesque in Art and Literature.* Tr. Ulrich Weisstein. New York: Columbia University Press, 1981.

Keats, Nathan, and An Keats, eds. *An Age of Kings: The Historical Plays of William Shakespeare.* New York: Pyramid, 1961.

Kelly, Henry Ansgar. *Divine Providence in the England of Shakespeare's Histories.* Cambridge, MA: Harvard University Press, 1970.

Kennedy, Dennis. "Performing Inferiority: Shakespeare's Lesser Plays in the Twentieth Century." In *Shakespeare and the Twentieth Century.* Ed. Jonathan Bate, Jill L. Levenson, and Dieter Mehl. Newark, DE: University of Delaware Press, 1998. 60–74.

Keyishian, Harry. *The Shapes of Revenge: Victimization, Vengeance, and Vindictiveness in Shakespeare.* Atlantic Highlands, NJ: Humanities Press, 1995.

Kinoshita, Junji. *Kinoshita-Junji-Shu (Collected Works of Junji Kinoshita)* Tokyo: Iwanami-shoten, 1989. Vol. 8.

King, John N. *English Reformation Literature: The Tudor Origins of the Protestant Tradition.* Princeton: Princeton University Press, 1982.

Kitchin, Laurence. "Shakespeare on the Screen." *Shakespeare Survey* 18 (1965): 72–75.

Knowles, Ronald. "The Farce of History: Miracle, Combat, and Rebellion in *2 Henry VI.*" *Yearbook of English Studies* 21 (1991): 168–186.

Knutson, Roslyn L. "The Repertory." In *A New History of Early English Drama.* Ed. John D. Cox and David Scott Kastan. New York: Columbia University Press, 1997. 461–480.

Kolve, V. A. *The Play Called Corpus Christi.* Stanford: Stanford University Press: 1966.

Kristeva, Julia. *Revolution in Poetic Language.* Tr. Margaret Waller. New York: Columbia University Press, 1984.

———. *The System and the Speaking Subject.* Lisse, Netherlands: Peter de Ridder Press, 1975.

Kröll, Katrin, and Hugo Steger, eds. *Mein ganzer Körper ist Gesicht: Groteske Darstellungen in der europäischen Kunst und Literatur des Mittelalters.* Freiburg im Breisgau: Rombach, 1994.

las Casas, Bartolomé de. *A Short Account of the Destruction of the Indies.* Ed. and tr. Nigel Griffin. London: Penguin, 1992.

Lee, Patricia-Ann. "Reflections of Power: Margaret of Anjou and the Dark Side of Queenship." *Renaissance Quarterly* 39 (1986): 183–217.

Leech, Clifford. "The Two-Part Play: Marlowe and the Early

Shakespeare." *Shakespeare Jahrbuch* 94 (1958): 90-106.

Leggatt, Alexander. *Shakespeare's Political Drama: The History Plays and the Roman Plays*. London: Routledge, 1992.

Lehner, Ernst, and Johanna Lerner. *Picture Book of Devils, Demons and Witchcraft*. Dover Pictorial Archive Series. New York: Dover, 1971.

Levack, Brian P., ed. *Renaissance Magic*. New York: Garland, 1992.

Levin, Harry. *The Overreacher: A Study of Christopher Marlowe*. Cambridge, MA: Harvard University Press, 1952.

Levin, Richard. "What's Wrong with His Feet and Tail and Her Face and Back?" *Shakespeare Newsletter* 47 (1997): 28–29.

Levine, Nina S. "The Case of Eleanor Cobham: Authorizing History in *2 Henry VI*." *Shakespeare Studies* 22 (1994): 104–121.

———. *Women's Matters. Politics, Gender, and Nation in Shakespeare's Early History Plays*. Newark, DE: University of Delaware Press, 1998.

Levy, F. J. *Tudor Historical Thought*. San Marino, CA: Huntington, 1967.

Liebler, Naomi Conn. "King of the Hill: Ritual and Play in the Shaping of *3 Henry VI*." In *Shakespeare's English Histories: A Quest for Form and Genre*. Ed. John W. Velz. Binghamton, NY: Center for Medieval and Early Renaissance Studies at SUNY Binghamton, 1996.

Light, Fred, Simona Tosimi Pizzetti, and David H. Weinglass, eds. *Fussli Pittore di Shakespeare, Pittura e Teatro 1775–1825*. Milano: Electra, 1997.

Link, Luther. *The Devil: The Archfiend in Art from the Sixth to the Sixteenth Century*. New York: Harry N. Abrams, 1996.

Loewenstein, Joseph. "The Script in the Market Place." In *Representing the English Renaissance*. Ed. Stephen Greenblatt. Berkeley, CA: University of California Press, 1988. 265–278.

Long, William. "Bookkeepers and Playhouse Manuscripts: A Peek at the Evidence." *Shakespeare Newsletter* 44 (1994): 3.

Loraux, Nicole. *Mothers in Mourning*. Tr. Corinne Pache. Ithaca, NY: Cornell University Press, 1998.

Lusardi, James P. "The Career of Robert Barnes." In Martz, Sylvester, and Miller. Vol. 8, part 3. 1367–1415.

Maguire, Laurie E. *Shakespearean Suspect Texts: The "Bad" Quartos and Their Contexts*. Cambridge: Cambridge University Press, 1996.

Magny, C. E. *Histoire du roman français*. Paris: Plon, 1950.

Manheim, Michael. "Duke Humphrey and the Machiavels." *American Benedictine Review* 23 (1972): 249–257.

———. "The English History Play on Screen." In *Shakespeare and the Moving Image*. Ed. Anthony Davies and Stanley Wells. Cambridge: Cambridge University Press, 1994. 121–145.

————. *The Weak King Dilemma in the Shakespearean History Play.* Syracuse, NY: Syracuse University Press, 1973.

Marcus, Leah. *Puzzling Shakespeare: Local Reading and Discontents.* Berkeley, CA: University of California Press, 1988.

Martin, Randall. "Elizabethan Civic Pageantry in *Henry VI.*" *University of Toronto Quarterly* 60 (1990–1991): 244–264.

Martz, Louis L., Richard S. Sylvester, and Clarence H. Miller, eds. *The Complete Works of St. Thomas More.* 15 vols. New Haven, CT: Yale University Press, 1981.

Marx, Karl. *Capital.* Tr. Ben Fowkes. New York: Vintage, 1977.

McKerrow, R. B. ed. *The Works of Thomas Nashe.* 5 vols. 1904–1910. Rpt. New York: Barnes and Noble, 1966.

McMillin, Scott. "Casting for Pembroke's Men: The *Henry VI* Quartos and *The Taming of A Shrew.*" *Shakespeare Quarterly* 23 (1972): 141–159.

McNeal, Thomas H. "Margaret of Anjou: Romantic Princess and Troubled Queen." *Shakespeare Quaterly* 9 (Winter 1958): 1–10.

McRae, Andrew. "Agrarian Communism." In *God Speed the Plough: The Representation of Agrarian England,* 1500–1660. Cambridge: Cambridge University Press, 1996.

Mebane, John S. *Renaissance Magic and the Return of the Golden Age, The Occult Tradition and Marlowe, Jonson, and Shakespeare.* Lincoln, NE: University of Nebraska Press, 1989.

Mills, David, ed., *The Chester Mystery Cycle: A New Edition with Modernised Spelling.* East Lansing: Colleagues Press, 1992.

Miner, Madonne. "'Neither Mother, Wife, nor England's Queen': The Roles of Women in *Richard III.*" In *The Woman's Part: Feminist Criticism of Shakespeare.* Ed. Carolyn Ruth Swift Lenz, Gayle Greene, and Carol Thomas Neely. Chicago: University of Illinois Press, 1983.

Mora, George, M.D. "Introduction." In Weyer. *De Praestigiis daemonum.*

Muir, Kenneth, and S. Schoenbaum, eds. *A New Companion to Shakespeare Studies.* Canbridge: Cambridge University Press, 1971.

Norton, Thomas, and Thomas Sackville. *Gorboduc.* In *Elizabethan and Stuart Plays.* Ed. Charles Read Baskervill, Virgil B. Heltzel, and Arthur H. Nethercot. New York: Henry Holt, 1934.

Olds, Sally B., Marcia L. London, and Patricia A. Ladewig. *Maternal-Newborn Nursing: A Family-Centered Approach.* 2nd ed. Menlo Park, CA: Addison–Wesley, 1984.

Ornstein, Robert. *A Kingdom for a Stage: The Achievement of Shakespeare's History Plays.* Cambridge, MA: Harvard University Press, 1972.

Otten, Charlotte F. "What's Wrong with His Feet?" *Shakespeare*

Newsletter 46 (1996): 87–88.

Palmer, Barbara D. "The Inhabitants of Hell: Devils." In *The Iconography of Hell*. Ed. Clifford Davidson and Thomas H. Seiler, Early Drama, Art, and Music Monograph Series 17. Kalamazoo, MI: Medieval Institute Publications, 1992. 22–27.

Pape, Walter, Frederick Burwick, et al, eds. *The Boydell Shakespeare Gallery*. Bottrop: Peter Pomp, 1996.

Paré, Ambroise. *On Monsters and Marvels*. Tr. and intro by Janis L. Pallister. Chicago: University of Chicago Press, 1982.

———. *Des Monstres et prodiges*. Ed. Jean Céard. Geneva: Librairie Droz, 1971.

Parkes, M. B., and A. G. Watson. *Medieval Scribes, Manuscripts and Libraries: Essays Presented to N. R. Ker*. London: Scolar, 1979.

Patterson, Annabel. *Shakespeare and the Popular Voice*. London: Blackwell, 1989.

Paxson, James J. "The Nether-Faced Devil and the Allegory of Parturition." *Studies in Iconography* 19 (1998): 139–176.

———. "Personification's Gender." *Rhetorica* 16 (1998): 149–179.

———. *The Poetics of Personification*. Cambridge: Cambridge University Press, 1994.

———. "Theorizing the Mysteries' End in England, the Artificial Demonic, and the Sixteenth-Century Witch-Craze." *Criticism* 39 (1997): 481–502.

Pearlman, Elihu. *William Shakespeare: The History Plays*. New York: Twayne, 1992.

Philips, Ambrose. *Humphrey, Duke of Gloucester. A Tragedy*. As it is acted at the Theatre-Royal in Drury Lane, By His Majesty's Servants. London: Printed and sold J. Roberts, near the Oxford-Arms in Warwick-Lane, 1723.

Pierce, Robert B. *Shakespeare's History Plays: The Family and the State*. Columbus, OH: Ohio State University Press, 1971.

Piers Plowman: The B Version. Ed. George Kane and E. Talbot Donaldson. London: Athlone Press, 1975.

Pitt, Angela, *Shakespeare's Women*. Totowa, NJ: Barnes and Noble, 1981.

Potter, Robert. "The Recovery of Queen Margaret: 'The Wars of the Roses,' 1963." *New Theatre Quarterly* 4 (1988): 105–119.

Pratt, Samuel. "Shakespeare and Humphrey Duke of Gloucester: A Study in Myth." *Shakespeare Quarterly* 16 (1965): 201–216.

Price, Hereward T. *Construction in Shakespeare. University of Michigan Contribution in Modern Philology* 17. Ann Arbor, MI: University of Michigan Press, 1951.

Pugliatti, Paola. "'More Than History Can Pattern': The Jack Cade Rebellion in *Henry VI, 2*." *Journal of Medieval and Renaissance Studies* 22 (1992): 451–478.

———. *Shakespeare the Historian*. New York: St. Martin's Press, 1996.

———."Shakespeare's Historicism: Visions and Revisions." In *Shakespeare and the Twentieth Century*, ed. Jonathan Bate, Jill L. Levenson, and Dieter Mehl. Newark, DE: University of Delaware Press. 1998, 336–349.

Purvis, J. S., ed. *The York Cycle of Mystery Plays*. New York: Macmillan, 1957.

Quinn, Michael. "Providence in Shakespeare's Yorkist Plays." *Shakespeare Quarterly* 10 (1959): 45–52.

Rabkin, Norman. *Shakespeare and the Common Understanding*. New York: Free Press, 1967.

Rackin, Phyllis. *Stages of History: Shakespeare's English Chronicles*. Ithaca, NY: Cornell University Press, 1990.

Rasmussen, Eric. "The Revision of Scripts." In *A New History of Early English Drama*. Ed. John D. Cox and David Scott Kastan. New York: Columbia University Press, 1997. 441–460.

Redford, Bruce. *The Origins of "The School for Scandal."* Princeton, NJ: Princeton University Press, 1986.

Reed, Robert R. *Crime and God's Judgment in Shakespeare*. Lexington: University Press of Kentucky, 1984.

Reese, M. M. *The Cease of Majesty: A Study of Shakespeare's History Plays*. London: Edward Arnold, 1961.

Ribner, Irving, ed. *The Complete Plays of Christopher Marlowe*. New York: Odyssey Press, 1963.

———. *The English History Play in the Age of Shakespeare*, rev. ed. Princeton: Princeton University Press, 1965.

Richmond, Hugh M. *Shakespeare's Political Plays*. New York: Random House, 1967.

Ricks, Don M. *Shakespeare's Emergent Form: A Study of the Structures of the "Henry VI" Plays*. Logan, UT: Utah State University Press, 1968.

Riggs, David. *Shakespeare's Heroical Histories: "Henry VI" and Its Literary Tradition*. Cambridge, MA: Harvard University Press, 1971.

Righter, Anne. *Shakespeare and the Idea of the Play*. London: Chatto & Windus, 1964.

Robbins, Rossell Hope. *The Encyclopedia of Witchcraft and Demonology*. New York: Crown, 1995.

Rosen, Barbara. *Witchcraft in England, 1558–1618*. Ann Arbor, MI: University of Michigan Press, 1991.

Rossiter, A. R. *Angel with Horns and Other Shakespeare Lectures*. Ed. Graham Storey. New York: Theatre Arts, 1961.

Rothwell, Kenneth S., and Annabel Henkin Melzer. *Shakespeare on Screen: An International Filmography and Videography*. New York: Neal-

Schuman Publishers, 1990.

Rowland, Beryl, ed. *Medieval Woman's Guide to Health: The First English Gynecological Handbook.* Kent, OH: Kent State University Press, 1981.

Rudnytsky, Peter L. "'The Darke and Vicious Place': The Dread of the Vagina in *King Lear*." *Modern Philology* 96 (1999): 291–311.

Rudwin, Maxmilian. *The Devil in Legend and Literature.* 1931; rpt. New York: AMS, 1970.

Russell, Jeffrey Burton. *Lucifer: The Devil in the Middle Ages.* Ithaca, NY: Cornell University Press, 1984.

Sanders, Wilbur. *The Dramatist and the Received Idea.* Cambridge: Cambridge University Press, 1968.

Sandoe, James. "A Director's Commentary on *Henry VI*." *Henry VI*. Dell Laurel ed. New York: Dell, 1963.

Sasaki, Takashi, ed. *Shakespeare in Japan Bibliography.* Tokyo: Nihon Tosho-shuppan, 1995.

Scholkwyk, David. "'A Lady's "Verily" Is as Potent as a Lord's'": Women, Word, and Witchcraft in *The Winter's Tale*." *English Literary Renaissance*, 22:2 (Spring 1992): 242–272.

Schuster, Louis A. "Thomas More's Polemical Career." In Martz, Sylvester, and Miller. Vol. 8, part 3. 1137–1194.

Sen Gupta, S. C. *Shakespeare's History Plays.* London: Oxford University Press, 1964.

Schiff, Gert. *Johan Helnrich Füssli.* 2 vols. Zurich: Verlag Berichthaus, 1973.

Shoyo Tsubouchi. *Shoyo Senshu (Collected Works of Shoyo).* 2 vols. Tokyo: Daiichi Shobo, 1977.

Shapiro, James. Commentary. *Public Access.* New York Shakespeare Festival. December 1996.

Silber, Patricia. "The Unnatural Woman and the Disordered State in Shakespeare's Histories." *Proceedings of the PMR Conference in Shakespeare's Histories*, Augustinian Historical Institute of Villanova University 2 (1979): 87–96.

Smidt, Kristian. *Unconformities in Shakespeare's History Plays.* Atlantic Highlands, NJ: Humanities Press, 1982.

Smiley, Jane. "Shakespeare in Action." *New York Times.* December 2, 1996, Azz.

Spector, Stephen, ed. *The N-Town Plays.* Oxford: EETS, 1991.

Sonnino, Lee A. *A Handbook to Sixteenth-Century Rhetoric.* London: Routledge: Kegan Paul, 1968.

Sterling, Brents. "Shakespeare's Mob Scenes: A Reinterpretation." *Huntington Library Quarterly* 8 (1944–1945): 213–240.

Spivack, Bernard. *Shakespeare and the Allegory of Evil.* New York: Columbia University Press, 1958.

Stevens, Martin. *Four Middle English Mystery Cycles: Textual, Contextual, and Critical Interpretations*. Princeton, NJ: Princeton University Press, 1987.

Stevens, Martin, and James J. Paxson. "The Fool in the Wakefield Plays." *Studies in Iconography* 13 (1989–1990): 49–80.

Sundelson, David. *Shakespeare's Restorations of the Father*. New Brunswick, NJ: Rutgers University Press, 1983.

Swander, Homer D. "The Rediscovery of *Henry VI*." *Shakespeare Quaterly*. 29 (1978): 146–163.

Talbert, Ernest William. *Elizabethan Drama and Shakespeare's Early Plays: An Essay in Historical Criticism*. Chapel Hill, NC: University of North Carolina Press, 1963.

Taylor, Gary. "Shakespeare and Others: The Authorship of *Henry the Sixth, Part One*." *Medieval and Renaissance Drama in England*, 7 (1995): 145–205.

Tertullian. "On the Apparel of Women. Ed. and trans. Alexander Roberts and James Donaldson. *The Ante-Nicene Fathers*, Vol. 4, Buffalo: Christian Literature, 1885.

Thomas Aquinas. *Summa Theologica*. Ed. Thomas Gilby. 9 vols. New York: McGraw–Hill, 1964.

Thomas, Keith. *Religion and the Decline of Magic*. New York: Scribner's, 1971.

Tillyard, E. M. W. *Shakespeare's History Plays*. 1944; rpt. New York: Collier Books, 1962.

Tobin, J. J. M. "Antony, Brutus, and *Christ's Tears over Jerusalem*." *Notes and Queries* 243 (1998): 324–331.

———. "Nashe and *Romeo and Juliet*." *Notes and Queries* 225 (1980): 161–162.

———. "Nashe and Shakespeare: Some Further Borrowings." *Notes and Queries* 237 (1992): 314.

———. "Nashe and Some Shakespearian Sonnets." *Notes and Queries* 244 (1999): 222–226.

———. "Nomenclature and the Dating of *Titus Andronicus*." *Notes and Queries* 229 (1984): 186–187.

Tomory, Peter. *The Life and Art of Henry Fuseli*. London: Thames and Hudson, 1972.

Traister, Barbara Howard. *Heavenly Necromancers, The Magician in English Renaissance Drama*. Columbia, MO: University of Missouri Press, 1984.

Turner, Robert Y. "Characterization in Shakespeare's Early History Plays." *ELH* 31 (1964): 241–258.

———. *Shakespeare's Apprenticeship*. Chicago: University of Chicago Press, 1974.

Urkowitz, Steven. "'All Things Is Hansome Now': Murderers Nominated by Numbers in *2 Henry VI* and *Richard III.*" In *Shakespeare's Speech-Headings: Speaking the Speech in Shakespeare's Plays*, Ed. George Walton Williams. Newark, DE: University of Delaware Press, 1997. 102–119.

———. "'Brother, Can You Spare a Paradigm?'": Textual Generosity and the Printing of Shakespeare's Multiple-Text Plays by Contemporary Editors." *Critical Survey* 7 (1995): 292–298.

———. "Five Women Eleven Ways: Changing Images of Shakespearean Characters in the Earliest Texts." *Images of Shakespeare: Proceedings of the Third Congress of the International Shakespeare Association, 1986.* Ed. Werner Habicht, D. J. Palmer, and Roger Pringle. Newark, DE: University of Delaware Press, 1988. 292–304.

———. "Good News About 'Bad' Quartos." In *"Bad" Shakespeare: Revaluations of the Shakespeare Canon*, ed. Maurice Charney. Rutherford, NJ: Fairleigh Dickinson University Press, 1988. 189–206.

———. "'If I Mistake in Those Foundations Which I Build Upon': Peter Alexander's Textual Analysis of *Henry VI Parts 2 and 3.*" *English Literary Renaissance* 18 (1988): 230–256.

Vatter, Hannes. *The Devil in English Literature.* Bern: Francke Verlag, 1978.

Walker, Barbara G. *The Crone: Woman of Age, Wisdom, and Power.* San Francisco: Harper Collins, 1988.

Wehr, Demaris S. *Jung and Feminism: Liberating Archetypes.* Boston: Beacon Press, 1987.

Weigle, Marta. *Creation and Procreation: Feminist Reflections on Mythologies of Cosmogony and Parturition.* Philadelphia: University of Pennsylvania Press, 1989.

Wells, Robin Headlam. "The Fortunes of Tillyard." *Essays and Studies* 66 (1985): 391–403.

Wells, Stanley. "Television Shakespeare." *Shakespeare Quarterly* 33 (1982): 261–277.

Wells, Stanley, and Gary Taylor, with John Jowett and William Montgomery, eds. *William Shakespeare: A Textual Companion.* Oxford: Claredon, 1987.

Werstine, Paul. "A Century of 'Bad' Shakespeare Quartos." *Shakespeare Quarterly* 50 (1999): 310–333.

Weyer, Johann. *De praestigiis daemonum.* Tr. John Shea. In *Witches, Devils and Doctors in the Renaissance.* Gen. ed. George Mora, M.D. Binghamton, NY: Medieval and Renaissance Texts and Studies, 1991.

White, Hayden V. *Tropics of Discourse: Essays in Cultural Criticism.* Baltimore, MD: Johns Hopkins University Press, 1978.

Wilders, John. *The Lost Garden: A View of Shakespeare's English and Roman History Plays.* Totowa, NJ: Rowan and Littlefield, 1978.

Willems, Michele. "Verbal-Visual, Verbal-Pictorial or Textual-Television? Reflections on the BBC Shakespeare Series." In *Shakespeare and the Moving Image.* Ed. Anthony Davies and Stanley Wells. Cambridge: Cambridge University Press, 1994. 69–85.

———. *Shakespeare à la Television.* Rouen: Publication de l'Universite de Rouen, 1987.

Williams, Gwyn. "Suffolk and Margaret: A Study of Some Sections of Shakespeare's *Henry VI.*" *Shakespeare Quarterly* 25 (1974): 310–322.

Williamson, Marilyn. "'When Men Are Rul'd by Women': Shakespeare's First Tetralogy." *Shakespeare Studies* 19 (1987): 41–59.

Willis, Susan. *The BBC Shakespeare Plays.* Chapel Hill, NC: University of North Carolina Press, 1991.

Wills, Garry. *Witches and Jesuits: Shakespeare's "Macbeth."* New York: Oxford University Press, 1995.

Wilson, Richard. "'A Mingled Yarn': Shakespeare and the Cloth Workers." *Literature and History* 12 (1986): 164–180.

Winny, James. *The Player King: A Theme of Shakespeare's Histories.* New York: Barnes & Noble, 1968.

Woodbridge, Linda. *The Scythe of Satan: Shakespeare and Magical Thinking.* Urbana, IL: University of Illinois Press, 1994.

———. *Women and the English Renaissance: Literature and the Nature of Womankind, 1540–1620.* Urbana, IL: University of Illinois Press, 1984.

Zitner, Sheldon P. "Wooden O's in Plastic Boxes: Shakespeare and Television." *University of Toronto Quarterly* 51 (1981): 1–12.

Index